Many Infallible Proofs

Many Infallible Proofs

Evidences for the Christian Faith

Henry M. Morris

with

Henry M. Morris III

Master Books

First printing: August 1974
Fourteenth printing, revised and expanded: August 1996
Eighteenth printing: October 2005

Library of Congress Catalog Number: 74-81484
ISBN: 0-89051-005-9

Cataloging in Publication Data
Morris, Henry Madison, 1918 –
Many infallible proofs: practical and useful evidences of Christianity
1. Apologetics 2. Bible—Evidences, authority, etc.   I. Title
                    239   74-81484

Printed in the United States of America.

Please visit our website for other great titles:
www.masterbooks.net

For information regarding author interviews,
please contact the publicity department at (870) 438-5288.

Table of Contents

Introduction

The first edition of *Many Infallible Proofs* was published in 1974, and has been widely used as both a textbook and reference book, and also for general devotional study. Since the book still seems to be in much demand, I finally decided it should be updated and then augmented with short chapters on the cults and the so-called New Age movement, both of which have greatly expanded their influence in the past two decades or more.

Most of the great evidences of the truth of Christianity are timeless. Such topics as the evidence for inspiration of the Bible, the evidence for the deity of Christ, the testimony of fulfilled prophecy, the argument for the existence of the God of the Bible, and other such evidences are much the same as always, so chapters in the book on topics such as these have required little change.

However, since "science" is very ephemeral in its arguments and pronouncements, those chapters dealing with creation and earth history *did* need updating. Actually, the evidence for special creation and the worldwide flood seems to become stronger every year, with each new scientific discovery. The same is true with the latter-day prophecies of the Bible. Changes in this second edition, therefore, apply primarily to those chapters dealing with these great themes. In addition, as noted above, two new chapters have been added.

The manuscript for the first edition had been reviewed and improved by two long-time friends and distinguished theologians, Dr. John Whitcomb and Dr. Charles Ryrie. This new edition has been reviewed with all its changes by my son and co-author, Dr. Henry Morris III, who has both the D.Min. degree and an MBA, as well as much experience in the pastor-ate and college teaching, and also in the business world. In addition, he has been the primary author of the two new chapters on the pseudo-Christian and New Age cults. He also has taught a number of courses on Christian evidences and has authored two Bible study books of his own.

It is our prayer that the Lord will use this new edition of *Many Infallible Proofs* not only to strengthen the faith and testimony of Christians, but also to help many sincere searchers to come to saving faith in the Lord Jesus Christ. The Christian faith is under tremendous attack in these latter days, and people need the Lord more urgently than ever before. We trust that God will use this book to answer their questions and bring solid Christian love and stability to their lives.

I wish also to thank my daughter, Mrs. Mary Ruth Smith, B.S., for her very efficient work in typing and editing the entire revised manuscript.

Henry M. Morris
Institute for Creation Research

Chapter I

Why Study Christian Evidences?

Introduction

The purpose of this book is to survey in systematic and comprehensive fashion the "many infallible proofs" of the unique truth and authority of biblical Christianity, together with a refutation of its alleged fallacies and a reconciliation of its alleged discrepancies. It will be seen that, not only is there no mistake or contradiction in the Bible, but also there are innumerable evidences of its divine inspiration and authority. Not only are there no legitimate objections to a true Christian theology, but rather there are overwhelming evidences that Christianity is uniquely and completely true.

As a matter of fact, the entire subject of evidences is almost exclusively the domain of *Christian* evidences. Other religions depend on subjective experience and blind faith, tradition and opinion. Christianity stands or falls upon the objective reality of gigantic supernatural events in history and the evidences that they really happened. This fact in itself is an evidence of its truth.

Definitions

The terms "apologetics" and "evidences," as they relate to the Christian faith, are often used more or less interchangeably. In the formal sense, however, the first is the broader of the two terms as understood by theologians. Apologetics involves the systematic scientific defense of the Christian faith in all its aspects against the intellectual attacks of its adversaries. There are various philosophical systems of apologetics, each attempting to build a logical defense of Christianity upon its own specific or implied presuppositions.

That aspect of apologetics which is more positive and objective, setting forth concrete reasons for accepting the Bible as God's word and Jesus Christ as Lord and Savior, is what is commonly understood as the field of Christian evidences.

This book does not deal with the various systems of philosophical apologetics. These are important in theological studies, especially at the seminary level, but our concern here is with practical and factual evidences supporting the Bible and the Christian faith. This approach should produce at least three very important and practical results.

1. It will confirm and solidify the faith of those who read it, enabling them to withstand the attacks of both rationalistic and irrationalistic unbelief.
2. It should prepare them to witness more knowledgeably and effectively to people of the present generation, influenced as they have been with the pervasive attitudes of skepticism and unbelief that are so characteristic today.
3. It will equip them to maintain a clear and uncompromising stand on the full integrity of God and His Word under all circumstances, despite the pressures of modern life.

Reasons for Studying Christian Evidences

Many people in professedly Christian circles today advocate an almost completely subjective approach to the discovery of Christian truth. Believing that the Bible is not really reliable in its traditional literal and historical sense, they feel the religious experience must be realized either through some sort of subjective "encounter" with Christ or else through involvement in social action movements. The emphasis is on "relevance" and "fulfillment," rather than truth.

Nevertheless, paraphrasing C.S. Lewis, the only really important question is not whether it works, but whether it's true! The criteria of feeling and personal satisfaction are highly unreliable as indices of truth. There are many false systems of belief (e.g., Christian Science, Spiritism, Buddhism, etc. — even Communism!) whose adherents often profess to have found real peace and satisfaction through submission to them, but this fact hardly proves that all such diverse and contradictory systems are therefore true!

Thus there is a clear need for criteria by which to establish the unique validity of biblical Christianity. A credulous faith in some artificial "Christ" of one's own imagination, rather than in the real Christ of biblical history, is not that faith by which men are saved.

Further justification for understanding and using Christian evidences is found in the following partial list of reasons:

1 The Bible commands it. Note especially 1 Peter 3:15: "Be ready always to give an answer to every man that asketh you a reason of the hope that is in you." In this verse, the Greek word for "answer" is *apologia*, from which is derived our English word "apologetics." This same word is translated "defense" in Philippians 1:7 and 1:17, in which Paul indicates his deep concern for the "defense and confirmation of the gospel." See also Jude 3 ("earnestly contend for the faith"), Colossians 4:6 ("know how ye ought to answer every man"), Titus 1:9 ("convince the gainsayers"), and others.

2. The early Christians consistently used Christian evidences in their witnessing. This was especially true of the evidential value of the resurrection of Christ (Acts 4:33; 1 Cor. 15:1-8, etc.), of the evidence of God in nature (Acts 14:15-17; Rom. 1:20), and of the objective testimony of their own transformed lives (Acts 26:9-22; 1 Tim. 1:12-16; etc.). Whenever they first approached pagans, who neither believed nor even knew the Old Testament Scriptures, they never began by quoting Scripture. Rather, they first approached them in reference to the physical creation and their intuitive knowledge of a primeval Creator (note especially Acts 14:11-17 and Acts 17:18-31).

3. The almost universal climate of skepticism and unbelief today, together with an appalling ignorance of the Bible and Christian doctrine, makes it almost mandatory that a sound exposition of Christian evidences accompany a presentation of the gospel if lasting results are to be obtained. It is often possible

to secure a quick emotional "decision for Christ" without this, but such a person is too often like "he that received the seed into stony places . . . that heareth the word, and anon with joy receiveth it; Yet hath he not root in himself, but dureth for a while: for when tribulation or persecution ariseth because of the word, by and by he is offended" (Matt. 13:20-21). Indeed, very often it is impossible today even to obtain a hearing for the gospel unless the ground has been prepared by clearing away some of the stones of misinformation about the supposed errors in the Bible and fallacies of Christian doctrine.

4. It is experimentally true that many who today are strong and fruitful Christians were either won to Christ initially in part by the judicious use of Christian evidences or else were materially strengthened in their faith and witness by this means. In our work at the Institute for Creation Research, for example, we have received very large numbers of testimonies — both written and spoken — from men and women and young people who have been led to Christ as a result of our creation seminars or books or other materials, all of which place strong emphasis on literal creationism and Christian evidences in general. Even more have testified that they have been enabled to win many others to Christ, partly through use of our books, videos or periodicals. The Christian faith *does work*, all right, but it works because it is based on *truth*, provides abundant evidence of its truth, and people everywhere need urgently to know that fact. On the other hand, those Christians who rely exclusively on their personal feelings and experiences in their belief in Christ and the Word, too often lose their zeal and settle into the rut of a routine and fruitless Christian life.

The Use of Evidences

While emphasizing the importance of knowing and using the evidences of Christianity, it is important to insert a few words of caution. If one is frequently in the arena of debate and polemics, there is the possibility that he or she may develop an overly argumentative, too-critical, possibly even bitter and sarcastic, attitude toward opponents. This by all means must be avoided.

Our purpose in using the evidences is not to win arguments but to win souls, and also to win a more favorable intellectual environment for the presentation of the gospel. Many of the Scriptures that enjoin the defense of the faith also give this same caution: "Be ready always to give an answer to every man that asketh you a reason of the hope that is in you with meekness and with fear" (1 Pet. 3:15). "Let your speech be alway with grace, seasoned with salt, that ye may know how ye ought to answer every man" (Col. 4:6). "And the servant of the Lord must not strive; but be gentle unto all men, apt to teach, patient, In meekness instructing those that oppose themselves" (2 Tim. 2:24-25).

Skill at persuasion and argumentation is no substitute for prayer and sincere concern for souls, and certainly no substitute for the use of the Word of God itself. At the same time, it is a serious mistake to teach, as many do, that the use of Christian evidences (in *addition* to prayer and concern and the *judicious* use of Scripture) is unnecessary. In a world of almost universal hostility to Bible Christianity, where unbelief in the Bible is only exceeded by ignorance of the Bible, it is obvious that to most people at least, the testimony of Scripture and personal experience alone (even *that*, of course, can be a form of Christian evidence) will be pointless. Some basis must also be given for believing the Bible to be true and the experience to be more meaningful than experiences offered by other religions.

Those who feel that only the Bible need be used in witnessing rely on the mystical power supposedly resident in the words of Scripture themselves. Charles Haddon Spurgeon's remark to the effect that the Bible is like a lion which can defend itself is often quoted in support of this belief. However, Spurgeon himself was a strong defender of the faith. He said on one occasion: "We *must* defend the faith; for what would have become of us if our fathers had not maintained it?"

The lassitude of Christians in contending intelligently and earnestly for the faith during the past century especially for the doctrine of special creation, has been one primary cause of the almost universal drift into a modernistic apostasy and a secularized society. This drift has occurred in spite of the widest dissemination of the written Word, as well as the preached and spoken Word, that the nation and the world have ever known.

Another caution to be noted by the Christian apologist is that his presentation may tend to become cold and intellectual; it may convince the mind, but leave the heart and conscience unaffected. One's witness should therefore concentrate, many say, only on his own inner experience telling what Christ has done in his heart, giving peace and joy and consciousness of sins forgiven and a changed life. Converts can more easily be won by making them feel that Christianity will work in their own lives than convincing them Christianity is true, so the argument goes.

By all means, the Christian *apologia* should be warm and interesting, manifesting a genuine concern for those to whom one is witnessing, as the Christians seeks to persuade others, even as he presents both the fallacies in their own philosophies and the evidences for Christianity. But a mere recital of one's own testimony, with a few gospel Scripture verses, will be adequate for the needs of only a small fraction of those he encounters.

Why should one presume that his or her own experience is the norm for all others? "The wind bloweth where it listeth . . . so is everyone that is born of the Spirit" (John 3:8). Furthermore, the appeal to an unconverted man strictly on the subjective basis of his own personal needs, rather than on the basis of objective truth, tends to produce converts who are self-centered rather than God-centered. If Christ is, for him, mainly a psychological entrance to an "abundant life," he may "anon with joy receive it," but "when tribulation or persecution ariseth because of the word, by and by he is offended" (Matt. 13:20-21). A solid evidential basis for faith in God's Word, accompanied by an intelligent and biblical presentation of the gospel, is far more likely to produce genuine and permanent results.

Another caution, however. No matter how sound the evidence and clear the scriptural exposition, a person who is unwilling to believe cannot be argued into believing. Christian evidences can never replace the convicting and illuminating work of the Holy Spirit. No matter how strong and irrefutable the evidence, it is always possible for the skeptic to find some new reason for not believing. It is a matter of basic attitudes and unrecognized pre-suppositions. The Christian witness and apologist "must not strive." It is possible to allow a presentation of evidence to degenerate into a heated argument, and in such an atmosphere, the Holy Spirit cannot be heard.

It is this type of situation that has led some Christian philosophers to conclude that a Christian witness to the unsaved should *never* use evidences. The gospel alone should be preached, allowing the Holy Spirit to work as He will in the hearts of those who hear. Evidences may then be of value as encouragement to those who have been saved, but they cannot persuade someone to be saved, so they maintain.

But one need not discard the baby with the bath water! The fact that *some* people are allergic to antibiotics does not thereby prove that antibiotics do not help *most* people. Although many people may be stubbornly unwilling to believe in God's truth, a great many more would be willing but have been hindered therefrom by the persuasive pressures of the unbelieving intellectualized society in which they live.

It must not be forgotten that the early Christians almost invariably used an evidential approach in their witnessing, especially the evidences of creation, of the resurrection of Christ, the miracles of Christ, God's provision in nature, and fulfilled prophecy. Indeed, until the New Testament Scriptures were completed, God even on occasion gave special evidences in the form of gifts of healing, prophesying, and other supernatural manifestations. Even when testifying of personal experience, as in the case of Paul before King Agrippa (Acts 26), the appeal to conversion was on the strength of the fact of prophecy fulfilled (Acts 26:22, 27), and of Christ's resurrection (Acts 26:8, 23, 26).

Thus the judicious use of Christian evidences, as well as Scripture and personal testimony, is based on biblical precept and example. In addition, it is known and proved in practice that this approach has been effective in the lives of many people, both before and after conversion.

There is a final caution, however. The effective use of Christian evidences requires diligent study and preparation. A glib, superficial recital of hearsay evidence, without any real factual, documented basis, may very well evoke a sarcastic, ridiculing rejection by those who hear it.

It is probably this factor — unwillingness to study and learn the evidential facts, and consequent fear of ridicule — that is really the reason why many argue against the use of evidences at all. It is so much easier, and less subject to embarrassment, simply to quote Scripture and give one's testimony, and nothing else.

But don't forget that Buddhists and Mormons and Christian Scientists and even Communists can also quote *their* scriptures and give glowing, happy testimonies of how much their religion has done for *them!* The question is, which is *true?* The answer requires a sound knowledge of the evidence.

Laziness and fearfulness are ill-fitting equipment for a Christian witness. "Study to shew thyself approved unto God, a workman that needeth not to be ashamed, rightly dividing the word of truth" (2 Tim. 2:15). "For God hath not given us the spirit of fear, but of power, and of love, and of a sound mind" (2 Tim. 1:7).

Selected books for further study:

Bible League, ed. 1984. *Truth Unchanged, Unchanging*. Abingdon, England: Bible League Trust. 503 p.

Chapman, Colin. *The Case for Christianity*. Grand Rapids, MI: Wm. B. Eerdmans Co. 313 p.

Clark, Gordon H. 1987. *God's Hammer: The Bible and its Critics*. Jefferson, MD: The Trinity Foundation. 200 p.

Frame, John M. 1994. *Apologetics to the Glory of God*. Philipsburg, NJ: Presbyterian and Reformed.

Geisler, Norman. 1976. *Christian Apologetics*. Grand Rapids, MI: Baker Book House. 393 p.

Groothvis, Douglas. 1994. *Christianity that Counts*. Grand Rapids, MI: Baker Book House. 224 p.

Henry, Carl F.H. 1983. *God, Revelation and Authority*, vol. I-VI. Waco, TX: Word Books. 500-plus pages, each volume.

Morris, Henry M. 1991. *Christian Education for the Real World*. Green Forest, AR: Master Books. 295 p.

Morris, Henry M. 1995. *The Defender's Study Bible*. Grand Rapids, MI: World Publishing Inc. 1,620 p.

Noebel, David A. 1991. *Understanding the Times*. Manitou Springs, CO. 896 p.

Van Til, Cornelius. 1955. *The Defense of the Faith*. Philadelphia, PA: Presbyterian and Reformed. 299 p.

Zuck, Roy B., ed. 1995. *Vital Apologetic Issues*. Grand Rapids, MI: Kregel Publishers. 263 p.

Chapter II

The Uniqueness of Christianity

The Exclusive Claims of Christianity

If Christianity is regarded as only one religion among many others, each possessing an uncertain mixture of truth and error, then, of course, the study of Christian evidences is futile and pointless. Acceptance or rejection of Christianity in that case becomes merely a matter of personal convenience, not conviction. Whether it is true or false is not even a relevant question.

Unfortunately for those who would like to view "religion" in such a detached manner, this option is not possible in the case of biblical Christianity. Its structure is such that it must either be absolutely and uniquely true or else be completely and grossly false. An attitude of indifference is precluded where Christianity is concerned, for here indifference is the same as repudiation. A few of these claims to exclusiveness and uniqueness are as follows:

The God of the Bible is claimed to be the only true God. Jeremiah 10:10-12 is typical of a host of Scriptures to this effect: "The Lord is the true God, he is the living God and an everlasting king . . . The gods that have not made the heavens and the earth, even they shall perish from the earth, and from under these heavens. He hath made the earth by his power, he hath established the world by his wisdom, and hath stretched out the heavens by his discretion."

Christ claims to be the only way to God, to salvation, and to heaven. "I am the way, the truth, and the life: no man cometh unto the Father, but by me" (John 14:6).

The Bible is claimed as the only true revelation from God. "To the law and to the testimony: if they speak not according to this word, it is because there is no light in them" (Isa. 8:20). The canon of Scripture closes with a fearful warning to any who would presume either to augment or delete any of the words recorded therein (Rev. 22:18-19).

The way of salvation presented in the Bible is claimed to be the only way. Peter said: "Neither is there salvation in any other: for there is none other name under heaven, given among men, whereby we must be saved" (Acts 4:12). Paul warned: "If any man preach any other gospel unto you than that ye have received, let him be accursed" (Gal. 1:9).

The Unique Historical Basis of Christianity

Alone among all the religions of mankind, Christianity (including its Old Testament foundations) is based upon historical acts and facts. Other religions are centered in the ethical and religious teachings of their founders, but Christianity is built on the great events of creation and redemption.

For example, the Moslem faith is based on the teachings of Mohammed, Buddhism is based on the teachings of Buddha, Confucianism on those of Confucius, and so on. Christianity, however, is founded not on what Jesus taught, but on who He is and what He did! His teachings indeed were wonderful. "Never man spake like this man" (John 7:46). But it is not His teachings, but Christ himself, who provides salvation.

This unique feature of biblical Christianity is a strong evidence of its truth. Since all other religions are based upon the teachings of men, there is necessarily a strong subjective element in all of them. No matter how intelligent or compassionate a man Mohammed may have been, or Zoroaster, or Buddha, he was still a man, beset by the same physical and mental limitations as other men. His teachings may have been ever so brilliant and satisfying, but the only assurance of their reliability is their personal appeal to us. Thus, such religions are subjective religions, both in their origin and in their acceptance by individual followers.

Christianity, on the other hand, is based on objective

facts, not subjective pressures. Its truth or falsity stands on the validity of the great facts of creation, fall, redemption, and resurrection, the historical records of which are subject to examination by the ordinary criteria of objective investigation. Thus, Christianity is the one and only religion which offers even the possibility of objective certainty concerning the question of its validity.

Its Unique Account of Origins

In trying to distinguish the truth about such basic issues as these, the question of origins is fundamental. Where did everything come from, and how did it get like it is? It is obvious that this question must be answered before any teaching concerning purposes and destinies can be more than pure speculation.

Strangely enough, the various religions of men all in effect confess their utter ignorance on this point. That is, although they all propose certain cosmogonic myths, none really is able to go back to the absolute beginning of things. All are basically evolutionary in their cosmogonies, beginning with matter in some form or other, and then trying to explain how this primeval matter may have gradually been transformed into the present world.

Thus, the famous Babylonian cosmogony *Enuma Elish* began with a primeval chaotic mixture of three kinds of waters. The ancient Egyptian cosmogony also assumes an initial watery chaos out of which everything else evolved. Likewise the early Greek myths, as transmitted by Hesiod, Homer, and Thales, drawing largely from the Sumerians, indicate a chaos of water at the beginning. So do those of many animistic tribes. Roman writers such as Lucretius assumed that in the beginning was a universal blind interplay of atoms, the Orphic myths suppose that the universe developed out of a primeval world-egg, and so on. Modern theories of evolution supposedly are more sophisticated, but they likewise begin with eternal matter in one form or another. Thus, no extra-biblical cosmogony, ancient or modern, is able to go beyond the present order of things to a real First Cause. In effect, therefore, they all end by confessing that they really do not know how the universe began. All begin with space, matter, and time already existing.

The Bible, and only the Bible, starts with the special creation of all things by an eternal, omnipotent, personal God.

This is an eminently reasonable solution to the problem of origins; an infinite and eternal God is an adequate cause to explain space and time; an omnipotent God can account for the vast sources of power and matter in the cosmos; an omniscient God can explain the innumerable evidences of intelligence and order; a personal God is capable of creating life and personality in His creatures; but primeval chaos and colliding atoms are capable of explaining none of these things.

The Person of Christ

Biblical Christianity is also absolutely unique in the nature of its central personage and founder, Jesus Christ. There is none other like Him in all history or even in all literature.

Some writers, of course, presume to place Christ as merely one in a list of great religious leaders, but this is grotesque and absurd. He stands in *contrast* to all others, not in line with them, not even at the head of the line. His uniqueness is illustrated in the following partial list of attributes.

Anticipation of His Coming. His coming was prophesied in fine detail, as to lineage, birthplace, time, career, purpose, nature of death, resurrection, and many other things, hundreds of years prior to His actual appearance. Of no other religious leader — indeed, of no other man — in all history was such a thing true.

The Virgin Birth. Although tales of demi-gods, the progeny of unions between men and the gods (actually demons) are common in ancient mythology, the narrative of Christ's virgin birth stands entirely alone; nothing like it was ever imagined elsewhere. God himself took up residence in embryonic human form in a virgin's womb, thence to be born in a fully natural human birth, with no actual genetic connection to human parents, even though legally the natural heir of a human father and embryologically the seed and fruit of a human mother. No other human birth was ever like this, in fact or fiction, yet it was uniquely and ideally appropriate and natural when God became man.

The Divine-Human Nature. Though men have

often thought of themselves as children of God, Jesus Christ was the *only begotten* Son of God. Although there have been power-crazed dictators and fanatics who have claimed to be God, even these individuals recognized and acknowledged that their assumption of divinity was only relative — they hardly imagined that they had created the stars or even their own mothers! But Jesus Christ was God in the highest sense, the Creator of all things (Col. 1:16), and He claimed to be God on many occasions and in many ways. He was also man in the fullest sense, except that He had no sin. He was not half-man and half-God, but rather all man and all God, in a perfect and indissoluble union. No other man was ever thus — indeed, no other man ever claimed to be thus.

Sinless Life. Of no one else in history could the claim ever be made in seriousness that he lived a whole lifetime without one sin, in thought or word or deed. But this very thing was claimed by Jesus' closest friends, by His worst enemies, by the greatest of the apostles, and by Jesus himself. Peter said, "[He] did no sin" (1 Pet. 2:22), and John said, "In him is no sin" (1 John 3:5). Judas said, "I have betrayed the innocent blood" (Matt. 27:4), and Pilate said, "I find in him no fault at all" (John 18:38). Paul said, "[He] knew no sin" (2 Cor. 5:21), and Jesus said concerning himself, "The Father hath not left me alone; for I do always those things that please him" (John 8:29). Jesus Christ was the one man who never sinned; He was the unique, representative Son of Man, man as God intended man to be.

Unique Teachings. Many non-Christians have acknowledged Christ to be the greatest teacher of all time. The Sermon on the Mount is without parallel, and the beauty and power of the Upper Room discourse, the compelling majesty of the sermon on the Mount of Olives, the power of His parables, and all His other teachings are separated by a great gulf from even the finest teaching of other men. And yet His teachings continually include both the claim and the internal awareness that He was uniquely God's Son, and that His teachings were absolutely true because of this. In no other religious writings does one find such a phenomenon as this.

His Unique Death. After a cruel mockery of a trial and a period of incomprehensible suffering in prison and on the cross, "He said, It is finished: and he bowed his head, and gave up the ghost" (John 19:30). Literally, He "dismissed His spirit." No one else can die like this. It is evidently quite a difficult task even to commit suicide, but certainly no one can simply decide to die and then, by his mere volition, proceed to die. But Jesus did! He said, "No man taketh it from me, but I lay it down of myself" (John 10:18).

The Resurrection of Christ

Not only did Christ die by His own power, but He rose again on the third day by His own power. "I have power to lay it down, and I have power to take it again." (John 10:18). The overwhelming proof of the bodily resurrection of Christ will be discussed later, but here it is merely noted that this constitutes the final and greatest proof of His absolute uniqueness. All other religious founders and leaders are dead. In most cases, their tombs are known and venerated. But the tomb of Christ was occupied only three days and thereafter became empty forever. Other men have been temporarily restored to life after dying, but only Christ is "alive forevermore" (Rev. 1:18). Death is man's last and greatest enemy (1 Cor. 15:26), which conquers all alike, no matter how brilliant or powerful. Christ alone conquered death, thereby demonstrating forever that He is "the resurrection and the life" (John 11:25).

The Book

The Bible (meaning "the Book") is not only the greatest and most widely read book ever written, but it stands in a class altogether by itself in several critical respects:

Unity in Diversity. Consisting of 66 separate books written by about 40 different authors over a time span of at least 2,000 years, brought gradually together into one volume by a process which no one has ever been able to describe in full, the Book presents a marvelous unity and a magnificent development of its great themes from beginning to end, with no errors and no internal discrepancies. There is nothing remotely comparable to this among all the millions of books written by man.

Fulfilled Prophecy. There are hundreds of prophecies recorded in Scripture which have been meticulously fulfilled, often hundreds of years later. This is a unique characteristic of the Bible, not found in the Vedas or the Koran or any of the other "scriptures" of mankind. The so-called prophecies of Nostradamus, Edgar Cayce, Jeanne Dixon, and others of like kind are of a completely different order than those in the Bible, always dark and ambiguous and, much more often than not, later proved wrong.

Accuracy. Not only has the Bible proved accurate in its prophecies, but also in its very frequent references to matters of history and principles of natural science. Although some problems remain, it is still true that not a single uncontroverted fact of history or science refutes a single statement in the Bible. It is also true that archaeological and historical research has confirmed the biblical references in hundreds of instances and that scores of now-known facts of science were written in the Bible long before men recognized them in nature. Once again, there is no other book ever written of which the above things can be said.

Unique Preservation. No other book has ever been the object of such antagonism as has the Bible. In both ancient and modern times, kings and priests have tried desperately to destroy it and unbelieving intellectuals to ridicule and refute it. Untold numbers of copies have been burned and mutilated, and hosts of its advocates persecuted and killed. But it has only multiplied the more, and today is read and believed by more people in more nations and languages than ever before, continually remaining for centuries the world's best seller.

Claims of its Writers. The writers of the Bible maintain again and again that their writings were inspired by God, often even consisting of the directly recorded words of God. Although other writers such as Mohammed have claimed divine inspiration for their writings, the frequency and variety of such assertions are unique to the Bible. And, still more remarkable, in the same Book and often in the same contexts in which such statements are made, the writers condemn falsehood and hypocrisy in terms of burning fury. It is inconceivable that writings with claims to divine authority could be intertwined with such exhortations to holiness and condemnations of deception unless either the writers truly were writing under the inspiration of the Holy Spirit or else were themselves monsters of hypocrisy and evil. The latter alternative, however, is utterly inconceivable in view of the unique character and history of the Book which they produced.

Salvation by Grace

The final proof of uniqueness to be offered in this section is that of the all-important teaching concerning salvation. The Bible uniquely teaches salvation through faith alone. All other religions teach salvation through faith plus works.

Of course, the specific objects of faith and the specific list of works required for salvation vary widely from one religion to another. But the basic principle is universal.

Biblical Christianity alone, among all the religions of mankind, teaches that eternal salvation is the free gift of God's grace, to be received by faith alone, apart from works of any kind. The watchword of other religions is "Believe and do"; of Christianity, the word is "Believe and live."

This does not by any means imply that Christianity has a lower or easier standard than other religions. To the contrary, the standard of works in Christianity is so high as to be unattainable by the natural man, so that no man could ever earn salvation by his own good works. "For all have sinned, and come short of the glory of God" (Rom. 3:23). "For whosoever shall keep the whole law and yet offend in one point, he is guilty of all" (James 2:10). "The soul that sinneth, it shall die" (Ezek. 18:4).

Nor does it imply that Christian salvation is cheap, for the price of redemption was the blood of Christ. "Ye were not redeemed with corruptible things, as silver and gold . . . But with the precious blood of Christ" (1 Pet. 1:18-19).

Although the idea of salvation by grace goes against the

grain of human nature, since man's pride is at stake here, it clearly must be of divine origin. Man would never invent a standard of righteousness which he could never hope to attain. It is significant that every one of the standards of works required in the many religions of men is quite capable of accomplishment by human effort. This fact clearly indicates they were originated by human ingenuity. Only God would ever prescribe a standard which could be attained only by God himself. The uniqueness of salvation by grace through faith alone clearly stamps the Christian gospel as divine in origin.

The World's Religions

In the same ways that Christianity is unique, the other religions of the world are homogeneous. Each was founded by men who were, unlike Jesus Christ, sinful men. These founders are all in their graves, defeated by man's last enemy. Christ alone rose from the grave and defeated death.

Similarly, there is a vast contrast between the Bible and the sacred books of the other religions, and between the gospel of grace of Jesus Christ and the dead works of other religions. A brief survey of the chief features of these religions will help emphasize these contrasts.

Though reliable statistics are impossible to obtain (who, for example, really knows the present population of Red China or the religious beliefs of these people?) the following tabulation will give at least an approximate idea of the religious complexion of mankind.

Christianity		1,000,000,000
Roman Catholic	600,000,000	
Eastern Orthodox	150,000,000	
Protestant	250,000,000	
Islam		500,000,000
Buddhism		200,000,000
Hinduism		450,000,000
Confucianism		400,000,000
Animism		750,000,000
Shintoism		75,000,000
Taoism		50,000,000
Judaism		15,000,000
Miscellaneous		60,000,000
	Total Population	3,500,000,000

Parenthetically, the missionary task still confronting Christians is obvious from the fact that only a third of the world's inhabitants are even nominal Christians. The number of "Christians" included in the tabulation is itself almost meaningless, since it includes most of "Christendom" and thus most of the population of Europe, and North and South America. The number of genuine, Bible-believing Christians who have been personally regenerated through faith in the Lord Jesus Christ would probably not be more than 5 percent of the world's population at most.

Islam (meaning "submission to God") was founded by Mohammed (A.D. 570–632). An orphan, given to mysticism (some historians think he was an epileptic), Mohammed's character was a mixture of generosity and cruelty, religious zeal and sensuality. He was the recipient of a series of "visions and revelations" which were purportedly an extension of the prophecies of the Old and New Testaments, with which he was superficially familiar. These collected writings, 114 "Suras" in all, became the Koran, the sacred book of the Muslims. Salvation and heaven are earned by the Muslim through belief in one God (Allah), angels, the Koran, the prophets (of whom Mohammed was the last and greatest), the final judgment and God's decrees, and through the faithful practice of prayer, fasting, almsgiving, recital of the creed ("No God but Allah and Mohammed his prophet"), and once in a lifetime, the pilgrimage to Mecca.

Hinduism has been from ancient times the national religion of India. It is extremely diversified in time and space, and generalizations are difficult. Most of it was originally brought into India by the Indo-Aryans, and was essentially identical with the theistic polytheism of the early Greeks and other ancient peoples. These beliefs were gradually written down as the four *Vedas* (Veda means "knowledge," and has the same root as the English "wisdom"). Much later, additional scriptures were appended, known as the *Brahmanas* and *Upanishads*. These became more and more philosophical, and eventually incorporated the two doctrines known as *Samsara* (reincarnation) and *Karma* (works, decreeing that a person's deeds in his current incarnation determine his type of existence in the next). The only release from these endless cycles is the attainment of *nirvana*, which in effect means cessation of existence, either by good works, transcendental philosophic understanding, or ritualistic devotion to the gods. For most Hindus, the latter is followed and India is a land of multitudes of gods and goddesses, temples, and rituals.

Buddhism was founded by Gautama (563–480 B.C.) partially in reaction to the popular Hinduism of his day. He received what he called "enlightenment" at age 35, attaining a foretaste of *nirvana* and rapidly won great numbers of disciples. Eventually Hinduism won out in India, however, and Buddhism has been stronger in other lands. He taught that *nirvana* could be achieved by the eightfold path of right beliefs, aspirations, speech, conduct, means of livelihood, endeavors, mindfulness, and meditation. There have, of course, been many offshoots of Buddhism, different in different countries. Gautama is not the only "Buddha" ("enlightened one") in the view of many; there have been other Buddhas before and since. Lamaism in Tibet and Zen Buddhism in Japan are examples of variant forms of Buddhism. The popular practice of Buddhism often is polytheistic and animistic. Shintoism is a specialized sort of national Buddhism in Japan. In China, it has been somewhat incorporated into Confucianism and Taoism.

Confucianism is named after the Chinese practical philosopher Confucius (551–478 B.C.). It is primarily an ethical system, rather than religious, and is silent, if not actually skeptical, toward the existence of God and a future life. The *Analects* of Confucius were collected by his disciples and form the guide book most used by Confucianists, although various other semi-sacred writings are attributed to him. He did teach ancestor worship and at least condoned the religious polytheism of the people, though probably he himself was strictly a humanist. Later, in many areas of Confucianism, he was himself deified and worshipped. The pantheism of Tao ("the way") and the polytheism of Taoism are commonly mixed with it and elements of Buddhism.

Animism is a sort of generic term for a great variety of religious beliefs, ancient and modern, centering in the worship of nature and the spirit beings who control the various processes of nature. Though it has no scriptures (except in the form of ancient traditions handed down in each tribe) and no common center or acknowledged founder, it nevertheless is essentially the same religion the world around, whether among the black tribes in Africa, the Indians of the Americas, the natives of the South Pacific, or the aboriginal tribes of Asia. In essence it is not much different from the polytheistic religions of antiquity, from the spirit and ancestor worship of the modern eastern religions, nor from the widespread spiritism and other occult religions found even in Christian countries today.

All of the above religions, as well as various other smaller systems, while diverse in many details, are really one religion of works-salvation, centered in man's own authority and philosophical insights. The same judgment could be lodged against even many so-called "Christian" systems, to the degree in which they also teach salvation by works, and interpose some human authority instead of the Lord Jesus Christ as a necessary mediator between man and God.

Selected books for further study:

Anderson, Norman. 1976. *The World's Religions*. Grand Rapids, MI: Wm. B. Eerdmans Publishing Co. 244 p.

Bavinck, J.H. *Introduction to the Science of Missions*. Phillipsburg, NJ: Presbyterian and Reformed.

Clarke, Andrew D., and Bruce W. Winter, eds. 1993. *One God, One Lord: Christianity in a World of Religions Pluralism*. Grand Rapids, MI: Baker Book House. 256 p.

Clendenin, Daniel B. 1995. *Many Gods, Many Lords*. Grand Rapids, MI: Baker Book House. 176 p.

Gaebelein, Arno C. 1927. *Christianity or Religion*. New York, NY: Our Hope Publications.

Kretzman, Paul E. 1943. *The God of the Bible and Other Gods*. St. Louis, MO: Concordia Publishing House. 196 p.

Lewis, C.S. 1948. *The Case for Christianity*. New York, NY: Macmillan. 56 p.

Lewis, C.S. 1960. *Mere Christianity*. New York, NY: Macmillan. 190 p.

McDowell, Josh, and Don Stavant. 1983. *Handbook of Today's Religions*. San Bernardino, CA: Here's Life Publishers. 567 p.

Morris, Henry M. 1988. *The God Who is Real*. Grand Rapids, MI: Baker Book House. 96 p.

Nash, Ronald H. 1994. *Is Jesus the Only Savior?* Grand Rapids, MI: Zondervan Publishing House. 176 p.

Sire, James W. 1976. *The Universe Next Door*. Chicago, IL: Inter-Varsity Press. 238 p.

Zwemer, Samuel M. 1945. *The Origin of Religion*. New York, NY: Loiseaux Brothers. 256 p.

Chapter III

The Authenticity of the New Testament

Importance of Historicity

As pointed out in the preceding chapter, an important aspect of the uniqueness of Christianity is the fact that it is founded on historical events rather than merely on ethical teachings. It is not surprising, therefore, that non-Christians and skeptics in general have consistently sought to attack and refute the true historicity of these events. If the events surrounding the life of Jesus Christ — His virgin birth, the miracles, the resurrection — did not actually happen, then the whole structure of Christianity collapses. "If Christ be not raised, your faith is vain; ye are yet in your sins" (1 Cor. 15:17).

The same is true concerning the history of the Early Church and the initial establishment and spread of Christianity as recorded in the Book of Acts and the Epistles. Critics have tried to persuade people that the books of the New Testament were written long after the period of the Apostles and that they, therefore, contain much that is legendary and non-historical, especially those parts which describe miracles. A great deal of this destructive criticism has been so successful that it has been adopted in considerable degree by most of the major seminaries, and has been tremendously influential in subverting the faith of multitudes of nominal Christians.

On the other hand, if it can be shown that the New Testament documents are authentic, written by the traditional authors, then the evidence for the truth of Christianity is overwhelming. This is because the writings, when examined carefully, give indisputable evidence of sincerity and accuracy of such high degree that there can remain no reasonable doubt that all the deeds and words of Christ and the Apostles, as recorded therein, really and truly happened.

This inference is not dependent upon the question of whether or not the documents are divinely inspired and verbally infallible. Although we do believe in the fact and importance of plenary verbal inspiration, the genuineness of the person and work of Christ can be established entirely apart from that assumption, provided only that the New Testament documents are accepted as valid and authentic historical writings, of the same sort as other historical documents.

Therefore, it is important to establish, first of all, the general historicity and reliability of the New Testament writings. Once this is done, then the genuineness of the portrait of Christ found in these writings can be established. When He is acknowledged as true God and only Savior, then He himself becomes sufficient authority and proof of all other doctrines.

Authenticity of the Documents

The witness of almost two thousand years of the Christian era, with its tremendous impact upon the history of the world, is itself proof that something of unique power and importance took place to get it started. Effects must have adequate causes.

Whatever men think of the New Testament, there is no doubt at all that this remarkable history of Christianity is intricately related to it. The ultimate explanation of Christian origins can only be understood when the origins of the New Testament are likewise understood. No one now living, of course, nor anyone living in many generations, has actually seen Christ or the Apostles, so that our knowledge of them now must come entirely or largely from the written records of their activities. The same, of course, is true with respect to any other men or events in ancient history.

It is at this point that the tremendous strength of the evidences for Christianity begins to be realized. The written records of Christian origins are in this respect available in far greater variety and antiquity than are those of any other personages or happenings in the whole history of the world prior to the invention of printing! No one, for example, ever doubts for an instant that a man named Julius Caesar once ruled as emperor of Rome. But the manuscript evidence for the New Testament events is incomparably superior to that for the existence of Caesar.

Before the invention of the printing press, books had to be copied by hand. Those that were in much use wore out quickly and required frequent re-copying. The manuscript copies of the New Testament or portions thereof that have actually been preserved to the present day are amazingly numerous. Some of these are on papyrus fragments that were copied before the middle of the second century. Altogether there are probably available today over 5,000 handwritten manuscript copies of portions of the New Testament in Greek and at least 15,000 more in other languages. Nothing remotely comparable to this abundance exists for any other ancient writing.

One of the greatest New Testament scholars of our generation was Sir Frederic G. Kenyon, director of the British Museum. Though not himself a believer in the infallibility of the inspiration and transmission of the Scriptures, Kenyon said after an extensive review of the manuscript evidence:

> It is reassuring at the end to find that the general result of all these discoveries and all this study is to strengthen the proof of the authenticity of the Scriptures, and our conviction that we have in our hands, in substantial integrity, the veritable Word of God.[1]

Although there are many individual differences found in the New Testament text as preserved in these 20,000 manuscripts, the very number of them provides a powerful means of checking and tracing the origin of the variant readings and thus of ascertaining the original text. Furthermore, the discrepancies, whether caused by careless copying or by deliberate alterations, are in almost all cases quite trivial,[2] affecting no important fact or doctrine. In particular, the person and work of Jesus Christ as represented are not changed in any respect by the variant readings. Not only do we have such a tremendous accumulation of manuscripts of the New Testament itself, but also we have several times as many manuscripts of writings from early Christian writers containing

---

[1] *The Story of the Bible*, Special U.S. Edition (Grand Rapids, MI: Wm. B. Eerdmans Publishing Co., 1967), p. 133.

[2] It is worth mentioning that two of the most ancient manuscripts (the Sinaitic and Vatican manuscripts) have many obvious errors, even though they have been used extensively in modern English translations. This is probably why they have been preserved so long, having been kept but not used.

quotations from the New Testament Scriptures. Certain of these men, known as the Apostolic Fathers, wrote originally during the period A.D. 90 to 160 and exhibited a remarkable grasp of the New Testament. Scholars agree that if all manuscripts of the New Testament had been lost, it would have been possible to reconstruct it altogether from quotations in the writings of these and other early Christians.

Since these church fathers in many cases lived in the years immediately following those of the Apostles themselves, in some cases even overlapping their times and in fact some papyrus fragments of the New Testament itself, notably in the Gospel of John, are dated from about A.D. 150, there can be no doubt whatever that the New Testament as we have it today is essentially identical with that possessed by Christians at the close of the first century.

Kenyon has said in another place: "The interval, then, between the dates of original composition and the earliest extant evidence becomes so small as to be in fact negligible, and the last foundation for any doubt that the Scriptures have come down to us substantially as they were written has now been removed. Both the authenticity and the general integrity of the books of the New Testament may be regarded as finally established."[3]

This being so, it hardly seems likely that there could have been any significant change in the writings during the relatively short interval between their original composition by the Apostles and their general distribution among the churches by the close of the first century. Any significant alterations would certainly have been quickly discovered and corrected. Men who had known and heard the Apostles were still living in considerable numbers at that time. In fact, John the Apostle himself lived through the end of the first century.

Even if we were to allow the possibility, for the sake of argument, that considerable changes could have taken place in the written records in the last half of the first century, there is still no way in which such changes could have been of sufficient magnitude to transform the person of Christ himself. The Roman world of the first century was a world of scholarship and skepticism, not of ignorance and gullibility, a world of abun-

---

[3] Frederick G. Kenyon, *The Bible and Archaeology* (New York, NY: Harper Brother, 1940), p. 199.

dant transportation and communication, not of isolation. The contention of religious "liberals" that the great truths of the character and work of Jesus Christ, as presented in the New Testament, were nothing but the gradual accretion of myths and traditions with no basis in fact is naive at best.

If we can believe anything at all that has been preserved for us from ancient history by the writings of men of those days, we are more than justified in believing that our New Testament was originally written in essentially its present form by the traditional authors. The world's foremost biblical archaeologist, William F. Albright, has said: "In my opinion, every book of the New Testament was written by a baptized Jew between the forties and eighties of the first century A.D."[4]

Indirect Confirmations

The general authenticity of the events reported in the New Testament has been amply verified by close examination of the internal consistencies of the writings and also by external researches in the history and archaeology of the time. The books of the New Testament individually make claims concerning their own authorship and it is absurd for modern skeptics to presume to deny these claims merely on the basis of their own anti-supernaturalistic presuppositions. The Apostle Paul, for instance, always begins his epistles with his own name, clearly claiming authorship, and each epistle contains great numbers of incidental allusions which support such claims. One of the great classic works on Christian evidences (William Paley's *Horae Paulinae*) consisted of an extensive volume of compilations of such undesigned coincidences which proved Paul to be the author of all the epistles bearing his name.

Similar studies on the internal evidences in each book likewise confirm that Peter was the author of his epistles, John of his, and so on. Events referred to in these epistles frequently tie in with the earlier histories of these men as recorded in the gospels and in Acts. For example, Peter refers to his experience on the Mount of Transfiguration (2 Pet. 1:16-18; Matt. 17:1-5), and Paul to his stoning at Lystra (2 Cor. 11:25; Acts 14:19). Examples of this sort could be added almost without number. Linguistic evidence also is consistent with the traditional authorship. For example, the vocabularies of the Gospel of

---

[4] William F. Albright, *Christianity Today* (January 18, 1963).

John, the three epistles of John, and the Revelation are all strikingly similar (note use of "the Word" as a name of Christ — John 1:1; 1 John 1:1; Rev. 19:13).

In addition to these and other internal evidences, archaeological studies have provided still further confirmation of the New Testament writings and their authenticity. The Book of Acts is especially important in this connection. Dealing as it does with the spread of the gospel in the first 30 years after Christ, it incorporates a large number of references to places, times, customs, and events of the Roman, Greek, and Jewish worlds of that time. If the book were an accumulation of uncertain traditions compiled long after the events, or if its writer, Luke, were merely a careless reporter, there would exist an abundance of opportunity for factual mistakes in the book.

So far is such from being the case, however, that the greatest of all New Testament archaeologists, Sir William Ramsay, who made the most extensive studies anyone has ever undertaken on the authenticity of these data recorded in Acts, finally said (even though he began his studies as a skeptic), "Luke is a historian of the first rank; not merely are his statements of fact trustworthy; he is possessed of the true historic sense. . . . In short this author should be placed along with the very greatest of historians."[5]

It might be noted in passing that this same very careful and accurate historian, Luke, was also the author of the gospel that carries the fullest account of Christ's virgin birth and resurrection.

The other books of the New Testament do not, of course, lend themselves as readily to archaeological investigation as well as does the Book of Acts. Nevertheless, the description of Jerusalem and other cities and regions of Judea and Samaria, references to customs and political situations, and many other such incidental allusions have frequently been confirmed and illustrated by archaeological and historical studies. On the contrary, no statement in the New Testament has to this date been refuted by an unquestioned find of science or history. This in itself is a unique testimony to the amazing accuracy and authenticity of the New Testament records.

Finally, it is important to note that the New Testament

---

[5] William Ramsay, *The Bearing of Recent Discovery on the Trustworthiness of the New Testament* (Grand Rapids, MI: Baker Book House, 1953), p. 80.

was not written in the classical Greek language as scholars once thought it should have been. Instead, it was written in the common language of that era, the *Koine* (i.e., "common") Greek, which had been actually forgotten until it was rediscovered by archaeology in modern times.

Implications of Authenticity of Documents

Once we establish the fact that the books of the New Testament are authentic historical documents, written by contemporaries and often eyewitnesses of the events they describe, we are then able to examine the events and personages with genuine confidence that we can determine their real nature and significance. We are not dealing with elusive theological or philosophical questions at all, but with matters of fact, determinable by objective investigation.

Such an investigation is still quite independent of the question whether or not these documents are divinely inspired. Rather, we are concerned at this point whether, as valid historical documents, they describe the person and work of Christ as divine in origin and essence, or rather as truly and only human.

If indeed He is shown forth in the writings as deity, then a number of options may still be considered. Were the various writers involved in a monstrous plot, with the purpose of establishing themselves as leaders in some new religious or political movement? Or, if not, were they merely under some kind of delusion, thinking that Christ was God when really He was not? If they had been deceived in this way, did Jesus intentionally deceive them? Or was He also deceived, either by His own enthusiasm or by the persuasion of others, that He was God? All of these possibilities can be evaluated by a study of the writings themselves, once they are recognized as authentic in date and authorship. Thus, we are in position to decide objectively whether or not Jesus Christ truly is the only Son of God and the only way of salvation, as Christians believe.

On the other hand, it is never really possible to free one's mind from subjective factors on an issue such as this. Even if we can show that all these witnesses agree completely in their testimony to the deity of Christ, a person may still decide on his own initiative not to believe it.

To any argument, an objection or further question can always be devised if the objector is clever enough. Even if he is backed into a corner from which there seems no logical escape, he can always get angry and avoid the issue, insist on delaying a decision until he can think more about it, take refuge in the fact that many others are unbelievers, insist that all such reasoning and logic are unrelated to the central issue of relevance, or else just change the subject. Anyone who is predisposed to accept and believe solid Christian evidence will find it in satisfying abundance along this line of study.

Sincerity of the New Testament Writers

The general authenticity of the New Testament documents as to date and authorship can, in view of the foregoing, be considered as established. Furthermore, the general accuracy of their records has been adequately confirmed by linguistic and archaeological studies, as well as by their own internal consistency.

Certain skeptics, however, have sought to escape the impact of their portrait of Christ and the gospel by charging the writers with fraud. That is, for purposes of their own, perhaps to establish themselves at the head of a new religious or political movement, they conspired to produce the marvelous tale of a supernatural Savior and King, whose representatives they were and whose authority they were to exercise in the world's affairs.

Such an incredible supposition, however, can commend itself only to those who will grasp at straws. Several considerations mentioned below are sufficient to discredit this notion:

1. The "conspiracy" involved a large number of people, of such diversity as to render such collaboration almost completely impossible. There were at least eight different writers involved, not to mention a great number of associated colleagues, and these lived and wrote at widely scattered times and places.
2. Evidences of collusion are notably absent in the writings themselves. Each writer gives his own independent witness, writing from his own perspective. Often, in fact, they appear on the surface to contradict each other, and such contradictions are resolved only by very close and careful examination and cross-examination of their testimonies.
3. Rather than confining their writings to generalities

and to private events in their own lives, which would make it, of course, more difficult to detect error or fraud, the records teem with references to public events, places, dates, and other matters of accessible knowledge.

4. A candid reading of the New Testament books surely does not suggest fraud or hypocrisy in even the slightest degree. Not only are such sins scathingly rebuked, but the very atmosphere of the writings is pervaded with the feeling of sincere conviction on the part of the authors. If the writings are actually wicked deceptions, these men were undoubtedly the greatest masters at deception who ever lived.

5. The crowning proof of sincerity is, of course, the fact that the New Testament authors were willing to suffer and die for their convictions. They did indeed "suffer the loss of all things," and all except John died as a martyr because of their testimony. Men may occasionally be willing to die for an unworthy cause which is false, but never if they know it to be so. It is impossible that all these would gladly sacrifice their lives for what they knew to be a gross deception.

The Sanity of the Writers

Granted, then, that the writers of the new Testament were sincere men, firmly convinced of the truth of what they wrote, could they have been simply mistaken? Were they subject to some form of mass delusion or hysteria? Were they either highly unstable, easily convinced by their own emotions that they were seeing supernatural manifestations, or else were they gullible, deluded by sleight-of-hand artistry and clever persuasion?

The events reported by the writers, however, especially the miraculous events supposedly hardest to believe, were not at all such as to be amenable to mass hallucination or mass deception, as they would have to be if such suggestions have any validity. The events were:

1. In the open, among crowds of people, not in isolation or in dark corners. (For example, note the amazing feeding of the 5,000, one of the few events in the life of Christ reported in all four Gospels.)

2. Reported in a great variety of times and places, by many different people of varied backgrounds and characteristics, unlike any other cases of mass delusion ever reported.

3. Written up by men who were clearly not the type of men subject to credulity or hallucinations — e.g., Paul, one of the best-educated men of his day, with a highly logical and careful mind; Luke, an exceptionally competent physician and historian; Peter and John, trained as hard and pragmatic fishermen; Matthew, a politician and tax-assessor; James, a stolid and practical individual, acknowledged as leader of the early church in Jerusalem; and Jude, brother of James.

4. Accepted by great numbers of people who, because of the intense persecution they endured for their faith, would have certainly had every reason to analyze and test very critically the claims made concerning Christ by the early Apostles. It is inconceivable they could have persisted in their faith if there were any grounds for believing the Apostles to be nothing but deluded fanatics.

The Character of Christ

The only remaining source of deception that could be a possible explanation must be in Jesus Christ himself. That is, we have seen that the New Testament documents are authentic, written around the middle of the first century by men who were intelligent and stable men, sincere in what they wrote; men who had full access to the facts they were reporting, and who were firmly convinced that the one about whom they wrote was God himself, perfectly in union with human flesh, as Son of God and Son of Man, the one whose words and deeds were uniquely perfect, who performed many mighty miracles, and who had triumphed over death itself by His bodily resurrection.

Now, if all this were not really true, the only remaining possible way of accounting for such beliefs is to say that Jesus Christ himself somehow deceived His disciples into believing them. He so dazzled them with His speech that they thought He was absolutely perfect in word and deed. Likewise, He somehow tricked them into imagining they had seen Him walking on water, giving sight to the blind, and restoring

Lazarus to life after four days in the tomb. And then, most marvelous of all, by some sort of incredible "passover plot," He persuaded them He had been crucified, buried and then raised again. Furthermore, He deceived them into thinking that after His resurrection, they saw Him ascending up through the clouds into heaven!

The mere recital of such absurdities is proof enough that they are impossibilities! If Jesus were of such absolutely unique skills in trickery and deception as such an explanation would require, He becomes a more marvelous enigma than if He actually did all the disciples claim for Him. Furthermore, He is surely the greatest charlatan and hypocrite in all history, if such an explanation is really true.

Yet even His enemies have continually acknowledged Him to be the greatest teacher, by precept and example, the world has ever known. The influence of His teachings and those He inspired in His followers have been the greatest force for good that man has ever encountered. Unless His character is truly as portrayed in the New Testament, there is no way ever to find that which is good and true in this world. Life is certainly devoid of any meaning, and God is dead, if Christ is not what the Scriptures declare.

The Witness of the Ordinances

Christian churches everywhere, of almost all denominations, practice two most remarkable ceremonies. Though the particular form of the observance of each may have changed in some respects with the passing years, the very fact of the observance is itself a strong testimony to the authenticity of the New Testament and Christianity. These two ceremonies are what are known as the ordinances of baptism and the Lord's Supper.

According to the gospel records (e.g., Matt. 28:19), baptism was commanded by Jesus Christ as an integral part of His Great Commission, to be given to each new convert won to himself by the preaching of the disciples. Similarly, observance of the Lord's Supper was commanded by Him as a regular observance to commemorate His sacrificial death (e.g., Matt. 26:26-28).

It is known, of course, from the literature of the Church through the ages that the churches have always practiced these two ordinances in one form or another. The authority for doing so comes from the New Testament. However, the ordinances do have a peculiar witness of their own, not shared by the other events recorded in the New Testament.

As a matter of fact, they antedate the New Testament, since they were established by Christ himself and have been practiced ever since. It is clear from the Book of Acts that converts always were baptized soon after conversion (Acts 2:41; 8:12; etc.). Also, the churches regularly observed the Lord's Supper (1 Cor. 11:20-26), even before they had the New Testament Scriptures which commanded them to do so.

To appreciate the significance of this fact, one should try to imagine what it was like to be in one of these first century churches when they first began to receive copies of the epistles and other writings which eventually were to be the New Testament. Say, for example, it was a church which had been established as the result of the preaching of Philip the evangelist. This church continued to exist for, say, about 20 years after its founding before it began to receive copies of some of Paul's epistles and perhaps another 10 years before it obtained a copy of one of the four Gospels.

During this time it was guided in its practice by the teachings of its founder and perhaps also by other teachers whom God sent its way or raised up from its own members. Among the instructions they were following were, of course, those pertaining to baptism and the Lord's Supper. Philip, who had been one of the original seven deacons, would certainly have been careful to emphasize the basic importance of these two ordinances in the life of the church. When they finally received the actual written accounts of how those ordinances were first established, this would merely strengthen and confirm them in what they were already practicing and knew to be in accordance with the verbal teachings they had received at first.

But, now, just suppose neither Philip nor any of their other teachers had ever told them anything about either ordinance and they had not practiced either baptism or the Lord's Supper before, and neither had any of the sister churches with whom they had contact. Suddenly they receive a document purporting to be from an Apostle (say, the Gospel of Matthew, or Paul's first Epistle to the Corinthians) in which these ordinances are discussed in such a way as to indicate they had been established by Christ and practiced by the churches ever since.

The obvious reaction by the church would be to assume the documents were fraudulent and to reject them forthwith. Their authors obviously could not have been the real Apostles, because they were proposing two ceremonies as having existed in the churches since the days of Christ himself, which the church receiving the documents knew, from their own previous contacts, did *not* exist in the churches. Thus, these documents would have been rejected as spurious by this church and by any other churches to which they came.

Thus, at no time after the days of Christ, could any such writings ever have gained acceptance as authentic records at all, unless these ordinances which they described were actually being practiced in the churches at the time of their writing and circulation. In this way the very existence of the two simple ceremonies of baptism and the Lord's Supper, both picturing and commemorating the sacrifice of the Lord Jesus in obedience to His commandment, is in itself a powerful witness to the authenticity of the New Testament documents which describe their establishment and perpetuation. There is no way of accounting for the initiation of either of the ordinances except as described in these documents. The churches could never have been persuaded to *begin* practicing them by books or teachers who told them they had *already* been practicing them since the days of Christ, if in fact they knew otherwise. Therefore, the ordinances *were* established by Christ, and the New Testament writings which tell about them are authentic.

Demonstration of New Testament Truth in History

A somewhat different, but nonetheless powerful, line of proof of the validity of the New Testament portrait of Christ is found in the historical vindication of certain amazing statements concerning His influence made by Christ himself.

For example, consider John 8:12 in which Jesus said (or, at least, the writer says that He said it!) "I am the light of the world; he that followeth me shall not walk in darkness but shall have the light of life." This seems absolute insanity, for a man to make a claim such as this! If such words were to come from the lips of some great world leader of the present day, he would not continue very long as a leader! And Jesus, of course, was nothing at the time except an obscure Galilean carpenter, with a motley handful of disciples.

Yet this ridiculous assertion, whether actually made by the carpenter's son himself in a moment of fanatical frenzy, or imagined by the gospel writer on the lips of a character he was creating, has been demonstrated for two thousand years to be a remarkably fulfilled prophecy! This man, whether insane or imaginary or what, has indeed been the "light of the world" ever since the words were written. The world's greatest literature, the most beautiful paintings, the most glorious music have all been inspired by Jesus Christ. Most of the hospitals, many or even most of the great educational institutions, and most of the world's charitable organizations have been founded originally in His Name. The same is true of genuine social reforms, such as abolition of slavery. Not only so, but literally millions of individuals over the centuries have found that in following Jesus, they indeed received "the light of life." Instead, therefore, of the ravings of a fanatic or the philosophizings of a fictional character, these words of the Lord Jesus Christ have been proved to be, in light of all subsequent history, the sanest and truest words that could be spoken!

Consider also the remarkable fulfillment of the words of Christ in Matthew 24:35: "Heaven and earth shall pass away, but my words shall not pass away." Such a claim, at the time it was made, must have seemed sheer madness! Who was this eccentric wanderer from an obscure village in a despised nation, that He should imagine anyone but His own circle of ignorant followers would ever be interested in what He had to say? Never pass away, indeed!

And yet, absurd and impossible though it may be, for two thousand years His words have not passed away! They have, in fact, been heard and read and loved and obeyed by more people in more nations that those of any other man who ever lived.

He also said: "And I, if I be lifted up from the earth, will draw all men unto me. This He said, signifying what death He should die" (John 12:32-33). One would think that the sight of the death of a condemned criminal on a Roman cross would present no great attraction, but rather a feeling of repulsion, to be erased from the memory as quickly as possible.

But once again, the prophecy has experienced a continuous fulfillment for two thousand years. Representative men from every nation, every walk of life, every degree of learning or ignorance, every age, every level of wealth or poverty, have been drawn to the cross of the Lord Jesus Christ. Such a phenomenon, utterly unique in history, could never have been anticipated by human reason. But there it is!

Then there is the prophecy concerning His church. "Upon this rock I will build my church; and the gates of hell shall not prevail against it" (Matt. 16:18). Again, this is an absurdly impossible claim that has nevertheless been fully accomplished in history. That the pitiful aggregation of disciples, for whom the spokesman and leader was an ignorant and impulsive fisherman like Peter, should somehow be perpetuated and multiplied despite intense and continuous opposition and persecution, seems a wild dream at best. Still more foolish would seem the notion that this persistence would be founded on Peter's belief that Jesus was the Son of the living God. Nevertheless, the dream has come true.

Jesus also predicted that these unlikely disciples would be witnesses for Him "unto the uttermost part of the earth" (Acts 1:8). This was, so far as known at the time, an utter physical impossibility, not to mention the intrinsic absurdity of the very thought that the disciples of such a teacher and such a message would be equal to such an assignment. And now, with radio, air travel, and other technological aids the Word is being taken to the most isolated tribes in the remotest regions, and has long since been preached as a witness in all the more accessible lands.

Many similar prophetic claims of Christ could be discussed in similar fashion. He made any number of claims and predictions which, coming from the lips of any other man who ever lived, would sound insane and impossible. But these words coming from *His* lips seem always right and natural and true, and in fact have always proved out to be true, whether on the stage of world history or in the realm of individual human experience.

This body of unequivocal facts, like it or not, has no rational explanation if Jesus is not actually God in human form, as the New Testament everywhere proclaims Him to be. It doesn't help any to allege, as some have done, that the writers may have misquoted Jesus and exaggerated His claims. This itself is a naive notion; the writers would rather have been shocked themselves by such claims and, if anything, would have tried to soften them and make them sound more rational.

But in any case the greater fact is that, whether Christ made
the claims or not, they have nevertheless been fulfilled. The
writers can hardly be charged with manufacturing the fulfillments! If Christianity is false, the existence of a fallacy of such
scope as this constitutes a greater miracle than if it were true.

Selected books for further study:
Bruce, F.F. 1954. *The New Testament Documents: Are they Reliable?* Grand
Rapids, MI: Wm. B. Eerdmans Publ. Co. 120 p.
Burgon, John W. 1990. *Unholy Hands on the Bible: An Introduction to Textual
Criticism.* ed. Jay Green. Sovereign Grace Trust Fund. 603 p.
Deissman, Adolph. 1927. *Light from the Ancient East.* New York, NY: Hodder and
Stoughton. 535 p.
Greenleaf, Simon. 1965. *Testimony of the Evangelists.* Grand Rapids, MI: Baker
Book House. 613 p.
Habermas, Gary R. 1984. *Ancient Evidence for the Life of Jesus.* Nashville, TN:
Thomas Nelson Publishers. 187 p.
Kenyon, Frederick G. 1940. *The Bible and Archaeology.* New York, NY: Harper
Brothers.
Kenyon, Frederick G. 1967. *The Story of the Bible.* Grand Rapids, MI: Wm. B.
Eerdmans Publishing Co.
Linnemann, Eta. 1992. *Is There A Synoptic Problem?* Grand Rapids, MI: Baker
Book House. 219 p.
Linton, Irwin H. 1943. *A Lawyer Examines the Bible.* Boston, MA: W. A. Wilde Co.
300 p.
Morris, Henry M. 1980. *King of Creation.* San Diego, CA: CLP Publishers. 239 p.
McRay, John. 1991. *Archaeology and the New Testament.* Grand Rapids, MI:
Baker Book House. 432 p.
Ramsay, William. 1953. *The Bearing of Recent Discovery on the Trustworthiness
of the New Testament.* New York, NY: Hodder and Stoughton. 427 p.
Ramsay, William. 1962. *St. Paul the Traveler and the Roman Citizen.* Grand
Rapids, MI: Baker Book House.
Thiessen, Henry C. *Introduction to the New Testament.* Grand Rapids, MI: Wm.
B. Eerdmans Publ. Co. 347 p.
Unger, Merrill F. 1962. *Archaeology and the New Testament.* Grand Rapids, MI:
Zondervan Publ. House. 350 p.
Waite, D.A. 1992. *Defending the King James Bible.* Collingwood, NJ: Bible for
Today Press. 306 p.

Chapter IV

The Authenticity of the Old Testament

The Canon of Scripture

Our present Old Testament Scriptures consist of 39 books, and there is little doubt that these were the same books accepted by the Jews of Christ's day as their divinely inspired Scriptures. The writings of Josephus, the Jewish historian, various statements in the Talmud, and numerous references in the New Testament all agree in focusing on these books, and only these, as the recognized Scriptures of the Jews. Likewise, it was these books that were accepted and used by the first Christians.

Whether or not they were all mistaken in this belief may be a matter for further discussion, but at least this was the belief, shared equally both by the early Christians and also by their Jewish opponents. Most importantly, at least to the Christian, this was the Jewish Bible as accepted by Jesus Christ.

The Old Testament was generally divided by the Jews of that day into three parts: (1) the Law of Moses, or the *Torah*, the five books of the Pentateuch; (2) the books of the Prophets, including the historical books; (3) the so-called Writings, or the "other books," the poetical writings, of which the Book of Psalms was considered most notable. This threefold division was noted by Christ, when He spoke of the prophecies, "which were written in the law of Moses, and in the prophets, and in the psalms, concerning me" (Luke 24:44).

The exact process by which these 39 books came to be "canonized" is not known, any more than is the process by which the New Testament books were later accepted. The most realistic conclusion, in both cases, is that each book was essentially self-authenticating from the very time it was written. They were acknowledged by the people of God to constitute the Word of God by the witness of the Spirit and the divinely authoritative character of the writings, right from the start. This is the only reasonable way to account for their universal acceptance in the absence of any official political or ecclesiastical determinations of their character.

The question, then, is how the scriptural writings could have ever become so universally accepted as authentic among the Jews if, in fact, they were *not* authentic. If Moses did not really write the books of Moses, if Isaiah was only one of several men who wrote the Book of Isaiah, if Daniel did not write the Book of Daniel, then how did such opinions ever become established among the people who used them? There is not the slightest answer to these questions among any of the ancient Jewish writings that have come down to us.

Reliability of the Old Testament Text

Although there is little doubt that the Old Testament as we have it today contains the same books that composed the Scriptures used by Christ, the Apostles, and the Jewish scribes of the first century, we still have the question of whether the text had been transmitted to them intact as originally written. It is obvious that, if we possess no "autographs" of the New Testament, we certainly could have none of the Old Testament.

The science that attempts to determine the original text of Scripture is known as *textual criticism*, or sometimes, the "lower criticism." We have already given reasons for our confidence that we do possess, for all practical purposes, the complete and accurate text of the New Testament.

For the Old Testament text, we are limited mainly to the Masoretic text, the Septuagint version, the Latin Vulgate, the Samaritan Pentateuch, the Syriac version, and more recently, the Dead Sea Scrolls. The text of the Old Testament which has been accepted as authoritative by both Christian and Jew is known as the Masoretic text. The Masoretes were a group of Jewish scribes who, sometime around A.D. 500, developed a more or less official text from the systematic sorting and comparison of the various manuscripts that had come down to them. In the margins of this text they were careful to write down all the variant readings which had been accumulated up to that time. These all amounted only to about 1,200 in number, or less than one per page of the Hebrew printed Bible.

As far as the transmission of the Masoretic text is concerned, prior to the printing of the first Hebrew Bible in A.D. 1526, there are about 1,000 manuscripts in existence. The oldest of these is dated at A.D. 916. However, of those that are available, there are scarcely any variations of significance, and support from other sources also warrants confidence that we have the original Masoretic text.

The basic text of the Old Testament originally consisted only of consonants, with vowels assumed to be understood by the reader from the context. However, in the present Hebrew Bible appear so-called "vowel points," indicating which vowels to use with the consonants. These were added by the Jewish scholars in about A.D. 700. Since they do not constitute a part of the original text itself, it is conceivable that these are wrong in some instances, and may need to be corrected if sound textual criticism justifies it.

As a check on the accuracy of the Masoretic text, there are several other channels of transmission of the Old Testament which can be examined. The most important of these is the Septuagint Version, so-called because it was supposedly produced by seventy scribes in about 280 B.C. These men translated the Hebrew Scriptures into the Greek language, for use by the Jews of the Dispersion. It is possible that this Septuagint translation was used by the Apostles and the other first-century Christians.

The Latin Vulgate was translated by Jerome from Hebrew and Greek into Latin in about A.D. 400. The Syriac Version was translated from the Hebrew about A.D. 200. The Samaritan Pentateuch (the Samaritans did not accept the rest of the Old Testament) had been handed down independently of the Jewish transmission line since the time of Nehemiah, about 400 B.C.

Although there are minor variations in all these versions, none are significant enough to change any doctrine or event recorded in the Old Testament. In almost all cases, the variations are trivial.

Furthermore, there are numerous ancient writings in which extensive quotations from the Old Testament were made, including the Book of Jubilees, the Book of Ecclesiastes, the Talmud, the writings of Josephus and Philo, the Zadokite Fragments, the Targums, and other early literature, as well as numerous quotations of the Old Testament in the New Testament. All unite in showing that the Old Testament text has always been essentially as we have it today, as far back as any direct evidence can take us.

This fact has been further confirmed by the discovery of the famous Dead Sea Scrolls, beginning in 1946 and continuing on to the present. These manuscripts actually date from the time of Christ or earlier and are the oldest actual manuscripts of any parts of Scripture found to date.

Many scrolls have been found, and these include, in one scroll or another, practically the entire text of the Old Testament. The agreement of all these with the received Masoretic text is remarkable, such variations as exist being insignificant.

There is thus no reasonable doubt that our present Old Testament, based on the Masoretic text, is practically identical extending back to the time when the last books of the Old Testament were originally written. That being true, there is no reason to doubt that all of the books have come down to us substantially as written. The scribes who copied the manuscripts are known to have taken extreme pains to insure accuracy of copying. Many numerical devices were used counting letters and gematria (numerical equivalents of the letters) in the various books as cross-checking devices.

Finally, it is significant that no other ancient writings of age comparable to the Old Testament have been so accurately transmitted or based on such an abundance of textual evidence. If we can rely on the accurate transmission of any ancient document at all, that document is the Old Testament.

The Strange World of Higher Criticism

The textual critic, working in the field of "lower criticism," performs a vital service as he seeks by scientific analysis of the manuscript evidence to determine as closely as possible the original text of the biblical writings. But there is another field of study, euphemistically called "higher criticism," the motivations for which are suspect, to say the least, and the results of which have been devastatingly corrosive to biblical faith.

This type of study (or, better, speculation) presumes to be able to reconstruct an accretion process by which ancient writings, especially the Bible, came to be assembled out of a miscellaneous assortment of fragments and forgeries, and then foisted on the people as divinely inspired writings of the fathers and prophets.

The "higher critics" profess to be scientific in this endeavor, but actually they are completely subjective, seeking by all means to find a naturalistic, evolutionary explanation for the Bible and the history of Israel and the Christian Church. Invariably they attempt to explain away all miracles and fulfilled prophecies, and almost always to attribute the authorship of the books to writers of much more recent date than claimed in the books themselves.

The Bible, to the higher critics, is thus a purely natural book, full of errors and contradictions and outright lies. It certainly cannot long retain any religious authority or moral value if this is its character, and yet this higher criticism has been taught as certain fact for a century or more, not only in secular universities but even in most of the theological schools of the western world.

One would think that, with an abundance of manuscript evidence confirming the textual accuracy of the Old Testament back to the very time of its completion, combined with its universal acceptance as authentic and divinely inspired, by both Jews and Christians, in the centuries closest to its writing and compilation, it would be taken at face value by those who use it, at least until some clear evidence of fraud or forgery comes to light.

But this is not the case. The higher critics insist that practically none of the Old Testament books were written by the traditional authors — all were written much later, by writers who had no direct knowledge at all of what they were writing. Claims of authorship were deliberately misrepresented to give the writings a spurious authority and, especially, to make their records of current events look like fulfilled prophecies.

This peculiar field of study began, as do most attacks on the Bible, with an attack on the two creation chapters of Genesis. Jean Astruc, an infidel French physician, in 1753 wrote that Genesis 1 and Genesis 2 were from two different and conflicting sources, since the name used for God was, in the first case, *Elohim*, and in the second, *Jehovah Elohim*. He was followed by the German rationalist Eichorn, who in 1779 noted differences of style also. DeWette in 1806 professed to distinguish four main writers of the "Hexateuch," writers now known as J, E, P, and D (referring, respectively, to the supposed "Jehovist," "Elohist," "Priestly," and "Deuteronomist" writers and editors). Various writers suggested still other documentary divisions, authors and "redactors." The Graf–Wellhausen "Hypothesis" (developed in 1866–78) worked out a very complex division of the first six books of the Bible, all supposedly written and edited in the period 900–600 B.C., whereas Moses died about 1450 B.C. Other prominent higher critics of the 19th century included Kuenen, Driver, Cheyne, Ewald, Coonhill, and others. All such men were, of course, evolutionists (though some antedated Darwin) and naturalists (though some professed Christianity and held professorships in theological schools).

The higher criticism does not, of course, stop with the books of Moses and Joshua, though these were the first to be attacked. Because of their fulfilled prophecies, Isaiah and Daniel have been particularly fought, but actually no book of the Old Testament has escaped these destructive critics.

Although these critical writings are full of high-sounding technical discussions about vocabulary and style, the real underlying presuppositions of such writers are as follows:

1. Moses could not have written the Pentateuch, because writing was unknown in his day (and, if Moses' books had to be moved to a late date, the others, that accepted Moses' authorship, had to be moved to still later dates).
2. The evolutionary theory of man's cultural developments precluded attainment of high civilizations and literary abilities as early in Israel's history as the Bible indicated.
3. The miracle stories of Genesis, Exodus, Kings, Jonah, etc., were derived from ancient mythologies. This must be so, since miracles are impossible scientifically.
4. Fulfilled prophecy is also a miracle, and therefore impossible.

But all these presuppositions are false! In recent decades,

many archaeological discoveries have confirmed that writing was very common, even among tradesmen and housewives, before even the time of Abraham. The boyhood home of the latter, Ur of the Chaldees, for example, has yielded thousands of stone volumes from its excavated library. Similarly, a great collection of business documents was unearthed at Nuzi, a city of the Horites, from the time of Abraham. The Ras Shamra tablets are examples of alphabetic cuneiform writing in the days of Moses. The Tel-el-Amarna letters have also shown widespread use of cuneiform writing at that time.

What is true of writing is also true of civilizations and literature. Even if evolution had been proved true (and exactly the opposite is the case), it certainly had attained a high state of culture long before Moses. More evidence comes in almost daily of an advanced state of technology in very ancient times, not only in Bible lands, but even in western Europe, America, the far East, and other areas.

As far as miracles and fulfilled prophecies are concerned, a bias against miracles and prophecy is, of course, a bias against God. To say miracles are impossible is atheism. The idea that the biblical miracles were derived from similar tales in other nations is pure assumption. Many such similarities (e.g., legends of the great Flood, the long day, etc.) are best accounted for as dim recollections of real events, the records of which are preserved accurately only in the Bible. Every one of the more local Bible miracles is very credible, in terms of both testimony and divine purpose, and there is no reason to reject any of them.

The higher critics deal at great length with details of grammar, vocabulary, and style, but none of these speculations can offset the universal testimony of the Jews and the Early Church, and especially that of Christ himself, that the writings are authentic. As far as style is concerned, it is pure presumption to think that one can distinguish different authors merely by their styles. The style and vocabulary of a single writer may and do vary widely from one book to another, depending on the subject being discussed and the purpose of writing. The style and vocabulary of the present writer's engineering publications, for example, are very different from those of this book, but they both have the same author!

With respect to the Book of Genesis, however, it is probable that differences in style and vocabulary actually are partly attributable to different writers. These are not the mysterious J, E, P, and D, however, but Adam, Noah, Shem, and the other patriarchs. The divisions of Genesis are marked off by the phrase "these are the generations of (author)." It is quite possible that these sections were thus originally written on tablets of stone by the patriarchal eyewitnesses themselves, handed down, and then finally compiled and edited by Moses.

Discussions of details of grammar and vocabulary are beyond the scope of our present purpose. It should be noted, however, that all such critical speculations have been thoroughly answered and refuted by conservative Bible scholars. The fact that these refutations have been completely ignored by liberals means only that such critics are either too lazy or too arrogant to read them, for they are unanswerable.

One such scholar was Dr. Robert Dick Wilson, long-time professor of Semitic philology at Princeton Seminary. Dr. Wilson was proficient in some 45 languages and dialects, and was probably more intimately familiar with the Hebrew Old Testament than any man of his generation. He died in 1930 after 50 years of continuous scholarly contributions to the study of the Old Testament. His devastating critiques of the higher criticism in all its details have never been answered.

Wilson was not alone. Numerous other conservative Old Testament authorities — men such as W.H. Green, A.H. Finn, James Orr, Oswald Allis, Melvin G. Kyle, Edward J. Young, and many others — have thoroughly answered and demolished every claim of the higher critics, if the critics would only read their writings! Dr. Wilson summarizes the situation as follows:

> In conclusion, we claim that the assaults upon the integrity and trustworthiness of the Old Testament along the line of language have utterly failed. The critics have not succeeded in a single line of attack in showing that the diction and style of any part of the Old Testament are not in harmony with the ideas and aims of writers who lived at, or near, the time when the events occurred that are recorded in the various documents. . . . We boldly challenge these Goliaths of ex-cathedra theories to come down into the field of ordinary concordances, dictionaries, and

literature, and fight a fight to the finish on the level ground of the facts and the evidence.[1]

The Geographical and Historical Accuracy of the Old Testament

There is no reason at all to question on a linguistic basis that Moses could have written the Pentateuch, that Daniel could have written the book that bears his name, or that any of the books of the Old Testament could have been written by their traditional authors at the time and places claimed. This contention is still further strengthened by the amazing historical accuracy of the Bible narratives, wherever they can be checked.

Critics, of course, are far more eager to cast doubt on the accuracy of the Bible than on that of any other ancient book, and they have systematically refused to accept its historicity at any point unless there is a large amount of external supporting evidence. Instead of assuming it to be true until proved false, almost invariably they assume it to be false until the incoming evidence compels them to change their minds.

The 19th century higher critics, for example, used to deny the historicity of the Hittites, the Horites, the Edomites, and various other peoples, nations, and cities mentioned in the Bible, for the expressed reason that other ancient historians did not mention them. This "argument from silence," however, has long since been silenced itself by the archaeologist's spade, and few critics any longer dare to question the geographical and ethnological reliability of the Bible.

The same is true of the histories of kings and empires. The Davidic-Solomonic empire, the histories of the kings of Israel and Judah, the Babylonian captivity, and the return from exile are all now considered to be historical, whereas once they were questioned or denied.

It is significant that the names of over 40 different kings of various countries, mentioned at various times in the Old Testament, have also been found in contemporary documents and inscriptions outside of the Old Testament, always consistently with the times and places associated with them in the Bible. By comparison with gross errors in such matters known

---

[1] Robert Dick Wilson, *A Scientific Investigation of the Old Testament* (Chicago, IL: Moody Press, 1959), p. 130.

to exist in other ancient histories, it becomes obvious that the writers of the Bible narratives not only were contemporaries of the people and events so named, but that they were extremely careful in what they wrote, and furthermore, all those who later copied and transmitted their writings were also extremely careful. Nothing at all exists in ancient literature which has been even remotely as well-confirmed in accuracy as has the Bible. Even those names which once were doubted by the critics (e.g., Belshazzar, Darius, etc.) have now long since been confirmed.

One of the earliest biblical events of sufficient geographical extent to be of possible interest to non-biblical historians is the record of the confederation of kings from the East who invaded Canaan and were defeated by Abraham, as recorded in Genesis 14. This story was long denied by the critics.

However, Dr. Nelson Glueck, once widely recognized as the dean of Palestinian archaeologists, president of the Hebrew Union College and the Jewish Institute of Religion, found abundant evidence of this invasion. He said, describing these events:

> Centuries earlier, another civilization of high achievement had flourished between the 21st and 19th centuries B.C., till it was savagely liquidated by the kings of the East. According to the biblical statements, which have been borne out by the archaeological evidence, they gutted every city and village at the end of that period from Ashtaroth-Karnaim, in southern Syria through all of Trans-Jordan and the Negev to Kadesh-Barnea in Sinai (Gen. 14:1-7).[2]

Dr. Glueck, though not himself a believer in biblical inerrancy, systematically explored the land of Israel for archaeological records, and found the Bible to be amazingly reliable at all points. Often he used it successfully to lead him to new discoveries, sometimes of significant economic value to the developing Israeli nation. All of this experience finally led him to make the following sweeping generalization:

---

[2] Nelson Glueck, *Rivers in the Desert* (New York, NY: Farrar, Straus and Cudahy, 1959), p. 11.

As a matter of fact, however, it may be stated categorically that no archaeological discovery has ever controverted a biblical reference. Scores of archaeological findings have been made which confirm in clear outline or in exact detail historical statements in the Bible. And, by the same token, proper evaluation of biblical descriptions has often led to amazing discoveries. They form tesserae in the vast mosaic of the Bible's almost incredibly correct historical memory.[3]

The Testimony of Christ

We have seen in the previous chapter that the New Testament records are historically authentic, and that they represent Jesus Christ to be the perfect and infallible Son of God. He was also the perfect Son of Man, sinless and without defect, as well as perfect in knowledge and power, all that the writers claim Him to be and that He himself claimed to be, or else the gospel records are inexplicable.

That being true, His own evaluation of the accuracy and reliability of the Old Testament Scriptures is of supreme determinative importance, especially to those who profess to believe in Christ. It is therefore significant, and there is no question at all about the fact, that Jesus Christ accepted the Old Testament Scriptures throughout as both historically authentic and divinely inspired. The same is true of all the writers of the New Testament.

There are at least 320 direct quotations from the Old Testament in the New, always cited as of absolute authority, in addition to hundreds of other allusions.

The Lord Jesus Christ said, among other things: "The Scripture cannot be broken" (John 10:35), and "It is easier for heaven and earth to pass, than one tittle of the law to fail" (Luke 16:17). He accepted Moses as the author of the Pentateuch (Luke 24:27; John 5:46-47), Isaiah as the author of both major "divisions" of the Book of Isaiah (Matt. 13:14 citing Isa. 6:9-10, and John 12:38 citing Isa. 53:1), and Daniel as the author of the Book of Daniel (Matt. 24:15).

---

[3] *Ibid.*, p. 31. The current crop of younger archaeologists are again promoting an anti-biblical view of Israel's history, but they have in no way matched the scholarship or refuted the conclusions of Dr. Glueck.

Christ accepted the historicity of Adam and Eve (Matt. 19:4-5), of Abel (Matt. 23:35), of Noah (Luke 17:26), of Abraham (John 8:56-58), and Lot (Luke 17:28). Likewise, He believed that the Genesis records of creation (Mark 10:6-9) and the Flood (Matt. 24:37-39) were historically true. He even believed in the *recency* of creation (Mark 10:6).

Neither did Christ have any problem in believing the Old Testament miracles, as do the modern critics. He believed in the supernatural destruction of Sodom and Gomorrah (Luke 17:29) and the calamity of Lot's wife (Luke 17:32). He accepted the miracle of the manna (John 6:32), the healing of the serpents' bites (John 3:14), the miracles of Elijah and Elisha (Luke 4:25-27) and the deliverance of Jonah from the whale (Matt. 12:39-40).

It is no light burden which modern liberal preachers and theologians assume, when they presume to know more about such matters than did the One whom they profess as their Master. To Christ and the Apostles, the Old Testament was absolutely reliable, authentic, and verbally inspired of God, and that should settle the matter for all who claim to be Christians.

The Continuing Witness of the Passover

We have noted in an earlier chapter that the ordinances of baptism and the Lord's Supper provided a continuing witness to the early Christians concerning the genuineness of the New Testament Scriptures. These ordinances were established by Christ himself and were enjoined upon the members of each local church as soon as they were won to Christ and organized into churches by the Apostles and evangelists traveling out from Jerusalem.

Had it not been so, the New Testament Scriptures, which describe the establishment and transmission of these ordinances, could never have been received as genuine and authentic when they first began to be circulated among the early churches. They would have been rejected immediately as spurious, describing as they did these ordinances as having been ordained by Christ and taught by the Apostles, if in fact they knew that no such ordinances were in effect at all.

In somewhat the same way, the observance of the Passover supper afforded a continuing testimony to the genuineness of the books of Moses which described it. The higher critics attribute these books to a number of priests or others who wrote them hundreds of years after Moses — if, indeed, Moses ever existed at all!

But the Book of Exodus describes in much detail God's instructions to the people through Moses concerning the Passover inauguration, along with His commands for its perpetual annual observance. It describes the first Passover and then the miraculous deliverance from Egypt, which the children of Israel were commanded to recall each year through the Passover observance.

Now, suppose that none of this had really happened. Then, suppose also that sometime around 700 B.C. a group of scribes and priests decided to formalize a system of worship which they had developed, and thus, to solidify their own control over the people. They therefore developed a body of religious literature, using various sources, in particular establishing on a formal basis their own priestly offices and powers, finally imparting to all of it an aura of sacred authority by attributing it to the great legendary founder and lawgiver of the nation, Moses.

But they soon would have realized they had slipped up, by including this unfortunate story of the founding and continuing observance of the Passover feast. When the people came to read this, they would immediately have rejected the writings because they had, in fact, not been observing any such thing at all, and neither had their ancestors, and they knew it.

Then, perhaps, the fabricators of the hoax may have attempted to persuade the people that the documents had somehow been lost for many years and thus their instructions forgotten until they were recently rediscovered. Although some may have been persuaded in this manner, surely many of the more skeptical and hardheaded Israelites, naturally reluctant to accept the expensive and demanding priestly rule and restrictions commanded in these spurious documents, would have demanded firm proof that they were genuine works of Moses before they would have even accepted them. The kings and rulers especially would have resisted them, since they described a theocracy, rather than a monarchy, as the governmental structure of the nation.

In fact, the readers would no doubt have responded indignantly by pointing out that, if indeed the documents and practices had been lost for so long, it was the priests and scribes themselves who were guilty, since the very documents they were using said they had been made responsible to maintain the religious institutions of Israel and they had, therefore, failed miserably and were thus hardly to be entrusted again with all this power.

The writings, of course, not only described the Passover, but also the establishment of other institutions, such as the tabernacle, the perpetual offerings, the annual feasts and other observances, and even the Levitical priesthood itself. It is inconceivable that all of these things could now suddenly be inaugurated simply on the basis of a purported "rediscovery" of ancient documents establishing them, without absolutely firm proof that the documents were genuine works of Moses.

Could it have been possible, on the other hand, that all of these institutions had somehow sprung up on their own, with no guidance from Moses, and that now, at this late date, one of them — the priesthood — decided to crystallize all of them by the development of a set of "Scriptures" describing them? Normally, in real life, effects require causes. It is far easier to believe that Moses himself originally set up all these things than to believe that, somehow, they all just happened. All of them are intimately tied to the deliverance from Egypt and wilderness wanderings commemorating them in one way or another. Could all this elaborate history and the corresponding rituals simply have been invented either by priests or anyone else, with no basis in fact? Since all of them are intimate reflections, in one way or another, of the great events associated with the nation's beginning, they must have had their start immediately after that time.

If the histories really took place, however, and if Moses actually was the great leader and lawgiver which the traditions indicated, then the documents describing the establishment of the Passover and other institutions could never have been accepted by the people unless they corresponded fully with what they already knew about the institutions and unless they gave every evidence of being genuine works of Moses.

The only other possibility is that the real writers and editors of the documents were the most unscrupulous and yet the most brilliant forgers and charlatans the world has ever encountered. They somehow contrived a marvelous story of creation and earth history, the moving narratives of the lives of the patriarchs, the thrilling tales of Israel's deliverance from Egypt and wanderings in the wilderness. Most amazing of all, these scheming liars devised the Ten Commandments and the greatest moral and ethical code in all history, and convinced everyone for three thousand years that all of it had come from God through Moses!

Now, however, thanks to the brilliant sleuthing of our modern higher critics, this ancient scheme has finally been exposed! Or perhaps it is only the higher critics themselves who have been exposed. Can men who would reason in such devious ways as this really be honest and intelligent men?

The Old Testament Scriptures still stand. The testimony of the Passover, the unanimous acceptance by the early Christians and their Jewish contemporaries, the careful linguistic studies of dedicated and highly skilled conservative Bible scholars, the penetrating discoveries of archaeology, the impact of the Old Testament on all subsequent world history, and the full confirmation by the Lord Jesus Christ of its historic and divine trustworthiness, all unite in certain assurance that the Book is true.

Selected books for further study:
Aalders, G. Charles. 1948. *The Problem of the Book of Jonah*. London: Tyndale. 30 p.
Adams, J. McKee. 1946. *Ancient Records and the Bible*. Nashville, TN: Broadman Press. 397 p.
Allis, Oswald T. 1949. *Five Books of Moses*. Phillipsburg, NJ: Presbyterian and Reformed. 355 p.
Allis, Oswald T. 1972. *The Old Testament: Its Claims and Critics*. Phillipsburg, NJ: Presbyterian and Reformed. 509 p.
Allis, Oswald T. *The Unity of Isaiah*. Phillipsburg, NJ: Presbyterian and Reformed.
Anderson, Sir Robert. *Daniel in the Critics' Den*. Grand Rapids, MI: Kregel Publishing House. 186 p.
Bruce, F. F. 1988. *The Canon of Scripture*. Downers Grove, IL: Inter-Varsity Press. 349 p.
Free, Joseph P., and Howard F. Vos. 1992. *Archaeology and Bible History*. Grand Rapids, MI: Zondervan Publishing House. 314 p.
McDowell, Josh. 1975. *More Evidence That Demands a Verdict*. San Bernardino, CA: Here's Life Publishers. 365 p.
Morris, Henry M. 1976. *The Genesis Record*. Grand Rapids, MI: Baker Book House. 716 p.
Thiele, Edwin R. 1977. *A Chronology of the Hebrew Kings*. Grand Rapids, MI: Zondervan Publ. House. 93 p.

Unger, Merrill F. 1954. *Archaeology and the Old Testament*. Grand Rapids, MI: Zondervan Publ. House. 339 p.

Whitcomb, John C. 1959. *Darius the Mede*. Grand Rapids, MI: Wm. B. Eerdmans Publishing Co. 84 p.

Wilson, Robert Dick. 1959. *A Scientific Investigation of the Old Testament*. Chicago, IL: Moody Press. 194 p.

Wilson, Robert Dick. 1925. *Studies in the Book of Daniel*, 2 vol. New York, NY: Revell. 850 p.

Wiseman, P.J. 1946. *New Discoveries in Babylonia about Genesis*. London: Marshall, Morgan and Scott. 143 p.

Young, Edward J. *An Introduction to the Old Testament*. Grand Rapids, MI: Wm. B. Eerdmans Publ Co. 432 p.

Chapter V

The Unique Birth of Christ

The Person of Christ

The bodily resurrection of Jesus Christ is, of course, the greatest proof of His deity and, therefore, of the truth of the Christian faith. However, there are many other aspects of His person and work which also warrant treatment in a study of Christian evidences. As already noted, Christianity is unique in that it is based upon its founder rather than upon its founder's teachings. "For other foundation can no man lay than that is laid, which is Jesus Christ" (1 Cor. 3:11). Therefore, it is essential that the believer understand thoroughly the nature of Jesus Christ and the basis for our certainty that Christ indeed is God himself.

In studying this subject, it is assumed that the New Testament portrait of the deeds and words of Christ is authentic and reliable. This assumption is not blind faith, as demonstrated in chapter 3, but rather is based on overwhelming evidence. Entirely apart from the question of the divine inspiration of the Bible, which will be considered later, we can be absolutely confident that the New Testament gives an accurate record of the important events and teachings in the life of Christ, as well as the beliefs concerning Him held by the first Christians. Therefore, we can base our discussion henceforth on relevant biblical statements without further digression to establish their authority.

The Pre-Incarnate Christ

Unlike all other men, the Lord Jesus Christ, according to

His own claims, did not begin His life at the time He was born of a human mother. "For I came down from heaven," He said, "not to do mine own will, but the will of him that sent me" (John 6:38).

He is shown in Scripture as the second person of the triune godhead, and thus as having life from eternity. "As the Father hath life in himself; so hath he given to the Son to have life in himself" (John 5:26). In His human career, He still had perfect consciousness of this relationship and could recall all the events of the eternal councils of the triune God. In His prayer in the upper room, He spoke of "the glory which I had with Thee before the world was" and of how the Father "lovedst me before the foundation of the world" (John 17:5, 24).

The New Testament, in fact, teaches that Christ was himself the Creator of all things. "For by him were all things created, that are in heaven, and that are in earth, visible and invisible, whether they be thrones, or dominions or principalities, or powers: all things were created by him, and for him" (Col. 1:16). Note also such Scriptures as John 1:3, 10; Hebrews 1:2-3; Ephesians 3:9; Revelation 3:14, etc.

After the creation of the world and of man, Christ in His pre-incarnate state occasionally came down for direct communication with man. In fact, whenever God appeared to man in any visible form, it was none other than Christ who thus appeared. "No man hath seen God at any time; the only begotten Son, which is in the bosom of the Father, He hath declared Him" (John 1:18). He is "Alpha and Omega" (Rev. 22:13), the living "Word" which "was God" and which "was in the beginning with God" (John 1:1-2). He thus has the office in the godhead of direct executive and communicational activity with respect to all of God's created works and beings. "All things were made by Him" (John 1:3), and He now is "upholding all things by the word of His power" (Heb. 1:3). Whenever we read such statements as "the Lord appeared unto Abram" (Gen. 12:7), we may properly understand this to be a *theophany*, in which the pre-existent Christ was making God and His will known to man by direct manifestation.

When John the Baptist came to announce the imminent appearing of the Messiah, he said: "He that cometh after me is preferred before me: for he was before me" (John 1:15, 30). He applied the terms "Lord" (*Jehovah*) and "God" (*Elohim*) in

Isaiah 40:3, both to Jesus Christ, whose coming he had been sent to proclaim.

A good example of Christ's claims to this pre-incarnate existence is found in John 8:56-58. On this occasion, He confronted the Jews with a remarkable claim: "Your father Abraham rejoiced to see my day: and he saw it, and was glad." They replied incredulously, "Hast thou seen Abraham?" Jesus answered with an emphatic claim, not to reincarnation, but to *pre*-incarnation: "Before Abraham was, I am!"

Quite probably this was a reference to Genesis 15:1, in which it says: "The word of the Lord came unto Abram in a vision." This is the first use of "word" in the Word, and thus stresses that God's Word is personalized in God himself, the living Word (John 1:1). On that historic occasion, the Word said, "I *am* thy shield and thy exceeding great reward," this constituting the first of the many great "I am's" of Christ.

The Descent from Heaven

Long before it actually occurred, the incarnation had been planned in heaven. Jesus Christ was "foreordained before the foundation of the world" (1 Pet. 1:20). Indeed, He was the "Lamb slain from the foundation of the world" (Rev. 13:8).

It was promised through the Old Testament Scriptures that God himself would enter the human family in order to suffer and die and rise again, to redeem the lost world and reconcile all things to himself.

The first of these promises was given immediately after man's first sin, concurrently with God's imposition of the great curse on man and his dominion. In Genesis 3:15 (known as the "protevangel" or "first announcement of the gospel"), God promised: "And I will put enmity between thee [i.e., the Serpent, or Satan] and the woman, and between thy seed and her seed; it [or, better, 'He'] shall bruise [literally 'crush'] thy head, and thou shalt bruise his heel." Since neither Satan nor "woman" could produce literal seed, it is clear that this promise refers to a spiritual seed in both cases. Nevertheless, the "seed of the woman" requires an actual birth into the human family. In some way, therefore, the promised deliverer would be born of woman, but without genetic connection to His human parents. Clearly implied, though in veiled terminology, is the supernatural entrance of God himself into human life, in a great incarnation.

This primeval promise was made much more explicit over three thousand years later, through the prophet Isaiah. "Behold, [the] virgin shall conceive, and bear a son, and shall call his name Immanuel" (Isa. 7:14). The use of the definite article (*the* virgin) is justified by the Hebrew original and thus implies a very specific virgin, most likely referring to the "seed of the woman" of Genesis 3:15. This primeval promise is seen reflected in the early traditions of many nations, and even in the primeval signs seen by man in the heavens, the zodiacal sign *Virgo* being a case in point. When Isaiah spoke of *the* virgin, there is little doubt that his hearers and readers would have tied it in with the ancient Edenic promise, and this, in fact, was exactly the interpretation placed upon it by the Rabbinic teachers of pre-Christian Israel.

As far as the word "virgin" is concerned (Hebrew *ha-almah*), modern liberal commentators notwithstanding, it means exactly what its King James translation suggests. It is used six other times in the Old Testament, and in every case *could* mean virgin, and in some cases *must* mean virgin. In the Septuagint translation of this verse, as well as its quotation in Matthew 1:23, the Greek *parthenos* is used, which can *only* mean "virgin." Also, the definite article, "*the* virgin" appears in the Greek translations as well.

The name Immanuel means "God with us," and clearly refers to a supernatural birth in which God would become one of humankind. The same thought is amplified in Isaiah 9:6: "For unto us a child is born . . . and His name shall be called Wonderful, Counsellor, the Mighty God, the everlasting Father, the Prince of Peace."

Even more specific is Micah 5:2, "But thou, Bethlehem Ephratah . . . out of thee shall He come forth unto me that is to be ruler in Israel: whose goings forth have been from of old, from everlasting." Note also the striking prophecy of Jeremiah 31:22: "The Lord hath created a new thing in the earth, A woman shall compass a man."

In due course, "When the fulness of the time was come, God sent forth His Son, made of a woman" (Gal. 4:4). Jesus frequently made reference to the fact that He proceeded "forth from the Father, and am come into the world: again, I leave the world, and go to the Father" (John 16:28).

John says, "God sent his only begotten Son into the world"

(1 John 4:9), and Paul says that God sent "His own son in the likeness of sinful flesh" (Rom. 8:3). "Without controversy great is the mystery of godliness: God was manifest in the flesh" (1 Tim. 3:16).

The Incarnation

In order to redeem man, therefore, God must somehow become man. He must enter His space-time cosmos in a finite, temporal form, yet without ceasing to be the infinite, eternal God. This apparent paradox is resolved in the triune nature of God. God's eternal Son can also become the Son of Man.

"The Word was made flesh, and dwelt among us, (and we beheld his glory, the glory as of the only begotten of the Father) full of grace and truth" (John 1:14). The classic passage on the incarnation of Christ is Philippians 2:6-7, which can be paraphrased as follows: "Christ Jesus, being in the outward form of God, not fearful of losing his deity, divested himself of that appearance, and took upon himself the outward form of a slave, and was made in the physical likeness of men."

This divestiture (Greek *kenosis*) of His heavenly glory, did not mean that He gave up His essential deity. He was still the infinite and holy God, and continued to manifest His divine attributes when occasion required. At the same time, He now became a man, perfect man. As God, He can do all things consistent with His character, and so He could, and did, become man also.

The importance of the Incarnation is incalculable. Satan had become the ruler of this world when he persuaded the first man to follow him. All men since had become through Adam, "children of disobedience" and "children of wrath," walking according to the "prince of the power of the air" (Eph. 2:2-3). In order for man to be reconciled to God and Satan to be crushed, God must become the "seed of the woman," taking up residence, first of all, in embryonic form in the womb of a prepared woman, and then undertaking His great work of redemption among men.

Not only, therefore, did Satan do all he could to prevent the Incarnation, but even yet refuses to let his hosts acknowledge that it was successfully accomplished. The very touchstone by which evil spirits are to be identified is this: "Every spirit that confesseth not that Jesus Christ is come in the flesh is not of God" (1 John 4:3 — note that the name Jesus Christ is equivalent to "God as Savior and anointed King"). Demons are willing to acknowledge that the one called Jesus is "the son of God" (Matt. 8:29), since they have known Him thus from ancient times, but not that He is truly man — the one Man not in bondage to Satan (note Heb. 2:14-18), and therefore capable of setting other men free from that bondage.

Great, indeed, is this mystery. How could the infinite God enter the family of finite men and become truly "in the flesh"? Since He is the God of absolute holiness, He could not come "in sinful flesh," bearing all the inherent corruption from many generations of sinful ancestors. Even from the biological point of view, the accumulation of harmful genetic mutations that must inevitably have resided in the germ cells of any parents God could choose would preclude His being "made flesh" (John 1:14) by any natural process of human generation.

Yet, in order to really "come in the flesh" (1 John 4:2) and to be "found in fashion as a man" (Phil. 2:8), He must undergo the whole human experience, from conception and birth through childhood, youth, and manhood. He must come altogether "in the likeness of sinful flesh," and then be "tempted in all points like as we are" (Heb. 4:15), and yet remain "holy, harmless, undefiled, separate from sinners" (Heb. 7:26).

The Virgin Birth

The only way in which these two conflicting requirements could be met was by a miraculous conception and virgin birth. His human experience must begin, as for all men, with conception, but the embryonic form so generated could have no genetic connection with either mother or father, both of whose heredities were contaminated by both biological defects and inherent sin. The promised "seed of the woman" (Gen. 3:15) could only come by special creation; the "seed" is always of the man under normal conditions. Yet he must also be of the "seed of David" (Ps. 89:3-4), and therefore begin His human life through a mother descended from David's line.

Therefore, by special creative power, God prepared a perfect human body for the incarnation. "Wherefore, when He cometh into the world, He saith . . . a body hast Thou prepared Me" (Heb. 10:5). Since the body had been prepared by God himself, it was biologically perfect, though embryonic, and must appropriately be placed in the womb of a virgin for care prior to birth and in the home of godly and loving parents for care in infancy and childhood.

The perfect choice for this ministry was the virgin Mary and her future husband Joseph. Accordingly, the angel Gabriel was dispatched to inform Mary. "The Holy Ghost shall come upon thee, and the power of the Highest shall overshadow thee; therefore also that holy thing which shall be born of thee shall be called the Son of God" (Luke 1:35). Skeptics have derided the doctrine of the miraculous conception as a biological absurdity, but Mary, who alone really knew the full truth about it, responded in joyous faith, "He that is mighty hath done to me great things; and holy is his name" (Luke 1:49).

The angel likewise assured Joseph: "Fear not to take unto thee Mary thy wife: for that which is conceived in her is of the Holy Ghost" (Matt. 1:20). He reminded Joseph also of the great prophecy which was now to be fulfilled, "Behold, the virgin shall be with child, and shall bring forth a Son, and they shall call his name Emmanuel, which being interpreted is, God with us" (Matt. 1:23).

The passages describing the supernatural conception and birth of Christ (Matt. 1:18–2:23 and Luke 1:26–2:40) are among the most familiar in all the Bible, each year at Christmastime confronting even those who never read the Scriptures any other time. No part of God's revelation, except His record of His supernatural creation of the world and the body for the *first* man has been derided and rejected by unbelievers more vigorously than this record of His special creation of the body for the "*second man*, the Lord from heaven" (1 Cor. 15:47).

The doctrine of the virgin birth has, in recent times, become essentially a watershed for distinguishing modernism and fundamentalism or, more recently, between evangelicalism and neo-orthodoxy. To be more precise, of course, it is the miraculous conception which is the issue, since the birth itself was normal in every way. Mary, of course, remained a virgin until after the birth of Jesus (Matt. 1:25), but it was the supernatural creation of the body in her womb that constitutes the great miracle of the virgin birth.

Note also that the virgin birth of Christ is altogether unique. Some writers have tried to compare it to known instances of so-called "parthenogenesis" among rabbits or other animals (some have even claimed examples among human women), in which the egg cell from the mother is somehow fertilized by artificial insemination or other purely naturalistic (though abnormal) processes. Such comparisons are irrelevant, however, since the body prepared by God for His Son had no connection genetically with either mother or father. It was formed by God himself, just as was the body for the first Adam.

The objections that have been raised by unbelievers against the virgin birth are pointless and trivial and, more than anything else, reveal the spiritual shallowness of these who raise them.

These criticisms are listed and briefly answered below:

The virgin birth is a biological impossibility. It is an impossibility only if there is no God. It is indeed a mighty miracle of creation, as is uniquely appropriate for the entrance of the infinite God into the finite body of His creature, man.

The virgin birth is mentioned only by Matthew and Luke. The fact that neither Mark nor John discusses the birth of Christ, however, does not mean they did not believe He had been born! The primary message of the early Christians, of course, was Christ's death and resurrection, not the details of His birth. The writings of Matthew and Luke are quite reliable in every respect, were accepted as such by the early church, and the information they gave concerning the birth of Christ was all that was needed. Paul also mentioned the supernatural incarnation (Gal. 4:4), and the whole sense of the gospels and epistles is perfectly consistent with the virgin birth, even though specific reference to it was not often required.

The idea of virgin birth came from mythology. Nothing in any way comparable to the miraculous conception and virgin birth is found in any pagan myth or religion. Certain "incarnations" of gods in men or animals, of course, are found everywhere in polytheistic pantheism. Also, there are numerous "demi-gods," supposedly resulting from the cohabitation of gods and men. Such things as these have no similarity to the virgin birth of Christ and could never have given rise to the simple, matter-of-fact histories written, and undoubtedly checked out with Mary and Joseph, by Luke and Matthew. The mythical stories more likely themselves developed as a corruption of the primeval records in Genesis 3:15 and Genesis 6:1-4.

There are contradictions in the birth narratives. The only significant contradiction between Matthew and Luke is in the two genealogies given for Jesus (Matt. 1:1-17 and Luke 3:23-38), and this has nothing in itself to do with the virgin birth as such. As a matter of fact, the two genealogies supplement and confirm each other. Matthew's entire account is written from Joseph's point of view (evidently Matthew had learned these events either directly or indirectly from Joseph himself) and Luke's from that of Mary. Matthew, directly concerned with Jesus' right to the throne of David, thus gives the genealogy of Jesus through Joseph, who was his legal (though not actual) father. Luke records Mary's genealogy, also from David, calling Joseph the "son" of Heli (who was actually the father of Mary rather than Joseph) in accord with Jewish custom, which permitted a man to recognize his daughter's husband as his own son. Heli, under the circumstances, aware of Joseph's devotion to Mary and willingness to compromise his own good name for her sake, had special reason to regard Joseph with parental love and gratitude. Further-more, the two genealogies provide the solution to an apparent contradiction in Old Testament prophecies concerning the Davidic line. The succession of kings of Judah from the seed of David was apparently termi-nated with Coniah (Jer. 22:30), and yet he is listed in the legal genealogy leading to Joseph (Matt. 1:11-12). Still, God had made a sure promise that David's seed should forever occupy the throne of Israel (Jer. 33:17). Thus, the requirements of both legal succession and divine prophecy were met in the union of Mary and Joseph, and the two genealogies in effect point this out.

Thus, the supposed difficulties with the virgin birth are really not to the point. Although such objections are often hedged about with platitudes about the "incarnation," it is almost always true that those who reject the virgin birth also reject the unique and full deity of Jesus Christ. On the other hand, no other completely appropriate manner exists for the eternal Word to be made flesh. A newly created body was necessary, free both from physical defects and transmitted depravity, "without blemish and without spot" (1 Pet. 1:19). Yet in order to be truly the Son of Man, He must experience the totality of human life beginning from the conception itself. "Wherefore in all things it behooved Him to be made like unto His brethren" (Heb. 2:17). The only way in which these requirements could all be satisfied was by miraculous creative conception and then virgin birth.

Selected books for further study:
Anderson, Sir Robert. n.d. *The Lord from Heaven*. Grand Rapids, MI: Kregel Publications. 118 p.
Hanke, Howard A. 1963. *The Validity of the Virgin Birth*. Grand Rapids, MI: Zondervan Publ. House. 122 p.
Machen, J. Gresham. 1965. *The Virgin Birth of Christ*. Grand Rapids, MI: Baker Book House.
Morris, Henry M. 1993. *Biblical Creationism*. Grand Rapids, MI: Baker Book House. 276 p.
Orr, James. 1907. *The Virgin Birth of Christ*. New York, NY: Charles Scribner's Sons.
Sabiers, Karl G. 1943. *The Virgin Birth of Christ*. Los Angeles, CA: Robertson Publ. Co.
Smith, Wilbur M. 1944. *The Supernaturalness of Christ*. Boston, MA: W. A. Wilde Co. 235 p.

Chapter VI

The Miraculous Life of Christ

The Perfection of Christ's Character

Certain aspects of the doctrine of Christ have already been considered and shown to be strong evidences of His deity and of the unique truth of Christianity. These include both His miraculous birth, conceived of the Holy Spirit and born of the virgin, and also a preliminary discussion of His bodily resurrection, the climactic and crowning proof that He indeed was God.

Between His birth and His resurrection, however, He lived a life of unique holiness and power. The sinless life He lived, the mighty miracles He performed, and the gracious words He spoke, all providing a matchless setting for the unparalleled claims He made, add still further to the evidence that Jesus Christ was uniquely the Son of God.

Consider the character of Christ, as manifest in His life described in the four gospels. The gospel writers all are concerned solely with describing the words and deeds of Jesus Christ, and everything else is incidental and contributory to that purpose. He is always, in every chapter, the central character and theme.

Yet, with all this attention, it is remarkable that two features are notably missing from these biographies, features which are invariably prominent in all other biographies of great men. First, there is not one line describing the human physical appearance of Jesus! Whether He was tall or short, dark or light, heavyset or thin, bearded or clean-shaven, we are not told. The color of His hair or His eyes, the manner of gait, the structure of His physique, the pitch of His voice — all these things, usually of such interest to writers and their readers, are amazingly omitted by the Gospel authors. Medieval portraits and statues and pious descriptive forgeries notwithstanding, we actually have not the slightest knowledge today of Jesus' human appearance. We do not even know that He had what might be considered Jewish facial characteristics, since He was born without direct genetic connection to either Mary or Joseph.

The reason for this reticence in describing Jesus may be twofold. First, as the son of Man, He is thus capable of identification with all men, not just with Jews or whites, or tall men or brown-eyed men or any other particular type of men. Secondly, man's perverse tendency to idolatry would quickly have made an idol out of His picture or image had we known what He looked like (even without this, many have made what amounts to a shrine or idol out of a "model" of what some have imagined He looked like).

This remarkable restraint on the part of the four Gospel writers can be explained only as a divine constraint by the Holy Spirit. A second restraint, even more amazing, is a complete absence of any eulogies of Christ by the writers. Their portrait of a man absolutely perfect in word and deed, completely lacking in any slightest weakness of character, is quite unique in all literature. Yet they achieve this portrait by a simple factual record of what He said and did. Never do they pause to comment on His perfections, to exclaim over the wisdom of His words or to point out how uniquely moral and correct all of His actions were. The portrait is painted with perfect clarity and beauty, but altogether without the aid of editorial adjectives or interjections. Nothing they could possibly say by way of explanation or description could be half so effective as simply to recount the words and deeds of Jesus.

No one else in all history, or even in fiction, lived in such a way as did the Lord Jesus. Note the following points, among many others that might be listed.

> He was always master of every situation, taking exactly the right action to fit the circumstances, never having to seek advice before acting and never having to retract or apologize after acting.
>
> He never had to ask either permission, since He

always spoke with authority, or forgiveness, since He never said or did anything amiss.

He had no consciousness of sins or shortcomings in His life, yet never conveyed any impression of pride or sanctimoniousness in His manner.

He was never fearful of anything and could be overpoweringly bold when occasion required, and yet He was gentle and meek in the highest degree.

His words were always perfectly chosen to fit the need, of absolute purity and wholesomeness, never trivial or banal, always relevant and meaningful.

He never complained about His circumstances, in spite of weariness, hunger, poverty, persecution and rejection, but instead provided continual encouragement and comfort to others.

He was equally confident and authoritative with friends and enemies, common people or leaders, never flustered or confused about what to say or do, regardless of the company or circumstances.

A list such as the above could be expanded almost endlessly. It would seem that every type of person or situation confronted Jesus in some way or another in some degree, and He always responded or reacted in the most perfect way. Never do we find a situation in which we feel that we could have done it better or that He was unduly harsh or weak or unreasonable or equivocal or at fault in any respect.

It is true that He had enemies and was hated and persecuted and finally put to death. This was not because of any fault in His own character, but because His very perfections illuminated and condemned the sins and hypocrisies of other men, and they could only react by opposing and crucifying Him.

Even without being told, the reader is impelled to the conviction that His life is our perfect pattern, the example we should continually seek to follow, even though we are painfully aware that we can never really attain it. We are without excuse, however, since He attained it and He is no less human than we. He is the Son of Man — man as God intended and created man to be.

Jesus, in fact, said as much. Without any semblance of conceit or boasting, He made it plain that His life is our perfect example, and that we should follow Him.

The disciple is not above his master, nor the servant above his Lord. It is enough for the disciple that he be as his master, and the servant as his Lord (Matt. 10:24-25).

He that loveth father or mother more than me is not worthy of me. . . . And he that taketh not his cross, and followeth after me, is not worthy of me (Matt. 10:37-38).

And why call ye me, Lord, Lord, and do not the things which I say? (Luke 6:46).

My sheep hear my voice, and I know them, and they follow me (John 10:27).

I have given you an example, that ye should do as I have done to you (John 13:15).

A new commandment I give unto you, that ye love one another; as I have loved you, that ye also love one another (John 13:34).

As my Father hath sent me, even so send I you (John 20:21).

That the disciples fully accepted this concept of Jesus as their example in all things is evidence from what they later wrote of Him. John said; "He that saith he abideth in him ought himself also so to walk, even as he walked" (1 John 2:6). Paul said; "Let this mind be in you, which was also in Christ Jesus" (Phil. 2:5).

Peter said, in a classic passage: "For even hereunto were ye called: because Christ also suffered for us, leaving us an example, that ye should follow his steps: Who did no sin, neither was guile found in his mouth: Who, when he was reviled, reviled not again; when he suffered, he threatened not; but committed himself to him that judgeth righteously" (1 Pet. 2:21-23).

Jesus was surely the one man in all human experience who lived a perfect, sinless life. He was perfect man, truly human, and yet fulfilling His humanness as no other man can do. He is thus capable of providing perfect guidance and help for us in every situation. "For we have not an high priest which cannot be touched with the feeling of our infirmities; but was in all points [tested] like as we are, yet without sin. Let us therefore come boldly to the throne of grace, that we may obtain mercy, and find grace to help in time of need" (Heb. 4:15-16).

Son of Man

The perfect humanity of Christ is implied in the singularly appropriate title "Son of Man." This was evidently His favorite expression for himself. He called himself "Son of Man" no less than 80 times in the four Gospels.

The title is, of course, in no sense a denial of the deity of Christ. He is also the Son of God and, in fact, He frequently used the "Son of Man" title itself in a way which could only be applied to God. Thus: "The Son of Man hath power on earth to forgive sins" (Matt. 9:6); "The Son of Man is come to seek and to save that which was lost" (Luke 19:10); "Ye shall see the Son of Man sitting on the right hand of power, and coming in the clouds of heaven" (Mark 14:62).

The title is thus itself an indication of deity. No one man could in himself represent all men; only God is capable of this. Jesus was not just *a* son of man; He was and is *the* Son of Man. That is, He is the second man, the last Adam (1 Cor. 15:45-47). He is the heir of man, the inheritor of all the promises to man.

He is the perfect man — man as God intended man to be. Furthermore, He is man as we shall someday become, when "we shall be like him, for we shall see him as he is" (1 John 3:2). It is as the Son of Man that John saw him in the vision of his glory (Rev. 1:13).

It was as the Son of Man that He was lifted up to die on the cross (John 3:14; 12:32-34), bearing in His own body the sins of all men. The human body in which God thus became incarnate as man is the body which was laid in the tomb and which on the third day rose again from the tomb. It was in that body He ascended into heaven. Stephen said, "Behold, I see the heavens opened, and the Son of Man standing on the right hand of God" (Acts 7:56).

It is thus as the perfect, resurrected, glorified Son of Man, eternally incarnate, that the Lord Jesus Christ exists today at the right hand of the Father. It is as Son of Man that He will come again (Matt. 24:30) "with power and great glory" and as Son of Man that He will receive "everlasting dominion" (Dan. 7:14).

By His very title, therefore, with all the realms of revelation it implies, Jesus Christ is both set above all other men and yet is made one with all men. He is and always will continue to be uniquely the Son of Man.

The Son of God

Although He spoke of himself most frequently as the Son of Man, Jesus Christ also claimed to be the Son of God. In speaking to Nicodemus, for example, He said, "He that believeth not is condemned already, because he hath not believed in the name of the only begotten Son of God" (John 3:18). Many other Scriptures show that Christ frequently claimed to be, in a very unique sense, the Son of God (note, for example, John 5:25; 9:35; 11:4; etc.).

It was, as a matter of fact, this very claim that gave his enemies the opportunity to have Him condemned to death. In the Jewish law, blasphemy was a capital offense. At His trial before the elders, chief priests, and scribes, the climax came when they asked Him, "Art thou then the Son of God? And he said unto them, Ye say that I am. And they said, What need we any further witness for we ourselves have heard of his own mouth" (Luke 22:70-71).

It had been prophesied in the Old Testament that the coming Savior and Messiah would be the Son of God. In the second Psalm, David speaks of the Lord and His Anointed (i.e., Messiah) in verse 2, and then quotes the Lord, in verse 7, as saying: "Thou art my Son; this day have I begotten thee." Other Old Testament Scriptures speaking of God's unique Son include 2 Samuel 7:14 and Proverbs 30:4.

John the Baptist said, "And I saw, and bare record that this is the Son of God" (John 1:34). Peter said, "Thou art the Christ, the Son of the Living God" (Matt. 16:16). Martha said, "Yea, Lord: I believe that thou art the Christ, the Son of God" (John 11:27). As soon as Paul the Apostle had been converted, "Straightway he preached Christ in the synagogues, that he is the Son of God" (Acts 9:20). In fact, all the disciples acknowledged, saying, "Of a truth, thou art the Son of God" (Matt. 14:33).

Even the centurion that carried out His execution said, "Truly this man was the Son of God" (Mark 15:39). Demons recognized Him as such. "And devils also came out of many, crying out and saying, Thou art Christ the Son of God" (Luke

4:41). Finally, none other than Satan himself acknowledged Him to be the Son of God. At two of the temptations in the wilderness, he began by saying, "If thou be the Son of God . . ." (Matt. 4:3, 6). The word "if" actually is better translated "since." It is interesting, in the light of 1 John 4:2-3, that Satan readily acknowledged Him as the Son of God, but refused Him recognition as the Son of Man.

It should be understood that Christ is not a Son of God in the sense that other men may be sons of God by a spiritual relationship to their Heavenly Father. Men are not born as children of God; they become sons of God by being "born again," through the Holy Spirit (John 1:12-13; 3:3-7).

Jesus Christ, however, is the *"only begotten"* of the Father (John 1:14, 18; 3:16; 1 John 4:9). He is not the *only* son of God, as many modern translations would have John 3:16 and other such Scriptures say, but the *only begotten* (Greek *monogenes*) Son of God. There are at least five ways in which the Scriptures identify Him as Son of God in a special sense:

> *By eternal generation.* He is "the image of the invisible God, the firstborn of every creature" (Col. 1:15). He was a Son with the Father before the world began (John 17:5, 24). He has been "going forth . . . from everlasting" (Mic. 5:2). Eternally, He has been in relation to the eternal Father as His Son.
>
> *By special creation.* The technical phrase "Son of God" is applied in Scripture in a formal way only to those whose bodies have been specially formed by God, and were not produced by natural processes of human generations. Thus angels are sons of God by creation (Gen. 6:2; Job 1:6; 2:1; 38:7; Dan. 3:25), and so was the first man Adam (Luke 3:38). The body of Christ was also formed directly by God (Luke 1:35).
>
> *By resurrection.* Jesus Christ was the "beginning, the first-born from the dead" (Col. 1:18). Paul preached: "And we declare unto you glad tidings, how that the promise which was made unto the fathers, God hath fulfilled the same unto us their children, in that he hath raised up Jesus again; as it is also written in the second psalm, Thou art my Son, this day have I begotten thee" (Acts 13:32-33). He has been "declared to be the Son of God . . . by the resurrection

from the dead" (Rom. 1:4). Finally, the apostle John, introducing the final book of the Bible, identified Him as "Jesus Christ . . . the first begotten from the dead" (Rev. 1:5).

By inheritance. As the son is the father's heir, in things human, so Christ is to inherit all things from the heavenly Father. He "hath been appointed heir of all things" (Heb. 1:2). "He that built all things is God . . . But Christ as a son over his own house" (Heb. 3:4-6).

By nature. The phrase "son of — " is a graphic expression denoting one's nature. Thus, James and John were "sons of thunder" (Mark 3:17), Elymas the sorcerer was called "son of the devil" (Acts 13:10), Barnabas was so named by the Apostles because he was "the son of consolation" (Acts 4:36); etc. Jesus Christ similarly was called the "Son of God" because His nature was that of God. He challenged the Jews: "Say ye of him, whom the Father hath sanctified, and sent into the world, Thou blasphemest; because I said, I am the Son of God? If I do not the works of my Father, believe me not. But if I do, though ye believe not me, believe the works: that ye may know, and believe, that the Father is in me, and I in him" (John 10:36-38.

The Teachings of Christ

By common consent, Jesus Christ is the greatest teacher who ever lived. Even many who reject His deity will acknowledge this. The Sermon on the Mount, the parables of the Kingdom, the Olivet discourse, the glorious messages in the Gospel of John, and others all contain wisdom and spiritual power of majesty and insight incomparably superior to any other words ever spoken.

He is the "Wonderful Counsellor" (Isa. 9:6). He is the one of whom it was prophesied that "grace was poured into thy lips" (Ps. 45:2). When He preached in Nazareth, it was said that "all bare him witness, and wondered at the gracious words which proceeded out of his mouth" (Luke 4:22).

When He concluded His Sermon on the Mount, it is recorded that "the people were astonished at his [teachings]: For he taught them as one having authority, and not as the scribes" (Matt. 7:28-29). In Capernaum, "they were astonished at his teachings, for his word was with power" (Luke 4:32).

Even His enemies were impressed with His teachings. When officers were commissioned to arrest Him, they came back to the chief priests empty-handed, with the simple explanation: "Never man spake like this man" (John 7:46).

The sermons, the parables, the commandments, and the promises of Christ are an inexhaustible mine of blessing and wisdom and guidance to all who explore them. Each new reading of them yields new truth and insight not seen in previous readings. No other teacher and no other teachings can compare with these.

And yet Jesus was apparently only a carpenter from an obscure village in a despised nation. He never studied in a university, nor any other school so far as we know. He never traveled more than a few miles from His home, never wrote a book or article, never taught in a school. The only ones who paid much attention to what He taught (the multitudes sometimes listened and were impressed, but they soon forgot) were a motley band of unimpressive disciples, and even they missed the point on His most important teachings concerning His coming death and resurrection.

That such an obscure itinerant preacher would leave a legacy of the greatest teachings the world has ever known would seem absolutely impossible. But such is the fact! The only explanation that makes sense at all is that He was "a teacher come from God" (John 3:2), and that, as He claimed: "Whatsoever I speak therefore, even as the Father said unto me, so I speak" (John 12:50).

The Miracles of Christ

A further evidence of the supernaturalness of Christ is that of the miracles He performed. As the "teacher of Israel," Nicodemus said: "No man can do these miracles that thou doest, except God be with him" (John 3:2).

The time and place in which Jesus lived were not characterized by superstition and gullibility, but rather by learning and skepticism. Miracles were quite as unexpected and marvelous then as the same miracles would be today. The present order of things, as ordained by God (Gen. 8:22) is one of basic uniformity, varied only on rare occasions by the supernatural when God's sovereign purpose so designs.

Even such a great influential man as John the Baptist never performed a miracle (John 10:41). Yet when Jesus came it is said that "his fame went throughout all Syria: and they brought unto him all sick people that were taken with diverse diseases and torments, and those which were possessed with devils, and those which were lunatick, and those that had the palsy; and he healed them" (Matt. 4:24). He sent word to John: "The blind receive their sight, and the lame walk, the lepers are cleansed, and the deaf hear, the dead are raised up" (Matt. 11:5). These miracles of healing were never selective, or partial, or temporary, or trivial, as is true with modern so-called "faith healers," but were always medically or psychosomatically impossible, yet instantaneous, complete, and permanent.

Nor were His miracles limited to healings. He transformed water into wine, prodigiously multiplied a small quantity of bread and fish on two different occasions, calmed a raging storm on the Sea of Galilee, walked on the water surface, caused a tree to wither away, extracted a coin from a fish, and directed a great draught of fishes into fishing nets, on two different occasions. On several occasions, He even restored the dead to life again.

His miracles were never merely for display or frivolity. Always they had the dual purpose of satisfying some serious human need which could be met in no other way at the time, and also of confirming His own authority and claims. In connection with the latter purpose, it was entirely of grace that He used miracles to vindicate His words. Men should have recognized Him through their study of the Scriptures, through the preparatory ministry of John the Baptist, and by the witness of His own life and teachings. Because of their blindness and hardness of heart, however, He made it easier for them to believe by use of miracles.

Thus it is noted that "many believed in his name, when they saw the miracles which he did" (John 2:23). He told the unbelieving Jews: "If I do not the works of my Father, believe me not. But if I do, though ye believe not me, believe the works" (John 10:37-38). He even told His disciple Philip: "Believe me that I am in the Father, and the Father in me: or else believe me for the very works' sake" (John 14:11).

On the other hand, He would not perform miracles simply to satisfy curiosity or carnality. When certain ones came seeking a sign from Him ("signs" and "miracles" are the same word in Greek), He said: "An evil and adulterous generation seeketh after a sign; and there shall no sign be given to it" (Matt. 12:39). He refused to perform before Herod, even to save His life (Luke 23:8-9). He knew that many would never believe regardless of miracles. "If they hear not Moses and the prophets, neither will they be persuaded, though one rose from the dead" (Luke 16:31). Note also John 12:37: "Though he had done so many miracles before them, yet they believed not on him."

It is, therefore, obvious that the Lord Jesus Christ did on occasion perform mighty miracles, but always with clear reason and results, never for display or personal gain. The miracles that He did perform were accomplished before many different people, out in the open, in crowds, and were of many different kinds. They were obviously not tricks of hypnosis or mass psychology, as some have foolishly suggested.

As a matter of fact, many were actually miracles of creation (e.g., the water into wine, the multiplication of the loaves, etc.) and of resurrection. None but the Creator himself could be competent for such mighty works as these. John, in fact, develops his whole Gospel around the framework of seven great miracles of omnipotence and, when he concludes, he says: "And many other signs truly did Jesus in the presence of his disciples, which are not written in this book: But these are written, that ye might believe that Jesus is the Christ, the Son of God, and that believing ye might have life through his name" (John 20:30-31).

The Claims of Christ

In view of the sinless life, the wonderful teachings, and the mighty miracles of Christ, the claims He makes concerning His own person and mission are extremely important. A man who could accomplish such things as these can neither be dismissed as hallucinatory nor rejected as a charlatan. Neither, as has already been shown, can the gospel writers have been mistaken in reporting what He claimed.

Therefore, these claims must be studied carefully and regarded with utmost seriousness. They were actually made by Christ himself and, by all rules of reason and logic, should be accepted as absolute truth. They amount *en toto* to an absolute and dogmatic claim that He, Jesus Christ, is himself the eternal God! If this be so, and it *is* so, then a person can ignore or reject this fact only at the cost of tragic and eternal loss to his own soul.

The claims are many and varied, but all add up both individually and collectively to affirmation of His own unique deity as the eternal Son of God. A sampling of these is given below, without comment (for none is needed):

I am the way, the truth, and the life: no man cometh unto the Father, but by me (John 14:6).

The Son of Man hath power on earth to forgive sins (Matt. 9:6).

Whosoever therefore shall confess me before men, him will I confess also before my Father which is in heaven (Matt. 10:32).

All things are delivered unto me of my Father: and no man knoweth the Son, but the Father; neither knoweth any man the Father, save the Son, and he to whomsoever the Son will reveal him (Matt. 11:27).

I am the resurrection, and the life: he that believeth in me, though he were dead, yet shall he live: and whosoever liveth and believeth in me, shall never die (John 11:25-26).

The Son of Man is Lord also of the sabbath (Mark 2:28).

Whosoever will lose his life for my sake, the same shall save it (Luke 9:24).

I am the light of the world: he that followeth me shall not walk in darkness, but shall have the light of life (John 8:12).

When the Son of Man cometh, shall he find faith on the earth? (Luke 18:8).

The Son of Man came . . . to give his life a ransom for many (Mark 10:45).

Whosoever drinketh of the water that I shall give him shall never thirst (John 4:14).

The Father . . . hath committed all judgment unto the Son (John 5:22).

Come unto me, all ye that labour and are heavy laden, and I will give you rest (Matt. 11:28).

The dead shall hear the voice of the Son of God: and they that hear shall live (John 5:25).

Heaven and earth shall pass away: but my words shall not pass away (Luke 21:33).

Before Abraham was, I am (John 8:58).

Upon this rock I will build my church, and the gates of hell shall not prevail against it (Matt. 16:18).

I am the door of the sheep. All that ever came before me are thieves and robbers (John 10:7-8).

I and my Father are one (John 10:30).

I am the bread of life: he that cometh to me shall never hunger (John 6:35).

Statements of this sort could be added in great numbers. Remember that He who was sinless would never deceive, and He who was the wisest Teacher could not be mistaken. The claims are true and the promises sure. In the face of such incontrovertible evidence, we can only say with the once-doubting Thomas, "My Lord, and my God" (John 20:28).

Selected books for further study:
Bellett, J.G. 1943. *The Moral Glory of the Lord Jesus Christ*. New York, NY: Loiseaux Bros. 80 p.
Edersheim, Albert. 1990. *The Life and Times of Jesus the Messiah*. Grand Rapids, MI: Wm. B. Eerdmans Co. 1,523 p.
Guthrie, Donald. 1972. *Jesus the Messiah*. Grand Rapids, MI: Zondervan Publ. House.
Kinney, LeBaron W. 1942. *He is Thy Lord and Worship Thou Him*. New York, NY: Loiseaux Bros. 230 p.
Lockyer, Herbert. 1961. *All the Miracles of the Bible*. Grand Rapids, MI: Zondervan Publ. House. 311 p.
Morris, Henry M. 1971. *The Bible Has the Answer*. Grand Rapids, MI: Baker Book House. 256 p.
Rice, John R. 1966. *Is Jesus God*. Murfreesboro, TN: Sword of the Lord Publishers.

Sheldrake, Leonard. 1950. *Our Lord Jesus Christ, A Plant of Renown*. Fort Dodge, IA: Walterick Publishers. 171 p.

Tatford, Frederick A. 1950. *The Master*. New York, NY: Loiseaux Bros.

Thomas, W. H. Griffith. 1948. *Christianity is Christ*. London: Church Book Room Press. 144 p.

Trench, R. C. 1949. *Notes on the Miracles of Our Lord*. Grand Rapids, MI: Baker Book House. 298 p.

Chapter VII

The Death of Christ

The Strange Attraction of the Crucifixion

One of the most amazing influences of the life of Christ has been the strange fascination associated with His death. Untold numbers of crucifixes have been erected in churches and other places, and even greater numbers of ornamental crosses are worn as pieces of jewelry. The death of Christ has received far more attention in literature, art, and music, than have all the deaths of all other great men combined.

There was certainly nothing beautiful about His sufferings and death. He died as a common criminal, on a cross between two thieves. He had been beaten almost beyond recognition, and then the death by crucifixion itself was one of the cruelest of all possible ways to die.

But He had said: "And I, if I be lifted up from the earth, will draw all men unto me. This he said, signifying what death he should die" (John 12:32-33). Also, he had said: "And as Moses lifted up the serpent in the wilderness, even so must the Son of Man be lifted up: That whosoever believeth in him should not perish, but have eternal life" (John 3:14-15).

Somehow, in spite of the shame and cruelty and apparent futility associated with His death, millions of people down through the centuries have been attracted to His cross. His words have been fulfilled, in spite of their apparent unreasonableness. And all those who have looked upon His cross with true eyes of faith (in the way that the ancient Israelites, dying from the sting of the serpents in the wilderness, looked upon the brazen serpent erected by Moses on the great pole in the center of their camp) have received assurance of cleansing and everlasting life.

This is surely a remarkable phenomenon, if that is all it is. Nothing like it exists in all human experience. That the ugly death of a man on a cross two thousand years ago — a man who, by all common standards, was uneducated, poor, and insignificant — should exert such a universal, age-long attraction for men of all nations and times and that faith in the meaning of His death should give joy and peace to multitudes, is something which simply can have no rational explanation at all — except the one that He himself gave, "I am the good shepherd: the good shepherd giveth his life for the sheep" (John 10:11).

The Prophecies of His Death

It is easy, of course, to prophesy that someone will die. Everyone must die sooner or later, and it surely takes no gift of prophetic insight to predict death. For that matter, many men and women, especially those who have a morbid interest in the occult, make death a very frequent subject of prophecy. Some of these (e.g., Jeane Dixon's famous prophecy of John Kennedy's assassination) seem to come true, perhaps suggesting that demonic forces do have some limited knowledge of human plans and can occasionally forecast the events which they bring about, though of course most such soothsaying predictions are never fulfilled at all.

There is nothing in all human history, however, comparable to the prophecies associated with the death of Christ. These were not vague and hidden, like those of fortune-tellers, nor were they given only a short time before they were fulfilled, as are those of modern occultists. There are scores, perhaps hundreds, of such prophecies in the Old Testament that focus on the death of the coming Messiah, and many of them are very detailed and specific. All were recorded hundreds of years, some over a thousand years, before they were fulfilled.

The time when He would come into Jerusalem to die was prophesied in Daniel 9:24-26, and this was fulfilled exactly 483 years later, as predicted, when He entered Jerusalem for His last week before death, as recorded in Luke 19:37-44. After this, as Daniel (or, rather, the angel Gabriel) had prophesied, He was "cut off, but not for himself."

His betrayal by one of His close friends was forecast in Psalm 41:9, and even the price of 30 pieces of silver for His betrayal was given in Zechariah 11:12-13. The shameful mockery of the judicial process which constituted His trial is prophesied in Isaiah 50:6 and 53:7-8. The false witnesses are mentioned in Psalm 35:11.

The awful details of His sufferings on the cross are portrayed graphically in the 22nd Psalm, written by David almost 1,100 years before its fulfillment. The Psalm begins with the cry from the cross: "My God, my God, why hast thou forsaken me?" (Ps. 22:1; Matt. 27:46). The darkness is pictured in verse 2 (perhaps also in Amos 8:9). The mocking by the priests and others at the foot of the cross is described in verses 7 and 8. The terrible bodily sufferings induced by the crucifixion process are recorded in verses 14 and 15. The piercings of His hands and feet to receive the nails binding Him to the cross are mentioned in verse 16. The stripping of His garments and gambling over their possession by the soldiers crucifying Him is predicted in verses 17 and 18. His awful thirst is mentioned in verse 15 (and even the vinegar which was offered to Him, in Ps. 69:21). The collapse of His heart cavity, leading to the strange emergence of mingled blood and water from His side, is suggested in verse 14 (note John 19:34). There is no need for a detailed exposition of Psalm 22 here, but it is surely one of the most marvelous passages in all the Word of God, and will richly repay detailed and prayerful study by each individual Christian.

The fact that, despite the intensity of His sufferings, none of His bones would be broken, is foretold in Psalm 34:20, as fulfilled in John 19:36. The piercing of His side is suggested in Zechariah 12:10. The wounds in His hands may also have been noted by Zechariah in 13:6.

The 53rd chapter of Isaiah (actually beginning at Isa. 52:13) is also a marvelous chapter devoted to the future death of the Savior, written by Isaiah 750 years before it came to pass. Especially emphasized in this chapter (which is quoted in at least six different places in the New Testament) is the fact that the death of the Messiah would be a substitutionary death, offered up in sacrificial substitution for the sins of others.

He is called by Isaiah, God's "servant" (52:13) and His "righteous servant" (53:11). Yet it is also said that "it pleased the Lord to bruise him," and to "put him to grief" (53:10). This apparent insult to the character of a holy and just God can only be resolved in light of the fact that this was God himself, in the "form of a servant" (Phil. 2:6) who was making "His soul an offering for sin" (Isa. 53:10).

This emphasis on substitutionary suffering is repeated over and over in this remarkable chapter. It says, for example, that "He hath borne our griefs, and carried our sorrows" (verse 4), that "He was wounded for our transgressions, he was bruised for our iniquities: the chastisement of our peace was upon him; and with his stripes we are healed" (verse 5). Verse 6 says "The Lord hath laid on him the iniquity of us all." Verse 11 says "He shall bear their iniquities," and verse 12 that "He was numbered with the transgressors, and he bare the sin of many, and made intercession for the transgressors."

As a matter of fact, the Christian gospel — that "Christ died for our sins" (1 Cor. 15:3) — find its clearest expression in the whole Bible right here in this Old Testament chapter, recorded long before Christ came into the world to bring it to pass. Herein is surely a most marvelous evidence of the truth of God's Word, and the sure fulfillment of all His promises!

Other details of his trial and death are also given in this chapter. The awful bruising He bore at the hands of the soldiers and others is graphically portrayed in 52:14: "His visage was so marred more than any man, and his form more than the sons of men." His silence before His accusers at His trial is predicted in 53:7. The result of His mock trial is given in verse 8, and His death with the criminals, and His burial by a rich man, is recorded in verse 9.

And then, after His cruel death, His resurrection is prophesied in verse 10: "He shall see his seed, he shall prolong his days." Again, as with Psalm 22, we cannot give a detailed exposition of this chapter, but it is certainly one of the richest and most profound in the Bible, and has been a great source of unique blessing to multitudes through the ages.

There are many other prophecies in the Old Testament Scriptures which were fulfilled when Christ died on the cross. It must be clear to even the most skeptical that this is an absolutely unique phenomenon. There is nothing else comparable to this in all the realm of literature or religion. The death of the Son of Man, on Calvary's cross, is an event of unique interest in heaven and of unique importance to man on earth.

The Miracles of Calvary

As clear physical evidence of the cosmic importance of the death of Christ, certain marvelous events occurred at that time, for which no naturalistic explanation will suffice. The records of these events as given in the gospels must be, as we have seen, based on eyewitness accounts. They are events which would have been known to multitudes of people and which, therefore, if they had not occurred, would quickly have given the lie to the gospel writers who reported that they *did* occur.

For example, there was a supernatural darkness which enveloped all the land, from the sixth hour until the ninth hour of that date (Matt. 27:45; Mark 15:33: Luke 23:44-45). It may be that this darkness veiled the entire earth, as God for a time withdrew even the physical evidence of His providential care for the earth, as His Son was bearing in His own body the sin of the world and suffering the judgment of separation from God.

There is no evidence in astronomical history of a normal solar eclipse at this time, though there are certain traditions in other lands of a period of darkness. Yet the fact of this supernatural darkness was apparently well known to all those that dwelt in Jerusalem, and to those who read first the accounts of it in the gospels.

Another miracle, of course, is the earthquake. In fact, there was an earthquake both at the time of the crucifixion and again at the time of the resurrection. Earthquakes are natural phenomena, so that the miraculous aspect of these quakes was in their peculiar timing. That they were significantly violent quakes is proved by the statement of Matthew: "The earth did quake, and the rocks rent" (Matt. 27:51).

Another notable miracle, recorded in three of the Gospels (Matt. 27:51; Mark 15:38; Luke 23:45), was the rending of the veil in the temple. This veil was a very heavy, thick drapery, that would have required tremendous force to tear, and it is recorded that it was "rent in twain from the top to the bottom."

No explanation suffices for this occurrence, and its recording in the gospels in this way, except that an unseen angelic hand ripped it in two, symbolizing that the way unto the holiest place, the very presence of God, was now open to all who would come. The veil had as its purpose the separation of the place where God met once each year with the high priest, keeping out all others. But now, Christ has opened the way for all to come to God by Him. "Having therefore, brethren, boldness to enter into the holiest by the blood of Jesus, By a new and living way, which he hath consecrated for us, through the veil, that is to say, his flesh. . . . Let us draw near with a true heart in full assurance of faith" (Heb. 10:19-22).

It is also important to note that Jesus died at exactly the time He was ready to die, not before, and not later. "When Jesus therefore had received the vinegar, he said, It is finished: and he bowed his head and gave up the ghost" (John 19:30). Before He could die, one last prophecy had to be fulfilled (19:28), and then He could simply dismiss His spirit (Luke 23:46) from His body.

Although the Jews and Romans condemned Him to death, and the soldiers carried out the death sentence, it was not really they who put Him to death. He had said: "Therefore doth my Father love me, because I lay down my life, that I might take it again. No man taketh my life from me, but I lay it down of myself. I have power to lay it down, and I have power to take it again" (John 10:17-18). Even at the time of His arrest He said: "Thinkest thou that I cannot now pray to the Father, and he shall presently give me more than twelve legions of angels? But how then shall the scriptures be fulfilled, that thus it must be?" (Matt. 26:53-54). When Pilate told Him that he had the power to have Him crucified, He answered: "Thou couldest have no power at all against me, except it were given thee from above" (John 19:11).

Now, although all men eventually die, no man can simply decide to die, and then die! It is not easy even to commit suicide, but certainly no one can simply expire by an act of his own will. But that is exactly what Jesus did. When every last detail of His mission had been accomplished, He committed His spirit to His Father and merely dismissed it from His body. The physical death of Christ is thus absolutely unique in history.

The Surprising Circumstances of Christ's Burial

The great central passage on the gospel is 1 Corinthians 15:1-4. Here, the gospel is defined as centered around the good news that "Christ died for our sins according to the Scriptures; And that he was buried, and that he rose again the third day according to the Scriptures." Thus the gospel involves three main parts — the death, burial, and resurrection of Jesus Christ — and further emphasizes his post-resurrection physical appearances in confirmation thereof.

It is obvious that the death and resurrection are basic to Christianity, but why should there be equal emphasis on the burial of Christ? Undoubtedly, the reason is that it is of vital importance for men to realize that Jesus Christ "is come in the flesh" (1 John 4:2). As His burial was an actual physical burial, with His body placed in a physical tomb, so His resurrection must therefore be a physical resurrection with His body coming out of the tomb. The deadly heresy of the Gnostics, as of numerous other ancient and modern philosophies, was that the man Jesus and the great "Christ-spirit" were somehow united only in a very superficial way, so that when Jesus died the Christ returned to the Father. Thus, Christ did not really die — only Jesus died. Further, Jesus did not really rise — only Christ arose!

Neither demons nor unbelieving men have been willing to acknowledge that "Jesus *is* the Christ," that "Jesus *is* the Son of God," and that "Jesus the Christ *is* come in the flesh" (1 John 5:1; 5:5; 4:3). The Son of God is also Son of Man, with both the divine power and the human nature enabling Him both to represent man and to set man free from the evil one.

It is absolutely vital for all men to *know* beyond any doubt that it was the human Jesus who rose from the grave. Therefore, it must be certain that His body was carefully buried after His death, and that this burial was known to all, both friend and foe. Then, on the great morning when He arose from the dead, the emptied tomb would stand forever as the infallible proof of His bodily resurrection.

Such an important ministry as the burial of the body of Jesus could not be entrusted by God to the Roman soldiers, who would merely further defile it and then throw it in with the bodies of other executed criminals, nor to the Jewish authorities who would probably do even worse. Nor would these authorities have permitted it to fall into the hands of His disciples, as they were afraid they would seek to hide it and then claim He had been resurrected (Matt. 27:62-66).

The solution was for God to have the body buried by one or more of the authorities themselves who were also disciples. For this purpose, God chose two of the members of the governing Jewish body, the Sanhedrin, Joseph and Nicodemus. Thus, they would have access to the necessary information about the time and circumstances of His death, they would also have access to the Roman governor in order to make the required arrangements to acquire the body before the soldiers could dispose of it, and they would have enough wealth of their own to be able to make the needed preparations for a suitable resting place for the body until it could be raised from the dead.

Of course, they would have to be prepared ahead of time for this ministry. God, therefore, somehow touched the heart of Nicodemus, as he listened to John the Baptist, then later to Jesus, and as He saw the miracles which Jesus did. Eventually, he made his way into the presence of Jesus one night where the Lord spoke to him of the necessity of being born again, even though he was already the greatest "teacher in Israel" (John 3:7, 10).

The Scriptures do not tell us the outcome of that interview, except that sometime later Nicodemus defended Jesus on one occasion before the Sanhedrin (John 7:50-51). Similarly, we read that Joseph did not concur in the decision of the Sanhedrin to condemn Jesus (Luke 23:50-51).

Somehow these two men had become friends and had resolved to make preparations for Jesus' burial. It seems likely that they may have had other interviews with Jesus, though the Scriptures are silent on this, and perhaps learned from His own lips about His approaching crucifixion. He had, indeed, told Nicodemus that He must be "lifted up," as Moses had "lifted up the serpent in the wilderness," in order that men might have everlasting life. It hardly seems likely that Nicodemus, Israel's great teacher, would not try to learn much more about these things, and where better than from Jesus himself? If nothing else, however, he would surely have gone back to an intensive study of the Messianic Scriptures to learn all he could about the prophesied sacrificial death of the coming Messiah. These earnest studies most likely would have been shared with his friend Joseph.

Some such background as this is necessary to understand the otherwise inexplicable prescience of Joseph. Why, for example, should he, a rich man of Arimathea, buy a burial ground in Jerusalem instead of his own home town? And, especially, why should he purchase it in such a place as this — adjacent to the hill of Golgotha, where day after day there would come the cries of dying criminals and the wails of mourning families? Furthermore, it was a brand new tomb, not one in which others of the family had been buried (John 19:41), one that Joseph himself had hewn out in the rock (Matt. 27:60), perhaps not wishing others even to know about its preparation.

Strange also was the fact that Joseph knew exactly when Jesus died, and was immediately able to rush to Pilate with the request for His body, before others even realized He was dead (Mark 15:43-44). Even stranger was the fact that immediately thereafter came Nicodemus carrying 100 Roman pounds[1] of ointment for the burial (one does not carry even 100 Roman pounds very far!). Then, while the women watched from a distance, no doubt in amazement, these two respected members of the Sanhedrin gently lowered the body from the cross, wound it in the linen clothes, applied the spices and ointments, laid the body in the tomb, and then departed. Never, so far as the biblical record goes, were they ever heard from again, but there can be no doubt that this one act cost them their positions and probably their possessions, and possibly even their lives.

Probably in their studies together during the many months following Nicodemus' first meeting with Jesus, the two friends spent much time in the 53rd chapter of Isaiah. There especially was the sacrificial and saving work of the Messiah foretold, and this had been the great theme of Jesus' words to Nicodemus (John 3:14-21).

And in the heart of that great passage is the statement: "And he made his grave with the wicked (thus near the execution and burial grounds of the condemned criminals), but (a better translation in this context than 'and') with the rich (therefore, a rich man must somehow provide a grave for him even in these unlikely circumstances) in his death" (Isa. 53:9).

Joseph somehow decided himself to assume this prophetic obligation. He proceeded to purchase the land, cut out the tomb, plant a garden, purchase the required materials for the burial and hide them there, and then wait there with Nicodemus until they could perform that service for the Lord for which they had been born.

---

[1] A Roman pound was equivalent to 12 ounces.

Selected books for further study:

Denney, James. 1948. *The Death of Christ*. Downers Grove, IL: Inter-Varsity Press.

Foster, R.C. 1962. *The Final Week*. Grand Rapids, MI: Baker Book House.

Krummacher, F.W. 1948. *The Suffering Saviour*. Chicago, IL: Moody Press.

Linton, Irwin. 1943. *The Sanhedrin Verdict*. New York, NY: Loiseaux Brothers.

Morris, Henry M. 1991. *Sampling the Psalms*. Green Forest, AR: Master Books. 269 p.

Nicholson, William R. 1928. *The Six Miracles of Calvary*. Chicago, IL: Moody Press.

Schilder, Klaas. 1940. *The Schilder Trilogy: Christ in His Suffering; Christ on Trial; Christ Crucified*. Grand Rapids, MI: Eerdmans Publ. Co. 467 p., 549 p., 561 p.

Chapter VIII

The Resurrection of Christ

Importance of the Resurrection

The bodily resurrection of Jesus Christ from the dead is the crowning proof of Christianity. Everything else that was said or done by Christ and the Apostles, no matter how great or marvelous, is secondary to the resurrection in importance. If the resurrection did not take place, then Christianity is a false religion. If it did take place, then Christ is God and the Christian faith is absolute truth.

Death is man's greatest enemy, and it has conquered all men but Christ. No matter how brilliant or rich or strong he may be, no man is wise enough to outwit death or wealthy enough to purchase freedom from death or strong enough to vanquish death. The grave always wins the victory, and man sooner or later returns to the dust.

In fact, the inexorable triumph of death applies not only to man, but to all things. Animals die and plants die, and even whole species atrophy and become extinct. Cities and nations, like people, are born and grow for a season, and then fade away. Homes and automobiles and clothes wear out and must eventually go back to the dust, just as do their owners. Even the universe itself is running down and heading toward an ultimate "heat death."

This universal reign of decay and death is called in the Bible "the bondage of corruption" (Rom. 8:21). In science it has come to be recognized as the Second Law of Thermodynamics. Also known as the Law of Increasing Entropy, this Second Law is now recognized as a universal law of science, with no known exception ever observed. It says, quite simply, that every system tends to become disordered, to run down and eventually die. Its entropy, which is a measure of disorder, always tends to increase.

The universality of the reign of decay and death is the measure of the absolute uniqueness of the resurrection of Christ. All other men, even the greatest men and the holiest men, have died. Buddha, Mohammed, Zoroaster, Confucius, Caesar, Marx — men who made a profound impact on the world in one way or another — are all dead.

But Jesus Christ is alive! It is true that He died and was buried, in common with all other men, but unlike other men He returned from Hades, resurrected His own dead body, made it henceforth immortal, and emerged from the tomb, alive forevermore! This was the greatest of all miracles, and could have been accomplished only if Jesus indeed is God, as He had claimed to be.

In this chapter we wish to examine carefully the actual evidence for His resurrection. If all of this is somehow a delusion and if Jesus of Nazareth did not really rise from the dead, then He is no different from other great men who are also dead. He is worse than they, in fact, because He is thereby branded as either a charlatan or a madman, since He staked all His claims to absolute deity on His promise to return from the dead.

On the other hand, if the resurrection is really a demonstrable fact of history, then not only are His claims vindicated, but so are His promises. Death is not, after all, the great victor, but is a defeated foe. He has "begotten us again unto a living hope by the resurrection of Jesus Christ from the dead" (1 Pet. 1:3). "Now is Christ risen from the dead . . . even so in Christ shall all be made alive" (1 Cor. 15:20, 22).

The Foundation of Christianity

Without the resurrection it is quite certain there would have been no Christian church. With the ignominious death of their Master, the disciples were utterly confused and afraid for their own lives. There is not the remotest possibility that they could have continued as teachers of the Nazarene's doctrines, and even less that others could have been persuaded to follow them, in those circumstances.

But with their assurance that Christ was alive, they went forth everywhere proclaiming the resurrection, and multitudes became believers in their living Lord. The importance of the resurrection in the preaching of the Early Church is quickly seen by scanning the Book of Acts (note Acts 2:22-36; 3:13-18; 4:10-12, 33; 5:29-32; 10:37-43; 13:27-37; 17:2-3, 30-32; 23:6; 24:14-16; 25:19; 26:6-8, 22-23; etc.).

Similarly in the epistles, the resurrection is paramount (e.g., Rom. 1:3-4; 6:3-9; 1 Cor. 15:1-58; 2 Cor. 4:10-14; Gal. 2:20; Eph. 1:19-23; Phil. 2:5-11; Col. 2:12; 1 Thess. 1:10; 4:14; 1 Tim. 3:16; 2 Tim. 2:8-11; Heb. 13:20; 1 Pet. 1:21; etc.). Even where the resurrection is not explicitly emphasized, it is always assumed. The final book, Revelation, opens with Christ's identification of himself as "the first begotten of the dead," and as the one "that liveth, and was dead; and, behold, I am alive forevermore" (Rev. 1:5, 18).

Predictions of the Resurrection

The resurrection caught the disciples completely by surprise. There is no indication that they had any hope after Christ's death. In fact, when they did see Him they were frightened, thinking they were seeing a ghost (Luke 24:37).

And this was in spite of the fact that they should have known that He would die and rise again, both from the Scriptures and from His own words. He later told them: "These are the words which I spake unto you, while I was yet with you, that all things must be fulfilled, which were written in the law of Moses, and in the prophets, and in the psalms, concerning me" (Luke 24:44).

Although the prophecies of His resurrection in the Old Testament were not evident to a superficial reader, they should have been correctly understood by those in Israel who diligently studied the Word. Such prophecies as found in Genesis 3:15; Psalm 2:7; Psalm 16:9-11; Psalm 22:14-25; Psalm 30:2-9; Psalm 40:1-3; Psalm 110:1; Psalm 118:21-24; Isaiah 53:9-12; Hosea 5:15–6:3; Zechariah 12:10; and others, if carefully studied, would have indicated that the coming Messiah would be put to death and then rise again.

Even if they had not been able to anticipate the resurrection from the Old Testament, however, they had the clear statements to this effect from the lips of Christ himself. Note John 2:19; Matthew 12:38-42; 16:21; 17:22-23; 20:17-19; 26:30-32; John 10:17-18; 16:16; and many other passages in the four Gospels.

One thing is certain: the disciples could not have fabricated the story of the resurrection from their own imaginations. On the contrary, they somehow failed to anticipate it even after such an abundance of prophetic preparation for it, both from the Scriptures and from Christ. It took the strongest of evidences to convince them it had actually taken place. But once they became convinced, their lives were wholly transformed, and they went forth to live and witness and even to die for their resurrected Lord.

The Empty Tomb

The first evidence the disciples had for the resurrection was that of the empty tomb, and this evidence is still unanswerable. As Peter and John entered the tomb, they saw an amazing thing. The heavy wrappings of linen clothes which Joseph and Nicodemus had wound around the body of Jesus (John 19:39-40) were still there, just as they had been, but the body had vanished out of them and the grave clothes had, as it were, collapsed inward on themselves. No wonder the record says that when John entered the tomb, "he saw, and believed" (John 20:8). His doubts and fears immediately gave way to an amazed faith; the collapsed grave clothes yielded no possible interpretation except that the body of the crucified Christ had returned to life, in such fantastic form that it could simply pass through the linen wrappings and enter henceforth into the power of an endless life!

Peter and John then rushed back to John's home, probably to tell Mary, the mother of Jesus, the tremendous news (note John 19:27; 20:10) and, shortly after, the women who had first come to the tomb entered it and also saw the tomb was empty (Luke 24:3).

The fact that the tomb was empty, of course, shows clearly that the resurrection of Christ was a bodily resurrection, not a spiritual resurrection. The latter idea is a self-contradiction, in fact, because the spirit does not die and, therefore, cannot be "resurrected." Indeed, resurrection takes place when the spirit *returns* to the body from which it has departed.

So powerful is the testimony of the empty tomb that the enemies of Christ have resorted to many strange and wonderful devices to try to explain it away. The first such attempt was the lie that the disciples had stolen the body (Matt. 28:11-15). Such a thing was utterly out of the question, of course. The disciples were hiding in fear of their lives and nothing could possibly have been further from their thoughts than this. Furthermore, the tomb had been sealed, a great stone rolled in front of it, and a watch of Roman soldiers set to guard it (Matt. 27:62-66).

Others, equally desperate for an answer, have suggested that Jesus did not die, but only fainted from weakness. He was buried in the mistaken belief that He was dead, and when He came back to consciousness in the tomb, He arose and left it. How, in His weakened condition, He managed to disengage himself from the great weight of wrappings and ointments, then break the Roman seal, roll away the giant stone at the entrance, overpower or elude the Roman soldiers, and then search out the disciples, is apparently of little concern to the proponents of this odd theory. Nor do they explain how such a pitiful sight as Jesus must have been, beaten almost beyond recognition and weak past endurance by loss of blood and horrible suffering on the cross, could have excited such a complete transformation in the cowering disciples. He must soon, or at least eventually, die anyhow, and thereafter any preaching of a resurrection could be nothing but fraud and hypocrisy.

Besides all this, there is no doubt that He died on the cross. Pilate was given assurance of this by the centurion (Mark 15:43-45). The savage spear thrust into His side by the soldier (John 19:34) made certain of His death, "and forthwith came there out blood and water," evidencing complete collapse of the heart cavity.

Some have thought that Mary Magdalene, then Peter and John, then the other women, all went to the wrong tomb. Such a stupid mistake was not very likely, however, especially since there was no other tomb there! This was a garden, owned by Joseph of Arimathea (Matt. 27:60; John 19:41), and no one else had been buried there.

Besides, if the body were still in any tomb whatever, it could have easily been produced by the Roman or Jewish authorities. A few weeks later, when multitudes were accepting Christ because of the preaching of the resurrection, these same authorities did everything they could to stop the spread of the new Christian faith, and they utterly failed. If they had simply produced the body of Jesus, on the other hand, the entire movement would have collapsed overnight. But this was the one thing they could not do! That body, raised from the grave, had ascended up to heaven.

The Appearances of Christ

Not only was the tomb empty, but the disciples actually saw their resurrected Lord, on at least ten separate occasions after He left the tomb. These appearances were probably as follows:

> To Mary Magdalene (John 20:11-18; Mark 16:9)
> To the other women (Matt. 28:8-10)
> To Peter (Luke 24:34; 1 Cor. 15:5)
> To the 2 on the road to Emmaus (Luke 24:13-35; Mark 16:12)
> To 10 of the disciples (Luke 24:36-43; John 20:19-24)
> To all 11 disciples, eight days later (John 20:24-29)
> To 7 disciples by the Sea of Tiberias (John 21:1-23)
> To 500 followers (1 Cor. 15:6)
> To James (1 Cor. 15:7)
> To the 11, at the ascension (Acts 1:3-12)

There were probably many other times He appeared to one or more of His disciples. Luke says: "He shewed himself alive after his passion by many infallible proofs, being seen of them forty days" (Acts 1:3). Finally, of course, He was seen by Paul (Acts 9:3-8; 1 Cor. 15:8) and once again by John (Rev. 1:12-18).

Now, of course, skeptics have tried to avoid the testimony of these numerous post-resurrection appearances of Christ by pointing out various contradictions in the six accounts which list them (Matt. 28:8-20; Mark 16:9-20; Luke 24:13-51; John 20:11–21:14; Acts 1:1-11; 1 Cor. 15:5-8), or else by charging the writings with fabricating the stories themselves. Of course, the mere fact that there does appear on the surface to be numerous superficial discrepancies and omissions in the account is clear proof that the writers were not engaged in some kind of collusion. If they were making up the tales, each one evidently was doing so independently of all others. This in itself would be quite a remarkable state of affairs, especially since these discrepancies begin to vanish when they are compared under close examination. It is a well-known rule of evidence that the testimonies of several different witnesses, each reporting from his own particular vantage point, provide the strongest possible evidence on matters of fact when the testimonies contain superficial contradictions which resolve themselves upon close and careful examination. This is exactly the situation with the various witnesses to the resurrection.

The only other possible device for explaining away the post-resurrection appearances is to assume that they were merely hallucinations, or visions, perhaps induced by drugs or hypnosis or hysteria. Such an absurd hypothesis is surely the last resort of cornered foes!

Such hallucinations, if this is what they were, are quite unique and should warrant careful psychological scrutiny. These were experienced by a considerable number of different individuals, all seeing the same vision, but in different groups, at different times, both indoors and outdoors, on a hilltop, along a roadway, by a lakeshore and other places. Furthermore, they were not looking for Jesus at all. Several times they didn't recognize Him at first, and at least once actually believed it was a ghost until He convinced them otherwise. He invited them to touch Him and they recognized the wounds in His hands (John 20:27; Luke 24:39). They watched Him eat with them (Luke 24:41-43). On one occasion, over 500 different people saw Him at one time (1 Cor. 15:6), most of whom were still living at the time when the evidence was being used.

The vision theory is thus quite impossible; and, therefore, the numerous appearances of Christ must be regarded as absolutely historical and genuine. This fact, combined with the evidence of the empty tomb, renders the resurrection as certain as any fact of history could possibly be.

The Witness of the Apostles

Many people at this point try to take refuge in the thought that the New Testament records may not be authentic, and that the various records of Christ's resurrection may have gradually grown through many years of verbal transmission and embellishment. But this possibility has already been thoroughly considered and refuted in chapter 3.

There is, as we have seen, no reasonable way of avoiding the conclusion that the New Testament documents are authentic as to date and authorship. They are, for all practical purposes, preserved in exactly the form in which they were originally written. Thus, they give us honest accounts of what the writers actually saw and heard. We can have absolute confidence that we are reading about what really took place.

Now it is impossible in the highest degree that the Apostles could have preached and written as they did unless they were absolutely sincere and under deep conviction of the truth of what they preached. They had instantaneously changed from craven runaways to bold, Spirit-filled proclaimers of Christ and the resurrection. Such preaching cost them the loss of their possessions, intense persecution, and finally the loss of their lives, but they kept preaching as long as strength permitted. Multitudes who accepted their preaching suffered the same persecutions.

If they were faking all this, if somewhere they had the body of Jesus hidden away, or if He were still barely alive on a sickbed somewhere, or if they were involved in some kind of plot, or if they were not really sure whether they had seen Him or some vision — is it conceivable that all of them (as well as their hosts of converts) would have continued this make-believe right up to the point of death itself? It would seem there must be some things in this world which no one in his right mind could possibly believe, and this should be one of them.

No wonder then, in view of the combined evidence of the empty tomb, the numerous appearances, the change in the disciples, and the authenticity of the records, not to mention the testimony of two thousand years of Christian history, that such a man as Thomas Arnold, formerly professor of history at Rugby and Oxford, one of the world's great historians, could say:

> I know of no one fact in the history of mankind which is proved by better, fuller evidence of every sort, to the understanding of a fair enquirer, than the great sign which God hath given us that Christ died, and rose again from the dead.[1]

In like manner, Simon Greenleaf, one of the most skilled legal minds ever produced in this nation, top authority on the matter of what constitutes sound evidence, developer of the Harvard Law School, after a thorough evaluation of the four

---

[1] Thomas Arnold, *Sermons on Christian Life; Its Hopes, Its Fears and Its Close*, 6th ed. (London: 1859), p. 324.

Gospel accounts from the point of view of their validity as objective testimonial evidence, concluded:

> It was therefore impossible that they could have persisted in affirming the truths they have narrated, had not Jesus actually risen from the dead, and had they not known this fact as certainly as they knew any other fact.[2]

---

[2] Simon Greenleaf, *The Testimony of the Evangelists* (New York, NY: Baker Book House, 1874), p. 28.

Selected books for further study:

McDowell, Josh. 1972. *Evidence that Demands a Verdict*. San Bernardino, CA: Here's Life Publishers. 387 p.

McDowell, Josh. 1979. *More than a Carpenter*. Wheaton, IL: Tyndale House Publishers. 128 p.

McDowell, Josh. 1981. *The Resurrection Factor*. San Bernardino, CA: Here's Life Publishers.

Milligan, William. 1894. *The Resurrection of our Lord*. New York, NY: Macmillan. 318 p.

Morison, Frank. 1944. *Who Moved the Stone?* London: Faber and Faber. 183 p.

Smith, Wilbur. 1945. *Therefore Stand*. Boston, MA: W. A. Wilde Co. 614 p.

Sparrow-Simpson, W. J. 1968. *The Resurrection and Christian Faith*. Grand Rapids, MI: Zondervan Publishing House.

Tenney, Merril C. 1963. *The Reality of the Resurrection*. New York, NY: Harper and Row.

Zwemer, Samuel M. 1947. *The Glory of the Empty Tomb*. New York, NY: Fleming H. Revell Co. 170 p.

Chapter IX

The Fact of God

The Necessity of Faith

The evidence for the existence of God is so overwhelming that the Psalmist exclaims, "The fool hath said in his heart, There is no God" (Ps. 14:1; 53:1). The writer of Proverbs says: "The fear of the Lord is the beginning of knowledge; but fools despise wisdom and instruction" (Prov. 1:7). The New Testament says "Even as they did not like to retain God in their knowledge, God gave them over to a reprobate mind" (Rom. 1:28). Also, it says: "For the invisible things of him from the creation of the world are clearly seen ... even his eternal power and godhead; so that they are without excuse" (Rom. 1:20).

Such strong language as this in the Word of God surely implies that there is an abundance of incontrovertible evidence that God exists. Why, then, do so many intelligent people, even brilliant scientists, profess to be atheists? How was it that an ideology squarely founded on atheism, as is communism, could have conquered half the world in one generation in the most enlightened and scientific age in history? Even in "Christian" countries such as the United States, a sort of practical atheism has gained almost complete control of the schools, the courts, the communications media, and the legislatures. The doctrine of religious freedom has been corrupted into freedom *from* religion in such institutions, and God is expelled and rejected just as if He did not exist at all.

This is an amazing state of affairs — that God, whose existence and supreme importance is abundantly evident and incontrovertibly real, could be so widely denied and ignored. It is plain that factual evidence alone cannot bring acceptance in minds which are set against believing it.

The element of faith — obedient faith — must be present, or else the evidence will simply be rejected. This is what the Scripture says, in fact: "Without faith it is impossible to please him: for he that cometh to God must believe that he is, and that he is a rewarder of them that diligently seek him" (Heb. 11:6).

Thus, no matter what evidence is presented for the existence of God, it is always possible for the unbeliever to counter with some objection or with another question. No argument or combination of arguments can ever convince someone who does not want to submit to God. Even if he is completely overpowered and silenced by the arguments, he will still be of an unbelieving *heart*, and this is what really counts. "A man convinced against his will is of the same opinion still."

Nevertheless, the evidence is *there*! For a person who sincerely desires the truth and is *willing* to believe, there is an abundance of proof concerning the fact of God and the character of God. The evidence is such as either to completely satisfy an open mind and heart or else to irrevocably condemn an unbelieving heart. For the latter, the only acceptable evidence may prove to be the heavy hand of God's chastening judgments, and even this may only harden it yet more.

Of course, in a way, the evidences for the deity of Jesus Christ, as already discussed, constitute an evidence for God. That is, if Christ is God, then God exists! On the other hand, an atheist might maintain that all the miraculous aspects of the person of Christ can be explained in other ways — the virgin birth was merely fabrication, the healings were psychosomatic, the fulfilled prophecies were accidental, the resurrection was a plot. Perhaps all were real supernatural occurrences which we, not knowing much about psychic and occult phenomena, don't yet know how to explain scientifically, but which somehow do have a logical explanation without God. There are many such dodges, unreasonable or impossible though they may be in terms of all logical criteria.

Therefore, it is also important to show, independently of the witness of Christ, the existence of strong reasons for believing in God — indeed, for believing in the God of the Bible. These reasons, as treated by theologians and philosophers, often take the form of intricate philosophical discourses requiring training in the specialized concepts and vocabulary in order to be comprehensible.

Sometimes these reasons are stated as the argument from *teleology*, the argument from *cosmology*, the argument from *ontology*, the argument from *aesthetics*, the argument from *volition*, and the argument from *morality*. Teleology is the study of goals or ends, and the argument is to the effect that the evidence of order and design in nature indicates purpose and therefore a Designer.

Cosmology is the study of the cosmos and its processes, and this argument proceeds especially on the idea that the existence of motion implies ultimately a prime mover. Ontology is the study of being. The ontological argument suggests that the existence of the idea of God can only be explained if God really exists.

Aesthetics is the study of beauty and truth. Since there are standards in the world of *relative* beauty and truth, there must be somewhere an absolute standard to which all things must ultimately be compared. Similarly, the argument from volition concludes that an infinite Will must exist if man experiences a multitude of individual, often clashing, wills. The existence of morality, an awareness of moral actions and the relative "rightness" or "wrongness" of those actions, can only be explained if somewhere there exists an absolute standard and arbiter of moral actions.

Now philosophical objections can be raised to each of these standard arguments for God. Nevertheless, when the phenomena which they explain in terms of God are tested in terms of other philosophical systems (atheism, pantheism, etc.) on a comparative basis with true theism, the latter emerges in far better light than the others. Though these arguments do not *prove* God, they do provide strong evidence when considered as a whole and when compared with other systems.

The Evidence from Causation

For one who desires to believe in God, or who, even though skeptical, is genuinely open and willing to believe, the evidence is full and satisfying. All such arguments as those above involve in one way or another the causal argument — that is, that only God is an adequate cause for the world as we observe and experience it.

Both scientist and logician work and think continually in terms of cause-and-effect relationships. Nothing happens in and of itself alone; it is invariably the effect of one or more proximate causes. In science, causality is always a basic assumption. In fact, this assumption is so obviously true to all observation and experience that it is called the Law of Cause and Effect. Every observed phenomenon is an effect, and its cause must be adequate to produce it. No effect can be quantitatively greater or qualitatively extrinsic to its cause. Every effect must be assimilated in principle to its cause. The scientists may not always be capable of elucidating this connection, but it must be there, somewhere. From nothing, nothing comes!

This is basically what science is. The scientist seeks to relate each given phenomenon to the combination of factors or causes which produce it, and then to describe this relationship if possible in quantitative terms, or at least in functional form. That is, he tries to state that a particular process or situation is a "function" of one or several "variables" which affect its behavior. He tries always to assimilate the effect to its cause, never doubting that the cause-and-effect relationship is logically and rigorously applicable.

Each effect, therefore, has a cause adequate to produce it. But that cause must itself have been an effect caused by an antecedent cause, and that by another cause, and so on back.

Logic compels us ultimately to one of two conclusions: either the chain of causes is infinite, with no beginning of the sequence at all, or else we must finally see the chain terminate in a great First Cause which itself was eternally un-caused, capable in and of itself to initiate the entire succession of secondary causes and effects. These are the only two possibilities if the Law of Cause and Effect operated in past ages as it does today.

The concept of an infinite chain of secondary causes is somehow fatiguing to our minds; we can find mental rest in an ultimate First Cause, but not in a never-beginning and meaningless infinite backward progression. We can count forward infinitely, but not backward. Time flows in one direction only.

A causing mechanism can easily be capable of accomplishing more than the particular effect it produces. An effect, on the other hand, can never be greater than its cause. In an infinite chain of effects and causes, there must, therefore, either be an eternal uniformity of effects (each cause producing an effect exactly equivalent to itself) or else the secondary causes successively increase in potency as they go backwards in time until, finally, they become infinite at infinite past time. Both possibilities are contrary both to reason and experience. In fact, the second alternative becomes to all intents and purposes, not the postulated infinite chain of second causes, but rather a chain leading finally back to a great infinite First Cause.

Consider, then, some of the effects observable in the universe. The vastness of the physical universe is inconceivably great, and its cause must be at least co-extensive with space and co-terminous with time. Therefore, the First Cause is *infinite* and *eternal*. Indeed, as the ontological argument would suggest, the existence of the very *ideas* of infinity and eternity, two absolutes (nothing can be more vast than infinity or longer in duration than eternity), is evidence enough that such absolutes have real existence.

Everywhere and always in space and time occur phenomena of energy and matter and motion. To cause and maintain such an infinite array and variety of power-producing systems (e.g., the galaxies) and power-converting processes (e.g., all of the earth's phenomena), the First Cause must be *omnipotent* and *omnipresent*. The fact that all such systems and processes are orderly and capable of systematic and intelligent description and mathematical formulation clearly bespeaks intelligent design. Causality, therefore, in this case indicates the First Cause to be intelligent — indeed *omniscient*.

Still further, one of the most obvious and significant effects in the universe is that of personality, at least on the earth. Although some materialists think that such phenomena are purely physico-chemical reactions, the very fact they "think" such thoughts demonstrates consciousness, which few people could really believe is only a chemical process. At least we know what we mean when we use such terms as "think," "feel," "desire," "decide," etc. These entities have meaning and, therefore, have some kind of reality. They do not exist independently and thus did not cause themselves. Therefore, thought, feeling, desire, will — all these and numerous similar phenomena are effects, and must have an adequate cause. Consequently, the First Cause is *conscious, emotional,* and *volitional* — in short is *personal*.

In like manner, the existence of moral and spiritual realities in the universe proves the First Cause to be essentially *moral* and *spiritual*. The existence of evil in the universe needs further consideration later, but at least the universal recognition that, by definition, "right" is better than "wrong" in itself proves the First Cause to be intrinsically *righteous*. Similarly, the universal consciousness that "love" is better than "hate," and that "justice" is better than "injustice," shows that the First Cause is *just* and *loving*.

The material discussed can perhaps be summarized in some such tabulation as below:

The First Cause of limitless space must be
  infinite in extent.
The First Cause of endless time must be eternal
  in duration.
The First Cause of perpetual motion must be
  omnipotent in power.
The First Cause of unbounded variety must be
  omnipresent in phenomena.
The First Cause of infinite complexity must be
  omniscient in intelligence.
The First Cause of consciousness must be per-
  sonal.
The First Cause of feeling must be emotional.
The First Cause of will must be volitional.
The First Cause of ethical values must be moral.
The First Cause of religious values must be
  spiritual.
The First Cause of beauty values must be
  aesthetic.
The First Cause of righteousness must be holy.
The First Cause of justice must be just.
The First Cause of love must be loving.
The First Cause of life must be living.

Thus, reasoning from cause-and-effect leads us to conclude that the great First Cause of all things, the prime mover, is an infinite, eternal, omnipotent, omnipresent, omniscient, personal, emotional, volitional, moral, spiritual, aesthetic, holy, just, loving, living being. And this, of course, is nothing less than a character description of the God of the Bible!

The cause-and-effect argument is so persuasive, in fact, that some scientists and philosophers have recently alleged that the universe did not have a cause! It just *happened*, as a fluctuation of nothing into something, and that order is continually arising out of chaos. The evidence for this remarkable notion exists only in the realm of mathematical metaphysics, and merely illustrates the extremes to which unbelievers will go to escape from God and reason.

The Triune God

The doubter might well respond to the argument as presented above with such a statement as: "Well, perhaps you have shown that there must be a personal God back of the universe, but this does not mean that He is the triune God of the Bible. Perhaps there are many gods, or even more likely God is a unity rather than a Trinity. Possibly there are two gods, one good and one bad, and they are competing with each other."

We cannot, of course, rigorously *prove* that God is a triunity, because this would leave no room for faith in God's revelation. Nevertheless, the concept of God as triune is fully in accord with both intuition and reason.

First, however, note that polytheism is *not* reasonable. If there is more than one God, then none of the "gods" can be either omnipotent or omnipresent, as we have seen the true God must be. Furthermore, the universe is not a "multiverse." Its intrinsic unity as a vast and glorious space-mass-time "continuum" is explicable only in terms of a unified First Cause, not as a conglomerate of first causes. The very notion of a vast assemblage of individual "gods" gathering together to apportion out their several segments of creative responsibility is its own refutation.

As we have observed previously, in fact, polytheism in practice is always merely the popular expression of pantheism, which identifies God with the universe, and is experienced primarily as animism. A God who is essentially synonymous with the universe and its varied components could never be the *Cause* of the universe.

What about dualism, the philosophy of two equal and competing gods, one good and one evil? In effect, this elevates Satan to the position he desires, equal with God. In this belief Satan is equally eternal with God and is the same intrinsic type of being, except that in his moral attributes, he is the opposite of God. Where God is love and holiness, Satan is hatred and evil, and the two are supposed to be eternally in conflict. Such a philosophy does have a superficial appearance of reasonableness. Evil is a very powerful force in the world; one could almost believe that evil is more potent than good, and Satan the more powerful and prominent of the two gods.

Nevertheless, there can really be only one First Cause, as we have already seen. The same arguments that militate against polytheism likewise apply against dualism. Even though there may be two competing principles in the universe, it is still a universe, and for a universe, there must be a universal First Cause. Either, therefore, God created Satan and he later became evil, or Satan created God and he later became good. They could not both be equally the First Cause of the universe.

Now even though we may believe that "truth is forever on the scaffold, wrong forever on the throne," we still have to reckon with the strange fact that we know that truth is "better" than deception, and right is "better" than wrong. If Satan is really the creator of all men and if, indeed, he has the world mostly under his own control, how is it that all men feel they ought to do right even when they find it so much more natural to do wrong? Somehow there is built into every man the deep awareness that love and justice and holiness constitute a higher order of reality than do hate and injustice and wickedness. Even men who do not believe in a God of love and righteousness at all seem to be continually troubled at the hatred and cruelty that abound in the world. The only reasonable explanation for such phenomena is that the true creation is "good," with "evil" only a temporary, though powerful, intruder. This in turn means, by cause-and-effect relationship, that God is the First Cause of all reality and Satan only a late-coming disturber of His creation. The Scriptures, of course, teach exactly this.

Therefore, neither polytheism nor pantheism nor dualism can meet the requirements for the First Cause. The latter must be One God, perfect in power and holiness, and none else. "I am the first, and I am the last; and beside me there is no God" (Isa. 44:6).

How, then, can God be a trinity? To understand this, one must remember that this doctrine does *not* mean three gods.

"Three gods" is as impossible and false a concept as any other form of polytheism. There can be only *one* God, and He is the great First Cause, the author of all reality.

But if He exists only in His ineffable unity, He could never be truly known. He is fundamentally the eternal, omnipresent, transcendent God, the great First Cause, the source of all being. Being present everywhere, however, He could never be really seen or heard or sensed anywhere. Yet, since He could not be frivolous in His creation, He must have a purpose therein, and that purpose must be communicable. He must, therefore, somehow be seen and heard. He must be a God who is both infinite and yet finite, who is omnipresent and eternal and still comprehensible locally and temporally. He must paradoxically be both source and manifestation, both Father and Son.

Not only must the invisible and inaudible God be seen and heard objectively, however, He must also be experienced and understood subjectively. The life of the creation must be maintained in vital union with that of the Creator. The Spirit of God must move over the creation and must indwell it and empower it. The activity of the Spirit is distinct from that of the Son and from that of the Father, and yet is indissolubly one with both.

God, therefore, is one God, and yet He must be Father, Son, and Spirit. He is source of all being, manifestation in all creation, experience and meaning in all reality. God is Father in generation, Son in declaration, Spirit in appropriation. The Son is the only begotten of the Father, and the Spirit is eternally the bestower of both the Father and the Son.

The doctrine of the Trinity, rather than being unnatural and self-contradictory, is deeply implanted in the very nature of reality and in man's intuitive awareness of God. Man has always felt and known in his heart that God was "out there," everywhere, that He was somehow the invisible source of all things. But this deep consciousness of God as eternal and omnipresent Father, he has corrupted into pantheism and then eventually into naturalism.

Similarly, man has always recognized that somehow God must and does reveal himself in human dimensions, so that man can see and discern the nature and purpose of his Creator. But this glorious truth of God as Son and Word, man has distorted into idolatry, seeking continually to erect some kind of model of God to his own specifications, either from material substance or metaphysical reasonings.

Finally, man has always desired to know God experientially and thus has sensed that God indwells His creation, manifesting himself in actual vital union with man in particular. This is the reality of God the Holy Spirit, but once again man has corrupted this glorious truth into mysticism and fanaticism and even demonism.

Man has thus always sensed, and could have understood had he desired, that God is Father, Son and Spirit, but instead he has corrupted the true God into pantheistic naturalism, polytheistic paganism, and demonistic spiritism. "When they knew God, they glorified Him not as God, neither were thankful; but became vain in their imaginations, and their foolish heart was darkened" (Rom. 1:21). "Lo, this only have I found, that God hath made man upright; but they have sought out many inventions" (Eccles. 7:29).

The doctrine of the triune God is thus not only revealed in Scripture, but is intrinsic in the very nature of things as they are.

The Witness of Creation

Since God is the Creator and sustainer of all things, it is reasonable to expect to find built into the structure of the creation a clear testimony of His character. "The heavens declare the glory of God, and the firmament sheweth His handiwork" (Ps. 19:1).

This, in fact, is the explicit claim of a remarkable and powerful verse of Scripture. "For the invisible things of Him from the creation of the world are clearly seen, being understood by the things that are made, even His eternal power and Godhead; so that they are without excuse" (Rom. 1:20).

The fact of God ("His eternal power") and the nature of God ("and godhead") are, according to this striking verse, "*clearly* seen" in the creation.

As a matter of fact, these two aspects of God are indeed set forth with amazing clarity in the basic structure of nature. The fundamental laws which control all natural processes clearly point to an omnipotent God and a primeval creation. Also, the basic framework within which all processes are structured likewise points directly to the nature of God.

But how can "invisible things" be clearly seen? Such a statement seems contradictory, but we have already noted how the invisible God is manifest visibly in the Son. "No man hath seen God at any time; the only begotten Son, which is in the bosom of the Father, he hath declared him" (John 1:18).

In the same way the "invisible things of him" are seen in "the things that are made." First, His "eternal power" is witnessed by the laws He created to govern His universe; and second, His "Godhead" is reflected by the structure of the creation.

The two basic laws of nature, as recognized intuitively through the ages and formalized scientifically in the past hundred years, are laws of universal conservation and universal decay. The law of conservation (First Law of Thermodynamics) is a law of quantitative constancy; nothing is now being created or destroyed. The law of increasing entropy (Second Law of Thermodynamics) is a law of qualitative decay; everything is tending toward disorder and death. The sun is a tremendous source of power, but its energy is gradually being dispersed through space, and the same is true for other suns. Eventually the universe seems destined to die a "heat death," all of its power uniformly scattered as low-level heat throughout the universe. The energy will all still be there, but no longer available to keep things going and the universe will die.

Now, since it has not yet died, it must not be infinitely old, and therefore it must have had a beginning. As time goes on, the available power decreases (by the Second Law) even though the total power in the universe remains constant (by the First Law). Therefore, the source of the tremendous power manifest throughout the universe must be outside and above the universe. It cannot be temporal power; it must be *eternal* power. The universe had a beginning, brought about by a great First Cause, a prime mover, an omnipotent God! The basic laws of the universe thus witness with great power to the fact of God.

In similar manner the structure of the universe witnesses to the nature of God, or better, to the "structure" of God, the godhead. The universe is (both as all men sense intuitively and as modern science has described dimensionally) a remarkable tri-universe, a "continuum" of space and mass-energy and time. Similarly, although the word "godhead" does not itself mean the divine Trinity, it does have reference to the nature or "godhood" of God, the form in which God exists as God. Since Scripture does clearly reveal God to be a triune God, theologians through the centuries have naturally interpreted the term to include the concept of His triunity — God, as Father, Son and Holy Spirit, one God in three persons.

Space is the invisible, omnipresent background of all things, everywhere displaying phenomena of matter and/or energy (which are inter-convertible) which are, in turn, experienced in time. Just so, the Father is the invisible, omnipresent source of all being, manifest and declared by the eternal word, the Son, who is, in turn, experienced in the Spirit.

It is not that the universe is a *triad* of three distinct entities which, when added together, comprise the whole. Rather each of the three is itself the whole, and the universe is a true trinity, not a triad. Space is infinite and time is endless, and everywhere throughout space and time events happen, processes function, phenomena exist. The tri-universe is remarkably analogous to the nature of its Creator.

Furthermore, each of the three entities is also itself a trinity. That is, for example, space is comprised of three dimensions, each of which occupies all space. The first dimension is the basic dimension by which space is identified (e.g., the linear dimension); it can only be "seen," however, in two dimensions and "experienced" in three dimensions.

Time also is a trinity. The future is the unseen, unexperienced source of time. As it "flows" forward, time becomes apparent to the senses, instant by instant, in the present. In the past, it has become "experienced," or historical time.

And everywhere in space and time things happen. The particular event or "happening" is evidenced to the senses as a motion, a space-time ratio. The particular type and rate of motion (or "velocity," the space traversed divided by the corresponding increment of time) determines the particular "phenomenon" that is experienced, whether light, or sound, or weight, or inertia, or some other quantity. The motion, however, did not generate itself; rather it is caused by intangible, unseen energy. Here again is a triunity. Energy, occurring everywhere in space and time, continually generates motion, which is experienced as a phenomenon. For example, sound energy generates sound waves which are experienced as the hearing of sound. Light energy begets light rays which are experienced in the seeing. Gravitational energy produces the acceleration of gravity which is experienced in the falling, or in the weighing. And so on.

These remarkable relationships can be visualized by means of the diagram below:

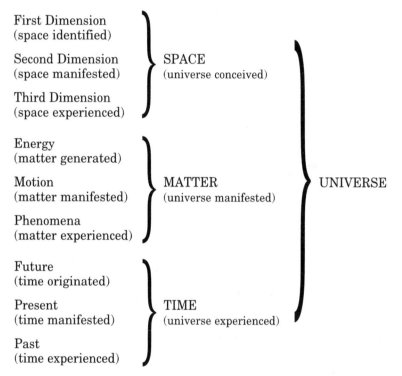

First Dimension
(space identified)

Second Dimension
(space manifested)

SPACE
(universe conceived)

Third Dimension
(space experienced)

Energy
(matter generated)

Motion
(matter manifested)

MATTER
(universe manifested)

UNIVERSE

Phenomena
(matter experienced)

Future
(time originated)

Present
(time manifested)

TIME
(universe experienced)

Past
(time experienced)

Thus, the entire physical creation is a marvelous trinity of trinities, clearly reflecting "even His godhead." The laws by which all processes function bear witness to the fact of God and the framework within which they function reflects the triune nature of God. These facts do not *prove* the existence of the triune God, but the latter is surely an adequate *cause* to explain the remarkable fact that the most basic laws of science imply the existence of an eternal omnipotent Creator, and that the structure of the physical universe is a trinity of trinities.

The Divine–Human Nature of Christ

We have shown the rational necessity of a personal God who created all things in the beginning. We have also considered the logical and scientific evidence that God is a triune God, one God in essence but existing in three persons, Father, Son, and Spirit.

It has also been shown that the second person of the godhead is the one who manifests God to man and to all His creation. Whenever and wherever God has been made visible or in any way manifested locally and temporally in His creation, it is the second person, the Word of God, who has so appeared.

His ultimate manifestation, in fact His permanent and final such manifestation, is as man himself. God became incarnate as man in the person of the Lord Jesus Christ. After His sacrificial death and resurrection, He is now forever the "man in the glory" at the right hand of the Father.

This "hypostatic union" of God and man in Jesus Christ is no doubt difficult to comprehend intellectually. A rational description of how it is possible for the infinite and eternal God to be indissolubly incarnate in finite and temporal man is quite elusive, and many people have considered such a union to be impossible. The Gnostic philosophers (including the modern "new-age" philosophers who separate the Christ "idea" from the man Jesus), whose influence in the apostolic period was so devastating to Christian truth, accepted the divinity of Christ but rejected His humanity. Most moderns, on the other hand, accept His humanity but reject His deity.

Nevertheless, as we have seen in the previous chapter, there are many compelling evidences that prove beyond all reasonable doubt that Jesus Christ was both perfect man and "very God of very God." However difficult such a union may be to comprehend scientifically, there is no other way to explain the actual facts associated with His life and testimony. In any case, it is instructive to note that the same type of paradox associated with the divine-human nature of Christ is also found impressed upon every aspect of the universe He created.

Consider the space-mass-time universe, which has already been shown to consist of a trinity of trinities, reflecting the trinitarian nature of God. In addition, each of the three entities exhibits a paradoxical complementarity very much analogous to that of the hypostatic union in Christ. For example, "space" is infinite and yet is comprehended and measured only in terms of finite regions of space. Similarly, "time" is eternal and yet is comprehended and measured only in terms of bounded increments of time. Although it sounds contradictory in a formal sense, it is nevertheless realistically true that "space" is both finite and infinite and that "time" is both temporal and eternal. As a matter of fact, these are the very terms with which we describe the divine-human nature of Christ. In His humanity, He is finite and temporal, confined to a given space at a given time. In His deity, on the other hand, He is infinite and eternal without "beginning of days, nor end of life" (Heb. 7:3), the one "that filleth all in all" (Eph. 1:23).

In the same manner there is a remarkable duality, or complementarity, of "mass-energy." It is well known that "mass" and "energy" are in principle inter-convertible, through nuclear fission or fusion reactions. The Einstein equation $E = Mc^2$ relates energy and mass to each other, by the constant "c," which is the velocity of light. The motion of light is thus the foundation of the whole complex of phenomena which occur in the space-time universe. The velocity of light is the ultimate motion in the physical universe, so far as we know, the velocity to which all lesser velocities must be referenced.

We can, therefore, speak of the universe as a "space-light-time" universe. Now, it is significant that this motion of light is famous for its mysterious and paradoxical complementarity. That is, the translation of light, moving at its immense velocity (300 million meters or 186,000 miles, per second), seems to take place both as a stream of particles and as a field of waves. It would seem that light could not be both waves and particles, and yet it definitely behaves as a wave motion under some conditions and as a particle motion under others. This duality applies both in radiations of electro-magnetic energy and in the atomic structure of matter, in which the orbiting electron likewise behaves both as a particle and as a wave. The two disciplines of modern physics known as *quantum mechanics* and *wave mechanics* have been developed from these two concepts.

This paradox has never been resolved in a manner satisfying to all physicists, but in any case is considered to be innately realistic. It has been developed, in fact, by Heisenberg into the famous "uncertainty principle" and by Born into his "complentarity principle." It has even been considered by such physicists as analogous to the paradox between determinism and free will in the moral realm.

One could say, therefore, that all physical reality has a dual nature, that the ultimate reconciliation of these apparently contradictory natures is involved in an intrinsic "uncertainty," but that they likewise exist in perfect "complementarity." Exactly the same statement can be made about the divine-human nature of Christ. Though it seems paradoxical, it is nevertheless harmonious in every respect with the nature of the world in which we live.

Escape from Reason

In this chapter we have seen that logical and rational analysis of the world which God created leads directly to the necessary existence of the Christian God. The witness of the universe around us (Ps. 19:1), and of our hearts within us (Rom. 2:14-15), provides clear evidence of the truth of God. Even the vast mysteries of God's triune nature and of the divine-human nature of Christ are so modeled in the structure of all physical reality that unbelievers are "without excuse" (Rom. 1:20; Ps. 14:1).

How, then, do skeptics justify themselves in rejecting the evidence of God? Basically, they fall back on one or both of two escapist techniques. The first is to raise objections to the doctrine of God because evil exists in the world, maintaining that if God exists and is really omnipotent and all-holy, He would never have permitted evil and suffering to enter the world. The second is to deny the validity of the reasoning process, especially when applied to the determination of ultimate causes.

The problem of evil is a very real problem and will be considered at some length in the next chapter. In itself, however, it fails altogether to deal with the *positive* evidence for God as outlined in this chapter. The argument from causation is still intact, whether or not we can adequately explain how a First Cause that is holy permits unholiness.

The argument from irrationality is more difficult to answer, however, since its very premise denies even the existence of an answer. Those who use this argument reject the possibility of meaningful reasoning from the finite to the infinite, insisting that other unknown factors may exist which would upset the apparent causal relationships.

For example, the argument based on the laws of thermodynamics is sidestepped by postulating either: (a) a "steady-state" cosmology, in which continual evolution of matter out of nothing is supposedly taking place in some unknown region in space to offset the continual decay of energy which is observed everywhere in the known universe; or (b) an "osclilating-universe" cosmology, in which the present reign of decay in the universe is supposedly offset by alternate cycles of growth, during which all things are somehow re-energized. Neither of these theories is capable of proof, since the postulated rewinding of the universe takes place outside of those regions of space and time which can be experimentally observed. Such theories are at best, therefore, speculative suppositions. The Second Law, on the other hand, has been experimentally observed to be true wherever and whenever it can be tested, without exception. The Second Law is *science*; the theories which attempt to circumvent it are strictly *fictions*, conceivable perhaps, but never observed in real life.

Similarly, the law of cause and effect is science; speculations which deny its applicability in relation to first causes are based on wishful thinking, not on present experience. The faith of atheism and pantheism is based on an irrational denial of uniformity in nature, despite its professed allegiance to experimental science.

The recent developments in mathematical cosmology which treat the entire universe as simply an "accident," a "quantum fluctuation" from the primeval nothingness, is a further example of this scientific escapism.

This strange irrationality in scientific philosophy may well be a contributing factor to the headlong flight from reason characterizing modern existentialism and its various offshoots. That is, scientists profess to have eliminated the need for God and yet to have no real explanation apart from God. It makes no sense that unfeeling, unthinking, dead matter (or even primeval "nothingness" could produce feeling, thinking, living beings, and yet that is what people are expected to believe. It is not too surprising that more and more people, especially young people, have concluded there is no rationality to anything. To such as these, the present moment of existence is all that has meaning and it is futile even to speculate about eternity or purpose or truth or any other ultimates.

Science, they think, has long since expelled God from any meaningful place in human life, and yet science is not itself a substitute for God, since it has led only to an imminent threat of nuclear extinction, to global pollution and to a wide variety of other socio-technologic perils. And so the cult of irrationalism and escapism grows, expressing itself in the amoral and a-mental productions of modern music, drama, literature, and art.

This is the dead end to which man's denial of the overwhelming evidences of God has led. True reason and true science will lead to God, but man does not want to submit to God and, therefore, denies the evidence of his own reason. "They became vain in their [reasonings], and . . . professing themselves to be wise, they became fools" (Rom. 1:21-22). "They have forsaken me the fountain of living waters, and hewed them out cisterns, broken cisterns, that can hold no water" (Jer. 2:13).

Another God

The cult of irrationality, manifest on different levels in the philosophy of existentialism, the theology of neo-orthodoxy and the tactics of destructivism and anarchy, only leads to chaos. Theoretical irrationalism in science and philosophy has naturally led to political and sociological confusion as well, for great numbers of people.

Men cannot long be satisfied with chaos, however. Each person is so conditioned by all his observation and experience to think in terms of causation and purpose that he must, even despite himself, look for some kind of ultimate order and meaning in the universe. If he has lost faith in the true God, and His Word, then he must sooner or later find another god.

Thus, the same tragic sequence is being repeated today that in varied ways has occurred often before. A solid and satisfying biblical theism declines to a compromising religious liberalism, then to confusion and anarchy, then onward to polytheistic pantheism and ultimately to satanism. It is no surprise that existential theology and philosophy produced the "beat generation" and this in turn the "drop out" hippie culture, leading not only to riot and revolution, but also to occultism and eventually into the worship of Satan himself. Yet they like to call this escape from reason the "New Age" movement!

Behind the scenes, no doubt, these movements are being manipulated by certain sinister forces, both human and demonic, who, unlike those they manipulate, are not at all confused about their aims and purposes. They promote atheism and irrationalism in order to persuade men and women to overthrow all prior institutions, remnant from the divine economy, and then to submit to a universal humanistic and pantheistic totalitarian government. More and more this final species of pantheism will be united with satanism, and all nations will consciously align themselves with Satan in his climactic effort to destroy God.

Man's innate spiritual and rational nature will impel him to believe and follow some god. If he will not believe the true God, he will inevitably follow a false god. "Because they received not the love of the truth, that they might be saved . . . God shall send them strong delusion, that they should believe the lie" (2 Thess. 2:10-11). "Even as they did not like to retain God in their knowledge, God gave them over to a reprobate mind" (Rom. 1:28). "And they worshipped the dragon" (Rev. 13:4).

Satan, together with the end-time leaders of his human conspiracy (called in the Book of Revelation the "beast" and the "false prophet") and with his angelic and human followers (Rev. 16:12-14), will finally prepare for one grand and mighty assault on the throne of God. But the outcome is never in doubt; "These shall make war with the Lamb, and the Lamb shall overcome them: For he is Lord of lords and King of kings" (Rev. 17:14).

Selected books for further study:
Clark, Gordon H. 1967. *The Philosophy of Science and Belief in God*. Phillipsburg, NJ: Presbyterian and Reformed. 95 p.
Clark, Robert E. D. 1949. *The Universe: Plan or Accident?* London: Paternoster Press. 192 p.
Crossley, Robert. 1978. *The Trinity*. Downer's Grove, IL: Inter-Varsity. 45 p.
Morey, Robert A. *New Atheism and the Erosion of Freedom*. Phillipsburg, NJ: Presbyterian and Reformed Publishing Co.
Morris, Henry M. 1988. *Men of Science, Men of God*. Green Forest, AR: Master Books. 107 p.
Paley, William. 1972. *Natural Theology*. Houston, TX: St. Thomas Press. 402 p.
Row, C. A. n.d. *Christian Theism*. New York, NY: Thomas Whittaker. 318 p.
Schaeffer, Francis A. 1979. *He is There and He is Not Silent*. Wheaton, IL: Tyndale Publishing House. 100 p.
Schaeffer, Francis A.. 1968. *The God Who Is There*. Chicago, IL: Inter-Varsity. 191 p.
Sire, James W. 1976. *The Universe Next Door*. Downer's Grove, IL: Inter-Varsity Press. 239 p.

Sproul, R. C. *If There's a God, Why Are There Atheists?* Wheaton, IL: Tyndale Publishing House. 137 p.

Wood, Nathan R. 1978. *The Trinity in the Universe.* Grand Rapids, MI: Kregel Publishing Co. 220 p.

Chapter X

The Character of God

The Problem of Pain

As seen in the last chapter, there is no real logical escape from the causal argument for God. Therefore, failing in this, atheists and skeptics take refuge in a diversionary argument, thinking that discovery of some imagined flaw in God's character will suffice to disprove His existence.

It must be emphasized, however, that our own ignorance of God's motives and purposes does not prove He has none, nor that they are not reasonable and right in the light of eternity. If God does exist, it is arrogant for His creatures to question His actions. "Shall the thing formed say to Him that formed it, Why hast thou made me thus?" (Rom. 9:20). Our very minds were made by Him, so how can we presume to formulate autonomous judgments as to His character? What God does must be absolutely right, *by definition*. That He does exist, as an omnipotent, personal, holy God, is proved to a high probability by causal reasoning, as well as by the evidence of the person of Jesus Christ and by the testimony of His written Word. The injection of extraneous questions concerning His character into the argument can in no way refute this fact.

Nevertheless, people do raise such questions. A world which is so obviously full of evil and suffering, they say, could not be attributed to an omnipotent, holy God. If God were omnipotent and yet allows evil to develop and continue, then He is not good. If God desires to rid the world of evil, but is unable to do so, then He is not omnipotent. In either case, He cannot be an omnipotent, all-righteous God, so the objection goes, and, therefore, the God of the Bible does not exist.

But to pronounce such judgments as these implies

omniscience on the part of the one judging. In effect, the skeptic is saying there is no possible explanation other than atheism for the present existence of both good and evil in the universe. Such people are professing to know so much about both past and future that there can be no possible justification for a holy God to allow evil to enter and thrive for a brief season. Since such knowledge must be infinite in breadth, they are therefore setting themselves up as God. This is somewhat presumptuous. The fact that they do not yet understand all of God's purposes does not prove there are none!

Unless one really does have infinite and infallible knowledge of all things (and therefore *is* God), it is obviously impossible to *prove* there is *no* God. Consequently, that one must at least confess the *possibility* that God exists. In the light of that possibility, it would then follow that we may ourselves have been brought into existence by God. Thus, our minds, our reasoning ability, our capacity to believe or not believe, may all likewise be creations of God.

In fact, the very attempt to reason things out and make value-judgments in this way in itself presupposes the existence of God. If there is no God, and our brains and thoughts are mere chance assemblages of atoms and forces, then obviously there is no such thing as any rational meaning or moral value in the universe. If logic and reason do have reality, however, and if good and evil do have any meaning at all, then there is order and purpose in the universe and a moral First Cause does exist. The evidence from causation is still *there*, like it or not. Therefore, God is still there.

Now, although it is really presumptuous for us to raise doubts about God's character, it is proper for us to seek to understand His actions within the limits set by His own revelation. We cannot comprehend their fullness, but we can at least obtain a partial and tentative understanding of them to the extent revealed in the Scriptures.

In the first place, it is clear that God has chosen to create *responsible* beings, both angelic and human. Men and women in particular have been created in His own image and, therefore, capable of love and holiness as well as intelligence and volition. Because of His own nature of infinite love and grace, it was His good pleasure to create beings on whom He could bestow His love and grace and who, being made in His image, would be capable of reciprocating and responding to that love. "Thou hast created all things, and for thy pleasure they are and were created" (Rev. 4:11). "We love him, because he first loved us" (1 John 4:19).

It is evident, however, that freedom to love also entails freedom not to love. Responsibility to obey implies also the ability to disobey. Thus, the creation of moral beings, in God's image, necessarily implies the possible, though not necessary, entrance of sin and evil into His creation. Each person was not to be a machine, but a responsible, thinking, decision-making being.

We *have* sinned, of course, as is evident from the age-long existence of suffering and death in the world, for these are the consequences of sin. God foreknew all this, but, rather than refraining from creating us on this account, He had already ordained and set in motion His marvelous plan of salvation.

Thus, a second reason for His allowing sin into His creation is that He might thereby manifest His redeeming grace. If we had never sinned and, therefore, never needed a Savior, we could never have known God in the fullness of His love. A redeemed sinner, saved through faith in One who died for him, would love Him with a love far deeper than one based only on His work in creating and providing for him.

These two reasons probably constitute the best explanation we can now give for God's allowing sin in His universe. They at least provide a framework within which we can tentatively understand the many individual problems that seem to exist in God's moral world.

Thus, the suffering and sorrow that are now such a part of human experience are directly related to sin. "For we know that the whole creation groaneth and travaileth in pain together until now" (Rom. 8:22). "Wherefore, as by one man sin entered into the world, and death by sin; and so death passed upon all men, for that all have sinned" (Rom. 5:12). Death (with suffering and sorrow that lead to, and follow from, death) came into the world only when sin entered into the world.

It is true, of course, that not every instance of suffering is directly related to a particular sin committed by the sufferer. The soldier killed in the war did not start the war, nor was the blind man "born blind" because his parents "did sin" (John 9:2). Nevertheless, "sin was in the world" and, therefore, "death reigned . . . even over them that had not sinned after the similitude of Adam's transgression" (Rom. 5:13-14).

The truth is that "all have sinned" (Rom. 3:23) and, therefore, all have earned the "wages of sin" which "is death" (Rom. 6:23), even though it is seldom possible to assign a particular death to a particular sin. Because of the universal reign of sin and death, "man that is born of a woman is of a few days, and full of trouble" (Job 14:1).

There would be a real problem here, of course, if this situation were to continue forever. In fact, the very existence of such inequities in the present moral universe is evidence that this present world does *not* last forever. God is allowing sin and suffering to exist for a season but eventually will settle all accounts and banish these intruders once and for all. "For our light affliction, which is but for a moment, worketh for us a far more exceeding and eternal weight of glory" (2 Cor. 4:17).

Here is one final clue as to why God permits evil. In some strange way, He makes the "wrath of man [to] praise him" (Ps. 76:10). As Joseph told his brothers, "Ye thought evil against me; but God meant it unto good" (Gen. 50:20). Somehow, in the scales of eternity, the character is purified and strengthened through suffering. "No chastening for the present seemeth to be joyous, but grievous: nevertheless afterward it yieldeth the peaceable fruit of righteousness unto them which are exercised thereby" (Heb. 12:11).

Within this general framework, we can at least suggest a tentative and partial answer to the problem of evil. This framework consists of God's sovereign grace, man's responsible freedom, the curse on man's dominion because of his sin, God's redemptive purpose in the death and resurrection of His Son, the present process of cleansing and preparation, and God's promised consummation and restoration of all things.

What About the Heathen?

One of the most common objections raised by skeptics to the biblical doctrine of God, especially in its exclusiveness, is that God is unfair. There have been multitudes of people, both in earlier ages and at the present time, who lived their entire lives without ever once hearing about the true God. "How then shall they call on him in whom they have not believed?" (Rom. 10:14).

This seems an especially vexing problem when expressed in terms of belief in Christ. Perhaps people could be expected to know about God through nature, but how could they ever learn about Jesus Christ without reading the New Testament or hearing a Christian preacher or missionary? Yet the Lord Jesus has said plainly: "No man cometh unto the Father, but by me" (John 14:6). And Peter said, "Neither is there salvation in any other: for there is none other name under heaven given among men, whereby we must be saved" (Acts 4:12). Doubters vigorously object to the idea of a God who requires faith in Christ for salvation without giving everyone equal opportunity to hear about Him.

This objection, however, refutes itself, for a completely equal treatment of all people in this respect would mean that all must be created exactly alike, with exactly the same genetic and environmental backgrounds and with exactly the same experiences throughout life. Otherwise, inevitably, there would be inequality of opportunity, and those who had lesser opportunity could still accuse God of favoritism toward those who had more. But for God to create all people exactly alike would insure that they would all respond exactly alike and, therefore, He would have created a race of automatons, with no real freedom at all, and everyone would have the same destiny, whatever it was.

In the real world, obviously, such is not the case. God has created men and women in infinite variety, with no two people alike at all. Individual abilities and opportunities vary widely, with respect not only to the gospel but also to every aspect of life. No one, in fact, would really want it to be otherwise.

People may complain about their individual lot, but no one would really wish everyone to be alike. Complexity and variety are clearly preferable to homogenized uniformity, but in the very nature of the case variety means non-equality.

Considered in these terms, it is obvious that this question of God's "fairness" is broader than just the problem of one's acquaintance with the gospel. It must deal with all types of differences and inequities, the entire spectrum of variability of human backgrounds and opportunities. In any case, it is clear that the existence of variety, and therefore inequality, is quite consistent with the creative power of God.

Each person is a free being and, therefore, capable of responding to God's will and purpose in whatever degree these have been made known to him or her. If some have more knowledge and opportunity than others, they are to that degree more responsible and, therefore, more culpable if they fail. "Unto whomsoever much is given, of him shall be much required" (Luke 12:48). Though inequalities are inescapable, God is perfectly able to evaluate all of these in relation to individual responses. He is also able to effect a system of graded rewards and punishments in the same proportion in a future life, and this is exactly what the Bible teaches He will do. "My reward is with me, to give every man according as his work shall be" (Rev. 22:12).

As a matter of fact, however, God is not obligated to any of us in any respect. No one has lived up to the light he has received, and thus no one deserves salvation. "For there is not a just man upon earth, that doeth good, and sinneth not" (Eccles. 7:20). "There is none that seeketh after God . . . there is none that doeth good, no not one . . . that every mouth may be stopped, and all the world may become guilty before God" (Rom. 3:11-12, 19).

Since all people are consciously sinners, even against whatever light they may have, they have no proper claim against God's justice. In perfect justice, God could consign everyone to eternal separation from himself. If He condescends to forgive and save anyone at all, it is entirely a matter of His grace, not of our merit.

That being the case, any criterion which God may establish as a basis for salvation is altogether of grace, and no one has a right to question it. God could, if He so elected, save only those people who were, say, over seven feet tall, and He would be completely righteous in doing so, at least in so far as any obligation He has to shorter people is concerned, for He has no such obligation. "Hath not the potter power over the clay, of the same lump to make one vessel unto honour, and another unto dishonour?" (Rom. 9:21).

By the same token, God is under no obligation to see that every individual man hears the gospel, since everyone has already rejected the earlier light God had given him. Even if no person ever heard the way of salvation and no one therefore ever accepted it, God would still be perfectly just in leaving all people in their lost condition. That is all anyone deserves.

On the other hand, it is wonderfully true that God is a God of love as well as justice. He earnestly desires "all men to be saved, and to come unto the knowledge of the truth" (1 Tim. 2:4). The criterion which He established for our salvation was not an arbitrary standard (such as whether a man was seven feet tall, or was able to acquire a Ph.D. degree, or to accumulate a million good deeds, or something else). Instead, God has established one which was uniquely consistent both with God's character and with His desire to bring the greatest number of lost souls to salvation.

The reasonableness and the necessity of the particular plan of salvation as ordained by God will be discussed in the next chapter. The point here is that any plan of salvation whatever is entirely due to God's mercy, and not in the least respect merited by anyone.

God in grace has provided a Savior, able and willing to "save them to the uttermost that come unto God by him" (Heb. 7:25) regardless of their sins or religious background or anything else. Because each person is still a free moral being, however, He will not force salvation on anyone, asking only that that person voluntarily receive salvation as a free gift, accepting Christ by faith as personal Savior and Lord.

The offer of salvation is utterly undeserved and completely free, needing only acceptance to become effective for anyone. But now, of course, before it can be accepted, it must be heard. Obviously, the one who never hears the gospel cannot accept it. Those who never hear will die in their sins. However, it should be remembered that they did not *deserve* to hear it or to be saved. Even if they *do* hear it, they may very likely reject it, thus adding even more to their weight of guilt before God.

Nevertheless, God does desire that every person hear the gospel and have opportunity thereby to be saved. The only problem, then, is how to convey the news to them.

It is conceivable that God could have thundered from heaven how to be saved. Or perhaps He could have dispatched His mighty angels to every corner of the globe to search out every man and woman and tell them about it.

Under such a barrage as this, there is no doubt they would have believed what they heard, for how under such circumstances could they do otherwise! But belief evoked in this way would be born out of necessity, just as one comes to believe in the burning ability of the flame when his clothes are on fire. For God's purpose to be fulfilled, on the other hand, He desires each person to respond in a faith which is founded on love and gratitude, not on compulsion.

Therefore, He has given those who believe on Christ the high privilege of conveying the good news of salvation to others. Each one who has been saved is to become a messenger to tell others, by whatever means and with whatever abilities God has given. There is no other means available. Neither God nor the holy angels can do it without inhibiting the freedom of men and women to reject it; neither Satan nor his wicked angels will do it because they by all means wish to prevent them from hearing it; unsaved people cannot do it because they either do not know it or do not believe it; the only ones who can serve as God's witnesses are those who themselves have been redeemed.

But it necessarily follows that, if each unsaved person must wait until he encounters some of God's human witnesses before he can hear the gospel, he may never hear it. It is true that God desires and urges believers to "preach the gospel to every creature" (Mark 16:15), even promising glorious rewards to those who do (1 Thess. 2:19; Dan. 12:3; etc.) and warning of sorrow and rebuke to those who do not (Ezek. 33:8; 1 Cor. 9:16; etc.). Nevertheless, it is sadly true that Christians have been stupid and fearful and slothful in implementing this commission, and multitudes have lived and died without once hearing of God's glorious provision of salvation.

Now the heathen or the skeptic may very properly and with full justification rebuke Christians for their negligence in spreading the gospel. But this does not justify them in rejecting it or in criticizing God for it. As we have seen, there was really no other way it could have been done and, anyway, God was under no obligation either to provide a Savior or to send a messenger at all. The message *is* going out this way, and multitudes *have* been saved this way, and that itself is sufficient proof that this was the best way.

In fact, there is some evidence that God may go even further than this in trying to reach lost people. God "is longsuffering to us-ward, not willing that any should perish, but that all should come to repentance" (2 Pet. 3:9). There is no doubt that the great majority of those who are without the gospel — whether animists or Muslims, or Hindus or whatever they are — not only do not know about Christ, but do not want to know!

They vigorously resist the gospel when they do hear it. It is not lack of opportunity to hear the truth, but unwillingness to respond if they do hear it; that is their real condemnation.

Nevertheless, it does seem that there may be some individuals in every nation and tribe who do have a real desire to know how to be saved and who would respond if they heard it with sufficient understanding. In view of the great lengths to which God has gone in order to provide salvation, it does seem conceivable that He might undertake in some special way, if necessary, to get the message to those who would really desire it. "For the eyes of the Lord run to and fro throughout the whole earth, to shew himself strong in the behalf of them whose heart is perfect toward him" (2 Chron. 16:9).

Missionaries frequently have told of entering new tribes or areas and finding individuals actually anticipating their arrival and eager to learn about the way of salvation. The experience of Cornelius in Acts 10 seems to have been paralleled in some degree in such instances. As Peter told Cornelius, "Of a truth I perceive that God is no respecter of persons; But in every nation he that feareth him, and worketh righteousness, is accepted with him" (Acts 10:34-35). As soon as Peter preached the gospel to Cornelius and his waiting household, they all immediately believed on Christ and received the Holy Spirit.

Suppose, however, that no missionary was available for God to lead into such an area where prepared hearts were ready and waiting. Is there any way in which the gospel message can reach such a person?

He does, of course, have the witness of his conscience that he has a basic responsibility to obey a higher power. Those who do not have God's written Word, Paul says, "Shew the work of the law written in their hearts, their conscience also bearing witness, and their thoughts the mean while accusing or else excusing one another" (Rom. 2:15). He should know by the witness of creation that there must be a God who created him and to whom, therefore, he is responsible. "For the invisible things of him from the creation of the world are clearly seen . . . even his eternal power and godhead" (Rom. 1:20).

Furthermore, since all people are descended from the three sons of Noah, God's primeval revelation was the common property of the ancestors of all present nations at one time. In every religion, distorted though it may have become through both demonic corruption and human invention, there can be traced elements of God's original revelation.

Most religious traditions, for example, preserve a record of the great Flood and of a primeval golden age at the dawn of history. All religions sense, too, that man is somehow alienated from God (or "the gods") and that something needs to be done to restore the lost fellowship. Most of them preserve the knowledge that God's favor can be restored only through sacrifice, and so various animals — sometimes even humans — are offered as a propitiatory sacrifice for this purpose.

Although this knowledge is often corrupted into the form of gross polytheism, with sacrifices made to idols and to demons, there still seems to be a vague awareness in most cases of a distant high god who is somewhere "out there." Many religions also retain the idea of a coming Redeemer, who will somehow restore all things to their primeval perfection, though now these beliefs often seem more descriptive of the coming Antichrist than of the true Christ. In any case, certain features of God's true program for man's salvation seem to have been preserved in vague and distorted form through mythologies, through the names and stories associated with stars and constellations, and through certain religious practices and traditions.

It is possible that an individual who desires to find the true God and is willing to believe His revelation may somehow be guided by the Holy Spirit (whose ministry is to "[convince] the world of sin, and of righteousness, and of judgment" (John 16:8) into an awareness of his own sin before his Creator-God? Since Jesus Christ is the "propitiation . . . for the sins of the whole world" (1 John 2:2), the price has been paid for his redemption. And since Christ also is "the true Light, which lighteth every man that cometh into the world" (John 1:9), there may yet remain in his understanding a dim hope that God must have somewhere provided a Savior.

He might also realize that he is unable to save himself and must rely completely on God to save him in whatever way He may have provided. If there does exist such a person, and if he does arrive at such an attitude of faith and trust in God as Savior, this is the same attitude with which one who does know about Christ must approach Him for salvation, and is, of course, produced only as the Holy Spirit "draws" him. Can we say that, like Abraham, "his faith is counted for righteousness" (Rom. 4:5)? "He that cometh to God must believe that he is, and that he is a rewarder of them that diligently seek him" (Heb. 11:6).

We do not know whether individuals like this have existed nor how God would undertake to get the gospel message to them if they did. God is both just and loving, and we must leave such matters in His hands. The Scriptures seem altogether silent concerning such hypothetical situations.

On the other hand, it is crystal clear that the heathen (whether highly cultured or grossly savage) are lost in the darkness of sin and rebellion, and that Christians have been commanded by Christ to carry the testimony of salvation "unto the uttermost part of the earth" (Acts 1:8).

The Question of Predestination

A common and very vexing problem associated with the character of God is the matter of predestination. Since God is both omniscient and omnipotent according to Scripture, then He knows everything that will ever happen, including, in particular, the names of those men who will reject Him and, therefore, be eternally lost. He knew this, in fact, before they were ever born — indeed, before the first man was ever created.

The problem is, since He knew that, why didn't He refrain from creating them? It seems as though, when we look at it this way, they were predestined to hell before they were born. Would it not have been more merciful and loving for God not to bring them into existence at all?

Furthermore, is it not somewhat artificial for Christians to be commanded to "preach the gospel to every creature" when God already knows who will refuse it and for whom, therefore, such preaching is bound to be futile? And, is it divine hypocrisy when God's Word says He is "not willing that any should perish, but that all should come to repentance" (2 Pet. 3:9)? If He does not want them to perish, why did He create them? If He really did not know for sure which way they would turn before He created them, then He is not omniscient. In any case, God's character is involved in a contradiction, and many think that, therefore, He doesn't really exist.

Doing away with God does not eliminate this particular problem, however. The theological enigma of predestination merely becomes the philosophical problem of determinism. According to the latter, everything that ever happens has been previously "determined," not by God, but by the inexorable laws of nature. Freedom of mind or will is only an illusion; man's brain, like all the rest of his physiology, is only a complex aggregation of chemicals, and what takes place there can in principle be altogether explained in terms of electric circuitry and chemical reactions. That being so, he is not responsible for his actions. The criminal steals because his genetic background and the interplay of forces in his environment make it inevitable. The good man deserves no praise, the wicked no blame, since both alike were predestined to be what they are by the inescapable sequence of cause and effect in all natural relationships.

And yet, though all such reasonings seem rigidly logical, everyone of rational mind is certainly aware that he *does* make decisions of his own. He may not have completely free will, of course — he cannot will himself to fly to Jupiter, for example — but he *is* free to decide whether to go to the other side of the room or not. In fact, most of our activities all day long involve a continuous decision-making sequence, from deciding to get up in the morning to deciding to go to bed at night.

All such things are such an integral part of our experience that, if they are not *real*, then it would seem nothing is real. In fact, our very brains, whether they are merely complicated electric circuitry or actually house an eternal intelligence, are the instruments by which we both make decisions and also devise reasonings which deny that we make decisions! How can we be sure that our thought processes are any more reliable when we are thinking "deterministically" than when we seem to be making free choices? Rigid logic seems to lead to determinism or predestination, whereas subjective experience assures us that we do really choose and decide things ourselves, at least within limits.

So which is right? It is obviously far easier to raise such questions than to answer them. It certainly does not help to use this problem as an argument against God, since the same problem is still there and, in fact, is even more inscrutable if there is no God. Besides, we have already seen that the evidence for God's existence is overwhelmingly strong, and it is not dissipated merely by raising questions about His fairness.

The solution to the paradox must, therefore, be in God himself. Since He is the source of all meaning and all reality, He is sovereign not only over all that ever happens but also over all that we ever experience. That is, the very consciousness we have of choosing and deciding is a reality, and not a delusion, because God made us and gave us this consciousness. At the same time, the choices and decisions we make are also part of God's creation and find their ultimate cause in Him.

The reason we cannot really comprehend this paradox is because we are finite and God is infinite. It is like the two sides of the door, both of them real, but which can be viewed only one side at a time. Or perhaps it is like the two parallel lines, which meet only at infinity. It is the scientist's "principle of complementarity," in the theological realm.

We cannot resolve the paradox by logical reasoning. Historically, the Calvinist-Arminian controversy seems always to founder on the rock of logic, even when carried out in terms of himself texts. The one will emphasize the ultimacy of divine sovereignty and those Scriptures that teach God's omnipotence; the other will stress the reality of man's experience of choosing and those Scriptures that emphasize human responsibility. Some Calvinists may contend that the "whosoever" Scriptures apply only to the "world" of the elect. Arminians will interpret the "predestination" Scriptures in terms of God's foreknowledge of man's free choice.

It would seem that the only way of resolving the conflict is to recognize that both doctrines — that is, God's sovereignty in election and man's responsibility in decision — are true. It is significant that there is a wealth of Scripture supporting each doctrine and, yet, somehow the writers of Scripture never seem aware that this poses a difficulty. The predestination-free will question as such is never discussed in the Bible, even though both concepts are frequently presented. Both doctrines are taught forcefully in Scripture, yet with no intimation that they contradict each other!

For example, the Lord Jesus in Matthew 11:27 said: "All things are delivered unto me of my Father: and no man knoweth the Son, but the Father; neither knoweth any man the Father, save the Son, and he to whomsoever the Son will reveal him." This statement stresses the divine prerogative in choosing man. Yet in the next breath, the Lord said: "Come unto me, all ye that labour and are heavy laden, and I will give you rest" (Matt. 11:28). Here apparently is a blanket invitation to one and all.

The classic predestination passage in Romans 9 says: "Therefore hath he mercy on whom he will have mercy, and whom he will he hardeneth" (Rom. 9:18). But Paul in the next chapter says: "For there is no difference between the Jew and the Greek: for the same Lord over all is rich unto all that call upon him. For whosoever shall call upon the name of the Lord shall be saved" (Rom. 10:12-13).

In Ephesians 1:11 the apostle Paul says we have been "predestinated according to the purpose of him who worketh all things after the counsel of his own will." He says that God "hath chosen us in him before the foundation of the world" (Eph. 1:4). Yet the same Apostle said that God "now commandeth all men every where to repent" (Acts 17:30). Also, he said: "Knowing therefore the terror of the Lord, we persuade men. . . . Now then we are ambassadors for Christ, as though God did beseech you by us: we pray you in Christ's stead, by ye reconciled to God" (2 Cor. 5:11, 20).

A striking example of the juxtaposition of God's sovereignty and man's responsibility in the very same act is found in Peter's pentecostal sermon: "Him, being delivered by the determinate counsel and foreknowledge of God, ye have taken, and by wicked hands have crucified and slain" (Acts 2:23). And also, "The kings of the earth stood up, and the rulers were gathered together against the Lord, and against his Christ. . . . For to do whatsoever thy hand and thy counsel determined before to be done" (Acts 4:26, 28).

What man's logical reasoning would seem to view as contradictory, Scripture thus treats as perfectly normal and natural. This, therefore, is the way we should approach this otherwise difficult and even inflammatory subject.

That is, both doctrines are completely true and highly practical in terms of spiritual understanding and motivation. The paradoxical aspects we can safely leave to God and eternity for solution.

From our human point of view, in this present world, we are fully capable of making decisions and responsible for the consequences of those decisions. "The soul that sinneth, it shall die . . . the righteousness of the righteous shall be upon him, and the wickedness of the wicked shall be upon him" (Ezek. 18:20). Paul says that God "will render to every man according to his deeds. . . . For there is no respect of persons with God" (Rom. 2:6, 11).

Furthermore, the death of Christ, as the infinite Word made flesh, was adequate price for the redemption of all men, even though it is ultimately effective only for the elect. He "tasted death for every man" (Heb. 2:9), even for those who "deny the Lord that bought them" (2 Pet. 2:1).

The Scriptures are clear in their teaching that anyone who so wills may come to Christ to receive salvation. "Whosoever will, let him take the water of life freely" (Rev. 22:17).

Each person also is completely responsible for the effects of his or her decision to accept or reject Christ. "He that believeth on the Son hath everlasting life: and he that believeth not the Son shall not see life; but the wrath of God abideth on him" (John 3:36).

Christian believers, furthermore, are commanded to "be witnesses . . . unto the uttermost part of the earth" (Acts 1:8). This witness is not to be a cold, matter-of-fact, take-it-or-leave-it, presentation of the gospel, but rather a prayerful, sincere, urgent message, calling men and women to Christ. The Apostle Paul, from whom we have received the strongest teachings on election, preached in such a way. "For though I be free from all men, yet have I made myself servant unto all, that I might gain the more. . . . I am made all things to all men, that I might by all means save some" (1 Cor. 9:19, 22). He reminded the Ephesians: "that by the space of three years I ceased not to warn every one night and day with tears" (Acts 20:31).

From our point of view, therefore, we must see reality in terms of human freedom and responsibility. God has made us thus and, therefore, this universal human experience is quite real and not an illusion. God is omnipotent and, therefore, can grant such responsibility to all of us without in any way compromising His own sovereignty.

Nevertheless, from God's point of view, all things are foreknown and therefore foreordained. "Known unto God are all his works from the beginning of the world" (Acts 15:18).

With respect in particular to the greatest of all decisions — that of accepting or rejecting Christ — we are told that Satan "deceiveth the whole world" (Rev. 12:9) and that he has "blinded the minds of them which believe not" (2 Cor. 4:4). Therefore, although an unsaved man may think and feel that he has complete freedom to choose as he wishes, he is really instead "the (bond) servant of sin" (John 8:34) and is not free at all. Before a man is free to choose, God himself must open his understanding. "If the Son therefore shall make you free, ye shall be free indeed" (John 8:36).

Therefore, not only must the price be paid for our salvation and then the gospel offer made to us, but we must also be prepared in heart and mind by God before we are free to respond to Him in faith. "No man can come to me, except the Father which hath sent me draw him" (John 6:44). Who are those, then, who choose to come to Him? "All that the Father giveth me shall come to me" (John 6:37). What happens to those who come to Him? "Those that thou gavest me I have kept, and none of them is lost" (John 17:12). But suppose that some whom the Father "draws" to Christ choose not to come? "Moreover, whom he did predestinate, them he also called; and whom he called, them he also justified" (Rom. 8:30). "Ye have not chosen me, but I have chosen you" (John 15:16).

The believer, after he has freely accepted Christ by his own decision, invariably can recall many events and circumstances which led him inexorably to that decision. From his viewpoint as an unsaved man, he voluntarily and freely trusted Christ as Savior and was born again. But from the divine viewpoint, he was one whom God had saved and called "with an holy calling . . . according to his own purpose and grace, which was given us in Christ Jesus before the world began" (2 Tim. 1:9). His name had been "written in the book of life . . . from the foundation of the world" (Rev. 13:8). He had been "chosen in him before the foundation of the world" and, therefore, one day he chose that day the One whom he would serve (Josh. 24:15).

The doctrine of election may, if misunderstood, lead both to lethargy in missions and evangelism and to indifference in Christian living. If the elect are bound to be saved anyway, some may think, why bother to evangelize them? Furthermore, what difference does it make how I live, since my election was settled long ago?

Those who reason in such a way as this, however, are likely not saved at all. That is why Peter, writing to professing

Christians, said: "Give diligence to make your calling and election sure" (2 Pet. 1:10). Indeed, we were chosen before the world began to be "holy and without blame before him in love" (Eph. 1:4). Our predestination is that we might be "conformed to the image of his Son" (Rom. 8:29).

Rather than a warrant for laxity, therefore, the truth of election is the strongest inducement to zeal and holiness. It stimulates patience in suffering, courage in danger, and thanksgiving in all things. "We know that all things work together for good to them that love God, to them that are called according to his purpose" (Rom. 8:28).

Furthermore, it is a strong incentive to true evangelism. We should "preach the gospel to every creature" (Mark 16:15) not only because Christ commanded it, but also because we know that God will always use it for His own purposes (Isa. 55:11) and that it will "prosper in the thing whereto I sent it." It is the highest of all privileges to be "ambassadors for Christ, beseeching men in Christ's stead to be reconciled to God" (2 Cor. 5:20). As the Lord told Paul when he entered Corinth: "Be not afraid, but speak, and hold not thy peace. . . . For I have much people in this city" (Acts 18:9, 10). This was while those people were yet unsaved. Similarly, when Paul preached in Antioch, the Scriptures say that "as many as were ordained to eternal life believed" (Acts 13:48).

Thus both doctrines, God's sovereign election and man's moral responsibility, are true. Though we cannot in our finite minds understand and reconcile them logically, we can sense their truth in our hearts, confident in faith that what God does, by definition, is right in the context of eternity.

The Severity of God

Even if we make all allowances for the general existence of suffering in the world as a consequence of the curse, and also for our own limited understanding of God's ways and purposes, there still appear to be a number of specific instances in the Bible where God seems unnecessarily cruel. Some of these incidents have, in fact, been offered by critics as proof that the God of Scripture could not really be God.

How, for example, could a loving God have ordered Moses to utterly destroy the inhabitants of Canaan (Deut. 7:2), even the children (Josh. 6:21)? And what about the time when Elisha cursed the children who were jeering him, and God sent two bears out of the wood who "tare forty and two children of them" (2 Kings 2:23-24)? On one occasion God commanded Saul to "go and smite Amalek, and utterly destroy all that they have, and spare them not; but slay both man and woman, infant and suckling, ox and sheep, camel and ass" (1 Sam. 15:3). Then, when Saul instead spared Agag, the Amalekite king, as well as all the best of the animals, God judged Saul severely, even deciding to take away his kingdom and instructing Samuel himself to execute Agag. "And Samuel hewed Agag to pieces before the Lord in Gilgal" (1 Sam. 15:33).

Similar instances of apparent divine cruelty are found throughout the Old Testament. All the inhabitants of Sodom and Gomorrah are destroyed by fire and brimstone out of heaven, and the entire world of the antediluvians is destroyed by water. Can such incidents possibly be reconciled with the idea of a God of love and mercy?

Though we may not understand fully all of God's dealings, we do well not to put ourselves in the position of judging God. "Shall not the judge of all the earth do right?" (Gen. 18:25). By definition, what God does is right, whether we understand it or not. God has established moral standards by which man is to be judged; man has no jurisdiction over God! He that established the Law is not thereby himself bound by the Law.

Nevertheless, we can partially understand the reasons for such incidents if we try to comprehend the situation as best we can from the divine viewpoint, especially considering the alternatives had God not acted in the manner described.

Take the destruction of the Canaanites, for example. The alternative in this case was the corruption of God's people and interference and long delay in the accomplishment of God's purposes. God had warned the Israelites this would be the case if they failed to carry out His command of complete destruction, and this is, of course, what happened.

When God first called Abram to go into the land of Canaan, He promised the land to him and his descendants. At that time, however, the promise was delayed in its implementation because, as God said, "the iniquity of the Amorites is not yet full" (Gen. 15:16). In Joshua's time, however, the Amorites and all the other inhabitants of Canaan had become so depraved that there was no remedy except destruction. The awful morass of idolatry and its accompanying moral wickedness, into which these nations had descended, is documented not only in Scripture but also by archaeology.

When the Israelites failed to carry out God's orders to execute all the Canaanites, the result was that they also were soon infected by the moral degradation of those they spared. The Psalmist later wrote about this tragedy in these words: "They did not destroy the nations, concerning whom the Lord commanded them: But were mingled among the heathen, and learned their works. And they served their idols: which were a snare unto them. Yea, they sacrificed their sons and their daughters unto devils, And shed innocent blood, even the blood of their sons and of their daughters, when they sacrificed unto the idols of Canaan: and the land was polluted with blood. Thus were they defiled with their own works, and went a whoring with their own inventions. Therefore was the wrath of the Lord kindled against his people, insomuch that he abhorred his own inheritance" (Ps. 106:34-40).

Who can calculate how many of the Israelites lost their eternal souls, as well as their lives, because of this contamination? Cruel though God's command may have seemed, it was more merciful for more people that the Canaanites be destroyed before their pollution could spread further.

It could even be considered an act of grace that the children of the Canaanites were to be slain by the Israelites. To be allowed to grow up in the environment in which they were born was certain moral and spiritual death. On the other hand, children who die before reaching an accountable age probably are taken into heaven immediately by virtue of the sacrificial death of Christ.

Another reason for God's apparent severity was to teach His chosen people both the exceeding wickedness of sin and also His own faithfulness and power. Although we may not understand fully all of the factors involved, it is at least clear enough that God had adequate reasons for commanding the destruction of the Canaanites.

If this was true in the case of the Canaanites, it was surely true also in the case of the antediluvians and of the people of Sodom and Gomorrah. In the case of the people of Noah's day (perhaps also the later Canaanites), there may well also have been still another factor, that of universal demonic control of the people to be destroyed.

Another frequently cited example of God's cruelty is that of Elisha's bears as found in 2 Kings 2:23-25. The great prophet of God, Elijah, had completed his ministry and Elisha had witnessed his miraculous translation into the skies on a chariot of fire (2 Kings 2:11-12).

The people of the Jericho-Bethel region, where the miracle had taken place, soon learned that the mantle of Elijah had fallen on Elisha and that, indeed, many of his miraculous gifts had already been manifested by Elisha. But then, according to the Scripture:

> As he was going up by the way, there came forth little children out of the city [i.e., Bethel], and mocked him, and said unto him, Go up, thou bald head; go up, thou bald head. And he turned back, and looked on them, and cursed them in the name of the Lord. And there came forth two she bears out of the wood, and tare forty and two children of them.

At first, this may seem an extraordinarily severe punishment for mere childish rudeness. However, there is more to this story than that.

Bethel was the place where Jeroboam had set up his golden calf, which had then become the center of idolatry in Israel. The revival that came later under Elijah, however, had evidently affected Bethel, because it was near there that Elijah's "school of the prophets" had been established (2 Kings 2:3). Consequently, by this time, the tension between the Baal-worshippers and the "sons of the prophets" had undoubtedly become bitter.

At this point, the translation of Elijah took place. "Elijah went up by a whirlwind into heaven" (2 Kings 2:11). Such an event as this, even associated with such a mighty man of God as Elijah, must have seemed completely unbelievable to the rationalistic Baalites. The reported "catching-up" no doubt had quickly become the butt of crude jokes in the households and on the streets of Bethel. Then, as Elisha approached Bethel, coming up from Jericho, a large crowd of the town delinquents came out and began to menace him.

The word "children" in the King James version (Hebrew *naar*) could actually have been rendered "young men," and it is frequently so translated. For example, King Rehoboam was said to have been "young" (same word, 2 Chron. 13:7), at a time when he was already 41 years old (2 Chron. 12:13).

These were not necessarily harmless little children that greeted Elisha, therefore, as he approached Bethel. At any rate, the youthful hoodlums, perhaps spurred on by their elders, were mocking not only Elisha, but also Elisha's God. "Go up, thou bald head," they jeered. "You claim old Elijah went straight up into heaven; let's see you prove it — you go up, too!" The shaving of the head was a religious practice of the pagan priests and was strictly forbidden to the people of God (Deut. 14:1), especially to the priests (Lev. 21:5). Thus, to call Elisha a "bald head" was in effect to call him a priest of Baal, and was an intentional blasphemous insult.

Furthermore, there is little doubt that they intended to harm him, perhaps to kill him. He, therefore, "cursed them in the name of Jehovah."

It is surprising that two bears could "tear" (literally "cleave open") 42 of these jeering youths. They must either have been animals of exceptional agility and ferocity or else (more likely) there was such a large mob of hoodlums that they stumbled over themselves and became hysterically confused and helpless as they scrambled to escape.

In evaluating this situation, we should again consider the alternative. Even if Elisha had not been killed by the mob, his authority and position as God's prophet and Elijah's successor in Israel would have been destroyed had God not acted decisively in the situation.

As far as Samuel's seemingly sadistic treatment of Agag is concerned, when he "hewed Agag in pieces" (1 Sam. 15:33), this action must be viewed in the light of Agag's previous career of bloodshed and wickedness. As king, he was primarily responsible for leading his people, the Amalekites, in their idolatrous degradation and implacable hatred of Israel. Samuel said, "As thy sword hath made women childless, so shall thy mother be childless among women." The Amalekites, though cousins of Israel (Amalek was a grandson of Esau), had fought them steadily for over 400 years, and were finally judged by God to be unfit to continue their national existence. Agag especially was not to be spared but rather to be made a particular example, for both Israel and their neighbors, of the unspeakable folly of continued rebellion against God and His purposes.

Other instances could be discussed, but those already mentioned are the most frequently quoted examples of God's supposed cruelty. The explanation given will perhaps not satisfy those who have a low concept of God's sovereign authority and awful holiness. We must not simply apologize for God's actions, as though we were somehow embarrassed by His severity. We must rather issue an urgent warning to those who presume to judge Him. "Is there unrighteousness with God? God forbid. . . . Nay but, O man, who art thou that repliest against God? Shall the thing formed say to him that formed it, Why hast thou made me thus?" (Rom. 9:14, 20).

The days of God's severity are not ended. "The Lord Jesus shall be revealed from heaven with his mighty angels, In flaming fire taking vengeance on them that know not God, and that obey not the gospel of our Lord Jesus Christ: who shall be punished with everlasting destruction from the presence of the Lord, and from the glory of his power" (2 Thess. 1:7-9).

Selected books for further study:

Benton, John. 1995. *How Can a God of Love Send People to Hell?* Phillipsburg, NJ: Presbyterian and Reformed.

Clark, Gordon H. 1995. *Predestination.* Phillipsburg, NJ: Presbyterian and Reformed Publ. Co.

Clarkson, E. Margaret. 1972. *Grace Grows Best in Winter.* Grand Rapids, MI: Zondervan Publishing House.

Craigie, Peter C. *The Problem of War in the Old Testament.* Grand Rapids, MI: William B. Eerdmans Co. 125 p.

Gerstner, John H. 1982. *Primer on Free Will.* Phillipsburg, NJ: Presbyterian and Reformed Publ. Co.

Guillebaud, H.E. 1941. *Some Moral Difficulties of the Bible.* London: Inter-Varsity Fellowship. 208 p.

Hart-Davies, D.E. 1946. *The Severity of God.* London: Pickering and Inglis. 124 p.

Lewis, C.S. 1972. *God in the Dock.* Grand Rapids, MI: William B. Eerdmans Co. 346 p.

Lewis, C.S. 1978. *The Problem of Pain.* New York, NY: Macmillan Company.

McDavid, Edmund R. 1991. *Let God Speak.* Birmingham, AL: Hope Publishing Co. 382 p.

Morris, Henry M. 1988. *The Remarkable Record of Job.* Grand Rapids, MI: Baker Book House. 146 p.

Myres, Edward P. 1978. *The Problem of Evil and Suffering.* Montgomery, AL: Apologetics Press. 132 p.

Peterson, Robert A. 1995. *Hell on Trial.* Phillipsburg, NJ: Presbyterian and Reformed Publ. Co.

Wilder-Smith, A.E. 1960. *Why Does God Allow It?* San Diego, CA: Creation-Life. 119 p.

Chapter XI

The Plan of God

God's Purpose in Creation

In the preceding chapters we have briefly examined the overwhelming evidence that God exists, and that He is an eternal, omnipotent, purposeful, personal God. He is a God of both absolute holiness and perfect love. Although He has allowed evil to enter and exist for a time, He is somehow overruling its effects for good and will eventually purge it completely.

In this chapter, we wish to consider the logical structure of God's overall purpose in creating man and then His plan for redeeming man and, ultimately, the entire cosmos. The gospel of Christ does seem to be profoundly offensive to the natural man and we need, therefore, to be able to give sound reasons for our hope of salvation through Him. Man longs to find a meaning and purpose for his existence and for that of the world around him, and the Christian believes that this is found only in Jesus Christ and the salvation which He provides.

In order to evaluate the validity of this conviction, the first question to consider is God's purpose in creation. God, being infinite, had existed from eternity without the creation and, therefore, was certainly under no necessity or compulsion when He created it. Being both omnipotent and omniscient, He did not create it by accident or by caprice. Therefore, His creation was by His own free choice, and must have been with a high and glorious purpose.

In trying to understand this purpose, it is obvious that men and women are at the heart of it. As far as the earth is concerned, we are highest of all creatures, the only ones capable in any degree of conceiving the idea of God and His purpose. And, of course, it is from the nature of phenomena on this earth that causal reasoning demonstrates the necessity of a purposeful God.

The question of possible extra-terrestrial life is, therefore, not to the point. We must be at the heart of God's purpose for at least that part of the universe comprehensible to us.

For that matter, there is no evidence that life comparable to human life exists anywhere else in the universe. Certainly no other planet in the solar system could support human life; our space exploration program has left no doubt whatsoever about this. Similarly, none of the stars are inhabitable, and there is no evidence (apart from statistical reasoning based on evolutionary considerations, which are quite invalid) that any of them have planets. Even if other such planets do exist, the probability that any of them could support human life is infinitesimally small. The complex of thermal, hydraulic, chemical, meteorologic, and other factors and processes which enable us to live on this earth is so unique and intricate that it would have to be duplicated almost exactly on some other planet before that planet could support life. We know by astronomic observations that no two galaxies are exactly alike and no two stars are exactly alike. It is even more unlikely that any two planets are alike, since planetary structures (and especially that of the earth) are tremendously more complex than those of stars, which are mostly nothing but burning hydrogen.

One can speculate about other forms of intelligent life than man, of course (and speculation is the appropriate word for it!). There is no evidence for "little green men" except in science fiction. The same chemical elements that exist on earth comprise the matter of the whole universe, and it is difficult to conceive of the chemical basis for biological processes being significantly different from that which prevails in biological processes on earth (e.g., DNA, carbon dioxide, water, air, etc.).

The possibility of spiritual beings (as distinct from physico-chemical life systems) is, of course, an entirely different matter. The criteria and techniques of physical science, so far as we know, are incapable of observing and measuring spirits. The only way we could know of the existence or purpose of either angels or demons, good spirits or evil spirits, would be either by divine revelation or by direct communication from the spirits themselves. As a matter of fact, the Bible indicates that even the angels were created as servants of man (Heb. 1:14; Ps. 34:7; 1 Cor. 6:3; etc.) as well as of God (Ps. 103:20; etc.).

It is reasonable to conclude that, within the limits of our ability to comprehend such things, God's purpose in creation directly involves human beings at its center. Our nature — intelligent, volitional, emotional, moral, spiritual — is somehow related to God's own nature. We have been created in the image of God.

This being so, it is obvious that communication and fellowship between people and God not only are possible but must actually have been a part of God's very purpose in creation. This fellowship is sadly missing in the present economy, but was undoubtedly present in the original plan.

This, in fact, is what the Scriptures teach as well. The primeval fellowship between man and God was broken when man first sinned and "Adam and his wife hid themselves from the presence of the Lord God" (Gen. 3:8).

But someday the lost fellowship will be restored. The best way to understand God's *original* purpose in creation is to study the final *consummation* of that purpose when all things have been reconciled. This present world is a temporary interruption in God's eternal plan. Eventually all His original perfect creation will be restored and His purposes fully accomplished.

In the "ages to come," God will "shew the exceeding riches of his grace in his kindness to us through Christ Jesus" (Eph. 2:7). We will then "ever be with the Lord" (1 Thess. 4:17). In the new heaven and new earth, after the first heaven and earth have passed away, it is promised that "the tabernacle of God is with men, and he will dwell with them, and they shall be his people, and God himself shall be with them, and be their God" (Rev. 21:3).

Thus, there will be perfect fellowship between man and God forever and, since this is the ultimate consummation toward which time is moving, there can be no doubt that this was God's primeval purpose when time began. He created men for fellowship with himself.

Since God is a God of love, such fellowship surely requires mutual love between man and God. God loves us because of His own nature of love and because He created us in His own image. We should have responded to that love in gratitude for our creation and for all God's gracious provisions for all our needs and desires. "We love Him because He first loved us" (1 John 4:19).

It is obvious, however, that now this fellowship is broken and God seems far away. Nevertheless, it is wonderful to know with confidence that God has a real purpose in bringing each person into the world. Whenever a child is conceived in the womb, at that instant does God create and implant an eternal spirit in that body. "Thou hast beset me behind and before, and laid thine hand upon me . . . for thou hast covered me in my mother's womb . . . in thy book all my members were written . . . when as yet there was none of them" (Ps. 139:5, 13, 16). For each of us, God has a wonderful purpose, and, in fact, "The Lord hath made all things for himself" (Prov. 16:4).

Separation from God

Although it is logically necessary to believe that we were created for the purpose of personal fellowship with God himself, it is true that no person in his natural state experiences any such fellowship. Not only are we alienated from God, but in greater or lesser degree we are alienated from our fellowmen. As a matter of fact, we are even struggling against the very environment which was created to be our home and dominion.

The only possible explanation for this state of affairs is that some factor alien to God's purposes has intruded His economy to generate this widespread alienation. This factor can be defined and identified as *sin*. In its essence, sin must be understood as anything contrary to God's will and purpose. Since we could only be aware of these in so far as God had revealed them to us, sin could more practically be defined as any action or attitude contrary to God's Word.

Not only did Adam and Eve sin, but so has every other man and woman. "There is not a just man upon earth, that doeth good, and sinneth not" (Eccles. 7:20). "For all have sinned, and come short of the glory of God" (Rom. 3:23).

Everyone is now a sinner both by heredity and practice. "Wherefore, as by one man sin entered into the world, and death by sin; and so death passed upon all men, for that all have sinned" (Rom. 5:12). Though not all have been direct recipients of God's audible commands, as was Adam, or have direct access to His written Word, as do most Americans and Europeans today, they have nevertheless received sufficient light in conscience (Rom. 2:15), in nature (Rom. 1:18-20) and through the preserved remnants of primeval revelation in their own traditions, so that they are "without excuse."

The question, of course, arises as to why God has allowed sin to enter the world, knowing that it must result in separating us from God and thus defeating His purpose in creation. The answer is, first, that real fellowship must be mutual and, therefore, we must each be free to reject it if we so choose. Second, since God is omnipotent, it is impossible for His purpose to be thwarted permanently, and, therefore, this separation must be only temporary and will somehow be sublimated into a higher order of benefit than had it never occurred at all.

Man, in his present state, is out of fellowship with God and is, therefore, living in an unnatural condition, not as God created and intended us to be. Not only man, but even his dominion, "the whole creation groaneth and travaileth in pain together until now" (Rom. 8:22).

As the first step toward reclaiming man from the chaos into which Adam's foolish choice had led him, God had to introduce the "curse" into the very elements of man's realm. "Cursed is the ground for thy sake," He said (Gen. 3:17).

God's purpose would not have been served by immediate annihilation of man, nor by an irrevocable and permanent banishment from His presence. But neither could man be allowed to settle contentedly into a state of eternal self-sufficiency, away from God's will. The curse of slow decay and ultimate death was the only solution, "lest he . . . live for ever" (Gen. 3:22) in his fallen state, and also lest he never look for a Savior to meet his need.

Salvation from Sin

The condition of every person since Adam is that he is lost and needs a Savior. This is the testimony not only of Scripture but also of true reason and experience. The question is — "How should man be just with God?" (Job 9:2). As David said: "In thy sight shall no man living be justified" (Ps. 143:2). "How then can man be justified with God? or how can he be clean that is born of a woman?" (Job 25:4).

The answer of atheism, materialism, monism, and such philosophies is that *no one* is saved. This answer, however, is utterly inconsistent with the doctrine of a God of omnipotent purpose and love, and we have seen overwhelming evidence that such a God indeed exists.

The answer of universalism is that *all* men eventually will be saved. But this simplistic solution ignores the holiness of God, as well as His decision to create man as a free moral being, capable of rejecting God's fellowship if he so chose. Shall a man who hates God be forced to "love" Him forever? Should a man who deliberately chooses to be separated from God be compelled to remain in His presence?

Another suggested answer is "conditional immortality." Those who desire to be saved and will accept God's offer of salvation will indeed be saved; others will eventually be annihilated. This is the belief of the Jehovah's Witnesses, Seventh-Day Adventists and others.

Such a solution perhaps has a sentimental appeal, but it has no basis in fact. There is surely no scientific reason for distinguishing between eternal spirits and terminated spirits. The inference of the law of conservation of energy would be that man's soul and spirit do not cease to exist when man's body dies. The atoms of the body do not cease to exist, and it seems unlikely that the higher components of man's being cease to exist just because the lesser components have gone through a change of state.

But, in any case, there is clearly no basis for saying that one category of souls is annihilated while another continues to exist in a dormant state until awakened at the resurrection. This type of information would have to come solely from revelation, and the Scriptures, of course, teach that both saved and unsaved exist forever (note Rev. 14:11; Dan. 12:2; Luke 16:23-26; etc.).

Furthermore, annihilationism would be inconsistent with God's justice. It is both reasonable and biblical that, in terms of future punishment, God "will render to every man according to his deeds" (Rom. 2:6), not the same punishment of annihilation to all unsaved alike.

Then there are all the various systems of "works-salvation," according to which salvation from sin and its effects may be earned by a certain set of good works and religious observances. The particular package of requirements varies from one religion or cult to another, but all are basically similar. The common street-corner variety typically supposes that if all of a man's good deeds outnumber his bad deeds, he will be saved. God is viewed as a cosmic bookkeeper or scale-tender, juggling ledgers or balances.

Such a view of God as this is an attempt to "bring Christ down from above" (Rom. 10:6), changing "the glory of the uncorruptible God into an image made like to corruptible man" (Rom. 1:23). Each such standard is entirely a man-made standard, capable of attainment by human efforts, and, therefore incapable of meeting the standard of God's perfection which true fellowship with Him entails.

Furthermore, any such system is insufferably arbitrary in its discrimination between the saved and the lost. Who is competent to decide that 1,000 good deeds, rather than 999 or 1,001, are just sufficient to pass the test? And with so many complex and intangible factors entering into every human action and decision, who is qualified to decide whether any certain deed is "good" or "bad" in the first place? God, no doubt, is capable of judging such things, but how can *we* be expected to make the fine distinctions involved in moral choices of borderline character?

Even assuming that one's good works clearly outweigh his faults and failures, can we assume that God, therefore, forgets the latter? Even one sin is sufficient to sever our fellowship with God, for this "comes short of the glory of God." Even this one sin, unresolved and unforgiven, would constitute an eternal barrier to that perfect fellowship for which we were created.

As far as the Bible is concerned, there is no doubt whatever that sin — any sin — results in condemnation, and that no amount of good works suffices to earn salvation. "Cursed is every one that continueth not in all things which are written in the book of the law to do them" (Gal. 3:10). "Now we know that what things soever the law saith, it saith to them who are under the law: that every mouth may be stopped, and all the world may become guilty before God. Therefore by the deeds of the law there shall no flesh be justified in his sight: for by the law is the knowledge of sin" (Rom. 3:19-20).

Both reason and Scripture, therefore, agree in concluding that all men are lost and that no man can possibly save himself or earn his own salvation.

Substitution and Redemption

We have seen, therefore, that God's holiness and justice preclude any type of reconciliation initiated and earned by man. On the other hand, God's omnipotent purpose and love require that salvation be provided by some means.

The only resolution of this impasse is that God himself must both initiate and consummate our salvation. There is no other way.

In so doing, there are several criteria that must be satisfied if the reconciliation thus offered is to be effective.

1. It must satisfy the requirements of divine justice, with the penalty of death and separation from God completely paid.
2. It must demonstrate God's love to man in such a way that man will freely reciprocate in love to God, in gratitude for the gracious provision of restoration to His fellowship.
3. It must be communicated and effected on the human level, in such a way that man can comprehend and appropriate it.
4. It must nevertheless be accomplished solely by God, in order to draw man's love and worship back to God alone, and not to some other creature.
5. It must provide assurance to man of complete forgiveness of the past and power to live in fellowship with God henceforth, with a purified conscience and confident hope.
6. It must be universal in scope, capable of saving all who wish to be saved, yet not compelling men against their wills.
7. Though the penalty of death must be paid, it must culminate in life and in the complete elimination of God's curse.

When these criteria, each of which must be satisfied if the desired reconciliation between man and God is to be accomplished, are carefully studied, it is evident that one and only one way exists by which it could ever be achieved. God himself must also become man, die in substitution for man's sin, and then rise from the grave in victory over sin, and death. This is the price for redeeming men and women from eternal separation from the love and fellowship of his Creator.

The seven criteria enumerated above are all satisfied by this means, and by this means alone. Thus:

1. As perfect man, living in fellowship with the Father, without sin, the incarnate Son is the only man not under condemnation for His own sins; as infinite God, He is capable of becoming the substitute for all men, suffering the righteous judgment of God on the sins of the whole world.

2. The sacrificial love of God in Christ, freely giving His own life in suffering and death in place of the guilty sinner, provides the maximum possible demonstration of God's love toward us, and, therefore, the greatest possible divine magnet to draw our love and gratitude to himself.

3. By himself becoming a man, He is able to demonstrate perfectly to us the holiness and love of God on a level comprehensible to us, providing the perfect example of a human life in fellowship with its Creator.

4. Since He is nevertheless God as well as man, the love so awakened in the heart of a redeemed sinner will be drawn to God, rather than to some other man or angel.

5. Since the penalty for sin has been completely endured and the redemption price paid in full, our guilty consciences can rightly be purged and our hearts filled instead with God's love, abhorring the sin which had heretofore separated us from God.

6. Since as both omnipotent God and perfect man, He has "tasted death for every man," He is able to offer free forgiveness and salvation to all who will receive it, while still not forcing acceptance of it by any whose hardened hearts even yet prefer to remain independent of God.

7. Though as man He died for the sins of the whole world, as God He conquered death and will ultimate rescind its curse.

Thus it becomes clear that it is only by substitutionary atonement that God can both be just, and the "justifier of him which believeth in Jesus" (Rom. 3:26). "God was in Christ, reconciling the world unto himself" (2 Cor. 5:19). The great plan of God is the one and only necessary and sufficient means by which we can be saved and made ready for eternal fellowship with God, knowing and loving Him now not only as Creator and provider, but also as Redeemer and Lord.

The Ages to Come

The plan of God, to create and then reconcile men and women to eternal fellowship with himself, will finally be consummated when Christ returns to earth. All rebellion, by men and angels, will be completely purged. In the measure of the eternal ages to come, "this present evil [age]" (Gal. 1:4), which now seems so long, will soon be recognized as only a very ephemeral period and will quickly be forgotten (Isa. 65:17) in the joyful activities of the endless future.

Not that this age is unimportant. On the contrary, this is the age of necessary preparation for eternity. Not only is this when God is creating and re-creating (2 Cor. 5:17) men and women to inhabit eternity, but this is also the age of probation and training, when the redeemed are in process of developing their gifts and characters for their future responsibilities in the millennial kingdom (Rev. 20:4-6) and ultimately in the new heaven and the new earth (Rev. 22:3).

The doctrine of eternal rewards might well be called the doctrine of eternal responsibilities. Salvation is entirely the gift of God's grace, to be received by faith alone. In God's glorious plans for the future, however, there will be an infinite complex of activities and responsibilities. "His servants shall serve him" in a wide variety of assignments and duties. The particular sphere of service and responsibilities will be determined by the way in which each person has discharged his or her responsibilities in the present age, as well as by the measure of love and fellowship with the Lord Jesus Christ, and the degree of conformity to His will and character achieved during this preparation. "He that is faithful in that which is least is faithful also in much" (Luke 16:10). To the faithful servant in this life, the Lord will say: "Well done, thou good and faithful servant: thou hast been faithful over a few things, I will make thee ruler over many things: enter thou into the joy of thy Lord" (Matt. 25:21). In the last message of the Bible, Christ says: "Behold, I come quickly; and my reward is with me, to give every man according as his work shall be" (Rev. 22:12).

But now, what about the unsaved? Their destiny is clearly revealed to be eternal suffering in hell, in the lake of fire (see Mark 9:43-48; Matt. 25:41, 46; Luke 16:23-26; 2 Thess. 1:7-9; Jude 7; Rev. 14:11; 20:12-15; 21:8; etc.).

This is one of the hardest doctrines for skeptics, and sometimes even for believers, to accept, in all the Word of God. The idea of God consigning men to eternal torment is profoundly offensive to sinful men and is one of the chief excuses offered for rejecting Christ and His Word. This problem — not science — was the main reason why Charles Darwin rejected God.

And yet, not only is the doctrine of eternal hell clearly taught in the Scriptures — especially by Christ himself— but it is really the only reasonable answer to the problem of unrepented sin. Every man is consciously a sinner, though in varying degrees of culpability, rejecting the Word of God and, therefore, under God's just condemnation. His measure of guilt becomes far greater, of course, if he hears and rejects God's offer of forgiveness and reconciliation through Jesus Christ. "And that servant, which knew his lord's will, and prepared not himself, neither did according to his will, shall be beaten with many stripes. But he that knew not, and did commit things worthy of stripes, shall be beaten with few stripes" (Luke 12:47-48).

It is obvious, in any case, that not all the unsaved are equally guilty. Each individual is a sinner, and, therefore, is lost without Christ, but some are relatively moral while others are unspeakably vile; similarly some have abundant knowledge of the way of salvation, others very little. It is necessary, therefore, in accordance with the principle of divine equity, that such differences be reflected in future degrees of suffering. The idea that this life is the end of everything, that those who die in their sins cease to exist, is thus clearly false. Annihilationism is nothing less than a slander against the holiness and justice of God. There is, therefore, a life after death, for the lost as well as for the saved.

Man's spirit, in fact, was created as an eternal spirit, in God's image, and its existence is independent of whether or not the body that houses it continues to exist. Even the body is not annihilated when it dies, but merely experiences a change in structure and state.

If a man has chosen to reject God and to remain independent of His purpose (and the fact he dies as an unsaved sinner demonstrates this), his character and attitude toward God have become fixed and thus he will continue forever with the same attitude. It would be unreasonable, even cruel, for God to force His fellowship upon him when he does not want it. In this sense, hell is more merciful as an eternal destiny for an unsaved man than heaven would be. One who does not love God, especially one who has ignored the love of God as manifest when Christ died for him, would be infinitely miserable if compelled to live in His presence forever.

Thus the nature of our creation and the requirements of God's justice dictate the continued existence of the unsaved man or woman after death. They will be less miserable separated from God than they would be in the company of God and the redeemed (Isa. 26:10).

That is what hell is — eternal existence separated from God. The fires of hell are quite literal fires, possibly a burning star in some infinitely remote corner of the universe, but physical fires, of course, do not destroy non-material spirits. Even if, in the second resurrection, the bodies of the unsaved are actual physical bodies, and thus quickly destroyed when cast into the lake of fire, their spirits would continue to exist. The fires of bitterness and hatred and all the myriad sins which they carried to the grave will continue to burn in their souls forever, and the lake of fire is an appropriate physical environment in which to give free rein for all these to develop without restraint from God, just as they wished it to be in their physical lives when on earth.

There will be degrees of suffering in these everlasting fires, in accordance with degrees of sin committed and degrees of light rejected. If nothing else, the fires of regret will be the more intense in proportion to the opportunities lost when in the flesh. Similarly, the intensity of hatred received from fellow inhabitants of the vast flaming sea will be in proportion to the degree of responsibility for their presence in such a place. (Think, for example, of the popularity of Adolph Hitler in the presence of the souls of multitudes of murdered Jews, or of apostate preachers or teachers in the midst of flocks of their parishioners or students whom they led astray.)

The natural mind recoils from such thoughts as these, and most men, therefore, either ridicule or ignore the biblical doctrine of hell. However, we have arrived at the conclusions above by straightforward logical reasoning, based on cause-and-effect relationships and on what we know about both physical and spiritual realities. Furthermore, all of this is either explicitly revealed or clearly implied in Scripture. Men and women ignore or reject these truths to their own eternal loss.

Selected books for further study:

Kevan, Ernest F. 1973. *Salvation*. Phillipsburg, NJ: Presbyterian and Reformed Publ. Co.

MacArthur, John F. Jr. 1988. *The Gospel According to Jesus*. Panorama City, CA: Word of Grace. 253 p.

MacArthur, John F. Jr. 1991. *Our Sufficiency in Christ*. Dallas, TX: Word Publishing Co. 282 p.

Machen, J. Gresham. 1937. *Christianity and Liberalism*. Grand Rapids, MI: Wm. B. Eerdmans Co. 189 p.

Morey, Robert. 1984. *Death and the Afterlife*. Minneapolis, MN: Bethany House.

Morris, Henry M. 1986. *Days of Praise*. Green Forest, AR: Master Books. 388 p.

Pieters, Albertus. 1949. *Divine Lord and Savior*. New York, NY: Revell Publishing House. 187 p.

Strombeck, J.F. 1936. *So Great Salvation*. Grand Rapids, MI: Kregel Publications. 160 p.

Wood, Nathan R. 1950. *The Open Secret of Christianity*. New York, NY: Revell Publishing House. 143 p.

Chapter XII

The Inspiration of the Bible

Introduction

Up to this point, we have been considering the evidences of Christianity without recourse to the authority of the Bible as the divinely inspired Word of God. Strictly on the basis of the Bible as a historical document, supported by evidence in nature and reason, there is a tremendous body of solid evidence demonstrating the divine origin and authority of Christianity. Although a number of difficulties can be lodged against this conclusion, there do exist reasonable solutions to all of these, and the difficulties do not in any case undermine the solid foundation of evidence supporting the Christian faith.

Thus, whether or not the Scriptures are divinely inspired, the basic facts of Christianity can be considered as firmly established — the triunity of the godhead, the omnipotence of Christ, the substitutionary atonement, the bodily resurrection of Jesus, the continuity of the Christian witness, and the fact of salvation by grace through faith in the risen Lord.

Now, however, we wish also to investigate the nature of the Bible itself. Is it only a collection of historical and religious writings of men, or is it, as Christians (and Jews, as far as the Old Testament is concerned) have always believed, actually the very Word of God? If it is the latter, does its inspiration apply only to its religious content, as many believe, or does it extend to the very words themselves, and to the descriptions of historical events and natural phenomena as well as to its spiritual insights?

The Unique Structure of the Bible

The word "Bible," of course, means *book*; and it is certainly one book; in fact, *the* Book. Yet it is also a library of many books, written by about 40 different authors over a period of at least 1,500 years. Its unity and continuity are so apparent, however, in spite of its diverse and protracted origin, that it is natural and easy to think of it also as having just *one* author! That one Author is none other than God himself.

Altogether, in its presently accepted form, it contains 66 separate books, not including the so-called Apocryphal books. The Old Testament has 39 books, the New Testament, 27. The authors of 55 books are well-identified by history and tradition. Authors of the other 11 books (Judges, Ruth, 1 and 2 Samuel, 1 and 2 Kings, 1 and 2 Chronicles, Esther, Job, and Hebrews) are not definitely known. Some books (e.g., Genesis, Judges, 1 and 2 Kings, 1 and 2 Chronicles) each cover such long periods of history that they probably represent collections of ancient records brought together and edited by some individual (e.g., Moses in the case of Genesis) near the close of the historical periods described in the books. If this is so, then the actual number of writers contributing to the Bible may be considerably greater than 40. Psalms and Proverbs both also have several authors, not all of whom are known.

All of the authors (possibly excepting Luke) were Jews and wrote in the context of the Jewish religion. Yet the words they wrote have the most universal appeal and interest, to people of all nations, of any words ever written. Two of the writers (David and Solomon) were kings; two were priests (Jeremiah and Ezekiel); Luke was a physician; two were fishermen (Peter and John); two were shepherds (Moses and Amos); Paul was a Pharisee and theologian; Daniel was a statesman; Matthew, a tax collector; Joshua, a soldier; Ezra, a scribe; and Nehemiah, a butler. Backgrounds and occupations of the other writers are largely unknown. Some were highly educated, but most were of ordinary circumstances. Their ministries were scattered over 1,500 years of turbulent history. But with all this diversity, the books they wrote form necessary components of a perfect whole, developing the same theme, never contradictory, speaking effectively to both mind and heart in every word.

Furthermore, the Bible contains history (fascinating and

always accurate), science (centuries in advance of its time), poetry (the greatest ever written), drama, medicine, ethics, practical wisdom — as well as the most wonderful story ever told, the great plan of salvation and the promise of eternal life.

There is no other book comparable to the Bible. In addition to the foregoing, the Bible is unique among all the writings of the ancient world, in all the following:

1. It is the only book of antiquity that gives an account of special creation of all things out of nothing; other ancient cosmogonies are never analyzed in relation to modern science, but many books have been written with such themes as "Genesis and Modern Science."
2. The Bible is the only book that gives a continuous historical record from the first man to the present era.
3. The Bible is the only book of ancient history whose history reveals a purpose in history.
4. The Bible is by far the purest religious literature, with the highest moral standards of all the religious books of the ancient world.
5. The Bible is the only religious book containing detailed prophecies of events to come.
6. The Bible is the only book from antiquity which has the power to convict men of sin and also is the only book which leads them to the only One who can free them from sin.

The Claims of the Writers

In view of the unique character of the Bible, as well as its incomparable influence for 3,500 years, the testimony of its own writers is of paramount significance. They claimed, of course, that they were writing the words of God. If they really *were* divinely inspired, then the unique nature and power of the Bible is easily understood. If not, however — if they were either lying or deluded — then we are confronted with the greatest mystery and paradox in all history. One way or the other, the Bible is utterly inexplicable in terms of criteria applicable to other writings.

In the Old Testament, the writers with great frequency claim to be recording the very words of the Lord, making such statements as "And the Lord spake unto Moses, saying . . ." or "The word of the Lord came unto me, saying . . ." or similar claims, over and over again.

Those who have attempted to count these and other similar statements in the Old Testament have come up with the following approximate figures:

Pentateuch: 680 claims of inspiration
Prophetical Books: 1,370 claims of inspiration
Historical Books: 418 claims of inspiration
Poetical Books: 195 claims of inspiration
Entire Old Testament: 2,600 claims of inspiration

Moses said, for example: "Ye shall not add unto the word which I command you, neither shall ye diminish ought from it, that ye may keep the commandments of the Lord your God which I command you" (Deut. 4:2). Almost half of the Book of Exodus consists of direct quotations from the words of God, and almost 90 percent of the Book of Leviticus.

David said: "The Spirit of the Lord spake by me, and his word was in my tongue" (2 Sam. 23:2). He wrote most of the Psalms, and these contain more evident marks of inspiration than perhaps any of the other writings of the Old Testament.

In the prophetical books, of course, again a very large part of each book is taken up with what the prophet claimed were the direct words of God. Jeremiah said: "His word was in mine heart as a burning fire shut up in my bones" (Jer. 20:9). Ezekiel said, "The word of the Lord came expressly unto Ezekiel the priest . . . and the hand of the Lord was upon him" (Ezek. 1:3).

It is true, of course, that such claims are not found in every one of the books of the Old Testament. One book, Esther, has no mention of the name of the Lord at all. Nevertheless, even these books were all accepted by the people of Israel as equal in divine inspiration and authority with those that did make such claims.

The historical books did not consist of the directly quoted words of God, of course, as did so many of the writings of Moses and the prophets. There was, therefore, no reason for the writers (often unknown) to make such statements. But divine inspiration need not mean divine dictation — it more often means divine preparation and direction of the writer and his natural abilities. Inspiration refers to the result, not the method. The result was such, in both accuracy and spiritual power, that both the teachers of Israel and Christian scholars have for thousands of years been convinced they all were part of the divinely inspired Holy Scriptures.

The same is true, as far as Christians are concerned, of the New Testament books. These only occasionally incorporate verbatim quotations from God. Nevertheless, the New Testament writings were both claimed by the Apostles and recognized by the early church as authoritative revelations from God. The Apostle Paul said, for example, "I certify you, brethren, that the gospel which was preached of me is not after man. For I neither received it of man, neither was I taught it, but by the revelation of Jesus Christ" (Gal. 1:11-12). Note also Paul's statements in 1 Corinthians 2:13; 1 Thessalonians 2:13; Ephesians 3:4-5; Romans 16:25-26; etc. In 1 Corinthians 14:37, Paul says, "If any man think himself to be a prophet, or spiritual, let him acknowledge that the things I write unto you are the commandments of the Lord."

Although the Apostles do not very often make explicit claims of inspiration for themselves, it is clear that they did regard their teachings as given by divine authority. This is evident, first, because they regarded the Old Testament Scriptures as fully and perfectly inspired, and second, because they insisted their own teachings completed — in some cases even superseded — the Old Testament.

The climactic claim to this effect is found at the very end of the Bible. The apostle John closes his writings (indeed, closes the very canon of Scripture) with these words: "For I testify unto every man that heareth the words of the prophecy of this book, If any man shall add unto these things, God shall add unto him the plagues that are written in this book; And if any man shall take away from the words of the book of this prophecy, God shall take away his part out of the book of life, and out of the holy city, and from the things which are written in this book" (Rev. 22:18-19).

The Old Testament in the New

There is no question that the Jews at the time of Christ revered the Old Testament Scriptures as fully inspired and authoritative, the very words of God. This faith was shared by the Apostles and writers of the New Testament.

There are, in fact, over 320 quotations from the Old

Testament recorded in the New, as well as over 1,000 clear and definite references to it. Always, the context indicates the belief of the speaker or writer that he was referring to the authoritative Word of God whenever he made such a quotation or reference.

The part of the Old Testament most severely criticized and ridiculed by modern liberals is that contained in the first eleven chapters of Genesis, dealing with events from the creation through the tower of Babel. Yet there are more than 100 quotations or clear allusions to this section in the New Testament. Every one of the New Testament writers (Matthew, Mark, Luke, John, Paul, James, Peter, Jude, and the writer of Hebrews) refers at least once in his writings to something recorded in these eleven chapters, and there is no doubt they regarded the events as true. Each one of these eleven chapters is alluded to in the New Testament.

Paul said, "For whatsoever things were written aforetime were written for our learning, that we through patience and comfort of the Scriptures might have hope" (Rom. 15:4). Peter said, "The prophecy came not in old time by the will of man: but holy men of God spake as they were moved by the Holy Ghost" (2 Pet. 1:21; note also 1 Pet. 1:10-12).

Not only did the Apostles accept the inspiration of the Old Testament, they also acknowledged the divine inspiration of other parts of the New Testament. Paul in 1 Timothy 5:18 quotes from both Testaments as Scripture. "For the Scripture saith, Thou shalt not muzzle the ox that treadeth out the corn. And, the labourer is worthy of his reward." In the first instance, he is quoting Deuteronomy 25:4 and in the second Luke 10:7. Similarly, Peter compares the writings of Paul and "all his epistles" to "the other Scriptures" (2 Pet. 3:15-16).

Peter unites the "words spoken before by the holy prophets" with "the commandment of us the apostles of the Lord and Savior" (2 Pet. 3:2). The writer of Hebrews begins by saying: "God, who at sundry times and in divers manners spake in time past unto the fathers by the prophets, Hath in these last days spoken unto us by his Son" (Heb. 1:1-2). Jude evidently quoted from 2 Peter 3:3 when he said: "Beloved, remember ye the words which were spoken before of the apostles of our Lord Jesus Christ; How that they told you there should be mockers in the last time, who should walk after their own ungodly lusts" (Jude 17, 18).

A very interesting indication of the reverence with which the Apostles regarded the Holy Scriptures is the way in which they introduce specific quotations from them. There seems to be a completely indiscriminate use of such phrases as: (1) "It says" (meaning "the Scripture says"); (2) "He says" (meaning "the human writer says"); (3) "God says" (meaning "the true divine author says"); and others. Evidently all are essentially synonymous.

For example, Romans 9:17 reads: "For the Scripture saith unto Pharaoh, Even for this same purpose have I raised thee up." Actually, he is quoting the words of God himself, in Exodus 9:16. Similarly, Moses is quoted in Romans 10:5 as saying, "That the man which doeth those things shall live by them," when actually it was God who said this, as recorded by Moses, in Leviticus 18:5.

Conversely, Hebrews 3:7 says: "The Holy Ghost saith, To day if ye will hear his voice, Harden not your hearts." But this is a quotation from Psalm 95:7-8, written by David. A more precise formula, yet amounting to the same thing, is found in such Scriptures as Acts 1:16, where Peter said, "The Holy Ghost by the mouth of David spake before concerning Judas," and then refers to David's writing in Psalm 41:9 apparently, even though he does not quote it directly. Similar examples could be added to all these types of references at great length.

There is, therefore, no doubt whatever that the writers of the New Testament all regarded the Old Testament Scriptures as absolutely divine in origin and authoritative in application.

The Testimony of Jesus Christ

Of most critical importance is the attitude of the Lord Jesus Christ to the Scriptures. We have previously seen that the evidence for His innate deity is quite compelling, entirely independent of the question whether or not the Scriptures are inspired. This being the case, as the only begotten Son of God, there can be no doubt that He knew and understood the true nature of the Holy Scriptures.

And it was He who said, "The Scripture cannot be broken" (John 10:35). He said, in His parable of the rich man, "They have Moses and the prophets: let them hear them" (Luke 16:29). He also said, "If ye believe not [Moses'] writings, how shall ye believe my words?" (John 5:47).

The Lord Jesus seemed almost to make a personal point of approving and citing passages of Scripture which might seem particularly difficult for the natural man to accept. He quoted from both Genesis 1:27 and Genesis 2:24 (the supposedly contradictory accounts of man's creation) in the same passage (Matt. 19:4-5). He referred to Noah and the great Flood (Luke 17:26-27; Matt. 24:37-39), the destruction of Sodom and Gomorrah (Luke 17:28-29), the miracles of the record of Jonah and the whale (Matt. 12:40). He accepted the prophecies of Daniel as true prophecies (Matt. 24:15) and regarded Isaiah as the true author of both parts of the book bearing his name (Matt. 4:16; 12:17). He accepted the writings of Moses and referred to some of the miracles recorded there — for example, the burning bush (Luke 20:37), the manna in the wilderness (John 6:32), and the lifting up of the brazen serpent (John 3:14).

After His resurrection, He rebuked the disciples in these words, "O fools, and slow of heart to believe all that the prophets have spoken: Ought not Christ to have suffered these things, and to enter into His glory? And beginning at Moses and all the prophets, He expounded unto them in all the Scriptures the things concerning himself" (Luke 24:25-27). Further, He said, "All things must be fulfilled, which were written in the law of Moses, and in the prophets, and in the psalms, concerning me" (Luke 24:44).

Just as the Apostles, there is no doubt that the Lord Jesus Christ regarded the Old Testament Scriptures as completely and perfectly consisting of the Word of God. This being so, it is mandatory that all true Christians, professing as they do to follow Him as their Master and Lord, do the same. It is sad to see professing Christians, concerned more about intellectual approbation by their contemporaries than approval by their Savior, questioning and compromising various parts of the book of Genesis and other sections of the Old Testament.

As far as the New Testament is concerned, Christ, of course, ascended back to heaven before any of it had been written. However, He did promise that it *would* be written: "The Comforter, which is the Holy Ghost, whom the Father will send in my name, He shall teach you all things, and bring all things to your remembrance, whatsoever I have said unto you" (John 14:26). "When he, the Spirit of truth, is come, he will guide you into all truth; for He shall not speak of himself: but whatsoever he shall hear, that shall He speak: and He will shew you things to come" (John 16:13). "After that the Holy Ghost is come upon you . . . ye shall be witnesses unto me . . . unto the uttermost part of the earth" (Acts 1:8). All these promises were fulfilled, as the Holy Spirit came, guided the Apostles in remembering the things of Christ, led them into new truth and showed them things to come. Through the resultant writings, the Apostles have literally been witnesses to the ends of the earth.

When the last book was written, the Lord Jesus came once again to put His seal upon it. "Write," he said, "the things which thou hast seen . . . blessed is he that keepeth the sayings of the prophecy of this book" (Rev. 1:19; 22:7).

We have assurance, therefore, from the Lord Jesus Christ himself that the Bible, from the first chapter of Genesis to the last chapter of Revelation, is the written Word of God.

Some modern liberals, and even some neo-evangelicals, have tried to explain Jesus' uncompromising acceptance of the Old Testament on the assumption that he was either ignorant of the true facts or else that he was merely accommodating himself to the ignorance of others. Both views, of course, grossly dishonor and caricature His nature — one charging Him with error, the other with deception. If we cannot rely upon His teachings on this basic subject, how can we trust Him in anything else?

Christ himself claimed that everything he taught was divine truth. "For I have not spoken of myself; but the Father which sent me, he gave me a commandment, what I should say, and what I should speak" (John 12:49). Furthermore, instead of "accommodating" himself to the beliefs of His contemporaries, He continually condemned them, nowhere more severely than when they had rejected or corrupted Scripture. "Why do ye also transgress the commandment of God by your tradition?" (Matt. 15:3). "For had ye believed Moses, ye would have believed me: for he wrote of me" (John 5:46).

It is certain, therefore, that the Lord Jesus Christ accepted the Old Testament Scriptures as the inerrant Word of God in every detail. A Christian who truly acknowledges Him as Savior and Lord can, therefore, do no less.

The Nature of Inspiration

There are several inadequate theories of inspiration which need to be recognized. At the risk of oversimplifying, these can probably be classified under four categories: (1) the naturalistic theory; (2) the partial theory; (3) the dynamic theory; (4) the encounter theory.

The *naturalistic theory* holds that the Bible is inspired only in the sense that great writers and artists are inspired when they produce great works of literature or music or art. This theory in effect denies inspiration in any special biblical sense altogether and need not be discussed.

The *partial theory* suggests that parts of the Bible may be inspired and other parts not inspired. Matters of fact, such as events of history and phenomena of science, are not recorded under inspiration, whereas spiritual and devotional passages may be supernaturally inspired. But the problem with this approach is how to tell the difference. Evidently there are no objective criteria established for this discrimination, and the reader himself (or his pastor, perhaps) must decide for himself. Furthermore, how can writers who make mistakes when they report simple matters of fact be trusted when they report visions and revelations?

The *dynamic theory* holds that the "thoughts" are inspired, but not the words. According to this idea, the important thing is that great spiritual truths be conveyed to the reader, and it really doesn't matter what words are used, or even whether the events described in the passage really happened or not. This theory may sound spiritual and pious, but actually, it is vacuous. It is possible to convey precise thoughts only by using precise words. If the words are unimportant, then the thoughts, which come through the words, are entirely subjective. One can read into a passage whatever he wishes.

The *encounter theory* holds that the Bible is a vehicle of revelation but is not itself a divine revelation. It becomes "inspired" when, and only when, it "inspires" the reader. It may be the medium through which a person "encounters" God in an act of faith, but otherwise it is a human document, subject to human error throughout. Inspiration, by this theory, becomes entirely subjective. One must have as much faith in his own encounter experience as the orthodox Christian does in Scripture. A passage which thus may be "inspired," so far as one reader is concerned, may be utterly uninspired to others, and there is no objective canon of evaluation at all.

It is obvious that each of the above theories makes man the sole judge of Scripture. Each person decides for himself whether a particular passage or message from the Bible is inspired. God's Word does not speak to him, except as he chooses. He is the final authority in deciding whether God is speaking and whether He is speaking truth. To all intents and purposes, therefore, any reader who approaches the Bible with one of the above theories is himself usurping the place of God. He is trying to judge the Word of God, whereas rightfully (and actually, whether he realizes it or not) the Word of God is judging him. "The Word is God is quick, and powerful, and sharper than any two-edged sword . . . and is a discerner of the thoughts and intents of the heart" (Heb. 4:12).

The only proper and true view of the inspiration of the Bible is that it is completely and literally inspired, altogether free of error and conveying exactly what God wished to say to man. This is the doctrine of *plenary verbal inspiration*. That there are problems connected with this high view of inspiration goes without saying, but this is nevertheless the teaching of Scripture itself. The problems can be resolved; but even if we cannot now answer all of them, we still must insist this is the only doctrine of inspiration which has any real substance. It is only by plenary (i.e., "full") inspiration and by verbal (i.e., "word-by-word") inspiration that God can objectively and accurately convey His Word to man. Any lesser theory leaves man to his own devices and, in effect, he becomes his own god.

In any case, this is clearly the teaching of the Scriptures themselves. Moses ended his great ministry with this admonition: "Set your hearts unto all the words which I testify among you this day, which ye shall command your children to observe to do, all the words of this law" (Deut. 32:46). Note also Proverbs 30:5-6: "Every word of God is pure: He is a shield unto them that put their trust in him. Add thou not unto his words, lest he reprove thee, and thou be found a liar."

The Apostles believed in verbal inspiration, as their frequent use of Scripture in specific support of specific teachings shows. Paul called the Scriptures the very "oracles of God" (Rom. 3:2; Heb. 5:12). A striking example of his use of Scripture is in Galatians 3:16: "Now to Abraham and his seed were the promises made. He saith not, And to seeds, as of many; but as of one, And to thy seed, which is Christ." Not only does Paul thus base his argument on a single word of Scripture, but on the fact that that word is singular, rather than plural! Similarly, he argues from a single phrase, "Yet once more," in Hebrews 12:27.

Most importantly of all, the Lord Jesus Christ himself believed in plenary verbal inspiration. He rebuked Satan by quoting: "Man shall not live by bread alone, but by every word that proceedeth out of the mouth of God" (Matt. 4:4; Luke 4:4; Deut. 8:3).

He rebuked the Sadducees on one occasion by calling their attention to a verse of Scripture in which the verb was "am" instead of "was." "Have you not read that which was spoken unto you by God, saying, I am the God of Abraham, and the God of Isaac, and the God of Jacob? God is not the God of the dead, but of the living" (Matt. 22:31-32). Shortly after, He silenced the Pharisees also with a single word, asking them "If David then called him Lord, how is he his son?" (Matt. 22:45). Again, he argued from a single words "gods" in John 10:35: "He called them gods, unto whom the Word of God came, and the Scripture cannot be broken."

No wonder, therefore, that the Lord Jesus said: "For verily I say unto you, Till heaven and earth pass, one jot or one tittle shall in no wise pass from the law, till all be fulfilled" (Matt. 5:18).

Some of the problems and objections that have been raised against belief in verbal inspiration will be discussed in the next chapter. Whether or not we can answer all the problems, however, it must be emphasized that this is the teaching of Moses, of Paul, of Christ, and of the Scriptures in general. If it is not true, we are left in effect with no reliable word of God at all. Man is a poor substitute for God, and he is acting directly against his own eternal interests when he tries to destroy the Holy Scriptures.

This chapter can best be concluded with the classic Pauline doctrine of Scripture: "All [thus refuting the partial theory of inspiration] *Scripture* [that is, the "writings," the actual words written, thus refuting the dynamic theory of inspiration] is *God-breathed* [thus refuting the naturalistic theory] and is profitable [and if all the writings are profitable, the encounter theory is refuted] for doctrine, for reproof, for correction, for instruction in righteousness: That the man of God may be perfect [that is, "complete" so that nothing more is needed than the Scriptures!], throughly furnished unto all good works" (2 Tim. 3:16-17).

Selected books for further study:
Carson, D.A. and John D. Woodbridge. 1995. *Hermeneutics, Authority and Canon*. Grand Rapids, MI: Baker Book House. 480 p.

Carson, D.A. and John D. Woodbridge. 1992. *Scripture and Truth*. Grand Rapids, MI: Baker Book House.

Gaussen, L. n.d. *The Plenary Inspiration of the Holy Scriptures*. Chicago, IL: Moody Press. 365 p.

Henry, Carl F.H., ed. 1958. *Revelation and the Bible*. Grand Rapids, MI: Baker Book House. 413 p.

Lightner, Robert P. 1970. *The Savior and the Scriptures*. Phillipsburg, NJ: Presbyterian and Reformed.

Lindsell, Harold. 1976. *The Battle for the Bible*. Grand Rapids, MI: Zondervan Publishing House. 218 p.

McDowell, Josh. 1972. *Evidence that Demands a Verdict*. San Bernardino, CA: Here's Life Publishers. 387 p.

Warfield, Benjamin B. 1948. *The Inspiration and Authority of the Bible*. Phillipsburg, NJ: Presbyterian and Reformed. 442 p.

Chapter XIII

Problems in Verbal Inspiration

The Nature of Inspiration

Many writers who reject the doctrine of the plenary verbal inspiration of the Bible criticize the doctrine as one of mechanical dictation, with the writer merely recording words which he heard in a dream or trance. They rightly point out that each writer has his own style of writing and that these styles are distinguishable one from the other, a fact which supposedly is inexplicable in terms of divine inspiration.

This type of argumentation, however, is very superficial, though frequently used. Even if the Bible were actually given by immediate dictation by God, there is no reason why God could not have couched His dictation in the style of the receiving scribe. God has no peculiar "style" of heavenly discourse. He is himself the Word, the Alpha and Omega, and *all* language and communication have their origin in himself. Since He must use the earthly language of the human writer as the medium of revelation, why could not He also use the earthly vocabulary and style of the writer?

Many of the biblical writings, in fact, were given in just this way, by direct dictation from God. This phenomenon is especially frequent in the writings of Moses and the prophets, as noted in the preceding chapter.

On the other hand, the historical and poetical books, as well as the epistles of the New Testament, were very definitely written by the human authors, using their own observations and researches and expressing their own feelings and convictions. This fact does not in any way negate the principle of verbal inspiration. They were so prepared by God, in terms of their family training, their own studies, their experiences in childhood and youth, and the circumstances under which they were living when they wrote, that finally the words they composed — entirely of their own volition and understanding — were those words desired by the Holy Spirit. They were words fully guarded against error and perfectly fitting and complete, even though the men who recorded them may have been much lacking in perfection themselves and even though their normal manner and content of writing may have been much less than perfect under natural circumstances.

The doctrine of inspiration, therefore, applies to the *result*, not the *method*. Inspiration may be defined as a supernatural influence, sometimes explicit and direct, sometimes indirect and unrecognized, exerted by the Holy Spirit on the human writers, such that their writings possess full divine trustworthiness. Inspiration is not the same as revelation, by which God directly reveals himself in some way to men. The Bible *is* revelation, of course, but God also has revealed himself in nature and in various other ways. Similarly, much of the Bible, though given by inspiration, did *not* come by revelation, but by simple recording of facts of observation.

A passage given by inspiration of God (that is, "God-breathed"), regardless of the method of inspiration, is thus necessarily true and appropriate and meaningful. Though phrased in the language and experience of the prophet, the words nevertheless are ultimately the words of God. In a sense, the Holy Spirit does, after all, "dictate" the words, though not in the same direct way as when God spoke directly from the glory cloud on Mount Sinai.

The Problem of Transmission

When the original "autographs" were written, therefore, they were perfect in content and free from error in every respect. These autographs have long since vanished and presumably have gone back to the dust. The preservation and circulation of the Scriptures, therefore, became the responsibility of Hebrew and Christian scholars specially trained and dedicated to the ministry of copying the ancient scrolls. Until the invention of printing, this had to be done by hand and was tedious and painstaking work, demanding a high degree of carefulness and consecration on the part of the scribe.

Nevertheless, the scribes *were* careful and dedicated to their task. They believed thoroughly that they were dealing with the very words of God. They were exceedingly careful in their work, and they developed various devices for checking and cross- checking their accuracy.

It is not our purpose here to study the science of textual criticism. This is the highly specialized science of comparing and sifting the ancient manuscripts of the Old and New Testaments that have come down to modern times with the purpose of ascertaining as closely as possible the text of the original autographs. It is sufficient to note that, in the opinion of most such scholars (including practically all *conservative* scholars), the text which we still have is practically identical with the originals. The text has certainly been established with far greater certainty than that of any other ancient writings.

In the New Testament, for example, authorities assure us that less than one word in a thousand is in any doubt at all. Although the many thousands of manuscripts do contain a great many variant readings, over 99 percent are nothing more than variations in spelling. Not more than a dozen verses in the New Testament could have their meaning affected by any of them and no doctrine would be affected. Some of the more ancient manuscripts (Sinaiticus, Vaticanus, etc.) do have a number of significant omissions (the first part of John 8, for example), but these may well represent defective manuscripts which have been preserved longer than others for the very reason that they were known to be unfit for use and set aside.

There is another factor to be considered, of course. The same God who prepared the original writers and protected them from error could as easily have prepared the copyists and safeguarded the Scriptures from later error. Jesus had said, "My words shall not pass away" (Matt. 24:35). There is good reason to believe He has fulfilled His promise.

Apparent Disclaimers of Inspiration

For our purposes, we can assume we have the Scriptures in the same form as that in which they originally were given. Obviously, this refers to the original Hebrew and Greek Scriptures, not directly to any specific translation into English or some other language, and we, therefore, do need to give attention to the accuracy of whatever translation we are using, particularly in dealing with problem passages. There are now numerous modern English translations available, but the beauty, power and accuracy of the familiar King James translation amply justify its continuing use today as our basic version and authority for faith and practice.

We have seen in the last chapter that the biblical writers believed and taught the doctrine of verbal inspiration. In particular, this is the doctrine of Scripture accepted and taught by Christ himself. Regardless of any problems or difficulties which it may entail, we must always remember that the Lord Jesus, as well as Peter, Paul, and the other Apostles, definitely taught this doctrine. Problems must always be considered, and solved if possible, in the light of this basic truth.

One of these problems is that, occasionally, a biblical writer seems specifically to deny the factor of divine inspiration in his writings, thus apparently contradicting his claims to inspiration on other occasions. The classic example of this phenomenon is found in 1 Corinthians 7, where Paul carefully distinguishes between his own instructions and those given by the Lord. At first glance, he seems to deny that some of his writings were inspired. However, closer examination of these statements proves exactly the reverse.

Paul, in writing to the Corinthians concerning marriage relations, says: "But I speak this by permission, and not of commandment" (1 Cor. 7:6). The meaning here is: "I speak this by way of permission." That is, this particular instruction to them was one of permission (by Paul to the church), not an order. He is certainly not disclaiming divine inspiration in so giving this permission.

In verse 10, he says: "And unto the married, I command, yet not I, but the Lord, Let not the wife depart from her husband." Then, in verse 12 he says: "But to the rest speak I, not the Lord: If any brother hath a wife that believeth not, and she be pleased to dwell with him, let him not put her away." In one case, he seems to claim divine authority, in the other to deny it.

Closer consideration, however, shows that he is rather putting his own teachings on the same level as those of the Lord Jesus. In verse 10, he merely refers to the fact that the Lord, for example, in Matthew 5:31-32, has already taught that marriage was to be permanent, with divorce permitted only for the cause of fornication. In verse 12, he then adds his own teaching, something not already specifically taught by the Lord, placing it on an equal plane with the Lord's previous teaching. Apparently the reason for this further clarification is that actually he is removing an Old Testament principle, when Jewish men were told to "separate yourselves . . . from strange wives" (Ezra 10:11). Rather than disclaiming divine authority, therefore, Paul actually is placing his own commands above those of the Old Testament Scriptures, something he would never dare to do had not God so directed.

In verse 25, he says: "Now concerning virgins I have no commandment of the Lord [that is, no specific Scripture, or specific revelation]: yet I give my judgment, as one that hath obtained mercy of the Lord to be faithful." This is Paul's counsel, as is the case in most of the practical-living parts of his epistles, but this does not mean that it is not *inspired* counsel. It is significant that he concludes this entire discussion on marital questions by saying: ". . . and I think also that I have the Spirit of God" (1 Cor. 7:40).

The Problem of Inexact Quotations

We have mentioned the frequent use which the New Testament writers make of the Old Testament, frequently quoting from it or making references to it as authority in the development of their own expositions. As seen already, there is no doubt that they regarded the very words of the Old Testament as divinely inspired and authoritative.

One problem, then, is why they occasionally seem almost careless in such quotations, quoting very loosely, or perhaps just paraphrasing the Scripture they are using. Does not the doctrine of verbal inspiration require word-for-word accuracy in such quotations?

The answer to this question is — no, it does not. Although the writers certainly accepted the verbal inspiration of these Scriptures, they were at liberty to make any legitimate application of them appropriate to their own teachings, so long as they did not contradict them.

As a matter of fact, they quite often draw spiritual lessons from them which, while not specifically spelled out in the original Old Testament passage, are nevertheless implicit therein, awaiting only the further light of New Testament revelation to bring it into view. An example is Hebrews 10:5: "Wherefore when he cometh into the world, he saith, Sacrifice and offering thou wouldest not, but a body hast thou prepared me." This is a quotation from Psalm 40:6: "Sacrifice and offering thou didst not desire; mine ears hast thou opened."

The explanation for this apparent mistake of quotation is that it was not a mistake at all but an expository interpretation and application. The opening-of-the-ears (or better, boring-of-the-ears) was an Israelite ceremony, described in Exodus 21:5-6, by which a servant dedicated his body to the will of his master forever. The passage in Hebrews tells similarly of the willing submission of the body of Christ to the will of the Father. "By the which will we are sanctified through the offering of the body of Jesus Christ once for all" (Heb. 10:10).

In precise argumentation, the writer could quite properly argue on the basis of the very words of Scripture, as we have seen. In exposition and application, on the other hand, it was appropriate to use only the deeper sense of a passage, so long as he did not contradict the literal meaning of the passage.

We make the same use of the Bible today. We use it both for precise study, in which we meticulously examine every word and its meaning, and for general devotional application in our lives. Each passage has a primary exegetical meaning, derived from its precise words, but it may also have almost innumerable secondary devotional and practical applications. And it is always legitimate to derive the latter from the former, provided only that we do not read some interpretation or application into it that is a contradiction or illegitimate extrapolation from its primary exegesis.

The New Testament writers, therefore, were quite justified in this sort of use of the Old Testament. Although they often used such generalized references and paraphrases, they were always careful never to use them in such a way as to constitute an improper extension or contradiction.

The important thing to remember, of course, is that *their* interpretations and applications of Old Testament Scriptures (unlike ours, which may be wrong) were given divine validity on the basis of the Holy Spirit's inspiration of their writings. Since in the ultimate sense, the Holy Spirit is the Author of both Testaments, He is free to quote himself, and to make application thereof, in any way He chooses.

Variant Reports

Another problem of verbal inspiration, somewhat similar to that of inexact quotations, is that of variant reports of the same event, or of the same discourse, by different writers. If two or more writers (e.g., the writers of 2 Kings and 2 Chronicles, or Matthew and Luke, etc.) happen to write about the same incident or to report the same sermon, and if both are verbally inspired by the Holy Spirit, then why don't they report them alike?

A classic example is the case of the Beatitudes, as reported by both Matthew and Luke (Matt. 5:1-12; Luke 6:20-23). Even a superficial glance at these indicates significant differences; for example, Matthew lists nine Beatitudes, Luke only four. Also, the wording is quite different. The same questions seem to apply to many other sections of the Sermon on the Mount, as reported in Matthew 5 through 7, and in Luke 6:20-49. There seem to be many discrepancies, both in order and content of this sermon, as recorded in these two Gospels.

This problem is easily resolved, however, by recognizing that Matthew and Luke are reporting two different sermons! The one in Matthew was preached only to His disciples, up on a mountain (Matt. 5:1). The one in Luke was preached down on the plain, to a multitude (Luke 6:17). The fact that there were certain similarities in the two sermons is explained by the fact there were certain truths He wanted both audiences to hear. It is quite common, of course, for a preacher or Bible teacher to bring similar messages to two or more different audiences, each time modified somewhat to fit the specific needs of each separate group.

Many of these so-called variant reports can thus be easily understood by postulating two different, though similar occurrences. There are some, however, which clearly refer to the same event. A case in point is the account of the temptation of Christ, as given in Matthew 4:1-11 and Luke 4:1-13. The main problem here is that the sequential order of the last two temptations is different in the two accounts.

In this case, unlike most such reports, none of the disciples were present. Consequently, the account of the temptation must either have been related to the disciples later by Jesus, or else given by direct revelation to Matthew and Luke. The former is more probable, being more consistent with the manner in which other historical sections of the Scriptures were assembled and written. In either case, neither alternative involves the recording of a chronological narrative, but rather the record of the Lord's victory over the same threefold temptation that caused the fall of Eve. Satan tempted both Eve and Christ with "the lust of the flesh, and the lust of the eyes, and the pride of life" (1 John 2:16), involving the whole being — body, soul, and spirit. The tree in the garden yielded fruit which supposedly was "good for food, pleasant to the eyes, and desirable to make one wise, as gods" (Gen. 3:5-6). In like manner, the temptation of Christ in the wilderness appealed to His need for food, His desire to rule the world, and His desire to be recognized as God. The temptation probably occurred throughout the 40 days (Luke 4:2), involving continuous repetition and urging in all three of its phases, so that the order is of little significance. In fact, all three aspects may well have been simultaneous and essentially continuous, carried out in the realm of the mind and spirit by Satan. Jesus then related the experience to His disciples later, and it would make no difference as to the order in which His listeners later wrote about it, so long as the threefold aspect was emphasized. Perhaps Matthew listed them in an order climaxing with the offer of all the world's kingdoms in harmony with his gospel's emphasis on Christ as King. Luke, on the other hand, emphasizing Christ as perfect man, chose to climax his account with the temptation to leap from the temple.

Many variant accounts, of course, merely reflect the different points of view and the different observations of the various witnesses. They supplement each other, so that a fuller picture is obtained of the entire event than is possible with only one account. The superficially different, but actually harmonious and complementary, accounts of the crucifixion and resurrection in the four gospels provide the best illustration of this.

There is still another factor which may be a partial explanation of some of the variant accounts of the discourses of Christ. These were originally spoken in an Aramaic dialect, and so had to be translated into Greek by the New Testament writers. Word-for-word translation from one language into another is impracticable, if not impossible, and no two interpreters would normally translate a given oral message in the same way. It is plausible, therefore, that when Mark and Luke, for example, translated and recorded the same saying of Christ, they might each render it differently, so long as neither distorts the meaning. Furthermore, both such renderings could well be verbally inspired by the Holy Spirit, each with just such distinct nuances as would be most appropriate for the particular gospel. Thus, Matthew continually uses the phrase "kingdom of heaven" and Mark uses "kingdom of God" (e.g., Matt. 13:31; Mark 4:30), even when it is almost certain they are both quoting the same statement. Evidently both expressions are legitimate translations of whatever Aramaic expression Jesus actually used, and each is more appropriate exactly as translated in the particular gospel.

There are many variant accounts such as these found in Scripture and, of course, each must be examined on its own merits. The above illustrations indicate, however, that an explanation of one kind or another, which is both reasonable and simple, can nearly always be found in full consistency with the doctrine of verbal inspiration. It must always be remembered that verbal inspiration applies to the result, rather than to the method. God has spoken "in divers manners" (Heb. 1:1), but always in truth.

Personal and Trivial Information

There are many sections in the Bible which seem to be of purely local and limited interest. Examples might include the various personal greetings in Paul's epistles, the details of the gifts from the various tribal princes in the book of Numbers, the lists of the temple signers in Chronicles, and other such information. Critics have often ridiculed the claim that such data were included in the Bible as part of the inspired Scriptures.

However, our ignorance of the intended purpose of some set of data does not mean that the Holy Spirit had no such purpose. In addition to the more obvious spiritual and ethical message of Scripture, there are also parts of it which have important historical, genealogical, chronological, geographic and other data, all of which may well have high significance relative to God's overall purpose for man and the earth.

If nothing else, the long lists of names, as well as the various personal references in the epistles, give us the assurance that God is personally, and eternally, interested in every single individual. The names of believers are recorded in heaven (Luke 10:20) and, perhaps as a token of this, the names of many of them and their services have been recorded in Scripture.

Any verse of Scripture, if studied closely enough, with prayer and meditation, will eventually yield real blessing and instruction, in one way or another. No one is unimportant, and no item of information is trivial and useless, either in God's great creation or in His even greater revelation. Whether we discern it or not, we can be absolutely certain that all Scripture is profitable.

Duplicate Passages

The four Gospels all are primarily biographies of Christ, and often describe the same events, frequently in very similar words. Nevertheless, each has a distinct emphasis and purpose, and is necessary in the complete picture. Each was written primarily with a particular set of readers in mind and, therefore, with a predominant theme corresponding. However, we now are inestimably enriched by having all four available, focusing on Christ, as it were, from all directions. We are able to see Him as king and as servant, as man and as God.

Critics have, as we have noted, objected when different accounts of the same event do not agree. However, these not only refute the idea of collusion between the writers, but also invariably upon close inspection turn out to be supplementary rather than contradictory.

Now, however, there are a few places in the Bible where different accounts *do* agree, and critics also object to this! For example, Psalm 14 and Psalm 53 are almost, though not quite, identical. Similarly, Jeremiah 52 is practically the same as 2 Kings 24:18–25:30. Second Kings 18–20 contains much that is identical with Isaiah 36–39. Micah 4:1-3 is a prophecy which is evidently identical with the prophecy in Isaiah 2:2-4. The question is why such duplicate passages are included, since they are practically identical and it would seem that one time each would suffice.

They are not *quite* identical. Each has certain differences from its apparent twin, and these differences will repay careful study. The similarities are too close to be coincidental, however. In each pair, one would have to conclude either that the same author had written both or else that the second author had merely copied from the first.

In the case of Psalms 14 and 53, both are ascribed to David. However, one was placed in Book 1 of the Psalms (Ps. 1-41), and the other in Book 2 (Ps. 42-72). Their importance is indicated by the fact that they are quoted by Paul in Rom. 3:10-12). The repetition of the psalm by the Spirit's direction may at least partially be explained by His ministry of "[convincing] the world of sin" (John 16:8), as this is perhaps the most graphic and convicting passage in the Bible in its emphatic declaration that the natural man, who despises God and His will, is a fool!

The passages in 2 Kings which are mostly duplicates of passages in Isaiah and Jeremiah were no doubt incorporated into Kings from the words already written by the prophets. Evidently Isaiah was the recognized prophet and record-keeper in Hezekiah's day, and Jeremiah in Zedekiah's. Their records of the histories of these periods were already included in their prophetical books when the unknown compiler of 2 Kings undertook his work. Rather than rewrite these histories, he simply incorporated them as appropriate in his own book, with such modifications and additions as necessary for his own purposes.

As to the underlying reason that the Holy Spirit may have had for this set of circumstances, one possibility might have been to confirm in a very concrete way that history and prophecy have the same Author. Isaiah and Jeremiah were the two prophets whose writings were placed at the head of the prophetical books, and thus represented in a sense all the prophets. Isaiah's prophecies to Hezekiah (Isa. 37:5-7, 21-35; 38:4-8; 39:5-7), and Jeremiah's prophecies to the last kings of Judah (note 2 Chron. 36:11-21), were quickly converted by God into actual histories, and these were then written by the prophets themselves, in demonstration of the fact that "what (God) had promised, He was able also to perform" (Rom. 4:21).

The parallel passages in Isaiah 2 and Micah 4 are different from the foregoing examples in that they were written by two different authors. Micah and Isaiah were contemporaries and were both prophets in Judah. It is believed that Isaiah's prophecy was written first, so that Micah's was evidently a quotation from Isaiah, and yet both are given as directly from the word of the Lord.

The explanation possibly is that Micah had just delivered his most disturbing prophecy, warning that Jerusalem would be utterly destroyed (Mic. 3:12). This prophecy made a profound impression, and indeed was quoted by the elders of Judah over a hundred years later (Jer. 26:17-19). It was fitting, therefore, that he should then immediately reaffirm God's glorious promise through Isaiah, with which the people must already have been intimately acquainted, that Jerusalem would yet be established above all the nations someday in a wonderful world of peace and godliness. The most moving way of doing this would be by simply quoting the great passage from Isaiah's prophecy.

Although we do not know all the answers and reasons for the inclusion of every verse of Scripture, we can always find at least a plausible tentative explanation. The biblical doctrine of plenary verbal inspiration is well grounded and quite capable of defense.

Selected books for further study:
Archer, Gleason L. 1982. *Encyclopedia of Bible Difficulties*. Grand Rapids, MI: Zondervan Publishing House. 76 p.
Engelder, Th. 1944. *Scripture Cannot Be Broken*. St. Louis, MO: Concordia Publishing House. 498 p.
Harris, R. Laird. 1969. *Inspiration and Canonicity of the Bible*. Grand Rapids, MI: Zondervan Publishing House. 316 p.
Hills, Edward F. 1967. *Believing Bible Study*. Des Moines, IA: Christian Research Press. 223 p.
Houghton, S.M., ed. 1984. *Truth Unchanged, Unchanging*. Abingdon, England: The Bible League. 503 p.
Stonehouse, Ned B. 1968. *The Infallible Word*. Phillipsburg, NJ: Presbyterian and Reformed.
Walvoord, John W., ed. 1957. *Inspiration and Interpretation*. Grand Rapids, MI: Wm. B. Eerdmans Publishing Co.
Warfield, Benjamin B. 1962. *Limited Inspiration*. Phillipsburg, NJ: Presbyterian and Reformed.

Chapter XIV

Fulfillment of Prophecy

The Testimony of Prophecy

One of the strong objective evidences of biblical inspiration is the phenomenon of fulfilled prophecy. The Bible is essentially unique among the religious books of mankind in this respect. Some of them contain a few vague forecasts, but nothing comparable to the vast number of specific prophecies found in the Bible.

The same is true of modern prophets, so-called. Such seers as Nostradamus, Mother Shipton, Edgar Cayce, Jeane Dixon, and others have made many predictions, but often they are nebulous and capable of various meanings. A few of their prophecies seem to have been fulfilled in a general way, but most of them completely failed.

As a matter of fact, this constitutes one of the claims of Scripture to its own uniqueness. "I am God, and there is none like me, Declaring the end from the beginning, and from ancient times the things that are not yet done" (Isa. 46:9-10). "We have also a more sure word of prophecy; whereunto ye do well that ye take heed" (2 Pet. 1:19).

Anyone can make predictions, of course, based on his own experience and judgment, and these may or may not come true. Scientific forecasters (of weather, of stock market trends, and the like) may, through careful statistical analysis of data, obtain a fairly good average of success on relatively short-range predictions. It is even possible that, through communication with demonic spirits who perhaps possess ways and means of ascertaining the near future on a limited basis, occultists may be able occasionally to prophesy successfully concerning certain imminent events. The few successful predictions made by fortune tellers, astrologers, spiritists, and similar seers are probably accounted for on this basis. To some very limited extent, demonic powers may be capable of influencing future events and, therefore, are able to foresee these events and to communicate this knowledge to those with whom they work.

But no man or angel or demon can predict specific events and personages that will appear scores or even hundreds of years in the future. Only God can do this, because it is He "who worketh all things after the counsel of his own will" (Eph. 1:11). Consequently, it is in His Word, the Holy Scriptures, *and only there*, that prophecies of this sort are found.

The Histories of Nations

The nations of the world come and go, and their rise and fall are controlled by God. "Behold, the nations are as a drop of a bucket, and are counted as the small dust of the balance: behold, He taketh up the isles as a very little thing" (Isa. 40:15). "The most High ruleth in the kingdom of men, and giveth it to whomsoever he will" (Dan. 4:17). Various nations have accordingly frequently been the subject of biblical prophecies.

Egypt was, with Babylonia, one of the two greatest nations of antiquity. Noph (Memphis) was the ancient capital of lower Egypt, and No (Thebes) the capital of all Egypt. The grandeur of their magnificent temples and images was tremendous. Yet Jeremiah said: "Noph shall be waste and desolate without an inhabitant" (Jer. 46:19), and Ezekiel said: "No shall be [broken up]" (Ezek. 30:16). The prophecies were fulfilled centuries later. Of Egypt as a whole, it was said "It shall be the basest of the kingdoms" (Ezek. 29:15). Egypt continued as a great and powerful nation for many centuries after the prophecy was written, but finally it became a backward, impoverished, weak nation and has remained so ever since. It was not condemned to extinction, however, as were many other ancient nations. Actually, it is amazing that the most ancient of nations, Egypt, is still in existence after over 4,000 years. Many Scriptures (for example, Isa. 19:21-22) indicate prophetically that Egypt is still a nation in the last days.

Edom (Idumea) was a small, but powerful, nation descended from Esau. Its stronghold was in Mt. Seir, and its capital was Petra, the rock-walled city, virtually impregnable, as well as rich. Yet many prophecies had been uttered against it, and all have been fulfilled. Obadiah 18, for example, said: "There shall not be any remaining of the house of Esau; for the hath spoken it." Today, the Edomites are gone, without a trace.

The same is true of the Philistines. Though Philistia continued to prosper until about A.D. 1200, Zephaniah had said: "The word of the Lord is against you; O Canaan, the land of the Philistines, I will even destroy thee, that there shall be no inhabitant" (Zeph. 2:5). The Philistines have now long since vanished.

What about Babylonia, the first great world-empire? The Greek historian Herodotus had reported that Babylon was 15 miles square, surrounded by walls 350 feet high and 87 feet wide. Its avenues, parks, and public buildings were a beautiful sight to behold. Yet Jeremiah had prophesied: "The broad walls of Babylon shall be utterly broken, and her high gates shall be burned with fire" (Jer. 51:58). Many other like prophecies were directed against her, and eventually they came to pass.

The Assyrian empire, with its great capital of Nineveh, was another colossus of antiquity. But God said: "He will stretch out his hand against the north, and destroy Assyria; and will make Nineveh a desolation, and dry like a wilderness" (Zeph. 2:13). Nothing could have seemed more unlikely than this when Zephaniah wrote, but it has been fully accomplished.

The two great cities of the Phoenicians were Tyre and Sidon. Of Tyre, God said: "They shall destroy the walls of Tyrus, and break down her towers: I will also scrape her dust from her, and make her like the top of a rock. It shall be a place for the spreading of nets in the midst of the sea" (Ezek. 26:4-5). Today, fishermen mend their nets on the barren rock where Tyre once stood. God also had said, in Ezekiel 26:14: "Thou shalt be built no more." The original site of ancient Tyre is quite suitable for habitation, but the prophecy has stood fulfilled now for over 2,000 years, and Tyre has never been rebuilt.

Tyre's sister city, Sidon, was the object of a different type of prophecy. "For I will send into her pestilence, and blood into her streets; and the wounded shall be judged in the midst of her by the sword upon her on every side" (Ezek. 28:23). Although Sidon has continued to exist as a city down even into the present, she has suffered more warfare and bloodshed than almost any other city in history. Sidon has been destroyed and rebuilt many times, and still exists today, in spite of all her suffering. Tyre, on the other hand, has never been rebuilt, thus confirming the prophecies.

Ashkelon was another great city, the birthplace of Herod the Great. It continued as a great city until finally destroyed in A.D. 1270. For, long before, Zephaniah had prophesied: "Ashkelon [shall be] a desolation" (Zeph. 2:4). The same prophecy had also warned of destruction upon two other Philistine cities, Ekron and Gaza. The modern city of Gaza is at an altogether different location, and is inhabited by Arabs rather than Philistines. In both cases, the prophecy was fulfilled.

Similar judgments were forecast for Bethel (Amos 3:14-15), Samaria (Mic. 1:6-7), Jericho (Josh. 6:26), and, in the New Testament, for Capernaum, Bethsaida, and Chorazin (Matt. 11:20-23). All have been fulfilled as written.

Many other prophecies dealing with these and other nations have been fulfilled. There are also many other prophecies dealing with individual cities in the nations. Their fulfillment is strong witness to divine inspiration.

The Sequence of Empires

A remarkable foreview of world history was given in Daniel 2, in the form of a dream which came to Nebuchadnezzar, king of Babylon. As interpreted by Daniel, the metallic image of the dream represented the entire subsequent course of world history, as influenced by four successive empires. Daniel's interpretation, as recorded in Daniel 2:37-45, indicated the first empire was the golden head of the image, Nebuchadnezzar's Babylonian empire. The second would be the breast and arms of silver (fulfilled in the Medo-Persian empire) and the third, the mid-section of brass (fulfilled in the Greek empire of Alexander the Great). The fourth was the Roman empire, represented by the iron legs, including the hips.

The order of metallic succession indicates both a successive decrease in value and a successive increase in strength. The former probably refers to the degree of personal control exercised by the emperor over the human and material resources of his kingdom, the latter to the power of his armies and extent of his conquests.

The Roman empire was not only the strongest of all but was to last the longest, as indicated by the greater lengths of the legs of the image. Its eventual twofold split into eastern and western divisions, with capitals at Rome and Constantinople, was pictured by the two legs. The break in continuity at the knees intimates the shift from political to religious unity of the two divisions, as maintained for so long by the Roman Catholic and Eastern Orthodox churches.

Thus, although the Roman empire did not persist indefinitely as a political unit, it still does persist in the present east-west division of the heirs of the Roman empire, western Europe and America in the west, Russia, eastern Europe and the middle eastern states in the east. The legal systems, the educational systems, the military systems, the religious systems, and many other facets of modern society are direct descendants of Rome, still retaining the same spirit and much of the same form.

The feet, however, indicate a decided change in direction, and the mixing of iron and clay clearly speaks of the mixture of Roman-style imperialism with mass revolutionary movements. The final form of this succession is indicated by the ten toes representing ten kingdoms, five in the east and five in the west. These will be destroyed and superseded by the kingdom set up by Christ himself over all the world when He returns.

This remarkable prophecy has been almost completely fulfilled. The sequence of world empires is now undoubtedly in the revolutionary "foot" stage, just before it finally assumes the "ten-toed" form prior to the establishment of Christ's kingdom.

While the great image prophesied the great sweep of empires throughout history, the prophecies given directly to Daniel himself, in the 8th and 11th chapters, forecast many of the specific details of the development of the Medo-Persian and Greek empires, as well as numerous events that would take place in their contacts with Egypt, Syria, and Israel. The prophecies in these chapters are so numerous and so specific that they constitute the main reason why critics refuse to accept the authenticity of the book of Daniel, insisting it must have been written after the events had taken place.

However, conservative scholars (for example, Dr. Robert Dick Wilson, of Princeton Seminary, in his classic *Studies in the Book of Daniel* have thoroughly refuted all such critical arguments and confirmed the traditional date of authorship.

The one and only reason today for questioning Daniel's genuineness any longer is the reluctance to believe in fulfilled prophecy. This, of course, is exactly the point. These prophecies confirm clearly and emphatically the fact of divine inspiration.

The Miracle of Israel

The continued existence of the Jews, after centuries of dispersal and persecution unique in human history, is a mute but eloquent testimony to fulfilled prophecy. The restoration of Israel as a nation among nations in our own generation is merely the most recent in a long line of prophecies dealing with the Jewish people which finally came to pass.

When the nation was first founded, through Abraham, God promised: "I will make of thee a great nation . . . And I will bless them that bless thee, and curse him that curseth thee: and in thee shall all families of the earth be blessed" (Gen. 12:2-3). Not only did Israel become a great nation under David and Solomon, but it is destined for even greater days in the future. The nations that have befriended the Jews (notably the United States and, to a lesser degree, England, France, and others) have indeed been blessed. Those that have persecuted the Jews (Egypt, Babylon, Assyria, Rome, Spain, Nazi Germany, and others — Russia's time is coming!) have eventually gone down to defeat and humiliation.

Through the Holy Scriptures, almost all written by Jews, and through Jesus Christ, the seed of Abraham has indeed become a blessing to all families of the earth. Some from every nation have found salvation and blessing through faith in Him.

God promised the children of Israel great blessing in the land of promise if they would remain faithful to Him. He also predicted great suffering, persecution, and worldwide dispersion when they forsook Him. These prophecies came to pass. Some of these warnings were as follows:

> The Lord shall scatter thee among all peoples, from the one end of the earth even unto the other . . . And thy life shall hang in doubt before thee; and thou shalt fear day and night, and shall have none assurance of thy life (Deut. 28:64-66).

> And I will deliver them to be removed into all the kingdoms of the earth for their hurt, to be a reproach

and a proverb, a taunt and a curse, in all places whither I shall drive them (Jer. 24:9).

My God will cast them away, because they did not hearken unto him: and they shall be wanderers among the nations (Hos. 9:17).

Numerous other such prophecies exist, concerning specific judgments and sufferings. But with all this, they would not be exterminated, like so many other nations of antiquity (indeed like *all* other nations who were driven from their homeland). "Though I make a full end of all nations whither I have scattered thee, yet will I not make a full end of thee" (Jer. 30:11).

Even more impossible than that a people could retain its identity without a homeland for two thousand years is that they should then return and establish their ancient nation once again. Yet this is exactly what the Bible had predicted.

Behold, I will take the children of Israel from among the heathen, whither they be gone, and will gather them on every side, and bring them into their own land (Ezek. 37:21).

And it shall come to pass in that day, that the Lord shall set his hand again the second time (note, the *second* time — the first was when he brought them back from the Babylonian captivity) to recover the remnant of his people, which shall be left . . . and shall assemble the outcasts of Israel, and gather together the dispersed of Judah from the four corners of the earth (Isa. 11:11-12).

The "wandering Jews" were without a national home for "many days" (Hos. 3:4-5), and it seemed impossible that such prophecies as these could ever be fulfilled. Even many Bible-believing Christians thought for centuries that God was through with Israel and that all the Old Testament promises to Israel should be spiritualized and applied to the church. But now, with the return of the Jews and the re-establishment of their nation, it is evident in a unique way that God's Word means exactly what it says.

Messianic Prophecy

Prophecies which were fulfilled in connection with the first coming of Christ could occupy a whole volume, as there are hundreds of them. There are over 90 such Old Testament prophecies which are specifically quoted by New Testament writers in a Messianic sense. Only a few of the best-known prophecies need be mentioned here.

The lineage of the Messiah was successively prophesied to be, first in the human family (Gen. 3:15), then through Shem (Gen. 9:26), Abraham (Gen. 22:18), Isaac (Gen. 26:4), Jacob (Gen. 28:14), Judah (Gen. 49:10) and, finally, David (2 Sam. 7:12-16). The fact that, in addition to His human lineage, He would also be uniquely the Son of God, was predicted in Psalm 2:6-7. He was called "the mighty God" in Isaiah 9:6, "whose goings forth were from everlasting" (Mic. 5:2).

His virgin birth was clearly prophesied in Isaiah 7:14 and intimated in several other passages. His birthplace in Bethlehem was given in Micah 5:2. The ministry of His forerunner, John the Baptist, was described in Isaiah 40:3 and Malachi 3:1.

Various aspects of His teaching and healing ministries were given in Isaiah 61:1-2; Isaiah 42:1-4, Isaiah 9:1-2; Psalm 40:7-10, and others. His so-called "triumphal entry" as the promised King of Israel, riding upon an ass, was prophesied in Zechariah 9:9-10; the rejection of His coming as such was prophesied in Psalm 118:22-24.

The date of His official coming as Judah's promised Prince was clearly spelled out in the great prophecy of the 70 weeks, as given in Daniel 9:24-26:

> Seventy weeks [i.e., "seventy heptads" or "seven-year periods"] are determined upon thy people and upon thy holy city . . . from the going forth of the commandment to restore and to build Jerusalem unto the Messiah the Prince shall be seven weeks, and threescore and two weeks: the street shall be built again, and the wall, even in troublous times. And after threescore and two weeks shall Messiah be cut off, but not for himself: and the people of the prince that shall come shall destroy the city and the sanctuary; and the end thereof shall be with a flood, and unto the end wars and desolations are determined.

The starting point of the prophecy is believed by most conservative scholars to be the date of the decree of Artaxerxes permitting the rebuilding of Jerusalem (Neh. 2:1-8), known from secular history to be approximately 446 B.C. The 70 weeks total 490 years. The first 49-year period was occupied in rebuilding the city and completing the Old Testament Scriptures (the book of Malachi was written about 400 B.C.). The "7-year" periods probably were meant to be understood as 7 years of 360 days each, as this was the customary Jewish and prophetic reckoning.

A 434-year period, added to the 49 years, gave 483 years (or 360/365 x 483 = 476 years) from the starting date to the coming of Messiah as Prince. This comes to about A.D. 30. Christ was actually born about 4 B.C., so that He was 33-1/2 years old (His probable age when He was crucified) in about 30 A.D. Note, of course, that there was no year "0," so that only one year separated 1 B.C. and A.D. 1.

Although there is some uncertainty about the exact dates involved, it is clear that the prophetic period terminated at very close to the time when Christ officially offered himself for reception as King of Israel. Instead of being crowned, however, He was crucified, "cut off, but not for himself."

Sometime after that, "the city and the sanctuary" were destroyed by "the people of the prince that shall come" — that is, the people in the territories subjugated and occupied by Rome, of whom eventually the great anti-Christian prince frequently mentioned in Daniel will come. Furthermore, the "end thereof" was "a flood." This word literally means "overflowing" and can apply both to overflowing waters and to overflowing armies or peoples. Probably in this case it refers specifically to the long-prophesied worldwide dispersion of the Jews.

Finally, "unto the end, wars and desolations are determined." Ever since the world, both Jews and Gentiles, rejected and crucified the Lord Jesus Christ, it has never known a lasting peace.

This great prophecy alone, given hundreds of years before its various fulfillments, is clear and unanswerable proof that "holy men of God spake as they were moved by the Holy Ghost" (2 Pet. 1:21).

But the light of biblical prophecy was focused more clearly

and intensively on the crucifixion of Christ than on anything else. The details so prophesied including the piercing of His side (Zech. 12:10), the darkness (Ps. 22:2), the vinegar (Ps. 69:21), the mocking (Ps. 22:6-8), the nakedness (Ps. 22:17), gambling for His vesture (Ps. 22:18), the unbroken bones (Ps. 34:20), the great cry from the cross (Ps. 22:1), and the broken heart (Ps. 22:14).

The substitutionary and sacrificial nature of His death on the cross was graphically portrayed in Isaiah 53, especially verses 4-6, 10 and 12. The shedding of His blood, as an offering for sin, was forecast in all of the Levitical offerings. The burial of Christ in a "rich man's grave," yet in proximity to the "wicked," was prophesied in Isaiah 53:9.

Finally, the resurrection of Christ from the grave was forecast in Psalm 16:10; Hosea 6:2; Psalm 30:3, 9; Isaiah 53:10; Psalm 40:1-2; and others. His ascension to sit at the right hand of the Father was then described in Psalm 110:1; Psalm 68:18; Proverbs 30:4; Psalm 16:11; and Psalm 24:3-10. And still there remain scores of fulfilled prophecies we have not even mentioned.

Prophecies of the Last Days

In addition to the hundreds of biblical prophecies that have been fulfilled in the past, there is a special class of predictions that focus on the events of what the Scriptures call "the last days," "the latter times," or other similar expressions. In some cases, these expressions are used in a relative sense only, but usually they apply specifically to the closing days of the present age, days associated with the second coming of Christ to the earth.

Our purpose here is not to study eschatology, but rather to stress that these prophecies also provide further evidence of biblical inspiration, since many of them are being fulfilled before our eyes today. In fact, as more and more of these ancient predictions are seen coming to pass, the evidence for the divine origin of the Bible is becoming stronger all the time.

We have already noted what is probably the most important of these end-time prophecies; namely, the re-establishment of Israel as a nation in its ancient homeland. That a nation could be completely destroyed as an organized entity by an invading army (as Israel was, by the Romans, in A.D. 70), its people either slaughtered or scattered from one end of the world to the other, its land occupied and ruled by aliens for over 1,900 years, and yet survive as a distinct nationality, and then finally regain its homeland and be recognized as a viable nation once more by the other nations of the world seems impossible. Yet it has happened in spite of the impossibilities, and to make it still more amazing, it was predicted to happen many centuries before it happened.

When Israel, including Judah, first went into captivity, in 588 B.C., the period known as "the times of the Gentiles" began. Babylonia, Medo-Persia, Greece and Rome were successive world empires, and their domain included the Land of Israel. After Rome destroyed the city and the temple in A.D. 70 (as predicted by Christ himself in Luke 19:41-44), the people of Israel were finally scattered in A.D. 135, "Among all people, from the one end of the earth unto the other" (Deut. 28:64).

In this context, we come to a remarkable prophecy made by Jesus Christ: "And they shall fall by the edge of the sword, and shall be led away captive into all nations: and Jerusalem shall be trodden down of the Gentiles, until the times of the Gentiles be fulfilled" (Luke 21:24).

Since the word "fulfilled" is the same word in the Greek as "finished," this prophecy clearly means that the times of Gentile world-rule will be ended when Jerusalem is no longer under Gentile control. But this can only be accomplished when Christ returns to banish the Gentile nations from Jerusalem and to establish His own world-kingdom capital there. Thus, the restoration of Jerusalem to the chosen people is necessarily accompanied by the coming of their Messiah to reign there. This is also clearly indicated in Zechariah 12–14, as well as other Scriptures.

The Jews began to return to Palestine in small numbers in the early part of the twentieth century, and then in much larger numbers after World War I and the Balfour Declaration. Jerusalem was still under British rule, however. After World War II, the Israeli nation declared its independence in 1948 and was soon recognized by most of the nations and by the United Nations. The new city of Jerusalem indeed did go back to the Jews at this time. However, the *old* city, including the all-important temple site on Mount Moriah, remained in the hands of the Jordanian Arabs.

In the "six-day war" of 1967, Israel finally recaptured

even the old city of Jerusalem, and the Israelis insist they will never let it go again. At this writing (1996), they have retained possession of all of Jerusalem for 28 long years.

Yet the Lord has not come! The times of the Gentiles are still in full sway, even though Jerusalem has apparently gone back to the Jews.

With one exception, that is! This exception makes all the difference, and indicates with what fine lines the Holy Spirit inscripturates His Word. Jerusalem is not, in God's judgment, a collection of houses and streets, like other cities. It is a temple where God dwells, where His people approach Him through sacrifice, and where He meets with them.

As Solomon built the temple, God said: "I have chosen Jerusalem, that my name might be there" (2 Chron. 6:6). But long before this, God had first spoken through Moses: "There shall be a place which the Lord your God shall choose to cause His name to dwell there; thither shall ye bring all that I command you; your burnt-offerings, and your sacrifices, your tithes, and the heave offering of your hand, and all your choice vows which ye vow unto the Lord" (Deut. 12:11).

This place was not just any place in Jerusalem; it was an exact spot, chosen by God. It was on Mount Moriah (2 Chron. 3:1), the spot which God told David to purchase from Ornan the Jebusite and to set up the altar there (1 Chron. 21:18). This was the same spot where Abraham had, almost a thousand years before, prepared to sacrifice his son Isaac (Gen. 22:2). It is only a short distance from Calvary itself.

This spot, to the Jews, and to God, *is* Jerusalem! And, amazingly, this one spot is the only spot in Jerusalem still controlled by Gentiles. It is on Mount Moriah that the Arabs have built their famous Dome-of-the-Rock, the second most holy place in the Muslim world. The Jews, for political or other reasons, have not yet dared to expel the Arabs from this site, raze it, and proceed to rebuild their temple, as they surely desire to do.

It is apparently by this exceedingly slender thread, therefore, that the "times of the Gentiles" are still suspended. As the Lord Jesus said: "One jot or one tittle shall in no wise pass from the law, till all be fulfilled" (Matt. 5:18).

There are many other prophecies dealing with the alignment of the Gentile nations in the last days. The emergence of an alliance of Eastern European and Muslim nations under the leadership and domination of Russia, all arrayed in opposition to Israel and the western nations, is prophesied in Ezekiel 38:1-16. The rise of a vast oriental confederacy of nations is described in Revelation 16:12. The development of a European union of nations comparable to the ancient Roman empire is suggested in Daniel 7:19-24 and other passages.

In response to the question: "What shall be the sign of thy coming, and of the end of the world?" (Matt. 24:3-8), the Lord Jesus answered: "Nation shall rise against nation, and kingdom against kingdom: and there shall be famines, and pestilences, and earthquakes, in divers places. All these are the beginning of sorrows" (or, more accurately, "the first birth pains"). The Hebrew idiom conveys the thought of a worldwide state of war. Thus, the prophetic sign entails a world war, accompanied by great physical calamities, as the initial sign that a new world is about to be born. This was clearly fulfilled in the decade from 1914 to 1924, when the first world war, followed by the world's greatest pestilence (the influenza epidemic of 1918), the world's greatest famine (leading to the starvation of hundreds of millions, especially in Russia and China, after the war and the communist revolution), and the world's most calamitous earthquakes (in China in 1920 and Japan in 1923), all took place. The world since that time has continued to experience these "birth pains," with World War II, the Cold War, great numbers of local wars, the Great Depression, continued deadly earthquakes, epidemics of polio, cholera, AIDS, and other diseases, and innumerable other "troubles" (Mark 13:8).

A fulfilled prophecy of an entirely different sort is found in 2 Peter 3:3-4. "There shall come in the last days scoffers . . . saying . . . all things continue as they were from the beginning of the creation."

This is the doctrine of *evolutionary naturalism*, which professes to explain the origin and development of all things in terms of the uniform operation of the same natural laws and processes which still "continue" today. The rise of this dogma took place in the 19th century, and has for a hundred years been the basic philosophy of the educational and scientific establishments. There was no way that Peter could have foreseen this development, 1,800 years in the future, apart from divine inspiration.

In relation to the realm of science and education, it was prophesied in Daniel that, at "the time of the end:" "many shall run to and fro, and knowledge shall be increased" (Dan. 12:4). The Hebrew words imply a vast increase in both frequency and speed of travel, as well as other forms of communication, along with great advances in science and technology.

Conflict in the economic and social realms in the last days is forecast in James 5:1-6. For ages, in all nations, the poor have been exploited by the rich, the working classes by the privileged classes. The uprising of the laborers in the latter days, leading to a "day of slaughter," is not only specifically predicted by James, but also implied in Daniel 2:41-43, Revelation 18:1-19, and other passages. These prophecies have been fulfilled in part, first in the French revolution, later in the Russian revolution and other communist-led upheavals. More is undoubtedly yet to come, especially when the ill-fed, poorly housed masses of the world come to realize that even their own revolutionary movements are financed and controlled in large measure by those "kings and merchants of the earth" who traffic in the "souls of men."

Moral conditions of the last days are prophesied to descend into the degradation of the "days of Noah" (Luke 17:26). But perhaps the most striking prediction associated with moral conditions in the last days is that the characteristics of professing religious people, in the realm of Christendom, will be essentially the same as those of the heathen in the old pagan world. That is, the catalog of the sins of those in the last days who have "a form of godliness" (2 Tim. 3:1-7, especially verse 5), is practically identical with that of the ancient godless rebels of Romans 1:28-31. Again, it seems impossible that Paul could have anticipated such a strange, sad development except by inspiration.

Religious apostasy in the ranks of professed Christian leaders is also prophesied in other Scriptures. Not only would false teachers deny the second coming of Christ (2 Pet. 3:3), they would even "deny the Lord that bought them" (2 Pet. 2:1). Not only would they, despite much education ("ever learning"), still never come "to the knowledge of the truth" (2 Tim. 3:7), but even "turn away their ears from the truth and be turned unto fables" (2 Tim. 4:4). All of these prophecies are being fulfilled today throughout the "Christian" world.

A particularly ominous form of apostasy is to be found in the rapid rise of demonism in the last days. "In the latter times some shall depart from the faith, giving heed to seducing spirits, and doctrines of [demons]" (1 Tim. 4:1). Jesus said: "There shall arise false Christs, and false prophets, and shall show great signs and wonders" (Matt. 24:24). During the great Tribulation period of the last days, these trends will culminate in a worldwide return to Satan worship (Rev. 13:4, 8). Before that, they will "worship [demons], and idols" (Rev. 9:20) and do so especially in connection with the use of drugs (the word "sorceries," in Revelation 9:21, is a Greek word from which we actually transliterate our English word "pharmaceutical," and means "magical incantations by the ritual use of drugs").

The amazing upsurge of spiritism, astrology, witchcraft and satanism all over the world in the past few years, along with the tremendous increase of drug use, especially by young people, certainly is an ominous sign of the imminent advent of Antichrist, but at the same time is a striking fulfillment of prophecy. That an age of scientific enlightenment could be followed so quickly by a widespread revival of paganism and occultism would seem paradoxical, but that is exactly what has happened, just as the Bible predicted.

We have only scratched the surface. There are scores of other biblical prophecies that either have already been fulfilled or are presently in process of fulfillment. There is no other book like the Bible.

"For the prophecy came not in old time by the will of man: but holy men of God spake as they were moved by the Holy Ghost" (2 Pet. 1:21).

Probability Analysis

Modern day forecasters of the weather, of sporting events, of political elections and other such things, often speak in terms of the "odds" on such and such a prediction. They try to assess all the various factors that might affect the outcome of the event under consideration, and then they conclude that "there is a 25 percent chance of rain tomorrow" or that "the Tigers have a 60 percent chance of winning the pennant" and so on.

One can analyze the biblical prophecies using a similar approach, in retrospect. That is, each prophecy can be studied in the light of the various events that brought about its fulfillment, and then an evaluation made as to how well the ancient prophet could have been able to take these factors into consideration in arriving at his forecast. Then, with this analysis, one can calculate roughly the probability that the prediction could have been made correctly without supernatural inspiration.

For example, consider the prophecy of Genesis 49:10, in which Jacob, while dying, predicted that Judah would be the one of his twelve sons who would exercise the rule over his brethren and from whom the Messiah would come. There was nothing in the immediate situation to warrant this prediction, and indeed it did not begin its fulfillment until David was crowned king 600 years later. How did Jacob know?

He could, of course, simply have guessed. Since he had 12 sons, he would have had a chance of guessing correctly equal to 1 out of 12. If he had tried to reason it out, or to go by his feelings, he would probably have picked either his oldest son, Reuben, or his favorite son, Joseph. Instead he picked Judah. At the least, therefore, the odds were 12-to-1 against his being right.

These are not impossible odds, however, so it might have worked out, just by chance. Next would be the question of where the coming King would be born. Micah predicted it would be in Bethlehem, and he made this prediction 700 years before it came to pass (Mic. 5:2). He could presumably have guessed the Messiah would be born in the land of Judah, since the kings at that time were descended from David and ruled over the land of Judah. Of course, it would have been quite possible for the coming King to be born anywhere in the world, and still to have been a descendant of Judah, and of David, in view of the extensive world trade carried on by Solomon and his descendants, and in view of the already-prophesied dispersion. It would be reasonable to say he had a 1-in-2 chance of being correct in assuming the Messiah would be born in the land of Judah.

But then, where in the land of Judah? The most likely place would be in the capital city of Jerusalem, but again, there was perhaps an equal chance He would be born somewhere in Judah *outside* of Jerusalem. Thus, Micah had a 1-in-4 chance of predicting correctly His birth to be in some Judean town other than Jerusalem.

As far as the rest of such towns were concerned, it probably would have been a toss-up. There were probably about a hundred towns and villages in Judah, and no one of them seemed a more likely candidate than any other. Thus, the odds against Bethlehem were 100 to 1. Possibly, for sentimental reasons, he might have leaned slightly toward Bethlehem, since David had originally come from there. For this reason, we might possibly lower the odds by a factor of 2, assuming that Micah was twice as likely to guess Bethlehem as any of the other towns in Judah outside of Jerusalem.

Putting this all together, the chance that Micah would guess Bethlehem by natural reasoning would be 1 out of 4 multiplied by 1 out of 50, or 1 out of 200. This would be extremely unlikely, but again, not completely impossible.

But what about predicting not only the place and the family, but even the *time* of Messiah's birth? In Daniel 9:24-26, we have just such a prediction. Although there may be some uncertainty about the exact chronology (some scholars have maintained, quite convincingly, that the fulfillment occurred on the precise day indicated by the prophecy), there can be no reasonable question as to, say, at least the century when it was fulfilled.

At the time of the prophecy, its fulfillment was still five centuries in the future. As far as Daniel knew, however, it could have been any time from his immediate present until the very end of the world. How did he happen to pick five centuries?

The chance of his guessing correctly would have been one out of the total number of centuries to come in the earth's history. From our present vantage point, we know that the world had at least 25 centuries yet to go, so we might reasonably assign his prophecy a 1:25 probability of being correct, as far as the century was concerned. If we accept the accuracy of the exact date as predicted for His so-called "triumphal entry" in this prophecy, we would have to multiply this number by the number of days in a century, making the probability of chance fulfillment 1:900,000.

Now, then, what is the probability that all three of these prophecies could have been fulfilled by chance? Each is independent of the others, and each was made by a different prophet at a different time in history, and yet all three prophecies converged on and were fulfilled by one person — Jesus the Messiah.

Statistical theory shows that if the probability of one event is x and the probability of another independent event is y, the probability of both events being fulfilled simultaneously is x multiplied by y. Therefore, the chance that the lineage, place and time of one individual could all be predicted in this way is equal to the product of the individual probabilities.

The three prophecies discussed above have a combined probability of chance fulfillment, therefore, equal to one out of 12 x 200 x 25, at the very most. This is one chance out of 60,000.

This might be conceivable, but is certainly unlikely. No gambler would wager much money that such a combination would ever occur. If we factor in the chance of guessing the exact date, the probability becomes one chance out of over two billion!

And these are only 3 prophecies out of over 300 that were fulfilled at the first coming of Christ. The odds against some of them (e.g., the virgin birth and the resurrection) are astronomical. Then, there are also the hundreds of other prophecies dealing with nations, cities, signs of the last days, and many others.

It seems reasonable to conclude that the phenomenon of fulfilled prophecy constitutes a unique and powerful evidence of the divine inspiration of the Bible.

Selected books for further study:
Anderson, Sir Robert. 1954. *The Coming Prince*. Grand Rapids, MI: Kregal Publications. 384 p.
Cooper, David L. 1940. *Future Events Revealed*. Los Angeles, CA: Biblical Research Society. 250 p.
Dyer, Charles H. 1993. *World News and Bible Prophecy*. Wheaton, IL: Tyndale House Publishers. 303 p.
Gaebelein, Arno C. *The Prophet Daniel*. Grand Rapids, MI: Kregel Publications. 218 p.
Lacey, Harry. 1942. *God and the Nations*. New York, NY: Loizeaux Brothers. 189 p.
LaHaye, Tim. 1972. *The Beginning of the End*. Wheaton, IL: Tyndale House Publishers. 198 p.
Lindsey, Hal, John Ankerberg, Henry Morris, Chuck Missler, and Don McAlvany. 1995. *Steeling the Mind of America*. Green Forest, AR: New Leaf Press. 304 p.
Morris, Henry M. 1991. *Creation and the Second Coming*. Green Forest, AR: Master Books. 194 p.
Morris, Henry M. 1983. *The Revelation Record*. Wheaton, IL: Tyndale House Publishers. 521 p.

Rowell, Earle Albert. 1933. *Prophecy Speaks*. Takoma Park, MD: Review and Herald. 127 p.

Smith, Wilbur M. 1951. *World Crises and the Prophetic Scriptures*. Chicago, IL: Moody Press. 384 p.

Stewart, Herbert. 1941. *The Stronghold of Prophecy*. London: Marshall, Morgan and Scott. 127 p.

Stoner, Peter B., and Robert C. Newman. 1976. *Science Speaks*. Chicago, IL: Moody Press.

Uprichard, Harry. 1994. *A Son is Promised*. Darlington, England: Evangelical Press. 144 p.

Urquhart, John. 1939. *Wonders of Prophecy*. London: Pickering and Inglis. 191 p.

Willmington, Harold L. 1981. *Signs of the Times*. Wheaton, IL: Tyndale House Publishers. 167 p.

Chapter XV

The Structure
of Scripture

Internal Evidences of Inspiration

A unique characteristic of the Bible is the fact that it bears innumerable marks of divine inspiration in its very structure. Such "internal evidences" are separate and distinct from the many external evidences found in such things as fulfilled prophecy, archaeological confirmations of its historical accuracy, scientific discoveries, and similar examples of its divine trustworthiness.

Although the Bible is a collection of 66 different books, written by 40 or more authors throughout a period of at least 1,500 years, each writer with his own particular style and from his own individual point of view, it is nevertheless clearly *one* Book, evidencing in countless ways its fundamental unity and continuity. Although there frequently appear to be points of disagreement and even contradiction, between different biblical writers, these all vanish upon closer study, and remarkable agreement and complementarity emerge again and again from these superficial discordances. Such phenomena as these are found in no other book or anthology. Not only, therefore, does the Bible have ultimately just *one* single Author, but that Author must be God the Holy Spirit!

In this chapter, we wish to examine a few of these internal evidences. Since these phenomena occur throughout the whole Bible, we cannot discuss them in full, but only select a few typical examples. In fact, new treasures of this sort are continually being discovered by those who explore the Bible country. As the Lord Jesus said: "Therefore every scribe which is instructed unto the kingdom of heaven is like unto a man that is an householder, which bringeth forth out of his treasure things new and old" (Matt. 13:52).

The Principle of First Mention

One of the remarkable evidences of biblical unity is its internal consistency. Nowhere is this more strikingly evident than in a phenomenon called the law of first mention. That is, the very first time an important word or concept of Scripture is mentioned in the Bible (usually, though not always, in the Book of Genesis), its usage in that passage provides the foundation for its full development in later parts of the Bible, especially in the New Testament.

This principle does not apply to every word, of course, but rather to certain key words — the "keynotes" of grand themes that are interlaced throughout the Scriptures, climaxing in a crescendo of power and beauty in the full revelation of Jesus Christ. No attempt is made here to present a complete listing of these words, nor a complete exposition of the development of any one of them in its biblical context, but a number of examples, with brief comment, will be indicated below.

Light. This word, of course, first appears in Genesis 1:3, and it is significant that it follows the first word spoken by God. The inference to be drawn immediately is that light is not dependent on the sun or moon or stars (which were created later, as "light-holders"), but rather comes through the Word of God. All else is darkness. When Jesus, the Living Word, finally came into the world, it was said that "light is come into the world" (John 3:19). Of the Written Word, the Holy Scriptures, it was said: "We have also a more sure word of prophecy; whereunto ye do well that ye take heed, as unto a light that shineth in a dark place" (2 Pet. 1:19). Finally, the word occurs for the last time in Revelation 22:5. "They need no . . . light of the sun, for the Lord God giveth them light: and they shall reign for ever and ever."

Love. This great word appears first in what seems like a strange context — the love of a father for a son whom he is about to slay. "Take now thy son," said God to Abraham, "thine *only* son Isaac, whom thou *lovest* (literally, 'thine only and beloved son') . . . and offer him three for a burnt-offering" (Gen. 22:2). Abraham, despite his great love for his son, was willing at any cost to obey God's will, knowing in faith that the greatest ultimate good for his beloved son must come in obedience to God's Word. Therefore, he "offered up his only begotten son. . . . Accounting that God was able to raise him up, even from the dead; from whence also he received him in a figure" (Heb. 11:17-19). The real significance of this event could be understood 2,000 years later, when it was realized that all this was a "figure" of a much greater sacrifice, when the heavenly Father would offer up His only begotten Son. This first mention of "love" tells us that the foundation of all love — was in the divine love existing within the Godhead from past eternity. Jesus, as He prayed to the Father, said: "Thou lovedst me before the foundation of the world" (John 17:24). It is thrilling to note that, in the New Testament, the first time the world "love" occurs in each of the synoptic Gospels, is when the Father calls out from heaven: "This is my beloved Son, in whom I am well pleased" (Matt. 3:17; Mark 1:11; Luke 3:22). Then, in the Gospel of the beloved disciple, the book in which the word "love" appears more often than in any other book, the word occurs first when the Lord Jesus says: "For God so loved the world, that he gave his only begotten Son, that whosoever believeth in him should not perish, but have everlasting life" (John 3:16).

Faith. After looking at the word "love," we should also look at the other two words in the great triumvirate of 1 Corinthians 13:13: "Now abideth faith, hope, charity [i.e., love], these three." The word "faith" occurs first in its verb form, and is found in Genesis 15:6: "[Abraham] *believed* in the Lord; and he counted it to him for righteousness." We are told, thereby, as it were, that righteousness before God comes not by works or rituals but only by faith. Furthermore, this saving faith is not some abstract faith in oneself or in society or in other men, but faith in Jehovah, the only true God, and specifically in His Word of promise. The

New Testament commentary on the event says: "[Abraham] was strong in faith, giving glory to God; And being fully persuaded that, what He had promised, He was able also to perform. And therefore it was imputed to him for righteousness" (Rom. 4:20-22).

Hope. This word is expressive of that expectation that God's plans, both for the salvation of the individual and for the redemption of the whole creation, will someday be perfectly accomplished, all present appearances to the contrary notwithstanding. All these expectations are centered in "that blessed hope, and the glorious appearing of the great God and our Savior Jesus Christ" (Titus 2:13). The corresponding Hebrew word first occurs, interestingly enough, in the story of Joshua and the battle of Jericho. Joshua (whose name is the same as "Jesus"), after a long period of delay and wandering, suddenly and miraculously crosses the Jordan River to destroy the hopelessly wicked and unbelieving inhabitants of Jericho. But there was one woman in the city, Rahab by name, who had come to believe in the true God, and was willing to act on that faith even though her action would incur the wrath of all her fellow-citizens. She and her family were saved when Joshua came, recognized only by a "line of scarlet thread in the window" (Josh. 2:18). This seemed a very slender hope, but it was sufficient. The word "line" is the word which everywhere else in the Old Testament is translated "hope," and it occurs here for the first time. The scarlet color, of course, represents blood, and therefore sacrifice. Her life was spared and her sin forgiven (she had been a prostitute) because of her trust in Jehovah evidenced by her treatment of God's emissaries and symbolized by the redemptive, blood-red "hope in the window" (Josh. 2:21).

Blood. And while thinking of the hope of redemption through the blood of Christ, we might note that the first occurrence of "blood" is in Genesis 4:10: "The voice of thy brother's blood crieth unto me from the ground." The first mention of blood, therefore, is in connection with the shedding of blood, innocent blood.

Abel was the first prophet and first martyr (Matt. 23:35; Luke 11:51). Cain was able to silence the prophesying voice of Abel by spilling his blood, but only to have the voice of his blood crying out from the earth itself. Similarly, the Jews clamored for the blood of Christ, saying: "His blood be on us, and on our children" (Matt. 27:25), but then later complained to the Apostles, "Ye have filled Jerusalem with your doctrine, and intend to bring this man's blood upon us" (Acts 5:28). The blood of Jesus, of course, "speaketh better things than that of Abel" (Heb. 12:24), not only condemning all those who, like Cain, reject God's Word and persecute those who speak it, but also sealing an eternal covenant of redemption and peace for those who receive and obey it. "The God of peace that brought again from the dead our Lord Jesus, that great shepherd of the sheep, through the blood of the everlasting covenant" (Heb. 13:20).

Grace. One of the most wonderful words of the Bible is "grace." Note some of the words that are used to describe it: "sufficient" (2 Cor. 12:9); "abounding" (2 Cor. 9:8); "glory" (Eph. 1:6); "exceeding riches" (Eph. 2:7); "manifold" (1 Pet. 4:10). It is , of course, "by grace ye are saved" (Eph. 2:8). And so it was with Noah. In a world of universal wickedness, destined for destruction, "Noah found grace in the eyes of the Lord" (Gen. 6:8). This is the first mention of "grace" in the Bible. God had, in sovereign grace, chosen Noah even before he was born, as evidenced in the prophecy of his father Lamech (Gen. 5:29). It is only *after* Noah found grace that the Scripture says he was a "just" and "perfect" man. That is, he was made "righteous" and "complete" (these two words also are first mentioned here in Gen. 6:9), on the basis of his receiving the grace of God. Just so, we are made "the righteousness of God in him" (2 Cor. 5:21) and we are "complete in him" (Col. 2:10).

Word. This brief study of the first mention of several key words in Scripture should also include notice of the first time the word "word" itself occurs in Scripture. It is most significant that it is not in connection with the words of men, but with the Word of the living God! "After these things the word of the Lord came unto Abram in a vision, saying, Fear not, Abram: I am thy shield, and thy exceeding great reward" (Gen. 15:1). The Word of the Lord is thus personified and indeed is the Living Word, the pre-incarnate Christ himself. Whenever in the Old Testament God is seen or heard or in some way is manifest to the physical senses, it is always the second person, the Word of God. "No man hath seen God at any time: the only begotten Son, who is in the bosom of the Father, he hath declared him" (John 1:18). Here also is the first of the great "I am's" of Christ. "I am thy shield and thy exceeding great reward." No wonder Christ said: "Your father Abraham rejoiced to see my day." Then, when His listeners scoffed at the thought that He had seen Abraham, He replied "Before Abraham was, I am" (John 8:56, 58). Furthermore, the word "vision" occurs first in this verse, indicating that only true revelation from God will show forth Christ, and so do the words "shield" and "reward." Thus, the promise also assures us that the Lord Jesus Christ is both our protection from every harm and our provision of every need. Finally, as the first mention of "word" in the Bible directs us to the Living Word, Jesus Christ, so the last mention conveys to us directly from Him the strong warning neither to add nor take away any word from His Written Word, "the words of the book of this prophecy" (Rev. 22:18-19).

Several other examples of first occurrences, all in the Book of Genesis (after the fifth chapter), are listed below. The reader is urged to study these words and their doctrinal development in subsequent Scriptures for himself.

Word	First Mention
Just (= righteous)	Genesis 6:9
Perfect (= complete)	6:9
Atonement (= pitch)	6:14
Covenant	6:18
Altar	8:20
Shed (= pour out)	9:6

Word	First Mention
Wine	9:21
Drunken	9:21
Praise (= commend)	12:15
Peace (= Salem)	14:18
Tithes	14:20
Vision	15:1
Shield	15:1
Reward	15:1
I am	15:1
Imputed (=counted)	15:6
Righteousness	15:6
Angel of the Lord	16:7
Worship (= bow down)	18:2
Mercy	19:16
Fire	19:24
Obey	22:18
Sow	26:12
Salvation	49:18

These are only a few examples of this remarkable principle of first mention in the Bible, and none of these has been at all fully expounded. They testify clearly and unmistakably that the whole Bible, from Genesis to Revelation, has one great Author. The coincidences are too striking to be attributed to chance and are completely beyond the reach of human contrivance. Once again, the only explanation for this phenomenon, as for fulfilled prophecy and so many others, is that "holy men of God spake as they were moved by the Holy Ghost" (2 Pet. 1:21).

Types and Shadows

Another evidence of unity and continuity in Scripture is found in the study of typology. The characters and events of the Old Testament frequently are seen to be "types" (or "models" or "patterns") of New Testament truths, especially as fulfilled in the person and work of the Lord Jesus Christ. "The New is in the Old concealed; the Old is in the New revealed. The New is in the Old contained; the Old is in the New explained."

This phenomenon is similar to that of fulfilled prophecy, except that prophecies are clearly stated and defined as such. A type, on the other hand, is recognized to have prophetic implications only after its anti-type, or prototype, has been revealed. But once the latter has appeared, then the remarkable analogies with its Old Testament "model" throw a thrilling light upon that model, and provide a striking evidence of divine foresight and planning.

These Old Testament types are very numerous, far too many to discuss here. In fact, in one way or another, practically every event in the Old Testament could be shown to have some kind of typological significance. As Paul says: "Now all these things happened unto them for ensamples [or, literally, 'as types']: and they are written for our admonition" (1 Cor. 10:11). "For whatsoever things were written aforetime were written for our learning, that we through patience and comfort of the Scriptures might have hope" (Rom. 15:4).

Of special interest, of course, are those which are specifically cited in the New Testament as types of Christ. Even these are too numerous to discuss here in detail. A few important examples will be mentioned and treated very briefly below.

Adam. The first man, Adam, is a *contrasting* type of Christ. "As in Adam all die, even so in Christ shall all be made alive" (1 Cor. 15:22). "The first man Adam was made a living soul; the last Adam was made a quickening spirit" (1 Cor. 15:45). "For as by one man's disobedience, many were made sinners, so by the obedience of one shall many be made righteous" (Rom. 5:19). As Adam was made in the image of God, so Jesus Christ is "the image of the invisible God" (Col. 1:15). Adam yielded to the temptation, but Christ was "in all points tempted like as we are, yet without sin" (Heb. 4:15). Adam died for his sin and returned to the dust, but "Christ died for our sins . . . and rose again from the dead" (1 Cor. 15:3-4).

Eve. Eve, formed from the side of Adam to be his bride, is a type of the Church, the bride of Christ. As Adam allowed God to place a "deep sleep" upon him, so Christ died in order that His own bride might be formed and be made a part of His body. "Christ also loved the church, and gave himself for it . . . that he might present it to himself a glorious church" (Eph. 5:25, 27). Christ is the Bridegroom (John 3:29; the Church is espoused to one Husband — to Christ (2 Cor. 11:2).

The Sun. As the sun is the source of all the earth's physical energy for maintaining its physical processes and organic life, so Jesus Christ is spiritually "the light of the world" (John 8:12), dispelling darkness and bringing the light of life. He is the "Sun of righteousness . . . with healing in his wings" [literally, 'rays'] who shall arise (Mal. 4:2). He is "the brightness [literally 'out-raying'] of his glory" (Heb. 1:3). "For God, who commanded the light to shine out of darkness, hath shined in our hearts, to give the light of the knowledge of the glory of God in the face of Jesus Christ" (2 Cor. 4:6).

The Tabernacle. The tabernacle in the wilderness was the center of Israel's worship, the place to which the people brought their sacrifices and offerings and the place where God met with His people. The details of its construction were all carefully specified by God himself, who told Moses: "According to all that I shew thee, after the pattern of the tabernacle, and the pattern of all the instruments thereof, even so shall ye make it" (Exod. 25:9). When it was all completed, "Then a cloud covered the tent of the congregation, and the glory of the Lord filled the tabernacle" (Exod. 40:34). The reason for such precise divine specifications for the tabernacle was fully understood when Christ came, for its details were all in some way representative of His person and work. "The first tabernacle," the writer of Hebrews says, "was a figure for the time then present" (Heb. 9:8-9). "But Christ" has now come "by a greater and more perfect tabernacle, not made with hands" (Heb. 9:11). There are numerous ways in which the tabernacle typifies Christ, but the most fundamental is that it speaks of the personal presence of God through the "Shekinah" glory-cloud that resided there. This symbol became a glorious reality in Jesus Christ. "The Word was made flesh, and dwelt [literally, 'tabernacled'] among us, (and we beheld his glory, the glory as of the only begotten of the Father,) full of grace and truth" (John 1:14). Ultimately, the type will find its eternal fulfillment in the New Jerusalem. When the holy city descends from Heaven to the new earth after the last judgment, God will say: "Behold, the tabernacle of God is with men, and he will dwell with them, and they shall be his people, and God himself shall be with them, and be their God" (Rev. 21:3).

The Offerings. The altar in the tabernacle, and later in the temple, received the blood of literally millions of sacrificial animals. Many chapters in Leviticus and other books are occupied with the procedural details for offering such sacrifices. In every case, it was understood by the person bringing the offering that it was to be received as a substitute for himself, being put to death in his place for his sins. "For the life of the flesh is in the blood: and I have given it to you upon the altar to make an atonement for your souls: for it is the blood that maketh an atonement for the soul" (Lev. 17:11). This was all symbolic (though the obedient faith which it required was quite real) of one great sacrifice which would one day be offered. "For it is not possible that the blood of bulls and goats should take away sins" (Heb. 10:4). "But this man . . . offered one sacrifice for sins for ever" (Heb. 10:12).

Bread from Heaven. God's faithful provision for the physical needs of His people was amply demonstrated by the daily dispatch of manna from heaven during all the years of wilderness wanderings. It was more than bread for the body, however, also speaking figuratively of God's provision for the daily spiritual needs of His people, satisfied only through His Word. "Man shall not live by bread alone, but by every word that proceedeth out of the mouth of God" (Matt. 4:4). It thus also symbolized the living Word, Jesus Christ. "I am the living bread which came down from heaven: if any man eat of this bread, he shall live for ever; and the bread that I will give is my flesh, which I will give for the life of the world" (John 6:51).

The Water of Life. In the original creation, "a river went out of Eden to water the garden" (Gen. 2:10). This river, with its life-giving waters, is a model for the great stream that flows out of the divine temple during the coming millennial age. "And it shall be in that day, that living waters shall go out from Jerusalem" (Zech. 14:8). This millennial river in turn is a type of the glorious river that flows from the throne of God in the eternal ages to come. "And he shewed me a pure river of water of life, clear as crystal, proceeding out of the throne of God and of the Lamb" (Rev. 22:1). And all of them are types of the water of spiritual life in Christ. "Jesus stood and cried saying, If any man thirst, let him come unto me and drink. He that believeth on me, as the Scripture hath said, out of his belly shall flow rivers of living water" (John 7:37-38). It is significant that the last invitation of the Bible is to drink: "Whosoever will, let him take the water of life freely" (Rev. 22:17).

The Brazen Serpent. Ever since Satan used the serpent's body to tempt Eve, the serpent has been symbolic of evil. On one occasion (Num. 21:6), because of their complaining, "the Lord sent fiery serpents among the people; and they bit the people: and much people of Israel died." When they repented, the Lord told Moses to erect a serpent of brass upon a pole, symbolizing sin judged and put to death. "And it came to pass that if a serpent had bitten any man, when he beheld the serpent of brass, he lived" (Num. 21:9). This was a type of Christ, who "bare our sins in his own body on the tree" (1 Pet. 2:24). Jesus himself said: "As Moses lifted up the serpent in the wilderness, even so must the Son of Man be lifted up: That whosoever believeth in him should not perish, but have eternal life" (John 3:14-15).

Each of the above types has been treated only in the sketchiest fashion, and the analogies between model and prototype could be greatly expanded over the summaries given above. Similarly, numerous other important types could be added. The water from the rock (1 Cor. 10:4), the Passover supper (1 Cor. 5:7), Melchisedec (Heb. 7:1-3), the rejected stone for the temple (Matt. 21:42-44), the firstfruits (1 Cor. 15:23), the high priest (Heb. 7:26-27), and many others are available for further study.

In addition to the definite spiritual value inherent in the study of the Old Testament shadows of New Testament truths, it is clear that they also add still further to our list of Christian evidences. The unity of doctrine and analogies of detail which they exhibit between the Old and New Testaments can only be rightly explained in terms of a single Author for the whole Bible.

Selected books for further study:

Fairbairn, Patrick. 1989. *Typology of Scripture*. Grand Rapids, MI: Kregel Publications. 918 p.

Habershom, Ada R. 1959. *The Study of the Types*. Grand Rapids, MI: Kregel Publications. 240 p.

Harrison, James. 1994. *The Pattern and the Prophecy*. Peterborough, Ontario: Isaiah Publications. 399 p.

Kinney, LeBaron W. 1939. *The Greatest Thing in the Universe*. New York, NY: Loizeaux Brothers. 211 p.

Lang, G.H. 1955. *The Parabolic Teaching of Scripture*. Grand Rapids, MI: Wm. B. Eerdmans Publishing Co. 400 p.

Marsh, F.E. *The Structural Principles of the Bible*. Fincastle, VA: Bible Study Classics.

Morris, Henry M. 1978. *That You Might Believe*. Westchester, IL: Good News Publ. Co.

Rimmer, Harry. 1938. *Internal Evidence of Inspiration*. Grand Rapids, MI: Wm. B. Eerdmans Publishing Co.

Saphir, Adolph. *Divine Unity of Scripture*. Grand Rapids, MI; Kregel Publications. 376 p.

Chapter XVI

Alleged Bible Contradictions

In spite of all the Bible's claims and the innumerable evidences of its inspiration, skeptics continue to reject it as the authoritative Word of God. Whatever may be the real underlying reasons for this attitude, the expressed excuses often center on the so-called contradictions in the Bible.

Indeed, if there really are contradictions in the Bible, our belief in plenary verbal inspiration would be difficult to maintain. God the Holy Spirit would not contradict himself.

There is no doubt, however, that it is easily possible to find a great number of *apparent* discrepancies in the Bible. Critics have been discovering and exploiting these for many generations. Most of these problems have been explained and reconciled long ago by conservative scholars, but the answers are commonly ignored and the same old supposed contradictions continue to be paraded by such critics.

Reasons for the Discrepancies

Since the Bible is indeed the inspired Word of God, and since there really are many of these superficial contradictions, it seems evident that God must actually have had reasons for allowing them in the Scriptures. We have already looked at much evidence that the very words of the Bible are divinely inspired and, if so, this can only mean that even those words which seem to create problems of this kind must be there for some good reason.

Certain possible reasons can be suggested. In the first place, the existence of so many apparent discrepancies certainly disproves the notion of collusion or intentional deception on the part of the writers. If it so happened that everything was in perfect agreement and this agreement between Moses and Isaiah, between Paul and Peter, between Matthew and John was all very obvious, right on the surface as it were, then skeptics would immediately seize on this as evidence of collaboration or forgery. Real people, separated by great spans of time or distance, simply do not write of their own volition in concert such as this, and perfect agreement would naturally generate suspicion. The apparent contradictions of the Bible, therefore, first of all serve the purpose of refuting this kind of objection.

But, furthermore, they also stimulate Bible study! God desires and commands us to study the Scriptures (2 Tim. 2:15), and there are few motives which can so stimulate us to diligently search the Scriptures as that of trying to find the answer to a problem or the solution to a difficulty. The Bible-believing Christian cannot be satisfied with the easy answer that the discrepancies are merely reflections of the fallibility of the human writers of the various books. He knows that these writers, being men, were fallible, and that their writings do manifest their respective backgrounds and viewpoints, but he also knows their writings were simultaneously guided by the Holy Spirit. Therefore, he is confident that, since the Holy Spirit is God and God does not contradict himself, the superficial disagreements of the Bible must invariably exhibit a deeper agreement which reveals in greater measure the full counsel of God. Consequently, the desire to find these broader and deeper truths in the Bible, manifesting in greater majesty the full purposes of God, is a strong incentive to systematic, in-depth study of the Word. And this is good!

When, in such a case, the solution finally is actually found, the Christian experiences a strengthening of his own faith in God's Word and of his love for the Lord, such as few other experiences can give. This must, therefore, constitute yet another reason why God has allowed these superficial problems and contradictions in His Word. Only a diligent and careful student of the Holy Scriptures can really understand the joy of discovery (comparable perhaps to finding a rich vein of gold in a great rock) and the instant response of thankful praise which such an experience generates.

But such motivation and such experience relate only to one who already either believes or is willing to believe the Bible. The apparent contradictions of the Bible also serve the contrary purpose of exposing the rebellious hearts of unbelievers. A person may either use such passages as justification for his unbelief or as stimulation to faith, and his response merely reveals what manner of person he is. On the one hand, there are those "which in an honest and good heart, having heard the word, keep it and bring forth fruit with patience" (Luke 8:15). On the other hand, there are those "which stumble at the word, being disobedient: whereunto also they were appointed" (1 Pet. 2:8). The Word of God, and the one who witnesses thereof, is "to the one . . . the savour of death unto death; and to the other the savour of life unto life" (2 Cor. 2:16). A person should examine the way he reacts when he hears about some new problem which somebody professes to have found in the Bible. Does he experience a subtle feeling of release from the restraint of Scripture and of triumph over its proponents? Or does he rest in faith that there is a good solution to the problem and set about to find it? The Bible is a mirror with which one can examine both his own heart and those of others, and this fact is nowhere more clearly revealed than in the reaction triggered by the apparent problems of the Bible.

Methods for Resolving the Discrepancies

Assuming the student really does desire to find a satisfactory solution to an apparent contradiction in the Bible, there are several guide lines which may help in his search. In almost every case, he will find that there does exist at least a possible plausible reconciliation of the problem. His solution may not satisfy the skeptic, but that becomes the skeptic's problem. If he has posed a supposed contradiction in the Bible as a reason for rejecting it, and he then is shown a possible solution which is consistent with all the facts (whether or not that solution can be proved to be the only correct solution), his continued rejection of the Bible merely demonstrates that this supposed contradiction was not his real problem after all. The burden of proof is on him to prove that the proposed reconciliation of the discrepancy is invalid. If he cannot show this, and if he nevertheless continues to reject the inspiration of the Bible, the skeptic openly demonstrates that he is in rebellion against God. His problem is spiritual, not intellectual, and he can no longer hide under a cloak of pseudo-intellectualism. Perhaps this forced confrontation with his own deeper motives can be used by the Holy Spirit to demonstrate to him his own sinfulness and need of cleansing.

To find plausible solutions to the apparent discrepancies in Scripture, one can keep in mind the following suggestions. These are not rigid rules, nor is this an exhaustive list, but they are at least often helpful.

1. Study closely the context of the passage in question. One can indeed prove most anything from Scripture (or any other book, for that matter) by lifting statements out of context. "A text without a context is a pretext." If one examines carefully the circumstances, the reason for writing, the person addressed, the person doing the writing, the time of writing, prior and later developments, and other such factors, he will often find there is a perfectly valid explanation for what may seem to conflict with something written elsewhere under different circumstances and for different reasons. There is no conflict, for example, between Genesis 1:31, where it is said that "God saw everything that he had made, and behold it was very good" and Genesis 6:5, where it is said that "God saw that the wickedness of man was great in the earth, and that every imagination of the thoughts of his heart was only evil continually." The difference in what God saw is explained by the different times and circumstances He was seeing.

2. Take into consideration the legitimate use of parabolic language and figures of speech. Much of the Bible (especially the Book of Psalms, for example) is written in poetry, and the manner of conveying a given truth may be different in poetry than in a straightforward prose narrative. When David speaks of the Lord as his rock (Ps. 28:1), as his shepherd (Ps. 23:1), as his light (Ps. 27:1), and as his shield (Ps. 28:7), these are not contradictory descriptions. God is not literally either a rock or a shepherd or a light or a shield, but, to the believer, He is symbolically all of these and much more. Skeptics make a practice of ridiculing "literalists" by using references of this

type. Actually, the literalist is one who believes the writer said what he *intended* to say, and does not try to intrude some alien figurative meaning of his own into the passage. When the writer clearly intended to convey a real fact by use of some figure of speech, he makes this clear in the context and by his manner of writing. This is true of secular writings, and it is true of the biblical writings. If the Bible scholar will simply try, as best he is able, to read the passage as the writer intended it to be read, he will find this approach will often reconcile any apparent disagreement with other passages.

3. The full truth regarding a particular situation can often be appreciated only if the different aspects of that situation are emphasized separately. Thus, an apparent contradiction between two doctrinal teachings (for example, the classic conflict between the "election" passages of Scripture and the "whosoever" passages) may be merely the surface expressions of two aspects of a much broader concept incorporating all the activities of the infinite God in relation to finite man. Like the blind men, each attempting to describe an elephant he could touch, we may see only a very small portion of the full truth and need to recognize that the apparent paradox may be merely an extension of our own limitations.

4. Some apparent discrepancies can be resolved by a critical examination of the particular translation or version. The doctrine of plenary verbal inspiration applies only to the original autographs, not to any specific translation and not to any specific copied manuscript. When difficulties are encountered, one of the first things to do is to try to ascertain, as closely as possible, whether the translation at hand really is expressing the original words and thoughts of the writer himself. The commandment "Thou shalt not kill" (Exod. 20:13), for example, does not conflict with another commandment in the next chapter, "He that smiteth a man, so that he die, shall be surely put to death" (Exod. 21:12), when one realizes that the word "kill" in Exodus 20:13 actually refers

to murder. As far as copies are concerned, it is possible that copyists' errors may inadvertently have crept into the transmitted text of Scripture, especially in the case of numbers. The "variant readings" of the different manuscripts indeed demonstrate that this was the case. Whereas errors of copying or translation can always be considered as *possible* explanations of apparent difficulties, this explanation only rarely needs to be employed, and then usually only as a last resort unless clear evidence of a positive nature does in some way favor this explanation.

5. The Bible was written for all people, not for scientists and scholars only. Therefore, it frequently employs approximations and everyday terminology, rather than exact quantities and precise scientific notation. When a series of events is narrated, the order may be either chronological or pedagogical, depending on the particular contextual purpose of the passage. The ages of men, durations of reigns, and other such data, are normally rounded off to the nearest year, rather than to months or days, though there are exceptions. Problems that may arise from the use of such popular language are fully explicably in harmony with verbal inspiration in view of the fact that the purpose of the Holy Spirit was to communicate God's Word and truth to man in the precise form that the reader could best understand and utilize.

The above suggestions, while not intended to form a comprehensive guide will normally suffice to lead the conscientious Bible student to a satisfactory solution of most apparent contradictions. The following sections give a few typical examples.

Doctrinal Contradictions

One major class of apparent contradictions in Scripture has to do with doctrinal problems. One writer seems to emphasize a certain doctrinal principle, and another will stress an apparently contradictory principle.

Perhaps the most familiar example is the classic discrepancy between Paul and James on the matter of salvation by faith or works. Paul says: "For by grace are ye saved through faith; and that not of yourselves: it is the gift of God: Not of works, lest any man should boast" (Eph. 2:8-9). James says: "Ye see then how that by works a man is justified, and not by faith only" (James 2:24).

This flagrant contradiction is easily resolved by application of suggestion (3) above, when the full passages in context are considered as in suggestion (1) above. Salvation is by faith, but saving faith inevitably is visibly expressed in works. James says: "I will show thee my faith by my works" (James 2:18). Paul says: "For we are his workmanship, created in Christ Jesus unto good works" (Eph. 2:10). One emphasizes the divine imputation, the other the human manifestation, but both are aspects of the whole truth regarding salvation. If there are no works, there is no salvation, but salvation is not earned by works. Salvation comes first, but if it is genuine, it is evidenced in works.

Another doctrinal difficulty involves God's immutability. According to 1 Samuel 15:29, God "is not a man, that he should repent." Yet in the very same chapter, it was recorded that God has said: "It repenteth me that I have set up Saul to be king" (1 Sam. 15:11). This same conflict between God's unchangeableness and His changeableness recurs in various ways in a number of other Scriptures.

This difficulty is also easily resolved by recognizing that God's "repentance" is necessitated by God's immutability. As God, He cannot change in His attitude toward sin and righteousness, punishing the one and rewarding the other. An unrighteous man deserves and receives the judgment of God, but when the man repents, he is no longer the unrighteous man he was, and God now blesses and rewards him. God has not changed, the man has changed. To the outward appearance, however, God's dealings toward that man have changed. His relationship with that man has indeed changed, but this "changeability" in God's actions is itself the proof of the "non-changeability" of His character. God cannot "repent" in character, but He must and does repent in His actions toward individual men, and that for the very reason that His character "changeth not." It is understood also that God's repentance is really only the *appearance* of repentance, popular language for the purpose of more effectually communicating truth. Since He knows all things, Saul's change did not take Him by surprise. Nevertheless, to the human eye, the change in His dealing with Saul obviously had the appearance of a change of mind toward Saul. Once God had chosen him as king, now he was rejecting him as king. This was the outward appearance of things, but actually there was no *real* change on God's part. His very holiness now required Him to curse the one He had blessed. Otherwise, there really *would* have been a change in the immutable God.

Another apparent contradiction that has often been charged against the Bible has to do with God's visibility or invisibility. The Scripture says: "No man hath seen God at any time" (John 1:18), and also that God dwells "in the light which no man can approach unto, whom no man hath seen, nor can see" (1 Tim. 6:16). Yet it also says: "And the Lord spake unto Moses face to face, as a man speaketh unto his friend" (Exod. 33:11). Jacob said: "I have seen God face to face" (Gen. 32:30), after his experience at Peniel, and there are a number of other instances recorded in the Bible in which men are said to have seen God.

Since God in His essence is spirit (John 4:24) and is omnipresent, "filling all in all" (Eph. 1:23), it is obvious that no finite man can actually see God with physical eyes. If God is everywhere, no one can really see Him as an entity distinct from His surroundings, since He is in those, also. Nevertheless, because He is also omnipotent, He can do all things as well as fill all things. Thus He is able, as and when He chooses, to manifest himself locally and temporally in whatever way He desires. Such a manifestation is called a "theophany." This theophanic presence of God is often identified as "the angel of the Lord" (e.g., in Judg. 6:12, 22; 13:20-22; etc.).

Furthermore, the doctrine of the Trinity recognizes that, though God is one God, He is also in three persons. The Father is "invisible" (1 Tim. 1:17), as is the Holy Spirit, but God the Son manifests God to man. "No man hath seen God at any time; the only begotten Son, which is in the bosom of the Father, he hath declared him" (John 1:18). "For in him dwelleth all the fulness of the Godhead bodily" (Col. 2:9). Whenever God has, in some finite, corporeal way, shown himself to man's physical senses, it has been as the second person of the godhead. Thus, although no man can see God in His omnipresence, many men *have* seen, and all men *shall* see (Rev. 1:7) God as He reveals himself in His only begotten Son.

Ethical Contradictions

There do appear also to be a considerable number of discrepancies of a moral and ethical nature in the Bible. Certain practices are commended or commanded under some circumstances, forbidden and condemned under others.

For example, capital punishment is authorized and even required in Genesis 9:6: "Whoso sheddeth man's blood, by man shall his blood be shed." Yet God's commandment says: "Thou shalt not kill" (Exod. 20:13). It is very clear, however, that the commandment applies solely to *murder*, one man killing another on his own initiative, taking the law as it were into his own hands. This, God forbids. The *government*, however, representing God in maintaining order and righteousness in human societies, has both the authorization and responsibility to enforce capital punishment under the terms established by God. A soldier or an executioner, acting under proper orders, is not breaking this commandment when he represents the governmental authority in carrying out this responsibility.

Many have puzzled over David's relation to God. God said: "I have found David the son of Jesse, a man after mine own heart, which shall fulfill all my will" (Acts 13:22). Yet David was guilty of adultery and, indirectly, of murder, as well as other acts of disobedience. The Bible says: "But the thing that David had done displeased the Lord" (2 Sam. 11:27). God said to David: "Wherefore hast thou despised the commandment of the Lord, to do evil in his sight?" (2 Sam. 12:9).

The changed circumstances explain this apparent contradiction. God by no means excused David's various sins. Rather, He punished him severely because of them. There were grave moral lapses on David's part; nevertheless, David's *heart* toward God was fundamentally right, and that is what God seeks (2 Chron. 16:9) above everything else. This was demonstrated in David's strong faith in God's Word, under the most difficult circumstances (e.g., Goliath, his attempted murder by Saul, the rebellion of his son Absolom, etc.). Even more clearly, however, was it demonstrated in the midst of David's condemnation itself. When most people are caught in an act of sin and are criticized or condemned for it, they respond defensively, in anger or self-justification, if not outright denial. When David was accused, however, he in repentance confessed his sin (2 Sam. 12:13; 24:10), and God forgave him, even though he still had to suffer its consequences. He later wrote: "I acknowledged my sin unto thee, and mine iniquity have I not hid. I said, I will confess my transgressions unto the Lord; and thou forgavest the iniquity of my sin. Selah" (Ps. 32:5). It is not the self-righteous man, but the repentant and humble man, who truly reaches the heart of God.

The so-called "imprecatory psalms" have troubled many people. In these, David and other writers invoke trouble and cursing on their enemies, as well as upon the wicked in general. There are many such passages. One typical imprecation is Psalm 58:6, 10: "Break their teeth, O God, in their mouth. . . . The righteous shall rejoice when he seeth the vengeance: he shall wash his feet in the flood of the wicked." Another is Psalm 6:10: "Let all mine enemies be ashamed and sore vexed: let them return and be ashamed suddenly." Even the souls under the altar, in Revelation 6:10, are said to cry out: "How long, O Lord, holy and true, dost thou not judge and avenge our blood on them that dwell on the earth?"

And yet Jesus said: "Love your enemies, bless them that curse you, do good to them that hate you, and pray for them that despitefully use you, and persecute you" (Matt. 5:44). "And be ye kind one to another, tenderhearted, forgiving one another, even as God for Christ's sake hath forgiven you" (Eph. 4:32).

Two important factors must enter into the proper evaluation of the biblical teaching on vengeance and forgiveness. First, we must remember that vengeance belongs to God (Rom. 12:19) and that it is God's intention to exercise this vengeance in His own good time. Jesus said: "Shall not God avenge his own elect, which cry day and night unto him, though he bear long with them?" (Luke 18:7). Since it is God's will to avenge all injustice and wickedness, especially as exercised upon His own people because of their stand for His Word, and since He exhorts us to pray according to His will (1 John 5:14), it is right to pray that His judgment be visited upon the ungodly.

Second, the Lord also teaches that forgiveness is conditioned upon repentance, both on the divine level and on the human level. "Let the wicked forsake his way, and the unrighteous man his thoughts: and let him return unto the Lord, and he will have mercy upon him; and to our God, for he will abundantly pardon" (Isa. 55:7). The same principle applies on the human level. Jesus said: "Moreover if thy brother shall trespass against thee, go and tell him his fault between thee and him alone: if he shall hear thee, thou hast gained thy brother. But if he will not hear thee, then take with thee one or two more, that in the mouth of two or three witnesses every word may be established. And if he shall neglect to hear them, tell it unto the church: but if he neglect to hear the church, let him be unto thee as an heathen man and a publican" (Matt. 18:15-17).

Thus, even in the ranks of believers, forgiveness is conditioned upon repentance. "Take heed to yourselves: If thy brother trespass against thee, rebuke him; and if he repent, forgive him" (Luke 17:3). At the same time, even though there be no repentance, and therefore no forgiveness, Christians are exhorted to "pray for them which despitefully use you" (Matt. 5:44). Forgiveness without repentance, when God's laws are involved, is as unwarranted in man as it is impossible with God. It is good for Christians to "love your enemies," with that love which earnestly desires their salvation or restoration, but not with a pseudo-"love" which is an excuse for weakness and tolerance of evil.

Finally, with respect to those who are true enemies of God and who, despite prayer and importunity, persist in their hatred of God and His people, it is only expressive of God's own viewpoint, shared by His people through the indwelling Holy Spirit, that the believer may well pray an imprecatory prayer. "Do not I hate them, O Lord, that hate thee? and am not I grieved with those that rise up against thee? I hate them with perfect hatred: I count them mine enemies" (Ps. 139:21-22).

It is not contradictory, therefore, but quite consistent, for a God-fearing man both to pray *for his* enemies and to pray *against* God's enemies. It is good to "turn the other cheek," so long as it is a personal injury to oneself which is involved, rather than a divine principle. It is also right to see and judge, by the indwelling Spirit, men and events in the way God sees them. This no doubt is the biblical meaning of the imprecatory psalms.

Another often-mentioned ethical contradiction has to do

with the story of Jephthah's daughter. Jephthah had vowed that, if God would give him victory over the Ammonites, "Whatsoever cometh forth of the doors of my house to meet me, when I return in peace from the children of Ammon, shall surely be the Lord's and I will offer it up for a burnt offering" (Judg. 11:31). God, of course, in other passages, strongly condemns and forbids the offering of human sacrifices (e.g., Deut. 12:30-31, etc.).

There is no doubt that, if Jephthah actually sacrificed his daughter in the fire, it was a crime, regardless of his vow. The Bible does not say God approved of this vow in any way nor, for that matter, does it say that Jephthah actually carried through the fiery sacrifice, though it does say that he "did with her according to his vow" (Judg. 11:39). The Law did require that, when vows were made, they were to be kept (Num. 30:2).

There is a strong possibility that, instead of dying, however, she was offered as a different kind of sacrifice, remaining a virgin the rest of her life. It is said that she and her companions "bewailed her virginity" (Judg. 11:38) rather than her death. Since she was Jephthah's only child (Judg. 11:34), this meant his entire house would die without descendants, and so was indeed a real sacrifice for both him and his daughter.

Long before, God had honored Abraham's faith by providing him a ram to offer up "for a burnt-offering in the stead of his son" (Gen. 22:13). Perhaps He accepted a similar substitute in Jephthah's case, along with the perpetual virginity of his only child, in satisfaction of his vow (Num. 30:2). This indeed was the very principle of the sacrifice of the firstborn (Exod. 13:2), for which the lamb, slain and burnt with fire, provided an acceptable substitute, with the dedication of the firstborn to God.

Factual Contradictions

Probably the most difficult of the apparent contradictions in the Bible are those which deal with matters of fact, rather than matters of doctrine or practice. Nevertheless, though there may be some that have not been adequately resolved, the great majority of these have been found, when examined closely by conservative scholars, to have satisfactory answers.

One of the most famous of these supposed contradictions is found in the first two chapters of Genesis. The first chapter makes it quite plain that all of the animals had been created before Adam and Eve were created. However, in chapter 2 we are told that "out of the ground the Lord God formed every beast of the field, and every fowl of the air; and brought them unto Adam to see what he would call them" (Gen. 2:19). It thus seems that Adam was already living when the animals were formed.

This problem arises, however, merely from an inadequate translation. There is no difference in the Hebrew between the translation "formed" and "had formed." The context governs the form of the verb rendering. That is, it is quite legitimate to translate the verse: "Out of the ground the Lord God *had formed* every beast of the field." When rendered in this way, the verse offers no contradiction at all to Genesis 1.

Skeptics have also quibbled about whether "the Lord hardened the heart of Pharaoh" (Exod. 9:12) or whether Pharaoh himself "hardened his heart, and hearkened not unto them" (Exod. 8:15). Both statements are true. Pharaoh volitionally hardened his own heart and refused God's command. Yet also *God* hardened his heart by commanding him to do what He knew he would refuse to do, thus compelling him as it were to make his choice of obedience or disobedience.

Another widely acclaimed discrepancy is the problem of Cain's wife. Immediately after Cain murdered his brother Abel (Gen. 4:8), God banished him to the land of Nod, where he "knew his wife . . . and he builded a city" (Gen. 4:17). This is supposed to be a glaring contradiction, since no one else except Adam and Eve were living at that time.

This supposition is unwarranted. The Bible does not say *when* these events took place. Elsewhere it says that Adam "begat sons and daughters" (Gen. 5:4) and that Eve was "the mother of all living" (Gen. 3:20). There was certainly no "pre-Adamic" tribe in the vicinity, since Adam was "the first man" (1 Cor. 15:45, 47). In order for man to fulfill God's command to "be fruitful, and multiply, and [fill] the earth" (Gen. 1:28), it obviously was necessary for this process to begin with the union of one or more of Adam's sons with one or more of his daughters. Such close unions were perfectly safe genetically in the beginning, even though later the accumulation of genetic mutations over many generations would make them sufficiently dangerous so that the actual legal prohibitions against incest (Lev. 18:6) had to be imposed by God.

Thus, Cain either married one of his sisters or a descendant of one of his sisters. Since he, like the other antediluvians, presumably lived for hundreds of years, a large population could easily have developed in the world during Cain's lifetime. God, in fact, specifically protected Cain against being killed by other men (Gen. 4:15), thus assuring him a long life, with ample time to establish his own family and civilization. Centuries later, of course, after the Flood, God instituted the system of human government and capital punishment (Gen. 9:6).

There are many more or less trivial apparent discrepancies in the Old Testament historical books. Except for the question of plenary inspiration, these would be of little concern to anyone. They do, as noted before, help demonstrate the absence of collusion or forgery in the writings. However, it will also be found, on closer examination, that there are always possible and reasonable ways of harmonizing them.

For example, 1 Chronicles 20:5 says that "Elhanan the son of Jair slew Lahmi the brother of Goliath the Gittite, whose spear staff was like a weaver's beam." The parallel passage in 2 Samuel 21:19 says "Elhanan the son of Jaare-oregim, a Bethlehemite, slew *the brother of* Goliath the Gittite, the staff of whose spear was like a weaver's beam." The contradiction arises from the fact that the words "the brother of" have been supplied by the translators, appearing in italics in the King James Version. Thus, Samuel says Elhanan slew Goliath, whereas the Chronicler, who wrote later, says he slew the brother of Goliath. Liberal scholars have discredited the story of the slaying of Goliath by David on the basis of that verse in Samuel.

One possible solution to this problem would be to assume there were two giants named Goliath, one of whom was slain by David. The other was then slain by Elhanan, who also slew his brother. There were two Elhanans of Bethlehem (2 Sam. 23:24), so why not two Goliaths of Gath? It is more likely, however, that the translators were perfectly correct in interpolating "the brother of" in 2 Samuel 21:19, as the more explicit and complete reference in 1 Chronicles 20:5 indicates plainly that Elhanan slew Goliath's brother, rather than Goliath himself. It has been argued very effectively by Old Testament scholars that the apparent discrepancy in this case with 2 Samuel 21:19 arose by a copyist's error in the latter. One other possibility, with some support in Jewish tradition, is that Elhanan was another name for David and Jair another name for Jesse. In any case, there is certainly no *proof* of a contradiction.

Numerous discrepancies have been imagined in the accounts of the life of Christ found in the four Gospels. Several of these have been discussed in previous chapters — the two genealogies in Matthew and Luke, the apparently different reports of the Sermon on the Mount, the two accounts of the temptation of Christ, the events at the Resurrection, and others. The differences are always superficial, with an underlying harmony which testifies to both the sincerity of the writers and the factuality of their testimonies.

One particular discrepancy, over which skeptics have made a great deal of fuss, is the question of the superscription placed on Jesus' cross at the crucifixion. These are listed as follows:

Matthew 27:37	"This is Jesus the King of the Jews"
Mark 15:26	"The King of the Jews"
Luke 23:38	"This is the King of the Jews"
John 19:19	"Jesus of Nazareth, the King of the Jews"

These are all slightly different in wording, and yet obviously refer to the same inscription. Actually, as John tells us (John 19:20), there were *three* inscriptions, in Hebrew, Latin, and Greek, and it is possible they were each slightly different, since the essential statement in each case would be simply "The King of the Jews," giving the charge under which He was being executed. Matthew would be likely to record the Hebrew inscription, Mark the Latin, and John the Greek, considering the readers for whom they were writing. Luke perhaps combined them. Or, possibly, the complete inscription was "This is Jesus of Nazareth, the King of the Jews," and each writer only recorded a portion of it. He would still be perfectly correct then in what he *did* record, since he did not claim to give the *complete* superscription.

Although this chapter could be expanded indefinitely, we have at least considered the major alleged contradictions of the Bible and suggested ways for resolving them. No matter what additional discrepancies might be suggested from time to time by the liberals, we are confident that satisfactory explanations can always be found if we study them carefully and empathetically. The Bible does not contradict itself, and still stands as the fully authoritative and verbally inspired Word of God.

Selected books for further study:
Arndt, William. 1932. *Bible Difficulties*. St. Louis, MO: Concordia Publishing House. 117 p.
Arndt, William. 1926. *Does the Bible Contradict Itself?* St. Louis, MO: Concordia Publishing House.
DeHoff, George W. 1950. *Alleged Bible Contradictions*. Murfreesboro, TN: DeHoff Publications. 303 p.
Haley, John W. 1975. *An Examination of the Alleged Discrepancies of the Bible*. Boston, MA: Estes and Lauriat. 473 p.
Torrey, R.A. 1907. *Difficulties and Alleged Errors and Contradictions in the Bible*. Chicago, IL: Moody Press. 125 p.
Young, Edward J. 1990. *Thy Word is Truth*. Grand Rapids, MI: Wm. B. Eerdmans Publishing Co. 287 p.

Chapter XVII

The Bible and Science

Introduction

Two widespread and very harmful misconceptions about the relation of science and the Bible are prevalent. One, very common among skeptics and unbelievers, is that the Bible is an antiquated religious book, filled with scientific fallacies and mistakes reflecting the naive cosmology of the primitive tribes of the Near East. The other misconception is widely held by professing Christian people, namely that the Bible is a book of true religion dealing solely with spiritual subjects and that, where it seems to touch on matters of science and history, it must be interpreted spiritually or allegorically rather than literally. The watchword of this school of thought is: "The Bible is not a book of science, but of religion."

The latter position appears to hold the Bible in higher repute than the former, but this is only superficial. If, whenever the Bible deals with matters of objective fact, capable of confirmation or refutation, it is assumed to mean something else than what it actually says, then the end-result is the same as if the reader frankly charged it with factual blunders. Furthermore, one must have a strange kind of faith if he can believe what the Bible says about salvation, eternal life, heaven and other spiritual truths (which neither he nor the Bible writer could check out for themselves) when he at the same time believes the Bible is wrong about practical matters of science and history, objective facts which do lend themselves to empirical investigation.

Either the Bible is wholly reliable on every subject with which it deals, or it is not the Word of God. The man who thinks he can winnow the wheat from the chaff in Scripture, passing judgment on which portions he will and will not believe, actually is claiming divine wisdom for himself, becoming his own authority, his own Word. He may as well write his own Bible. The same could be applied to one who allows any other man or group of men to decide for him what he can or cannot believe.

The real truth of the matter is that the Bible indeed is verbally inspired and literally true throughout. Whenever it deals with scientific or historical matters of fact, it means exactly what it says and is completely accurate. When figures of speech are used, their meaning is always evident in context, just as in other books. There is no scientific fallacy in the Bible at all. "Science" is *knowledge*, and the Bible is a book of true and factual knowledge throughout, on every subject with which it deals. The Bible *is* a book of science!

The Bible Account of Creation and the Basic Principles of Science

Obviously, the Bible is not a scientific handbook filled with tables and equations. If it were this kind of a book of science, it would quickly go out of date; any standard scientific textbooks or handbooks must be frequently updated or else replaced, and the Bible is not at all restricted in this way.

Nevertheless, the Bible *does* contain all the basic principles upon which true science is built. These principles do not pass out of fashion and have always been valid. They were recorded in Scripture long before scientists learned them through their scientific research.

Science seeks to understand and describe the nature of the universe and all its components, the processes that take place therein, the nature of life and all living creatures, and especially the character and meaning of human life. Commonly, the various sciences are, for convenience, grouped into the physical sciences, the life sciences, and the social sciences, although obviously every field of scientific study is related in some way to every other field.

Science is concerned, first of all, with the fact that the universe does exist and that things do happen there. It must deal, therefore, with those *things* (matter) and the *happenings* (energy). However, there must also be a matrix *in which* (space) and *during which* (time) those things can happen. It is difficult to separate, of course, between the "things" and the "happenings." Each necessarily involves the other and complements the other, so that matter-energy could be considered, as it were, a unitary phenomenon occurring everywhere in space and time.

The universe, therefore, in essence must be a *continuum* of space, time and matter-energy. No one of the three can exist without the other. Therefore, the entire continuum must have existed simultaneously from the beginning.

This fundamental truth is taught explicitly in the very first verse of the Bible, which is the foundation of everything else. "In the beginning [time], God created the heaven [space] and the earth [matter]" (Gen. 1:1). The foundation verse of the Bible thus yields the foundational fact of science!

The first "thing" that "happened" was a vast energy "conversion," a portion of God's limitless power being converted through the process of *creation* into the space-mass-time tri-universe which reflects His own godhead (note Rom. 1:20). In a sense, perhaps, we might think of the universe as being a sort of materialization of the thoughts and purposes of God. The Father is the omnipresent background of all things, reflected in the stretching-out of space; the Son is the omnipotent Creator, reflected in the manifestation of His creation in mass and energy; the Spirit is the omniscient interpreter in the experience of all things, reflected in the passage of time.

Space and time were evidenced initially by the appearance of an aggregation of elemental matter, "without form" (unstructured) and "void" (no life) (note Gen. 1:2). No manifestation of energy was yet present (thus "darkness") and all matter was in suspension or solution in a vast and formless mass of water (the "deep") (see also 2 Pet. 3:5).

But if things were going to happen on the earth, then energy would also have to be present, not only as locked up within the structure of matter but also in form immediately available for the "work" of causing things to happen. Therefore, the spirit of God immediately began to "move (that is, *vibrate*[1]) upon the face of the waters." From this omnipotent vibrating energy source began to flow out energy waves — waves of heat and sound and magnetism, as well as water waves. Thus, the

---

[1] The Hebrew word means "shake" or "flutter" and thus exactly parallels our modern technical term "vibrate."

created universe was *energized*, and the processes of the cosmos activated in proper order.

Most important of all, waves of Light began to spread out over the unformed earth. The first spoken Word of God issued forth: "Let there be light" (Gen. 1:3). This was specifically the *visible* part of the light spectrum, since it was clearly set over against the previous darkness. "God called the light day, and the darkness He called night." This light emanated from a distinct source, since there henceforth ensued a cyclical succession of days and nights. The necessary rotation of the earth on its axis also began at this time, evidently another response to the "moving" energy of the spirit of God. Possibly the light source was also this same vibrating energy of God, centered somewhere out in the heavens above the material earth. Or possibly the light waves were created in transit, as it were, from the light sources which were not actually to be organized until later.

The presence of visible light, of course, also implies the simultaneous presence of ultra-violet and infra-red light and, therefore, indeed of the entire electro-magnetic energy spectrum. The entire complex of energetics, the energy which sustains all the processes of the cosmos, is thus implied in this primal command of the living Word with the moving Spirit.

Both energy and matter were now present in the space-time framework. However, if "things" were now going to start "happening," some orderly system must be established to govern the relationships of the components of matter to each other, of the phenomena of energy to each other and of the interaction of matter and energy. These relationships are identified by modern scientists as the three basic types of "force fields": gravitational forces, electro-magnetic forces, and nuclear forces.

It is significant that these three forces, which embrace all other forces commonly associated with physical phenomena, all "act at a distance." Even so-called "contact forces" (e.g., tension, compression, shear, etc.) actually are electro-magnetic forces operating at the molecular and atomic levels.

But how can forces "act at a distance"? Nobody knows. Scientists can describe mathematically how the force of gravity acts, but they do not know why. They same is true of the electro-magnetic forces and, even more, of the nuclear forces.

There is no better answer than, simply, "the power of God." As far as gravity is concerned, the Scripture says, enigmatically, He "hangeth the earth upon nothing" (Job 26:7). The nuclear and electro-magnetic forces are summarized by saying that He is "upholding all things by the word of his power" (Heb. 1:3). There is no better scientific explanation.

Thus the fundamental aspects of the universe are delineated in outline form in the first verses of the Bible, and these are fully in accord with the observations of modern science (although not with all the varied speculations of many scientists). We have already seen, in chapter 9, how this fundamental triunity of space, matter and time reflects the triunity of the godhead, such that all processes of nature — everything that "happens" — continually bear witness in their very dimensional structure to the Creator who upholds them.

The establishment of the earth's original atmosphere ("the firmament"), its lithosphere ("the dry lands"), its hydrosphere ("the waters below the firmament"), and its former protective envelope of water vapor ("the waters above the firmament") took place on the second and third days of creation. Although a number of evolutionary theories have appeared attempting to describe on a naturalistic basis the pre-organic development of the earth, none has been successful. No other planets have the type of lithosphere, hydrosphere, and atmosphere possessed by the earth; only the earth is capable of sustaining life, in any higher form at least. The formation of these basic components of earth's structure by the direct energizing acts of God is the only adequate way of accounting for them.

The same is even more necessarily true of the biosphere, the complex world of plants and animals inhabiting the earth. According to Genesis, plant life was created on the third day, animal life in the hydrosphere and atmosphere on the fifth day, and animal life on the dry land on the sixth day.

This is not the place to discuss the theory of organic evolution, which attempts to explain the origin and development of every type of plant and animal on a purely naturalistic basis, except to mention that it is fundamentally an anti-theistic theory, designed to relegate God to only a secondary role in creation or even to eliminate Him altogether. It has been notably unsuccessful in demonstrating any mechanism competent to produce a transmutation of one kind into another. Ten times in the first chapter of Genesis does the phrase "after its kind" or "after their kind" appear, stressing the intended permanence of each basic kind of plant or animal (though allowing for variation within the kind), and all firm scientific evidence to date confirms that this is a fundamental law of nature.

In the atmosphere of evolutionary philosophy that pervades modern society, it seems strange at first that Genesis 1:14-19 should describe the creation of the sun, moon and stars on the fourth day of creation, when the earth had been created on the first day and even clothed with vegetation on the third day. Nevertheless, it is really the most logical and scientific point of view.

The earth is absolutely unique in the universe, so far as we know scientifically, as an abode for life. The space program has shown rather conclusively (although this was obvious without the space program) that there is no higher form of life anywhere in the solar system except on earth. There is no observational evidence that any other star in the universe has a planet like Earth. The evolutionist reasons, of course, that, with so many other stars in the universe, some of them must have developed planetary systems and some of these planets must have developed environments suitable for life, and so life must have evolved at various other points throughout the universe.

But this kind of reasoning is wishful thinking, not science. Science deals with observational, experimental evidence, of which there is absolutely *none* indicating other inhabited worlds or even habitable worlds. At best this argument is statistical in nature, but this kind of statistics applies only to randomized data. It thus presupposes that the universe and its components (including earth and life) have all arisen by random processes out of primeval chaos. This assumption, of course, begs the question. Not only does the Word of God teach that the earth was specially *designed* for man, but the earth itself, with its uniquely suitable environment, proclaims the same thing.

The earth, therefore, as implied in Genesis 1:1, was the original material component of the space-mass-time continuum created by God. It comprised all the necessary atomic elements and particles for all processes and materials which would be utilized in any aspect of the physical universe. These fundamental entities are called "the dust of the ground," and it was out of these that even living flesh was to be made, along with the water which was uniquely available on earth (note Gen. 2:7, 9, 19).

The sun and moon were created specifically for the earth and its inhabitants, as "lights" (literally "light-holders") to serve thenceforth as physical bearers of the basic "light" which had been emanating from an unknown source during the first three days. As incidental corroboration of the independent origin of the earth, moon, and sun may be mentioned the strong indications from the lunar landings data that the moon's structure is drastically different from that of the earth. The moon did not come out of the earth, nor did the earth come out of the sun. Each was created independently by God for its own function, and there is no fact of observational science which indicates otherwise. Each of the eight planets and their eighty or more satellites is uniquely different from all the others.

On the fourth day of creation, God "made the stars also" (Gen. 1:16). The stars, though much larger than the earth, are much simpler in structure than the earth, being composed mostly of hydrogen and helium. Complexity rather than size is the indicator of position in the hierarchy of God's creative design, and the earth is quite appropriately placed at the head of the list, with the stars only of incidental significance as they serve the earth "for signs, and for seasons" (Gen. 1:14) and "to give light upon the earth" (Gen. 1:17).

Theories of stellar and galactic evolution, as taught by modern cosmologists, are speculative only. As long as man has been observing the sky, the stars have stayed absolutely the same. As the Scripture says, "one star differeth from another star in glory" (1 Cor. 15:41). No two stars are alike and there is unending variety in the stars and galaxies, but there is no slightest evidence that they are in any kind of evolutionary flux. The exact purpose God may have had in creating such variety in the heavens (other than for man's fascinated appreciation of their beauty) must wait for manifestation in the ages to come, when "they that be wise shall shine as the brightness of the firmament; and they that turn many to righteousness as the stars for ever and ever" (Dan. 12:3).

The Laws of Thermodynamics and the Genesis Record

Once the universe has been created, its processes were designed to operate in an orderly fashion. All the different phenomena of nature and life were to be sustained by the three forces controlling the interactions between and among units of matter and energy. No further creation was contemplated for the present, since "God ended his work which he had made" (Gen. 2:2).

This complete cessation of creative activity has been inadvertently recognized by modern science in its formulation of the First Law of Thermodynamics, the Law of Conservation of Mass-Energy. This is the most universal and certain of all scientific principles, and it states conclusively that, so far as empirical observation has shown, there is *nothing* now being created anywhere in the known universe.

This is a principle that is stated in various ways in Scripture, and actually seems broader than the formal statement of the Law of Energy Conservation.

> The thing that hath been, it is that which shall be; and that which is done is that which shall be done; and there is no new thing under the sun. Is there any thing whereof it may be said, See, this is new? it hath been already of old time, which was before us (Eccles. 1:9-10).

This obviously does not preclude new combinations of elements (e.g., a new house, a newborn babe, etc.) and so evidently refers to the impossibility of creating any "new thing," a new element of matter or energy or a new form of life.

> That which hath been is now; and that which is to be hath already been; and God requireth that which is past (Eccles. 3:15).

This principle of the completeness of creation applies also to the various kinds of plants and animals, so that no new "kind" can be generated from some existing kind.

> God said, Let the earth bring forth grass, the herb yielding seed, and the fruit tree yielding fruit

after his kind, whose seed is in itself, upon the earth: and it was so (Gen. 1:11).

This is the first mention in the Bible of *seed*, the marvelous mechanism by which God assures the continuance of each form of life *after its kind*. Each organism *whose seed is in itself* is a mute but eloquent witness against the age-long scientific belief in "spontaneous generation" and "transmutation of species." Modern genetic research, with its amazing insights into the pre-programmed "genetic code" of each organism (the intricately structured molecular system which is designed to transmit hereditary "information" and to assure the continuance of the specific kind), has strongly confirmed, though unwillingly, this primeval divine injunction. There is an illuminating New Testament commentary on this:

> That which thou sowest, thou sowest not that body that shall be, but bare grain, it may chance of wheat, or of some other grain: But God giveth it a body as it hath pleased him, and to every seed his own body. All flesh is not the same flesh: but there is one kind of flesh of men, another flesh of beasts, another of fishes, and another of birds (1 Cor. 15:37-39). Can a fig tree ... bear olive berries? either a vine figs? (James 3:12).

Now the principle of conservation states not only that nothing is being created, but also that nothing is being destroyed. This fact is also clearly stated in Scripture, long before modern science discovered it, even though it might superficially seem contrary to common experience (e.g., destruction by fire, etc.). Note such Scriptures as the following, among others:

> Thou hast made heaven, the heaven of heavens, with all their host, the earth, and all things that are therein, the seas, and all that is therein, and thou preservest them all (Neh. 9:6).

> Lift up your eyes on high, and behold who hath created these things, that bringeth out their host by number ... for that he is strong in power; not one faileth (Isa. 40:26).

> I know that, whatsoever God doeth, it shall be for

> ever: nothing can be put to it, nor any thing taken from it: and God doeth it, that men should fear before him (Eccles. 3:14).

> Every good gift and every perfect gift is from above, and cometh down from the Father of lights, with whom is no variableness, neither shadow of turning (James 1:17).

> The heavens and the earth, which are now, by the same word are kept in store (2 Pet. 3:7).

> And he is before all things, and by him all things consist (literally "are sustained") (Col. 1:17).

> Who being the brightness [literally "out-radiating"] of his glory, and the express image of his person and upholding all things by the word of his power (Heb. 1:3).

Thus the principle of conservation of mass and energy, which embraces everything in the physical universe, was anticipated and elaborated in Scripture long ago. Since everything that exists and everything that happens is included in this sustaining principle, we are continually experiencing His power. He is "not far from every one of us: for in him we live, and move, and have our being" (Acts 17:27-28).

There is also, of course, a Second Law of Thermodynamics. This is the law of increasing entropy or disorder. This also is a firmly proved, universal law of science, which governs all processes and to which there is no known exception. Although mass-energy is not now being annihilated, it *is* running down, always becoming less "available" for the "work" of maintaining the processes of nature. According to the implications of the Second Law, the whole universe is inexorably heading toward an ultimate state of randomness and disorder, of maximum probability. Its total energy will still be the same, but will be in the form of uniform, randomly distributed, heat energy, incapable of performing any more work. All processes will cease and the universe will be "dead."

God will not die, however! "With [Him] is no variableness, neither shadow of turning" (James 1:17). The word "turning" in this verse is the word *trope* in the Greek, from which we derive our English word "entropy," meaning "in-turning." God, the source of all energy, is certainly not himself subject to the law of increasing entropy.

It seems, in fact, very unlikely that God would create the universe with such a built-in death sentence. At the end of the creation period, it is recorded that "God saw every thing that he had made, and, behold, it was very good" (Gen. 1:31). How could everything be very good, if everything was doomed to die before it began?

The answer can only be that this was *not* the way God created the world. Death is an intruder, not an inhabitant. "Sin entered into the world, and death by sin" (Rom. 5:12).

"In the day that thou eatest thereof thou shalt surely die" (Gen. 2:17). Adam was not subject to death as originally created, but warning was given that should he cut himself off from the out-radiating power of the Word of God by disobedience to that Word, the principle of death would at once begin to work in his members. And, since he was given dominion over all creation, the whole world would likewise be brought under this reign of death by Adam's defection.

"Cursed is the ground for thy sake," God told Adam (Gen. 3:17). The very ground, the dust of the earth, the basic elements, all were brought under the principle of decay and death, of increasing entropy, because of one man's disobedience.

There is no other scientific explanation for the Second Law. Science knows that entropy increases, but it does not know why. "For the [creation] was made subject to vanity, not willingly, but by reason of him who hath subjected the same in hope. Because the [creation] itself also shall be delivered from the bondage of corruption into the glorious liberty of the children of God. For we know that the whole creation groaneth and travaileth in pain together until now" (Rom. 8:20-22).

The "bondage of corruption" is, literally, the "bondage of decay." This is the great Adamic curse on the whole creation, with everything subject to "vanity," or "futility."

Since the curse of decay and death, or increasing entropy, was not a part of the original creation, the principle of conservation must have originally extended to "order" as well as mass and energy. The total entropy, as well as energy, of the universe, must have been a constant.

Such a system is now very hard to visualize, accustomed

as we are to living in a world of increasing entropy. In a world of constant entropy, presumably homes and automobiles and clothing would always remain as new as when they were purchased. Every machine and process would operate at 100 percent efficiency and, in fact, it would be quite possible to design perpetual motion machines if needed. Whenever frictional forces were needed in connection with specific processes, the heat so generated would not be lost but would be convertible to some other form of useful work. Perhaps, through some conversion process now lost, it would be converted back into some other form of electro-magnetic energy, possibly to assist in the process of photosynthesis by which plants would grow.

When fruits and vegetables or other plants were consumed by men and animals, any waste products resulting would not be wasted, but fully converted into useful chemical energy for the soil or other natural uses. Since plants have no conscious life, of course, their use as food is not "death" for the plants, but only an energy-conversion process. All natural cycles — the carbon cycle, the nitrogen cycle, the hydrologic cycle, *et al.* — would always remain in perfect balance with the increasing number of men and animals on the earth. There would thus be no pollution of air or land or water, since all processes would maintain a worldwide "steady-state" balance.

Disease-producing organisms — bacteria, viruses, parasites, *et al.* — evidently were not created with this as their intended function. Neither were animals which are now carnivorous originally created as carnivores. "To every beast of the earth, and to every fowl of the air, and to every thing that creepeth upon the earth, wherein there is life, I have given every green herb for meat" (Gen. 1:30). The plant kingdom presumably did not include weeds and noxious plants.

The extent of the great curse was thus far-reaching. Definite physiologic changes took place among plants which led to the production of "thorns and thistles" (Gen. 3:18). Possibly related changes took place in the animal kingdom which led to the production of fangs and claws and the gradual development of carnivorous appetites. Bacteria and parasites left their first estate, whatever it was, and began to accelerate the decay process in other organisms. The whole creation — physical, biological, social — began its long descent into the dust of death, "groaning and travailing together in pain until now."

This Second Law is alluded to in numerous Scriptures. Nearly always it is set over in these passages in contrast to the non-entropic nature of the life of God and those who have been redeemed from the curse through faith in Christ. Note the following tabulation:

Scripture	Dying Things	Undying Things
Psalm 102:25-27	Heaven and earth	God
Psalm 103:14-17	Man	God's Mercy and righteousness
Isaiah 40:28-31	Young men	Those who wait on God
Isaiah 51:6	Earth and its inhabitants	God's salvation
Hebrews 12:26-28	Earth and heaven	God's kingdom
1 John 2:17	World and its lusts	Those who do God's will
Matthew 24:35	Heaven and earth	Christ's words
Psalm 37:35-37	Wicked men	Upright men
1 Peter 1:24-25	All flesh	Word of God
Romans 8:21-22	Whole creation	Children of God

Before concluding this discussion of the Second Law, it is well to note that it will be in effect only temporarily. It is an intruder, and will be banished once the great work of redemption has been consummated by Christ. The "new heavens and new earth" (Isa. 65:17; 66:22; 2 Pet. 3:13; Rev. 21:1) will be established by the creative power of God once again. All the age-long effects and evidences of sin and death will be purged out and the earth and its environs made new again.

In the new earth, a number of characteristics of the present earth are listed as banished forever. These are:

"No more curse"	Revelation 22:3
"No more death"	Revelation 21:4
"No more tears"	Revelation 21:4
"No more sorrow"	Revelation 21:4
"No more crying"	Revelation 21:4
"No more pain"	Revelation 21:4
"No more regrets"	Isaiah 65:17
"No more exile"	Isaiah 65:22

"No more trouble"	Isaiah 65:23
"No more hurting"	Isaiah 65:25
"No more destruction"	Isaiah 65:25
"No more decay"	Isaiah 66:22
"No more unrighteousness "	2 Peter 3:13
"No more sea"	Revelation 21:1
"No more temple"	Revelation 21:22
"No more night"	Revelation 21:25
"No more sinners"	Revelation 21:27

Thus far we have noted that the most basic truths and principles of science not only are in full harmony with Scripture, but that they were anticipated in Scripture thousands of years before scientists formally recognized them. There are a host of other Scriptures that allude to various details of specific sciences.

Scientific Allusions in Scripture

The Bible abounds with references to nature and natural processes, and thus frequently touches on the various sciences. Those who say the Bible is not a book of science have not read it very attentively.

The writers, of course, do not attempt to formulate these statements in the terminology of a modern chemical or biological treatise. They use everyday language comprehensible to all readers, describing the phenomena in simplest terms. Nevertheless, they are always amazingly accurate, even when tested by the most vigorous scientific requirements. The so-called scientific mistakes of the Bible are not mistakes at all, nor do they have to be allegorized or explained as cultural accommodations or conventionalities.

Before looking at the alleged errors, however, let us note some of the anticipatory scientific insights in Scripture. It would take an entire book to discuss these in detail, so each will only be listed as a key phrase, with pertinent Bible reference. Even then, the list is only a sampling of the many such passages that might be cited.

Science	Phenomenon or Process	Scripture
Hydrology	Hydrologic cycle	Ecclesiastes 1:7; Isaiah 55:10

	Evaporation	Psalm 135:7; Jeremiah 10:13
	Condensation Nuclei	Proverbs 8:26
	Condensation	Job 26:8; 37:11,16
	Precipitation	Job 36:27-28
	Run-off	Job 28:10
	Oceanic reservoir	Psalm 33:7
	Snow	Job 38:22; Psalm 147:16
	Hydrologic balance	Isaiah 40:12; Job 28:24-26
Geology	Principle of isostasy	Isaiah 40:12; Psalm 104:5-9
	Shape of earth	Isaiah 40:22; Psalm 103:12
	Rotation of earth	Job 38:12, 14
	Gravitation	Job 26:7; 38:6
	Rock erosion	Job 14:18-19
	Glacial period	Job 38:29-30
	Uniformitarianism	2 Peter 3:4
Astronomy	Size of universe	Isaiah 55:9; Job 22:12; Jeremiah 31:37
	Number of stars	Jeremiah 33:22; Genesis 22:17
	Variety of stars	1 Corinthians 15:41
	Precision of orbits	Jeremiah 31:35-36
Meteorology	Circulation of atmosphere	Ecclesiastes 1:6
	Protective Effect of atmosphere	Isaiah 40:22
	Oceanic origin of rain	Ecclesiastes 1:7
	Relation of electricity to rain	Jeremiah 10:13
Biology	Blood circulation	Leviticus 17:11
	Psychotherapy	Proverbs 16:24; 17:22
	Biogenesis and stability	Genesis 1:11, 21, 25
	Uniqueness of man	Genesis 1:26
	Chemical nature of flesh	Genesis 1:11, 24-27; 3:19; 1 Peter 1:24-25
Physics	Mass-energy equivalence	Hebrews 1:3; Colossians 1:17
	Source of energy for earth	Genesis 1:14, 17; Psalm 19:6
	Atomic disintegration	2 Peter 3:10
	Radio waves	Job 38:35

Alleged Scientific Mistakes

As mentioned earlier, the so-called errors in the Bible will invariably be found, on closer examination, to be accurate scientific insights. A good example is the often repeated charge that the Bible teaches that p (the ratio of the circumference of a circle to its diameter) is only 3, when it ought to have been given as 3.1416.

This interesting observation is based on the statement in 1 Kings 7:23, in the description of Solomon's Temple: "And he made a molten sea, ten cubits from the one brim to the other; it was round all about, and his height was five cubits; and a line of thirty cubits did compass it about."

Thus, Solomon is charged with saying that the circumference of a 10-cubit diameter circle is only 30 cubits, when it should be 31.416 cubits. However, those who make this charge are themselves being unscientific.

It is quite important that the scientist be accurate in his statement of the *precision* of measurements. To assure this, he uses a conventional technique called "significant figures." It is only correct to state a measurement to the number of significant figures warranted by the accuracy of the measurement. Thus, if the number is stated as 10 cubits, it is accurate only to two significant figures, and might actually be anywhere between 9.5 cubits and 10.5 cubits. If the writer had said it was 10.0 cubits, it would supposedly be accurate to three significant figures.

Similarly, the 30-cubit circumference is accurate only to two significant figures, and might really be anything from 29.5 cubits to 30.5 cubits. It served no purpose to specify the dimensions to a higher degree of precision than two significant figures, and so the writer simply rounded them off.

For example, say the actual measurement of the diameter gave 9.67 cubits, accurate to three significant figures. This should then be multiplied by 3.14, which is p to the third significant figure. The result is 30.4 cubits, to the third significant figure. There cannot properly be more significant figures in a product than in any of its factors. It may not even be this accurate (if the diameter had been 9.665 cubits), multiplying by 3.14 would give 30.3 cubits instead of 30.4. It is quite common for this reason to retain one more significant figure in each factor than is needed in the product, which is then rounded off to one less significant figure than the factors have.

It would be perfectly proper and scientific, therefore, to round off the diameter of 9.67 cubits and the circumference of 30.4 cubits to 10 cubits and 30 cubits, respectively. The writer of 1 Kings was more scientific than his critics.

Another scientific mistake is supposed to be the biblical picture of a flat earth with four corners. The Bible gives no such picture, however. There is a reference in Revelation 7:1 to the "four corners of the earth," as translated in the King James translation. However, the phrase, "four corners," in the Greek, means simply "four quarters," and is so translated in Revelation 20:8 and other Scriptures. It obviously refers to the four directions as measured from the particular focal point of interest, and is the standard convention used in surveying and mapping to this day.

A similar convention, used by astronomers and cartographers even today, is that of measuring the motions of the sun, moon and stars relative to the earth. Thus, when Joshua said: "Sun, stand thou still upon Gibeon" (Josh. 10:12), and when David said: "[The sun's] going forth is from the end of the heaven, and his circuit unto the ends of it" (Ps. 19:6), they were not just writing of the "pre-scientific" notion of a fixed earth and an orbiting sun. All motion is relative motion, and the sun is no more "fixed" in space than the earth is. Since all heavenly bodies are in motion relative to each other, it is impossible to specify their *absolute* velocities.

The scientifically correct way to specify motions, therefore, is to select an arbitrary point of assumed zero velocities and then to measure all velocities relative to that point. The proper point to use is the one which is most convenient to the observer for the purposes of his particular calculations. In the case of movements of the heavenly bodies, normally the most suitable such point is the earth's surface at the latitude and longitude of the observer, and this therefore is the most "scientific" point to use. David and Joshua are more scientific than their critics in adopting such a convention for their narratives.

A different type of scientific mistake has been ascribed to Moses in Leviticus 11:6, when he forbade the Israelites to eat "the hare, because he cheweth the cud, but divideth not the hoof." The objection is that the hare does *not* chew the cud. This is evidently a mistake, but not a mistake by Moses. The translators should not have translated the Hebrew *arnebeth* by "hare." The arnebeth is evidently now extinct, so that we do not know exactly what it was, but at any rate, it was not a hare.

Other examples could be discussed, but the above are typical of the more frequently cited scientific "errors" in Scripture. In every case, it can be shown that the Bible is scientifically accurate. The problem sometimes results from an inaccurate translation, or from the use of figures of speech, but more commonly simply results from the critics' carelessness in treating scientific speculations as if they were scientific facts. This especially is the case with the two most important alleged scientific errors in Scripture, the records of creation and the Flood. These two events are treated separately later.

One important point should be made in closing this section. The Bible stands alone among the religious books of antiquity in the matter of scientific accuracy. All other ancient religious writings abound in obvious scientific fallacies, and no one would think of writing a study on modern science in relation to, say, the Babylonian or Hindu or Greek sacred books. Only the Bible can make a serious claim to being in accord with modern science, and this is in itself a witness to its uniqueness.

Miracles

A special class of scientific problems in Scripture has to do with the biblical miracles. Skeptics frequently charge that such-and-such a miracle — the long day of Joshua, the ten plagues of Egypt, the deliverance of Jonah from the whale, the preservation of the three Israelites in Nebuchadnezzar's furnace, the passage through the Red Sea, and many others — are scientifically impossible. Often, Christians have tried to avoid this issue by proposing some naturalistic process which might have been involved in the supposed miracle.

But all scientific objections to miracles merely beg the question. To say miracles are scientifically impossible is one thing, but to say they cannot happen is another thing. We might even define a miracle as an event which is scientifically impossible, but which happens anyhow. Science, after all, is merely the accumulated body of empirical knowledge of how things are normally observed to happen.

Science necessarily is empirical and the body of this empirical knowledge is continually growing. Nevertheless, it would be presumptuous folly to say we know everything about how things must happen in the world. If God is the Creator and sustainer of all natural processes, then He can surely change those processes when and as He wills. Thus, to say that miracles are impossible is simply to deny God. Anti-supernaturalism is atheism.

Thus the investigation of alleged miracles must be a historical investigation rather than a scientific investigation. *Did* the miracle occur — not *could* it occur? Is there adequate testimonial evidence that it really happened? Whether or not we can explain it in terms of known scientific processes is beside the point. In some cases, indeed, it may well be possible to understand a particular miracle as a providential timing of a natural phenomenon or as a particularly wide fluctuation of a statistically varying natural process. In many others, it may be quite impossible to explain the miracle on such a quasi-naturalistic basis as this at all, without doing unwarranted violence to the record thereof.

The point is that a miracle does not need to be explained. It needs to be verified as actually having occurred, but that is all. Its miraculous nature is specifically intended as a testimony that supernatural power is present in the event, and it cannot be denied simply by the dictum that science precludes miracles!

The investigation of an alleged miracle should take approximately the following form:

1. Are the witnesses and reporters of the event reliable observers and trustworthy narrators?
2. Is the event something which is unique, not reproducible by specific techniques employed by or at the direction of human practitioners?
3. Does the event contradict the basic laws of nature, especially one of the two laws of thermodynamics?
4. Does the testimony associated with the event honor the Lord Jesus Christ and support the clear teaching of the Scriptures?

If the answer to any one of the above questions is either "no" or "not sure," then there is reason to question whether a real divine miracle has indeed taken place, at least a miracle requiring the *direct* power of God. If all the answers to the questions are unequivocally "yes," then there is adequate reason to believe "that indeed a notable miracle hath occurred" (Acts 4:16).

If the answer to the first two questions is "yes," but the third and fourth are answered "no," then there may be reason to consider the possibility of a satanic, rather than a divine miracle. Since creative power would be necessary to set aside the laws of thermodynamics, it seems impossible that demonic powers could produce this kind of miracle, though they might be able to counterfeit creation by some hallucinatory deception in the mind of the beholder.

If the first, second, and fourth questions can be answered "yes," but the third is "no," then a secondary type of miracle can still be considered, one which does not require God to set aside His basic laws, but does involve an unusual statistical deviation in a natural process or an unusually timed occurrence of a natural process. This type may be called a *miracle of providence*, whereas a miracle involving a special creation of matter or energy or order, thus superseding one or both of the two laws of thermodynamics, is a *miracle of creation*.

All of the biblical miracles satisfy the criteria at least for providential miracles, and many of them for creative miracles, with the exception of certain events which are clearly implied to be satanic miracles. There is no reason to doubt, for scientific or other reasons, that any of the miracles recorded in Scripture actually took place in just the way they are described.

Selected books for further study:

Ackerman, Paul D. 1990. *In God's Image After All*. Grand Rapids, MI: Baker Book House. 101 p.

Andrews, Edgar H. 1986. *Christ and the Cosmos*. Phillipsburg, NJ: Presbyterian and Reformed Publishing Co. 128 p.

Barnes, Thomas G. 1993. *Science and Biblical Faith*. Norcross, GA: Creation Research Society. 191 p.

Bartz, Paul. 1990. *Creation Moments*. Minneapolis, MN: Bible-Science Association. 260 p.

DeYoung, Donald B. 1989. *Astronomy and the Bible*. Grand Rapids, MI: Baker Book House. 146 p.

_____. 1949. *Science and the Bible*. Grand Rapids, MI: Baker Book House. 110 p.

_____. 1992. *Weather and the Bible*. Grand Rapids, MI: Baker Book House. 162 p.

Gish, Duane T. 1992. *Dinosaurs by Design*. Green Forest, AR: Master Books. 88 p.

Morris, Henry M. 1984. *The Biblical Basis for Modern Science*. Grand Rapids, MI: Baker Book House. 516 p.

Mulfinger, George, ed. 1983. *Design and Origins in Astronomy*. Norcross, GA: Creation Research Society. 151 p.

Nelson, Ethel R., and C.H. Kang. 1979. *Discoveries in Genesis*. St. Louis, MO: Concordia Publishing House. 139 p.

Taylor, Charles V. 1984. *The Oldest Science Book in the World*. Assembly Press. 182 p.

White, A.J. Monty. 1985. *Wonderfully Made*. Phillipsburg, NJ: Presbyterian and Reformed Publishing Co. 128 p.

Wilder-Smith, A.E. 1968. *Man's Origin, Man's Destiny*. Wheaton, IL: Harold Shaw Publishers. 320 p.

Williams, Emmett L., ed. 1981. *Thermodynamics and the Development of Order*. Norcross, GA: Creation Research Society. 141 p.

Chapter XVIII

Scientific Fallacies of Evolution

Evolution and Science

One of the strangest paradoxes in the history of science is that a theory so barren of scientific proof as evolution could be so universally accepted as scientific fact. Science is *knowledge* and the essence of the scientific method is experimentation and observation. Since it is impossible to make observations or experiments on the origin of the universe, the origin of the earth, the origin of life, or the origin of any of the basic kinds of organisms (not to mention the origin of consciousness or the soul), the very definition of science ought to preclude use of the term when talking about evolution. Nevertheless, by far the most influential argument against the Bible is the widespread belief that science has proved evolution and, therefore, disproved the biblical account of creation. Consequently, this chapter will be devoted solely to showing that evolution is itself unscientific.

A more comprehensive definition of natural science might be as follows:

> The systematic observation and correlation of present physical relationships and natural processes involving the properties of matter, the forces of nature and the phenomena of life.

A key word is "present." Scientists may speculate about the past or the future, but they can only *observe* the present. The study of origins — whether by creation or evolution — is necessarily outside the scope of science in its real sense.

Therefore, the theory of evolution is not science but is rather a belief, a religious philosophy of origins. This becomes more evident when men try to define evolution. The classic definition of Sir Julian Huxley is typical.

Evolution in the extended sense can be defined as a directional and essentially irreversible process occurring in time, which in its course gives rise to an increase of variety and an increasingly high level of organization in its products. Our present knowledge indeed forces us to the view that the whole of reality *is* evolution — a single process of self-transformation.[1]

Anything which embraces the "whole of reality" is intrinsically philosophical or religious. Huxley was probably the world's leading evolutionist, but we should also, to be fair, let another prominent evolutionist speak, this time Theodosius Dobzhansky, a prolific author on evolutionary genetics, second only to Huxley in influence in the 20th century.

Evolution comprises all the stages of the development of the universe: the cosmic, biological, and human or cultural developments. Attempts to restrict the concept of evolution to biology are gratuitous. Life is a product of the evolution of inorganic nature, and man is a product of the evolution of life.[2]

In the minds of its leaders, therefore, evolution is a complete cosmology, purporting to explain the origin, meaning and destiny of all things. As such, one would suppose that careful *scientists* would acknowledge its fundamentally religious character. Instead, they insist it is a fact of science! Huxley said:

The first point to make about Darwin's theory is that it is no longer a theory, but a fact. No serious scientist would deny the fact that evolution has occurred, just as he would not deny the fact that the earth goes around the sun.[3]

---

[1] J.R. Newman, ed., "Evolution and Genetics," *What is Science?* (New York, NY: Simon and Schuster, 1955), p. 278.

[2] Theodosius Dobzhansky, "Changing Man," *Science*, vol. 155 (January 27, 1967), p. 409.

[3] Sol Tax (ed.), *Issues in Evolution* (Chicago, IL: University of Chicago Press, 1960), p. 41.

We might then ask Dr. Huxley whether we could at least consider evolution to be God's method of creation. If we have to accept all his views about natural selection, the evolutionary history of the geologic ages and all the rest, would it not then be all right to believe that God started and maintains the process? Sir Julian's answer was adamantly negative.

> Darwinism removed the whole idea of God as the creator of organisms from the sphere of rational discussion. Darwin pointed out that no supernatural designer was needed; since natural selection could account for any known form of life, there was no room for a supernatural agency in its evolution. . . . I think we can dismiss entirely all idea of a supernatural overriding mind being responsible for the evolutionary process.[4]

This opinion was expressed at the great Darwinian Centennial Convocation in 1959 at the University of Chicago, where Huxley was keynote speaker and where all the world's leaders (and even more followers) of evolutionary thought had gathered to pay homage to Darwin's memory. Huxley's opinion is important in its own right, of course, but the most significant point about this particular statement is that none of the assemblage of evolutionists who heard it raised any question about it. It is evident that neither the leaders of evolutionary thought nor those of their followers with courage to question their pronouncements were theistic evolutionists. The latter speak with more authority than they possess when they tell Christians to accept evolution as God's creative process.

The Testimony of Present Relationships

True science, as we have noted, traditionally included particularly the systematic study of present relationships between different natural systems and phenomena. With respect to the organic world and the possibility of evolution, we are especially interested in the various extant kinds of organisms and their individual characteristics with respect to each other.

These relationships have been codified in the form of a classification system originally developed by the great naturalist, Carolus Linnaeus (1707-1778). In this system, the basic

---

[4] *Ibid.*, p. 45.

unit is the *species*, which is conceived as a more-or-less stable reproductively isolated group of plants or animals usually incapable of inter-breeding with other species. Linnaeus was a strong believer in the original creation of the Genesis "kinds," and he attempted to delineate these "kinds" in his species concept (recognizing, of course, that he could be corrected as to the true identification of particular species). Within the species, however, wide variation is possible, and many particular varieties may be developed by different breeding processes. Although such varieties may be developed as reproducing units with distinctive characteristics, these are all still freely inter-fertile and, if left alone for several generations to mix freely, will tend to revert back to the ancestral species.

Perhaps the most familiar example is the dog. Everyone is familiar with the great number of different dog varieties which exist — St. Bernards, poodles, bulldogs, dachshunds, etc. Superficially, these varieties are very different from each other. Yet they are all one species and freely interbreed. There is little doubt that they all developed from one original type, probably the wolf, just a few thousand years ago.

This type of variation is, of course, quite common in most species. It does not take millions of years, but only a few generations, following fixed genetic laws.

However, the evolution of new species is a different matter altogether. The higher categories of organisms especially — genera, families, orders, phyla, etc. — are not based on empirical breeding studies at all, but on arbitrary criteria of classification. It is gratuitous to regard these higher units as merely various stages of evolutionary relationship, since no observational evidence has ever shown that genera evolve into families, and families into orders, and so on.

This is not to say that the species unit is the same as the biblical "kind" and thus incapable of change. No one knows exactly what the "kind" (Hebrew *min*) may have represented, and neither do modern taxonomists agree on exactly what a species is. If and when a so-called "species" is shown conclusively to change into another "species," it therefore does not in any respect show that one "kind" can evolve into a different "kind." More likely it shows that the original "species" was only a "variety" or "sub-species." The species is, after all, strictly an arbitrary category devised for taxonomic convenience and may or may not have permanent validity in a given case. The same is even more true for genera and higher categories.

Even at the species level, arbitrary though it is, real evolutionary change is almost never observed, especially among higher animals. In all human recorded history, no one has even observed true speciation taking place. Nevertheless, practically all modern creationist scientists would accept it as having probably occurred in the past, within limits.

The fittest individuals usually dominate the population and, therefore, they tend to perpetuate their own kind and the species' characteristics remain fixed. Only the less-fit individuals might be isolated from the group and, therefore, become capable of establishing a new variety in a natural-selection context. The new variety (or possibly "species") would have *de*-volved, rather than evolved upwards into a more complex and vigorous form, and would quite likely eventually be eliminated altogether.

The basic kinds of organisms, therefore, are quite stable, if left to interbreed in a natural environment. If the habitat changes, or the population is forced to move to a new habitat, the variational and adaptive potential resident in its fundamental genetic system may permit it to change its characteristics to some degree, but it will still be in essence only a new variety of the same basic kind. If the habitat should revert back to its former nature, then very likely the species will also revert back to its former characteristics. The frequently cited example of the *peppered moth* in England, which altered its white color to gray with the coming of the industrial revolution and its smoky atmosphere, is a good case in point. The basic kind was still unchanged — the moth was still the same species of moth. Natural variation with selection is thus a conservative process, enabling a given kind of organism to be preserved even though the nature of its habitat has been altered.

Artificial selection may increase the number of varieties considerably, as in the case of the dog and cat, but it cannot produce a new kind. And if this is true of scientifically controlled selection processes, how much more true must it be of the random processes associated with natural selection. The latter is very clearly a *conservative*, rather than *innovative*, mechanism.

The clear testimony of all present relationships in the organic world is, therefore, one of stability of the basic kinds (or "stasis") with provision for ample variation within the kinds. There are evidently unbridgeable gaps between the kinds, and no amount of variation has made even a start at crossing these gaps.

On the other hand, if evolution is the true cosmology, the gaps should not be there at all. That is, if all organisms have really descended by slow development from a common ancestor, under the same conditions in the same world, they ought now to be all inter-connected by imperceptible gradations from one form into another. In fact, it would be impossible to develop any kind of classification system at all, since we could never tell where one kind of organism stopped and the next began.

Furthermore, if evolution were really true, there also should now be continuous flux in the organic world, instead of the very stable species that we actually encounter. Cats should be turning into dogs and dogs into sheep, since all are supposed to share the same ancestral gene pool, and evolutionary transformism is supposed to be the basic law of nature. The actual stability of the kinds and the conservative character of the genetic processes, on the contrary, give powerful testimony that the evolutionary assumption is false. Modern evolutionists are abandoning the concept of gradual change in favor of what they call punctuationism. That is, a species may remain unchanged for 100,000 generations, say, and they suddenly evolve into a new species by some as-yet-uncertain process.

In the real world, however, tales about fishes and frogs turning into men are found only in books of fables and fairy tales; they have no proper place in books purporting to be textbooks of science. When a beast is transformed into a man in a moment, it is called magic; when the beast becomes a man over a million years it is called evolution. The factor of *time* becomes the fairy's magic wand! It seems that for a person to believe in evolution, he must "turn away [his ears] from the truth and shall be turned unto fables" (2 Tim. 4:4).

As a matter of fact, the only reasonable and adequate explanation for the actual relationships that do exist in the organic world is that of special creation. The many similarities that are obviously present among different organisms are easily explained in terms of creation by the same Designer. It is appropriate and logical that He would create similar structures for similar functions. Both men and fishes have eyes, for example, since both must see, but fishes have gills and men have lungs because they must live in different environments.

Thus, similar anatomy or similar embryonic structure or similar blood sera or similar DNA does not at all mean a common evolutionary ancestor but rather a common Creator. Furthermore, the *differences* are explained only by creation, and never by evolution. "God giveth it a body as it hath pleased him, and to every seed its own body" (1 Cor. 15:38).

The Testimony of Present Processes

Another part of the definition of science involves the study of present natural processes. The question is, simply, whether these processes tend to develop new and higher kinds or tend to preserve existing kinds.

The processes of biologic reproduction are intricate and marvelous processes. There seems not the slightest scientific evidence that they could ever have developed by innate evolutionary processes. Be that as it may, the most obvious fact about the reproductive process is that it always produces an organism of the same kind as its parents. Cats invariably beget cats and acorns produce oak trees. Like begets like; this is the basic law of biogenesis. There is, of course, wide variation possible within the reproductive process, as already discussed. No two individuals are alike, even with the same parents. Nevertheless, in normal reproduction all characteristics of the offspring are already present implicitly in the parents. The assemblage of genes in the parental chromosomes includes all the possible factors, either dominant or recessive, which might possibly find expression in the progeny.

The phenomenon of "recombination" is considered to be very important in evolution. Ernst Mayr, in fact, recognized a key principle of variation, a principle still valid today.

> Recombination is by far the most important source of genetic variation, that is, of material for natural selection.[5]

However, as the term itself implies, recombination of genes does not introduce something new but only rearranges factors that are already present. Undoubtedly, it accounts for much of the variation leading to new adaptive varieties, but it

---

[5] Ernst Mayr, *Populations, Species and Evolution* (Cambridge, MA: Harvard University Press, 1970), p. 103.

could never develop new and more complex kinds.

Another process of biologic change is that of *hybridization* (introgression). However, this process is likewise of no real significance in evolution. Hybrids are nearly always sterile, for one thing. More importantly, it is obvious that hybridization is merely another form of recombination, with nothing present in the hybrid form that was not already present in one or both parents. In fact, it is possible that in most cases the parents themselves may have been merely stable varieties of the same original kind.

In order to generate real novelties, some mechanism must be available which can add a structure or feature which was not present in either parent, even in recessive or latent form. Apparently the only possible mechanism is that of mutation. The effectiveness of mutations, therefore, is critical in the evaluation of evolution as a possible explanation of biologic origins.

A mutation is a definite change in the genetic structure, either in the structure of the chromosomes or in the structure of the DNA molecule (the latter essentially the same as a "gene" mutation). A mutation, or a combination of mutations, will definitely have a heritable effect on the organism and, if it proves to be beneficial, will presumably be preserved by natural selection.

The necessity of mutations for evolution to occur is stressed by Ernst Mayr, who is by any accounting, as the Agassiz professor of zoology at Harvard, still a leading authority on the subject.

> It must not be forgotten that mutation is the ultimate source of all genetic variation found in natural populations and the only new material available for natural selection to work on.[6]

Similarly, Francisco J. Ayala, one of today's top geneticists, has said:

> Mutation provides the raw materials of evolution.[7]

---

[6] Ernst Mayr, *Populations, Species and Evolution* (Cambridge, MA: Harvard University Press, 1970), p. 102.

[7] Francisco J. Ayala, "Teleological Explanations in Evolutionary Biology," *Philosophy of Science*, vol. 37 (March 1970), p. 3.

In order for mutations, followed by recombination and gene flow in populations, to be truly effective in evolution, however, they should be positive in character. That is, most mutations should be such as to increase the viability and organization of the plant or animal experiencing them, since evolution presumably has resulted in an overall upward progress in the evolutionary chain.

In actuality, however, mutations are nearly always harmful. Ayala pointed out that:

> Mutations are random changes of the hereditary material. . . . Most new mutations are in fact harmful to the organism.[8]

Another leading geneticist, Christopher Wills, says:

> Some mutations are "beneficial," that is, the individual in whom they are expressed is better able to adapt to a given set of environmental circumstances. The large majority of mutations, however, are harmful or even lethal to the individual in whom they are expressed. Such mutations can be regarded as introducing a "load," or genetic burden, into the pool.[9]

Not only are most mutations harmful; they are also quite rare. According to Ayala:

> It is probably fair to estimate the frequency of a majority of mutations in higher organisms between one in ten thousand, and one in a million, per gene per generation.[10]

This basic stability, of course, is obvious from the fact that the kinds (even the species) generally have remained the same all during recorded history. Since mutations are relatively rare events, and since practically all of those that do occur are harmful to the host organism, one must be very credulous to

---

[8] *Ibid*. Ayala is at the University of California at Davis.

[9] Christopher Wills, "Genetic Load," *Scientific American*, vol. 222 (March, 1970), p. 98. Professor Wills is at the University of California at San Diego, and was one of the team of evolutionary scientists that tried in 1990 to get the ICR Graduate School closed, since it was teaching science in terms of creation instead of evolution.

[10] F.J. Ayala, *Philosophy of Science*, p. 3.

believe that the marvelous integrated complexity of the entire organic world has been developed through this process. Yet this is the best evolutionary explanation there is!

The faith of evolutionists in their philosophy is profound. This faith persists despite the complete lack of positive evidence and the abundance of evidence against it. Ayala revealed the usually unspoken reason for this insistence.

> Darwin substituted a scientific teleology for a theological one. The teleology of nature could now be explained, at least in principle, as the result of natural laws manifested in natural processes, without recourse to an external Creator or to spiritual or nonmaterial forces. At that point biology came into maturity as a science.[11]

It is commendable that this remarkable statement of faith was qualified with the reservation "at least in principle." Darwinism may be a fine theory "in principle," from the perspective of those who wish to avoid "recourse to a Creator," but it does suffer when compared with facts.

Somehow, evolutionists have confidence that the infrequency and harmfulness of mutations are sublimated by time and natural selection. Even though mutations are very rare and good mutations very, *very* rare, geologic time is long and selection pressures will weed out all the bad mutations and gradually accumulate enough good ones to produce evolution. Creationists are considered unreasonable and unscientific to ask for actual scientific evidence that this is really taking place, since it requires millions of years in which to demonstrate itself.

That is, since it is impossible to *prove* that trans-specific evolution takes place, we consequently ought to accept it as a proved fact of science! Or, putting it another way, since it is possible for us to conceive of a way in which it *might* have taken place, therefore, it must be true, even though we can never observe it experimentally. With this profound insight, biology has, so to say, "come into maturity as a science."

Modern research has shown that earlier ideas about gene mutations and their preservation or elimination by natural

---

[11] Francisco J. Ayala, "Teleological Explanations in Evolutionary Biology," *Philosophy of Science*, vol. 37 (March 1970), p. 2.

selection were over-simplified. The effect of any one mutation on the fitness of the adult organism is now believed too small to have any significant selection value. The effects of many mutations at various "loci" must all combine to produce any significant change in the total organism in its reaction to the environment. Furthermore, a particular mutation may have various effects on various aspects of the life of the organism. As Mayr noted:

> Every character of an organism is affected by all genes and every gene affects all characters.[12]

This being true, it would seem difficult even to learn very much about any particular gene and its mutations. Furthermore, since it is necessary for many mutations to combine in order to produce any visible effect on the organism, and since most of these are bound to be harmful, it is still more difficult to see how the combined effect could ever be beneficial.

We have already mentioned the concept of the "genetic load," according to which every species is operating under a genetic handicap representing the accumulation of many generations of mutant genes. The very existence of such a concept is proof that the overall effect of mutations on organic species is harmful, not beneficial. If evolution were really produced through mutations, then it is as plain as can be that any mechanism which increases the mutation rate should, in the long run, further advance the evolutionary process.

The alarm continually expressed by evolutionists over mutations in man caused by radiations in the environment is a strong argument that they do not really believe their story. Wills says, for example:

> The most important actions that need to be taken, however, are in the area of minimizing the addition of new mutagens to those already present in the environment. Any increase in the mutational load is harmful, if not immediately, then certainly to future generations.[13]

---

[12] Ernst Mayr, *Populations, Species and Evolution* (Cambridge, MA: Harvard University Press, 1970), p. 164.
[13] Christopher Wills, "Genetic Load," *Scientific American*, vol. 222 (March, 1970), p. 107.

Summarizing, the only known biologic mechanism capable of producing genuine evolutionary novelty is that of mutations, but mutations are very rare and almost always (probably *always*, if understood fully) either neutral or harmful to the organism. The factors of gene flow and natural selection tend strongly toward the conservation of existing kinds, not the introduction of new ones. It is obvious that present processes, as actually observed, are *not* processes which tend to develop new and higher kinds of organisms. Rather, they tend to conserve present kinds against the tendency toward decay and disintegration of those kinds. The scientific *facts* always support special creation and repudiate evolution.

The Origin of Life

One of the key factors in evolution is that of the origin of life. Evolutionists believe that the first living organisms were developed naturally, by innate processes, from non-living chemicals. The purpose of evolutionary theory is to explain the development of all things without divine intervention, and so by all means God cannot be invoked at this most critical point in the theory.

However, "spontaneous generation," as it used to be called, is certainly not occurring in the present world, and even evolutionists agree with creationists on this. In terms of *science*, therefore, there is no such thing as the origin of life. Science deals with present processes, and these do not generate life from non-life, and that is that! The origin of life can neither be observed in present phenomena nor predicted from present phenomena.

The evolutionist, therefore, has to assume that the processes themselves have evolved, and that at some time in the past they could change inert matter into living matter, even though they cannot do it now. For this to be possible, the entire terrestrial environment with its hydrosphere and biosphere must have been drastically different from what it is now.

In other words, to explain the origin of life in naturalistic terms, the evolutionist has to assume an atmosphere which does not exist, an oceanic composition which does not exist, and processes which no longer exist, to explain the generation of hypothetical primitive organisms which no longer exist! This is no doubt material for interesting conversation, but it is not science.

There are, of course, many scientists today actively trying to, as it were, "create life in a test tube." Some very brilliant experiments have been made which have thrown some light on how organic chemicals might be synthesized in living systems. Stanley Miller of the University of California at San Diego showed that certain amino acids (which are basic components of proteins) could be generated by discharging electricity through a mixture of methane, water vapor, and ammonia. But this does not prove that amino acids were generated three billion years ago in a primeval soup this way.

Similarly, Sidney Fox at Florida State University showed that under certain artificial conditions, a number of amino acids could be randomly linked together. These "coacervates," as they were called, were supposed to be analogous to protein molecules, though they were, of course, *not* protein molecules. But even if they were, this would not prove that protein molecules ever had actually been formed this way under natural conditions.

Other scientists have been able to make DNA replicate itself, after extracting if from a living cell and placing it in a bath of the four nucleotides which constitute DNA, provided the proper enzymes and other constituents are also present. Whether anything similar had ever happened in the past, without human assistance, is quite unknown. Furthermore, the DNA and enzymes must both be present for the replication to take place, so this type of experiment throws no light on how either component ever came into existence originally.

Others later showed that virus DNA could be made to reproduce outside a host cell, contrary to usual virus behavior, provided again that the proper enzymes were present. A virus, however, is not a living cell, so this experiment has nothing to say about the origin of life, especially considering the fact that both DNA and the necessary enzymes were already available to start with.

Even genes have been synthetically copied, with the presence of proper enzymes. However, this accomplishment, brilliant as it may have been, was not in any sense a "creation of life," or even the "creation of a gene," since both the original gene and the essential enzymes had to be present first.

These and other related experiments no doubt have contributed to the understanding of life processes, and possibly even to future "genetic engineering" know-how, but they have not even approached the true creation of life. The day when men will start with simple inert chemical elements and from them build a living and reproducing cell, without any seeding or catalytic action from other living sources, is still a long way off and probably will never come.

Even if someday, crowning the efforts of hundreds of brilliant and trained scientists spending millions of dollars of tax money, such a synthesis is finally attained, this still will not prove that the random intermingling of inanimate materials and processes produced the same wonderful accomplishment three billion years ago by chance.

Furthermore, even the true synthesis of a living cell would be a very simple thing compared to the manufacture of a many-celled plant, for example, bearing seeds by which to propagate its kind. But even this would be nothing compared to the creation of an animal, with intelligence and consciousness. This consciousness, incidentally (Hebrew *nephesh*) is what the Bible means by *life*. And before man will ever create life of this category, a chipmunk will design and build a digital computer.

To conclude the discussion of this esoteric subject, note the statement of Leslie Orgel, who is everywhere recognized as one of the world's leading authorities on origin-of-life studies.

> It is extremely improbable that proteins and nucleic acids, both of which are structurally complex, arose spontaneously in the same place at the same time. Yet it also seems impossible to have one without the other. And so, at first glance, one might have to conclude that life could never, in fact, have originated by chemical means.[14]

Orgel cannot leave it there, of course, because he is committed by firm faith in total naturalism, to a non-theistic origin of life. At one time, he and Francis Crick (co-discoverer

---

[14] Leslie E. Orgel, "The Origin of Life on the Earth," *Scientific American*, vol. 271 (October 1994), p. 76. Dr. Orgel is on the science faculty at the University of California at San Diego.

of the famous DNA molecule) proposed that life was brought to Earth from some other planet. Currently (1996), he is pinning his hopes on the so-called "RNA" molecule, but he has acknowledged that this idea has little or no evidence to support it.

The Fossil Record

We have noted that the organic relationships and processes in the present world give no support to evolution. There are clear-cut gaps between the various basic kinds of plants and animals, rather than a continuous gradation between them as the evolutionary hypothesis would predict. The processes of biologic reproduction, rather than tending continually to develop new and higher kinds, are very efficient in conserving the present kinds against an innate tendency toward decay and disintegration.

Were it not for the fossil record, the evolutionist would indeed be hard put to show any evidence whatever for evolutionary progress of any significant magnitude. As Stanley says:

> While many inferences about evolution are derived from living organisms, we must look to the fossil record for the ultimate documentation of large-scale change. In the absence of a fossil record, the credibility of evolutionists would be severely weakened. We might wonder whether the doctrine of evolution would qualify as anything more than an outrageous hypothesis.[15]

However, the fossil record turns out to be a very unconvincing witness for "macro-evolution," since it is marked by the ubiquitous absence of any truly transitional forms between different basic kinds of organisms.

Evolution of the higher taxa (including not only classes and phyla, but also orders, families, genera, and most species) has not been observed to occur during the historical period, so it is essential to the evolutionary system that it be supposed to occur during the pre-historic period. The only evidence that exists concerning life in earlier ages is in the fossil record, and,

---

[15] Steven M. Stanley, *Macroevolution: Pattern and Process* (San Francisco, CA: W.H. Freeman Co., 1979). Dr. Stanley, at Johns Hopkins University, is a leading paleontologist, and his book is one of the most widely used references in this field.

therefore, it is mandatory that this record be interpreted as an actual documented account of the history of organic evolution on the earth.

It is felt that since the geologic ages are so long — almost five billion years, in fact — there is ample time for total evolution to have occurred, even if its rate is immeasurably slow right now. The evidence that it has occurred is the supposed change in life forms in the fossils with the advance of geologic time.

The various geologic ages, with their associated fossil indicators, are commonly summarized in what is known as the "standard geologic column," or the "geologic timetable." In this system, life is believed to have evolved from non-life in the Precambrian period, about three billion years ago. The Cambrian period, beginning somewhat over 600 million years ago, marked the emergence of abundant marine invertebrates. Fishes began to appear 100 million years later, in the Ordovician. Amphibians first evolved in the Permo-Carboniferous periods. The Mesozoic Era, from about 250 to about 70 million years ago, was the age of dinosaurs. Mammals and birds became dominant in the Tertiary period, beginning in the Paleocene Epoch following the extinction of the dinosaurs.

Finally, man, in essentially his present form, appeared about one million years ago. With this remarkable record of life preserved in fossil form, evolutionists believe they have adequate evidence of the historical fact of evolution, even though its present mechanisms are obscure.

However, it must be remembered that actual written records go back only a few thousand years. Time durations and biological events earlier than this must be deduced by indirect evidence, not by human observation. The very existence of the geologic ages, as well as their order and their duration, must be based on speculation and arbitrary extrapolation from the present. This system is quite properly open to criticism on this basis alone. In the following chapter, the evidence for the reality of these geological ages will be critically examined.

However, for our immediate purposes in this section, let us assume for the sake of argument the validity of the standard geologic column. That is, life first appeared in the Precambrian, fishes in the Ordovician, and so on, just as assumed by paleontologists.

Even allowing this premise, the fossil record does not show evidence of evolution. The fact that one assemblage of organisms lived in one geologic period and another assemblage of organisms lived in the succeeding geologic period hardly is *proof* that the second evolved out of the first. Indeed the clear-cut gaps in the fossil record between these assemblages and between the various basic kinds of organisms seem to prove exactly the opposite.

For if evolution is really true, and there has been uniformity and continuity of geologic processes over the ages, there ought to be no such gaps. The fossils ought to show continuous intergradations from one kind into another, at least on a statistical basis in relation to the abundance of fossils recovered. But this is not the case.

Furthermore, if evolution is a universal process of nature, and organisms are in a perpetual process of transformation, one would suppose that the forms of life in one age would be completely different from those in another. But so much is this not the case that animals and plants in the present world usually have easily identifiable relatives in the fossil world, often very far back in geologic time.

A prime example of this situation is the earliest and most primitive form of life yet discovered. These are the one-celled organisms found in the Precambrian rocks of southern Ontario, and later found still living today.

> Among single-celled organisms, the discovery, during the past decade, of survivors from a very remote past has been equally remarkable, though here it is partly a matter of finding essentially modern forms as Precambrian fossils. The most remarkable of these, and also one extraordinary form first known as a fossil and then discovered living today, came from the Gunflint Iron Formation of southern Ontario, which is about 1.9 billion years old.[16]

This is not an exceptional case by any means. Numerous types of so-called "living fossils" are known, from all the geological ages, including others even in the Precambrian. This fact is still more obvious if the comparison deals with basic

---

[16] G. Evelyn Hutchinson, "Living Fossils," *American Scientist*, vol. 58 (September-October, 1970), p. 534.

kinds, rather than specific marine species, which are the usual index fossils.

That is, for example, sponges, snails and jellyfish lived in the Cambrian, clams and starfish in the Ordovician, scorpions and corals in the Silurian, sharks and lungfish in the Devonian, ferns and cockroaches in the Carboniferous, dragonflies and beetles in the Permian, pines and palms in the Triassic, crocodiles and turtles in the Jurassic, ducks and pelicans in the Cretaceous, hedgehogs and rats in the Paleocene, rhinoceroses and lemurs in the Eocene, beavers and squirrels in the Oligocene, camels and wolves in the Miocene, horses and elephants in the Pliocene, and man in the Pleistocene. The above are only random listings, of course, and could be considerably expanded.

Except for the many now-extinct animals, such as the dinosaurs, it looks as though the fossil world was not greatly different from the present world. As far as the extinct animals are concerned, it should be pointed out that extinction is not evolution!

If the marine invertebrates of the Cambrian evolved into the fishes of the Devonian, which evolved into the amphibians of the Permian, which evolved into the reptiles of the Jurassic, which evolved into the apes of the Tertiary, which evolved into the man of the present, one wonders why marine invertebrates and fishes and amphibians and reptiles and apes still continue to live together with man in this present world. If natural selection converted the crossopterygian fish into the first amphibian, for example, as evolutionists allege, why didn't natural selection eliminate the crossopterygian fish in the process? How can one have his cake and eat it too?

Though many kinds of animals in the fossil column have become extinct (or at least have not yet been found living in the modern world), there is no indication of how they came into existence. All the basic kinds appear suddenly in the records, with no prior history of gradual development from other simpler kinds. This is particularly true of the complex assemblage of forms in the earliest of the geologic ages.

> The introduction of a variety of organisms in the early Cambrian, including such complex forms of the arthropods as the trilobites, is surprising. . . . The

introduction of abundant organisms in the record would not be so surprising if they were simple. Why should such complex organic forms be in rocks about six hundreds million years old and be absent or unrecognized in the records of the preceding two billion years? . . . If there has been evolution of life, the absence of the requisite fossils in the rocks older than the Cambrian is puzzling.[17]

It would be easy, though tedious, to bring together abundant documentation of the fact that this same absence of transitional forms characterizes the entire fossil record. There are no transitional forms evolving into the first vertebrates, no transitional forms between fish and amphibians, none between amphibians and reptiles, between reptiles and birds, between reptiles and mammals. No fossil has halfway wings or any other incipient structures leading to fully developed functioning structures on new kinds. Some organs have been cited as possible "vestigial organs," but none as "incipient organs."

This universal absence of true transitional forms in the fossils is attested by Tom Kemp, curator of the Oxford University Museum in England, though he himself is another doctrinaire evolutionist.

> As is now well known, most fossil species appear instantaneously in the record, persist for millions of years virtually unchanged, only to disappear abruptly — the "punctuated equilibrium" theory of Eldredge and Gould.[18]

Niles Eldredge at the American Museum of Natural History, and Stephen Jay Gould, professor of paleontology at Harvard University, to whom Kemp refers, have become famous as originators of the theory that evolution proceeds only by rapid "punctuations" in the equilibrium after long periods of evolutionary "stasis," when no change is taking place. The main evidence for this odd theory of evolution, offered in place

[17] Marshall Kay and Edwin H. Colbert, *Stratigraphy and Life History* (New York, NY: John Wiley and Sons, 1965), pp. 102-103.
[18] Tom Kemp, "A Fresh Look at the Fossil Record," *New Scientist*, vol. 108 (December 5, 1985), p. 67.

of the "slow-and-gradual" changes postulated by the previously predominant theory of neo-Darwinism, is the lack of gradual transitions in the fossil record. Stanley, another advocate of the theory (he calls it "quantum speciation") says:

> Evolution happens rapidly in small localized populations, so we're not likely to see it in the fossil record.[19]

It does seem that these modern evolutionists, having abandoned the old Darwinian ideas of gradual change by slow accumulation of beneficial mutations preserved by natural selection, are saying that the main evidence for evolution is that there is *no evidence we can see* — either in the present world or the fossil record of the past!

Gould and Eldredge admit as much (no doubt unintentionally) when they say:

> Nevertheless, contemporary science has massively substituted notions of indeterminacy, historical contingency, chaos and punctuation for previous convictions about gradual, progressive, predictable determinism.[20]

The usual evolutionary explanation today for this phenomenon is, therefore, that each transition took place in a small population of organisms over a small period of geologic time and, therefore, we would be unlikely to find any of the relevant fossils. The evolutionary process thus continues to be elusive, showing no evidence of its existence in the present and no indications of its operation in the past. Therefore, so the argument seems to go, we ought to accept it on faith, otherwise we might have to believe in creation!

In the absence of actual evidence, of course, it is always possible to devise some kind of explanation for anything in terms of some kind of evolution. The concept is very flexible and can be adapted to any situation. If there were an abundance of transitional forms, this would, of course, be cited as strong evidence for evolution. Since there is, however, a profound

---

[19] Steven Stanley, "Resetting the Evolutionary Timetable." Interview by Neil Campbell, *Bioscience*, vol. 36 (December 1986), p. 725.

[20] Stephen Jay Gould and Niles Eldredge, "Punctuated Equilibrium Comes to Age," *Nature*, vol. 366 (November 18, 1993), p. 226.

absence of such forms, this is taken as evidence of *rapid* evolution. Heads, I win; tails, you lose.

Some evolutionists have recognized this peculiar characteristic of evolutionary theory. Although he was a strong evolutionist, Peter Medawar admitted:

> There are philosophical or methodological objections to evolutionary theory. . . . It is too difficult to imagine or envisage an evolutionary episode which could not be explained by the formulae of neo-Darwinism.[21]

But if it is impossible to *falsify* a theory, it is impossible to *confirm* it. There is no test which could be applied to demonstrate whether evolution is true or false. Indeed, the foregoing discussion makes it clear that, even as a scientific "model," evolution fails to fit the facts, without large numbers of secondary qualifying assumptions. The simplest, most logical and most scientific model of origins is still that of special creation.

---

[21] Peter Medawar, *Mathematical Challenges to the Neo-Darwinian Interpretation of Evolution* (Philadelphia, PA: Wistar Institute Press, 1967), p. xi.

Selected books for further study:

Bird, Wendell R. 1984. *The Origin of Species Revisited.* 2 vol. Nashville, TN: Thomas Nelson Co. 1149 p.

Chittick, Donald. 1984. *The Controversy.* Portland, OR: Multnomah Press. 280 p.

Frair, Wayne, and Percival Davis. 1983. *A Case for Creation.* Chicago, IL: Moody Press. 155 p.

Gish, Duane T. 1990. *The Amazing Story of Creation.* Green Forest, AR: Master Books. 112 p.

Gish, Duane T. 1993. *Creation Scientists Answer their Critics.* San Diego, CA: Institute for Creation Research. 451 p.

Gish, Duane T. 1995. *Evolution: The Fossils Still Say No!* San Diego, CA: Institute for Creation Research. 391 p.

Ham, Ken. 1987. *The Lie: Evolution.* Green Forest, AR: Master Books. 168 p.

Lester, Lane P., and Raymond G. Bohlin. 1984. *The Natural Limits to Biologic Change.* Grand Rapids, MI: Zondervan Publishing House. 207 p.

Lubenow, Marvin. 1992. *Bones of Contention.* Grand Rapids, MI: Baker Book House. 295 p.

Morris, Henry M. 1981. *Evolution and the Modern Christian.* Phillipsburg, NJ: Presbyterian and Reformed. 72 p.

Morris, Henry M. 1963. *The Twilight of Evolution.* Grand Rapids, MI: Baker Book House. 103 p.

Morris, Henry M., and Gary E. Parker. 1987. *What is Creation Science?* Green Forest, AR: Master Books. 336 p.

Parker, Gary E. 1994. *Creation: Facts of Life.* Green Forest, AR: Master Books. 215 p.

Remine, Walter J. 1993. *The Biotic Message*. St. Paul, MN: St. Paul Science. 538 p.

Wilder-Smith, A.E. 1987. *Scientific Alternatives to Neo-Darwinian Evolutionary Theory*. Costa Mesa, CA: TWFT Publications. 198 p.

Wysong, Randy. 1976. *The Creation-Evolution Controversy*. Inquiry Press. 455 p.

Chapter XIX

Creation and the Flood

The Biblical Framework of Pre-History

By far the most significant area of apparent conflict between the Bible and science is that which concerns origins. As long as we are dealing with presently observable phenomena, there is no problem. In fact, as discussed in chapter 17, there are numerous descriptions of natural phenomena in the Bible which not only are scientifically accurate, but which were written in the Scriptures thousands of years prior to their discovery and description by modern scientists. The Bible is remarkably accurate as a basic reference book of scientific principles, and is incomparably superior to any other religious book of antiquity in this respect.

However, in its record of special creation and the world-wide Flood, both only a few thousand years ago, there is no doubt that the Bible runs headlong into almost a solid wall of contrary scientific opinion. Most modern scientists flatly reject and even ridicule both stories. They believe instead that the framework of pre-history is structured around *evolutionary uniformitarianism*, the concept that all things have developed into their present form by the same slow, natural processes that function at present, acting over billions of years of time.

Thus there are two contradictory and competing models of origins and early history, the *evolution model* and the *creation model*. These should be considered as scientific "models" rather than theories or hypotheses of science, since neither is capable of being scientifically confirmed or falsified. Creation cannot be studied in a laboratory, since it was completed in the past and is non-repeatable. Evolution cannot be studied in a laboratory, since its assumed mechanisms operate so slowly as to require millions of years for demonstrable results. No experiment can be devised which could, even in principle, demonstrate either creation or evolution to be either true or false. The small variations that *do* occur today (e.g., different breeds of dogs) are compatible with either model. "Horizontal" changes or "downward changes" say nothing at all about the origin of the kinds in the first place.

Nevertheless, the two models can be very effectively compared on the basis of their abilities to correlate and systematize known scientific facts into a meaningful and self-consistent whole. The creation model can do this at least as effectively as the evolution model. In fact, all the direct and obvious "predictions" of the creation model will be found to correspond directly and simply to all the observed facts in the real world.

The evolution model, on the other hand, continually encounters contradictions which require a multitude of auxiliary assumptions and exceptions to be imposed upon its basic formulation. For example, as discussed in the preceding chapter, its assumption that life has evolved from non-life encounters the stubborn fact that life is not evolving from non-life at present; therefore a secondary assumption is made that environmental conditions in the past were drastically different than at present, despite the utter lack of evidence supporting such an assumption and despite the contradiction of this assumption with the evolutionist's first assumption of uniformitarianism. The fact that life is not evolving from non-life at present, however, is exactly and directly what the creation model predicts!

This is only one example. The evolution model encounters similar problems in every aspect; the creation model encounters no such problems. Nevertheless, the great majority of scientists and intellectuals continue to insist that evolution is scientific and special creation is unscientific, apparently merely because the latter requires the direct activity of God and evolution does not!

Now, although the creation model fits the facts of the real world better than does the evolution model, this does not mean that we can "prove" scientifically that creation is true. These great events of the past are non-repeatable and non-observable, and, therefore, are beyond the scope of the scientific method. They are *history*, not laboratory science. To *know* the real truth concerning them (and remember that "science" means *knowledge*), we must rely on the written record of the One who was there! The biblical record of creation, the Flood, and the other events of earth's primeval history is the only real source of certain knowledge concerning them.

When this biblical framework, including the recent special creation of all things in six days, the universal curse on the world because of man's sin, the global hydraulic cataclysm in the days of Noah, and the miraculous linguistic dispersion of the nations at Babel is taken as simple historic truth and used as the basis for correlating all other relevant data from the so-called historical sciences, it will be found uniquely powerful and satisfying, fitting all true facts and correcting all errors.

The Geologic-Age System

The standard system of orthodox historical geology has been entrenched in scientific literature for over 150 years and is the real strength of the evolution model. The idea that the earth is billions of years old and the forms of life on the earth have been gradually changing and increasing in complexity during those vast ages seems to be *prima facie* evidence of evolution and against the Bible. The almost universal indoctrination in this geologic-age concept is beyond question the major barrier against acceptance of the divine inspiration of the Bible and the truth of Christianity. People have numerous moral and spiritual reasons for rejecting Christ, but their main intellectual justification will usually be found, if one probes deeply, in the assumption that the early chapters of the Bible have been proved scientifically false.

The geologic-age system, as presently structured, can be outlined briefly as below:

Time	Event
Eternal past	Existence of matter and/or energy in primal form
About 20 billion years ago	Origin of elements, stars, and galaxies
About 5 billion years ago	Origin of earth and solar system
About 3 billion years ago	Evolution of replicating chemicals (= "life")
About 1 billion years ago	Evolution of multi-cellular life
About 600 million years ago	Evolution of complex marine invertebrates

Time	Event
About 350 million years ago	Evolution of marine vertebrates and land plants
About 250 million years ago	Evolution of amphibians and insects
About 200 million years ago	Evolution of reptiles and flowering plants
About 100 million years ago	Evolution of mammals and birds
About 50 million years ago	Branching of evolutionary ancestors of apes and men
About 3 million years ago	Evolution of modern man

This remarkable outline of the history of the earth and its inhabitants has been so widely accepted that, until recently, anyone who questioned it was considered either ignorant or irrational. It is taught as proven fact in practically every public school and college and even in most religious schools, even though it squarely and clearly contradicts the Bible.

In this form, it obviously seems to be a powerful evidence for evolution. In fact, it is fair to say that this geologic-age system constitutes *the* evidence for evolution, since all other so-called evidences are strictly circumstantial and fit the creation model better than the evolution model. Evolution requires vast amounts of time to produce significant results, and the geologic-age system alone provides the time.

This system of geologic ages is based primarily upon the fossil record found in the sedimentary rocks of the earth's crust. The concept is that the fossil remains found in the rocks occur in the order of increasing complexity with the passage of ages of time. That is, simple fossils occur in old rocks, complex fossils in young rocks.

This supposed order does, of course, *suggest* evolution, though it certainly would not *prove* evolution. Even if the geologic-age system were basically correct, the universal absence of transitional forms between the major kinds of organisms in the fossil record, as discussed in the preceding chapter, constitutes a major barrier to the evolutionary model. Nevertheless, the geologic-age system does provide at least a superficial framework upon which to erect the evolutionary model and there is no doubt that it does constitute its main evidence. The biblical creationist must understand this fact and know how to deal with it if he is to have satisfactory answers in this field.

Accommodationist Theories

Bible students have attempted in various ways, by various exegetical devices, to accommodate the geologic-age system within the biblical framework of history, but further study has shown this to be impossible. In addition to the artificial exegesis required by such theories, they raise more serious scientific problems thān they resolve. That is, by forcing the geologic ages into Genesis, they in effect require the elimination of the evidence on which the geologic-age system is based.

For example, a theory that has been widely taught among fundamentalists for over a hundred years is the so-called *gap theory*, which pigeonholes the geologic ages in a supposed time gap between Genesis 1:1 and 1:2. According to this concept, the earth was devastated with a global cataclysm at the end of these ages, leaving the earth "without form and void," covered completely with water and "darkness upon the face of the deep," as described in Genesis 1:2. Following this cataclysm, the earth was "re-created" in the six days of the creation week of Genesis 1:3-31.

However, one cannot accommodate the geologic ages by destroying their foundation. No "ages" geologist accepts the gap theory for the simple reason that his entire system is built around uniformitarianism, the assumption that there was *no* worldwide cataclysm such as required by the theory. A cataclysm which would destroy the mountains and continents, sliding them into the waters of the deep, and which would propel the multiplied billions of tons of debris and dust into the air required to envelop the earth in total darkness, would necessarily be a cataclysm that would destroy the very structure of the earth's sedimentary crust, with all its fossils. And it is these fossils and these alone which identify and supposedly prove the existence of the geologic ages! The gap theory thus destroys itself.

The *day-age theory*, which has been held even more widely, is really no more help scientifically. There are numerous contradictions (at least 20 serious ones) between the order of evolution in the geologic ages and the order of creation in Genesis. The evolutionary geologist and astronomer certainly would not agree that the initial state of the earth was one of a universal ocean surrounded by total darkness, as described in Genesis 1:2. Nor does he for a moment imagine that this "deep" was in the next age divided into two great deeps, one above and one below the "firmament of heaven" where the birds were to fly, as described in Genesis 1:6-8, 20. And certainly he could not accept the biologically-impossible idea that an abundance of plant life, including even fruit trees, thrived on the earth for a great age (i.e., "day" three) before the earth was receiving any light from the sun, which was set at its task of "giving light on the earth" only on "day" four.

Remember that the geologic ages are identified by their fossils. If the days of creation are to be identified as the ages of geology, the fossils are almost completely out of place. Note the following table:

Creative "Day"	Life forms produced to make fossils
One	None
Two	None
Three	Grass, herbs, fruit trees
Four	None
Five	Fishes, birds, marine invertebrates
Six	Mammals, insects, reptiles, man

The lack of any significant correlation with the fossil sequences in the geologic ages is obvious.

Furthermore, the fossils are found in sedimentary rocks, which are formed primarily by transportation and deposition of sediments by water. This phenomenon first requires erosion of sediments and erosion requires rain — heavy rain. This requirement is flatly refuted by the Genesis record which says there was no "rain upon the earth" during these periods (Gen. 2:5). Without rain there could have been no rocks of terrestrial sediments and, therefore, no land fossils, thus no evidences of these geologic ages! Even many marine fossils are found in land-derived sediments, but the absence of rain would have made them impossible.

There is thus no way the geologic ages can be harmonized scientifically with the Genesis record of creation, regardless of whether or not the Hebrew exegesis will allow "day" to be equated with "age" or a gap to be inserted between the verses. As a matter of fact, however, such equivocal exegesis is itself precluded by the unequivocal commentary on these verses made by God himself in Exodus 20:11.

This important verse is a part of the Ten Commandments,

which were written by God's own hand directly on a table of stone (Exod. 31:18). In a very unique way, therefore, this verse was not only inspired, but actually inscripturated, by God himself. It was given as divine justification for the very rigidly enforced commandment for man to work six days and rest on the seventh day, and thus was meant by God to be plainly understood. "For," God said, "in six days the Lord made heaven, and earth, the sea, and all that in them is."

There is clearly nothing in the universe, therefore, that was made before or after the six days. There could be no leftover fossils or minerals or seeds from any kind of a pre-world, nor are there are parts of the cosmos still being created today. All was done in the six days of creation week. No statement could possibly state this fact more explicitly than this statement.

Furthermore, He says He made everything in six *days*, not six ages, the same kind of days in which man was also to do his work. If man's six days are not commensurate with God's six days, the statement is a *non sequitur*, and words convey no meaning. Furthermore, the Hebrew word for "days" (*yamim*), occurring in plural form as here, always means literal days, never indefinite periods, so far as its Old Testament usage is concerned.

There is one other consideration which makes the geologic ages totally unacceptable theologically, regardless of biblical or scientific attempts at correlation. This is their gigantic, worldwide, age-long testimony to the prevalence of suffering and death in the world during those ages. The very existence of the geologic ages is based on the fossil record, and the very existence of fossils is a testimony of death. Fossils are dead things!

Every geologic "age" from the Cambrian onward is identified by its characteristic fossils. These often occur in great masses, giving evidence of sudden and violent death and burial. Often the fossils give evidence of disease. Often they are contorted and distorted, indicating convulsive attempts to escape the sudden death that was engulfing them. Fossils in many cases testify not only of the extinction of individual lives, but even of whole species and kinds of animals.

A god who would use such wasteful, inefficient, cruel methods in the "creation" of man hardly seems to be the God of power, wisdom, and mercy described in the Bible. Indeed, a god who could in retrospect survey this whole monstrous spectacle of waste and suffering and then pronounce it all "very good" (Gen. 1:31) is more likely devil than god.

The existence of the geologic ages, therefore, is not only incongruous with the biblical record, but even with the very existence of the God of the Bible. The geologic ages and the evolutionary system are essentially synonymous, and one cannot logically accept one of them without accepting the whole package, including the universal prevalence of suffering and death as a basic component of the origin of all things. Consequently, the only legitimate and proper course for a serious Bible-believing Christian to take is to reject and oppose the entire system.

The Rocks and the Fossils

To reject the geologic ages, however, does not mean to ignore the actual data of the geologist. The empirical study of geologic processes, the measurement and identification of rock systems, the classification of fossils, and many other aspects of geo-science are all legitimate and vital scientific concerns, but these data simply need to be studied and correlated in the framework of the creation model.

The fossil-bearing sedimentary rocks cannot, as we have just seen, be attributed either to the creation period or to any hypothetical period before the creation period. Therefore, they must be explained in terms of events *after* the creation period. They speak eloquently of *death*, and the Bible says there was no death in the world until man brought sin into the world (Rom. 5:12; 1 Cor. 15:21), and God imposed the curse on man's dominion (Gen. 3:17; Rom. 8:20-22).

It seems evident, therefore, that at least the major part of the great sedimentary rocks must be attributed to events associated with the great Flood, as described in Genesis 6–9. This was the greatest visitation of death upon the world's inhabitants since the world began. The apostle Peter, describing it, said: "the world that then was, being overflowed with water, perished" (2 Pet. 3:6).

The creation model thus also includes as another major component the global cataclysm of the Deluge. It maintains that the actual facts of geology, including the sedimentary rocks and their fossils, as well as the present structure of the earth's crust and surface features, can be more easily and naturally explained in terms of the Flood than they can in terms of the uniformitarian model. The various rock systems do not represent evolutionary ages at all, but rather diluvial stages.

It is necessary first to emphasize that geologists determine the geologic ages of rocks solely on the assumption of evolutionary relationships between the fossil contents. One might naively suppose there should be some difference in the *physical* character of old rocks from that of young rocks. But this is not so: "The physical-stratigraphical criteria alone . . . are devoid of any generally recognizable geologic time significance."[1]

That is, rocks of any type — limestone, shale, sandstone, granite, basalt, etc. — may and do occur in all geologic ages. Similarly, rocks may be either loose and unconsolidated or hard and indurated and still correspond to any age. They may have any type of structure, any suite of minerals, any combination of petrography, any degree of tilt or fracture, any type of inorganic contents, and none of these determine their geologic ages.

> Physico-geometrical data (apart from radio- metric) can do no more than provide a crude local relative chronology.[2]

But what about radiometric dating? Don't uranium or potassium dating methods provide reliable geologic dates? No, they do not, and the most obvious proof of this is the fact that the entire system of geologic ages and the relative dates of all its various subdivisions had all been completely settled long before radioactivity was even discovered! A radiometric measurement never determines whether a rock belongs in, say, the Cambrian period or the Ordovician period. At most, such radiometric calculations are used to assign a tentative date in years to a formation whose geologic date (that is, its position in the evolutionary time scale) is already known. And if, as is frequently the case, there is a serious contradiction between

---

[1] J.A. Jeletsky, "Basis of Practical Geochronology," *Bulletin, American Association of Petroleum Geologists* (April 1956), p. 684.

[2] T.G. Miller, "Time in Stratigraphy," *Paleontology*, vol. 8 (February, 1956), p. 128.

the evolutionary date and the radiometric date, it is always the latter that is thrown out. Radioactive dating thus is certainly not the means by which ages are determined.

It is also significant that there is no physical boundary that discernibly separates one geologic age from another:

> It is, indeed, a well-established fact that the (physical-stratigraphical) rock units and their boundaries often transgress geologic time planes in most irregular fashion even within the shortest distances.[3]

A hundred years ago, geologists believed that the termination of each geologic age was marked by a worldwide mountain-building "revolution," and that this event was marked by a great "unconformity" at the interface between the sedimentary rocks for the age before and after. But no more.

> The employment of unconformities as time-stratigraphic boundaries should be abandoned.[4]

"Unconformities" are distinct physical or geometric changes in the characteristics of the rock strata above and below. These, however, have no necessary correlation with the supposed "ages" of the rocks.

What about the principle of superposition? Can't we at least assume that strata on the bottom of a vertical column of sediments are older than those near the surface?

Not necessarily, it seems. One would think this relationship, at least, would be self-evident, but it appears there are numerous exceptions.

> Early studies of mountain geology revealed that mountains are sites of tremendous folding and thrusting of the earth's crust. In many places the oceanic sediments of which mountains are composed are inverted, with the older sediments lying on top of the younger.[5]

---

[3] J.A. Jeletsky, "Basis of Practical Geochronology," *Bulletin, American Association of Petroleum Geologists* (April 1956), p. 684.

[4] H.E. Wheeler, and E. M. Beesley, "Critique of the Time-Stratigraphic Concept," *Bulletin, Geological Society of America*, vol. 59 (1948), p. 84.

[5] "Mountain-building in the Mediterranean," *Science News*, vol. 98 (October 17, 1970), p. 316.

These out-of-order strata are quite common, and are found in all parts of the world and in all parts of the geologic column. They are commonly explained in terms of the "overthrusting" of old sediments from one region on top of young sediments from another region. Often there is a complete lack of any physical evidence of such overthrusting, not to mention the problem of the source of the tremendous energy required to move such gigantic blocks of rock around in this way.

A modern twist on this idea has now been provided by the new theories of plate tectonics, according to which young sediments on the ocean bottom are "underthrust" beneath older sediments while still on the sea bottom. Examples of out-of-order submarine sediments have been found by oceanographic coring and explained in this ingenious manner:

> In one location they found limestones 120 million years old directly above oozes only 5 to 10 million years in age.[6]

The exact combination of forces, by which great thicknesses of oozes can be induced to ooze underneath solid limestone way down on the bottom of the sea, is not quite clear, but must be complex and wonderful.

In any case, it is true that vertical position in the local geologic column is not necessarily determinative of relative geologic age. In the strange world of geologic dating, any combination of geologic ages can occur in any vertical order. Any ages may be present or missing, normal or inverted, thick or thin, unique or cyclic.

There is one, and only one, criterion used to determine the geologic age of rocks, and that is the testimony of its fossils.

> Thus it appears that the only presently available rational geochronological indices are biostratigraphically based — i.e., *biochronologic.*[7]

Similarly, E.M. Spiker, professor of geology at Ohio State University, after discussing the various factors that might contribute to identification of a geologic age, concluded:

---

[6] "Mountain-building in the Mediterranean," *Science News*, vol. 98 (October 17, 1970), p. 316.

[7] T.G. Miller, "Time in Stratigraphy," *Paleontology*, vol. 8 (February, 1956), p. 119.

And what essentially is this actual time scale? On what criteria does it rest? When all is winnowed out and the grain reclaimed from the chaff, it is certain that the grain in the product is mainly the paleontologic record and highly likely that the physical evidence is the chaff.[8]

Dr. H.D. Hedberg, in a survey of the geologic age system made while he was president of the Geological Society of America, said:

That our present-day knowledge of the sequence of strata in the earth's crust is in major part due to the evidence supplied by fossils is a truism.[9]

But there are great numbers of different kinds of fossils and actually only certain special fossils are used in this important task of identifying rocks and their geologic ages.

In each sedimentary stratum certain fossils seem to be characteristically abundant: these fossils are known as *index fossils*. If in a strange formation an index fossil is found, it is easy to date that particular layer of rock and to correlate it with other exposures in distant regions containing the same species.[10]

Fossils, therefore, are the means of dating rocks. But just how do we know which fossils to use to date which rocks? How can we know that the "index fossils" lived only in certain ages, and not in others?

The answer is *evolution*! Since evolution is non-repeatable, each evolutionary stage is unique to the age in which it was attained, and thus can identify the rocks formed in that age. Hedberg notes this:

Fossils have furnished, through their record of the evolution of life on this planet, an amazingly effective key to the relative positioning of strata in widely

---

[8] E.M. Spieker, "Mount-Building Chronology and the Nature of the Geologic Time-Scale," *Bulletin, American Association of Petroleum Geologists* (August 1956), p. 1806.

[9] H.D. Hedberg, "The Stratigraphic Panorama," *Bulletin, Geological Society of America*, vol. 72 (April 1961), p. 499.

[10] J.E. Ransom, *Fossils in America* (New York, NY: Harper and Row, 1964), p.43.

separated regions and from continent to continent.[11]

How is it, then, that fossils determine the relative positioning of strata and, therefore, the dating of geologic age? *"Through their record of the evolution of life!"*

> Once it was understood that each fossil represented a biologic entity, instead of a special divinely created life form, it became quite obvious that the plants and animals of each stratigraphic division had simply evolved from those of the preceding epoch through gradual adaptation. They were, in turn, ancestral to those that followed.[12]

The quotations cited in the foregoing discussion are from authoritative sources. Even though they are older, the methods have not changed, as may be confirmed by looking at any recent textbook in historical geology.

Most index fossils are marine invertebrate animals, assumed to be of worldwide provenance and relatively restricted in time span. In more "recent" geologic ages, vertebrates are often used, but here also their assumed evolutionary status is the key.

Perhaps this reliance on evolution as the key to dating rocks would be quite reasonable if we really knew evolution to be true. But, as we have already pointed out, evolution is *not* true and, indeed, the only evidence supporting it is the imagined evolutionary succession of the fossils in the sedimentary rocks. Now we see this "succession" is not based on any kind of geometric or physical relationships in the rocks themselves, but rather on the assumption of evolution. Thus the only evidence of evolution depends completely on the assumption of evolution! Such evidence is certainly not compelling evidence, but might still be of value if it were entirely self-consistent. All reasoning is, to some extent, circular reasoning, and this type of reasoning may be quite legitimate in certain cases. In this case, however, the geologic age system built upon this assumption is so loaded with contradictions and inconsistencies that it seems incredible that it has been blindly accepted by so many people for so many years!

---

[11] H.D. Hedberg, *Bulletin, Geological Society of America*, p. 499.
[12] Ransom, *Fossils in America*, p. 43.

To the objection that the standard order of the fossils had already been worked out before Darwin's day, it should be noted that evolution had been accepted by many people long beforehand. Even the progressive creationists of the 18th century believed that all organisms had appeared on earth in order of increasing complexity. This idea was based on the old Greek pantheistic philosophy of "the great chain of being," which became popular during the Renaissance.

Deluge Stratigraphy

The stratified rocks of the crust, with their fossil contents, do not conform to the evolution model, but exactly what do they represent? To answer this question, one should remember that there is no way of distinguishing any one "geologic age" from any other, except by the implicit assumption of evolution as applied to fossil interpretation. For all physical evidence to the contrary, the entire fossil assemblage could well have belonged to only *one* age, instead of a long series of ages. Since the organic world of the present includes invertebrates, vertebrates, fishes, amphibians, reptiles, birds and mammals, there is no *a priori* reason (apart from evolution) why the world of the past should not also have contained all these types of creatures.

If they represent essentially only one age, then, of course, the tremendous sedimentary beds must be explained in terms of catastrophism rather than uniformitarianism. Present depositional rates would obviously require great ages to produce such thicknesses of sediments. Catastrophism is not unreasonable, however, as many have thought.

The concept of local and regional catastrophes has again become quite respectable in geological circles, even though catastrophism was considered geological heresy for a hundred years. Geologists do not feel as defensive about uniformitarianism as they once did, both because of their confidence that everyone has now accepted it and also because increased knowledge of present processes has made it obvious that present rates are not adequate to account for most geologic formations.

The very existence of fossils, in fact, is proof of catastrophism on at least a local scale.

> To become fossilized a plant or animal must usually have hard parts, such as bone, shell, or wood.

It must be buried quickly to prevent decay and must be undisturbed throughout the long process.[13]

Rapid burial obviously means at least a local flood, or perhaps some other catastrophe such as a volcanic eruption. Especially is this fact evident in the case of the great fossil graveyards of the world, such as the fish beds in California and Devonshire, the mammoth bones in the permafrost, the great dinosaur beds on every continent, and similar phenomena all over the world in every so-called geologic age.

Historical geologists now commonly think in terms of local catastrophism in an overall context of uniformitarianism. However, these exceptional events are actually the ones that account for the fossils, and the fossils are the means of identifying the rocks. Therefore, the real key to geologic interpretation is catastrophism, even for those who claim to be uniformitarians!

One of the leaders in this neo-catastrophist movement, as it has been called, has been Derek Ager, former president of the British Geological Association. In the most recent edition of his widely used book, *The Nature of the Stratigraphical Record*, he deals at length with the ubiquitous nature of catastrophism in all the structures and contents of the rocks of the geologic column. Then he closes his book with the following summary.

> In other words, the history of any one part of the earth, like the life of a soldier, consists of long periods of boredom and short periods of terror.[14]

This pithy saying has not become a sort of cliché among the younger geologists. Everywhere one looks in the rock formations of the geologic column, one finds evidence of catastrophism.

In another recent book, Professor Ager says:

> We cannot escape the conclusion that sedimentation was at times very rapid indeed.[15]

---

[13] F.H.T. Rhodes, H.S. Zim and P.R. Shaffer, *Fossils* (New York, NY: Golden Press, 1962), p. 10.

[14] Derek Ager, *The Nature of the Stratigraphical Record* (New York, NY: John Wiley and Sons Publ., 1993), p. 141.

[15] Derek Ager, *The New Catastrophism* (Cambridge University Press, 1993), p. 49.

A reviewer of the latter book, a fellow geologist, has observed:

> The last 30 years have witnessed an increasing acceptance of rapid, rare, episodic and catastrophic events . . . the geological record is dominated not by slow, gradual change but by episodic rare events causing local disasters. . . . this volume may mark the arrival of catastrophism as the status quo.[16]

Local disasters may be rare events, relatively speaking, but geologic processes are completely inadequate to explain the fossils otherwise.

Putting all the above observations together, it becomes clear that the best explanation for the entire fossil record and the sedimentary rocks in which they are found is the one great cataclysm of the Noahic deluge. The scientific principle known as Occam's Razor suggests that the simplest model to explain a given set of data is the best. Thus a single worldwide cataclysm is more probably a correct model than ten thousand local catastrophes!

We have noted that no physical or geometrical criteria distinguish one age from another age and the evolutionary paleontological criterion for such dating is invalid. We also have seen that each significant fossil deposit must have been laid down rapidly in order for the fossils to have been preserved. Furthermore, each "age" must immediately follow the previous "age," as there are no worldwide unconformities between the ages. If each fossil deposit is catastrophic and each section of the strata follows quickly after the previous section, then all the fossil deposits must have been formed quickly and catastrophically. All ten thousand local catastrophes, therefore, occurred concurrently or consecutively as part of a global cataclysm.

This concept is fully in keeping with the biblical record of the Flood. The "very good" world formed by God as man's home precluded storms, floods, volcanic eruptions and other catastrophes. A "greenhouse" environment was assured by the "waters above the firmament" (Gen. 1:7), probably a vast blanket of invisible water vapor above the troposphere and

---

[16] Warren P. Allmon, "Post Gradualism," *Science*, vol. 262 (October 1, 1993), p. 122.

extending far into space. With no significant differences in temperature, there could have been no massive air movements, therefore, no rainstorms and no floods. With the "great deep" restrained beneath the crust (the "fountains of the great deep" were "broken up" only at the time of the Flood), neither were there any earthquakes or volcanic eruptions. When the Flood came, however, "the same day were all the fountains of the great deep broken up, and the windows of heaven were opened, and the rain was upon the earth forty days and forty nights" (Gen. 7:11-12). "And the waters prevailed exceedingly upon the earth . . . And all flesh died that moved upon the earth, both of fowl, and of cattle, and of beast, and of every creeping thing that creepeth upon the earth, and every man" (Gen. 7:19-21).

Such a flood as this was obviously not a *local* flood! Noah's ark finally grounded on one of the mountains of Ararat (Mount Ararat today is 17,000 feet high) after 150 days of floating freely on the waters of the Flood, but it was still more than two more months before the tops of other mountains could be seen from the ark (Gen. 8:4-5). Only a worldwide Flood could cover 17,000-foot high mountains for almost a year. It is a sad commentary on the state of evangelicalism that the local flood theory could ever have been proposed by serious Bible scholars. The apostle Peter indicated that it affected the heavens and the earth which "were of old," saying that "the world that then was, being overflowed with water, perished" (2 Pet. 3:5-6).

Thus both the Bible and geology (rightly interpreted) agree in pointing to a worldwide hydraulic cataclysm as the true explanation for the sedimentary fossiliferous strata. The hydraulic aspects of the Flood were, of course, necessarily accompanied by tremendous volcanic and tectonic upheavals and followed by great winds and glaciers, as well as further hydraulic and volcanic activity for perhaps many centuries to come. This complex of phenomena provides a most effective model for correlation of the geologic strata.

The details of stratigraphy are, however, too complex to be treated adequately in a short study such as this. Each locality has a different combination of rocks and fossils in its own local geologic column. An extreme heterogeneity of deposits is, in fact, only to be expected in a complexly heterogeneous phenomenon such as the Genesis Flood. Much study still is needed by creationist geologists for full interpretation of the local strata in terms of the great cataclysm.

In general, however, the data will approximately fit the following model, permitting translation of uniformitarian age-categories into diluvial stage-categories.

Earth's core and mantle, as well as the crystalline rocks of the "Archaeozoic"	Creation week
"Proterozoic" and early "Paleozoic" rocks	Early deposits of the Flood, mostly submarine
"Mesozoic" rocks, including later periods of the "Paleozoic"	Intermediate deposits of the Flood, with inter-mixing of continental and marine environments
Early "Cenozoic" rocks, including most of the "Tertiary" period	Final stages of the Flood, mostly continental and shelf deposits
Later "Tertiary" and all of "Quaternary" periods	Residual catastrophism of the post-Flood period

This classification is obviously over-simplified and each deposit should be evaluated on its own merits, but it may provide a general outline for initial categorizing of deposits. It bases regional correlation of major rock systems primarily on the factor of *ecological zonation*, rather than evolution. The vertical order of the strata is thus primarily a function of vertical elevation of environmental habitat, and not evolutionary progress. This model recognizes that, if a worldwide flood were to come on the present world, it would certainly tend to produce sedimentary beds in just this order, with those simple marine organisms dwelling at the lowest elevations buried at the lowest elevations, and so on up the scale.

Another important factor operating during the Flood must have been that of *physiological mobility*. That is, animals with ability to move rapidly would tend to escape burial longer, and thus be buried at higher elevations, other things being equal. Again, such mobility is approximately proportional to organic complexity, resulting in the more complex animals being found higher in the strata. Very few human fossils would be preserved in true deluge sediments, because men usually could escape such burial altogether, with their dead bodies gradually decaying into dust on the barren land surfaces or ocean surfaces after the Flood.

On a local basis, the marine fossils from any given source area would tend to be segregated into assemblages of similar size and shape by the factor of *hydrodynamic sorting*. Simpler, more nearly spherical and streamlined objects would offer less hydraulic resistance to water flow and thus would tend to be transported slower and deposited deeper than organisms of more complex geometry.

These three factors, therefore — ecological zonation, physilogical mobility and hydrodynamical sorting — would all operate to produce a statistical order of the fossils increasing in complexity from bottom to top, an order which has been misinterpreted to suggest evolution. There is, therefore, every reason to conclude that the real key to stratigraphy is not evolution over many ages but rather the cataclysmic termination of the one antediluvian age.

The Date of Creation

Probably no scientific claim has more insistently opposed biblical teachings than that of the age of the earth. The Bible indicates that all things were created several thousand years ago. Figures recorded in Genesis 5 and 11, as derived from the standard Massoretic text of the Old Testament, add up to a total of 1948 years from the creation of Adam to the birth of Abraham. However, it is possible that at least one generation may have been omitted from these lists (compare Gen. 11:12-13 and Luke 3:35-36). Since secular historians and archaeologists agree that Abraham's time, as described in Genesis, was sometime around 2000 B.C., it is obvious that the Bible date for Adam is approximately 4000 B.C. Perhaps, if additional gaps exist in the genealogical lists, this date could be stretched to, say, 10,000 B.C. The creation of the earth itself, according to Genesis 1, took place only six days earlier.

Most scientists, however, believe that the earth is approximately 4.6 billion years old, and that even modern man is at least one million years old. These dates are based primarily on the uranium-lead and potassium-argon methods of radiometric dating.

These and other radioactive decay processes are widely held to be so uniform and certain as to leave no doubt that the geologic ages really occupied billions of years. The idea that the earth is very old has become such a part of our culture that advocates of a young earth are considered almost as antiquated as if they advocated a flat earth!

The much-maligned Ussher chronology, however, may have been discarded too quickly. As a matter of fact, Archbishop James Ussher was an outstanding scholar in his day, thoroughly conversant with the Old Testament and with secular historical data, and no doubt knew much more about ancient chronology than do most of those who ridicule him today. Although we would not insist on his exact date for creation, his general approach was soundly biblical, using the numbers given in the Bible itself, together with written historical records of ancient secular historians that have been preserved, as the basis for his calculations.

Even today, there are *no written* records of early man that go back more than a few thousand years. The king-lists of ancient Egypt and Sumeria, as well as other early civilizations, all begin at about 2,500 years before Christ. Most historians today place the beginning of civilization at about 5000 B.C., but much of this is based on radiocarbon dating, or other uniformitarian techniques, rather than actual records.

However, even allowing this possibility (along with the inference that there may be gaps in the genealogical lists of Gen. 5 and 11), it still is very significant that the origin of human civilization is to be dated in terms of a few thousands of years rather than millions. This is strong support for at least the order-of-magnitude accuracy of biblical chronology.

To date any part of the earth's structure prior to the time of human records, of course, requires extrapolation of some physical process, using uniformitarian assumptions. Since these assumptions are both untestable and unreasonable, there is no reason why we should place confidence in them, especially in view of the immense extrapolation necessary. Rates which have been measured over a very few years in the present must be projected for millions or billions of years into the past. This type of extrapolation would be unthinkable and abhorrent in any other type of scientific study, but evolutionists accept it with little question when it supports their beliefs.

Since it serves as the standard against which other radioactive methods have been calibrated, the decay of uranium into lead is the most important of these radiometric methods for estimating the age of the earth. It is based on the assumption that the decay rate has never changed, but this assumption in turn requires that the cosmic ray flux reaching the earth and the shielding effect of the earth's atmosphere and magnetosphere have never changed. A supernova (and there have been a significant number in the past few thousand years) in a nearby constellation, or a reversal of the earth's magnetic field (and most geologists now are saying this has happened often in the past), would certainly increase drastically for a time the flux of high-energy neutrinos. The chemist Fred Jueneman has pointed this out:

> There has been in recent years the horrible realization that radio decay rates are not as constant as previously thought, nor are they immune to environmental influences. And this could mean that the atomic clocks are reset during some global disaster, and events which brought the Mesozoic to a close may not be 65 million years ago but, rather, within the age and memory of man.[17]

More specifically, by thus accelerating all decay rates, such events would make all the apparent ages derived by these methods immensely older than the true ages. Another absurd assumption made in connection with these methods is that, when each radioactive mineral was first crystallized, it contained only the "parent" and none of the "daughter" element. Uranium minerals are found exclusively in igneous rocks, and these have been formed by the upwelling of liquid magmas from the mantle below the earth's crust. Radiogenic lead that was already associated with the uranium in the mantle (either by radioactive decay, or more likely as a result of the primeval synthesis of the elements, which presumably was essentially a reverse process to that of decay) would in most cases have been transported with it and, therefore, be already present with it when the magma cooled. Exactly this situation is known to be

---

[17] Frederick B. Jueneman, "Secular Catastrophism," *Industrial Research* (June 1982), p. 21.

true in the case of recent volcanic rocks of known historic age.[18] The question is this: if igneous rocks known to be only a few hundred years old are invariably dated by uranium dating to be hundreds of millions of years old, then why is it not reasonable to think that other igneous rocks of unknown age, similarly dated by uranium dating to be hundreds of millions of years old, are also only a few hundreds or thousands of years old?

Thus, the relative amounts of uranium and lead in a given mineral are a function, not of the time since the mineral crystallized, but rather of the processes by which the elements were originally formed and brought together, as well as external effects that have modified these amounts since the mineral was formed. Numerous other fallacies in the uranium method could be listed if necessary.

Similar criticisms could be lodged against the potassium-argon, rubidium-strontium, thorium-lead, and other similar methods. The potassium method is perhaps more widely used than any other, but suffers the additional difficulty of having a daughter product (Argon-40) which is a gas, and thus able to move quite easily both in and out of a potassium system. There is far more argon in the earth's crust than could possibly have been derived by the decay of potassium at present decay rates, so it is very likely that excess argon is present in most potassium minerals.

It is obvious that incorporation of excess Argon-40 may lead to significant errors in the age, particularly in the case of very young minerals or rocks, or of those with low potassium contents.[19]

Furthermore, any given rock may yield several different potassium-argon ages!

It is now well-known that K-Ar ages obtained from different minerals in a single rock may be strikingly discordant.[20]

---

[18] For an extensive listing of such cases, see: "A Critical Examination of Radioactive Dating of Rocks," by Sidney P. Clementson (*Creation Research Society Quarterly*, vol. 7, 1970), p. 137-141.

[19] A. William Laughlin, "Excess Radiogenic Argon in Pegmatite Minerals," *Journal of Geophysical Research*, vol. 74 (December 15, 1969), p. 6684.

[20] Joan C. Engels, "Effects of Sample Purity on Discordant Mineral Ages Found in K-Ar Dating," *Journal of Geology*, vol. 79 (September, 1971), p. 609.

As in the case of uranium dating, potassium dating also commonly yields great ages on rocks known to be very young.

> The radiogenic argon and helium contents of three basalts erupted into the deep ocean from an active volcano (Kilauea) have been measured. Ages calculated from these measurements increase with sample depth up to 22 million years for lavas deduced to be recent . . . it is possible to deduce that these lavas are very young, probably less than 200 years old.[21]

And again we ask how it is possible to be sure that potassium ages are correct when determined for rocks of unknown age, when the same method gives ages 100,000 times too great for rocks whose age we know!

The radiocarbon method likewise is plagued with many uncertain assumptions. The formation rate depends on the cosmic ray flux, and the decay rate depends on the neutrino flux, both of which almost certainly were different in the past than they are at present. The most serious fallacy, however, is the assumption of a worldwide "steady state" in the proportion of radiocarbon (C-14) to natural carbon (C-12) in the environment. A steady-state would require constant formation and decay rates to have been in operation for approximately 30,000 years.

Measurements do not indicate, however, that the process has been going on long enough to attain this equilibrium.

> There is strong indication, despite the large errors, that the present natural production rate exceeds the natural decay rate by as much as 25 percent.[22]

Other writers have found indications of even greater discrepancies than 25 percent. These data suggest that the true model for radiocarbon dating should be a non-equilibrium model. When the equation is corrected in this way, it can yield as a boundary value the time when the entire process began that is, presumably, when the atmosphere first assumed its present form. When this is done, the age of the atmosphere

---

[21] C.S. Noble and J.J. Naughton, "Deep-Ocean Basalts: Inert Gas Content and Uncertainties in Age Dating," *Science*, vol. 162 (October 11, 1968), p. 265.

[22] Richard E. Lingenfelter, "Production of Carbon-14 by Cosmic Ray Neutrons," *Reviews of Geophysics*, vol. 1 (February, 1963), p. 51.

turns out to be at the most 12,000 years, and more likely about 7,000 years.

At this point, it is appropriate to raise another question: Why is it that the only processes which are used to measure such ages are processes that give large ages; in other words, processes which operate at very slow rates? It isn't necessary to use such processes. There are many other processes which, even with similar uniformitarian assumptions, will give much younger ages. There is almost an infinite number of processes operating in the earth, and each one could serve to measure time, since each one involves changes with time. Why, then, select only a few special processes which move with almost infinitesimal slowness?

For example, we have just considered the build-up of radiocarbon. This process, even when we assume constant rates and an initial radiocarbon content of zero, will yield a maximum age for the atmosphere (where radiocarbon is formed) of about 12,000 years. If the atmosphere is only 12,000 years old, it is certain that air-breathing plants and animals can be no older!

As another example, consider the earth's magnetic field. The strength of this field has been measured for over 150 years and thus provides a process with exceptionally good records, far better than those upon which radioactivity time measurements are based. In an important study,[23] Dr. Thomas G. Barnes demonstrated that the strength of the magnetic field is decaying exponentially at a rate corresponding to a half-life of 1,400 years. That is, 1,400 years ago the magnetic field was twice as strong as it is now. Furthermore, 4,200 years ago (right after the Flood, by the Ussher chronology), it was eight times as strong as it is now! At 7,000 years ago, it would have been 32 times as strong as now. It seems impossible that it could ever have been much stronger than this, and so the earth's core (where the magnetic field originates) must be no older than about 7,000 years.

Recent speculations on so-called paleomagnetic reversals are rendered irrelevant by this study, since the most recent such reversal has been postulated at about 700,000 years ago.

[23] Thomas G. Barnes, Origin and Destiny of the Earth's Magnetic Field (San Diego, CA: Institute for Creation Research, 1973), 64 p.

Magnetic field decay is a worldwide process (not localized, as a radioactive mineral in a certain rock), is based on a measured record far longer than those upon which most geochronometers are based, and requires only very limited extrapolation (not a million-fold extrapolation as in the case of uranium dating). Consequently, it is clearly a much better method than these others, and it indicates that the earth is young.

There are many other processes which similarly will indicate an age for the earth far less than its popularly promoted five-billion year age. All such calculations, of course, require the assumption of uniformitarianism, whether they yield large ages or small ages. Uniformitarianism is a reasonable assumption over a short period of time, but the likelihood of a significant interruption in uniformity increases as the length of time increases. Consequently, those processes which give a young age are more likely to be correct than those which yield a large age. Furthermore, there are many processes which give a young age, only a few which indicate an old age. Even the latter can easily be correlated with a young age,[24] as discussed above.

One other evidence of a young age, at least as far as people are concerned, will be noted in this chapter. This is the evidence of population statistics. It is possible to postulate a number of different population growth models, but a simple exponential model will fit the known data as well as any other. Thus, if the initial population is two people and the average annual growth rate is G percent per year, then the world population P after Y years is as follows:

$$P = 2 \left(1 + \frac{G}{100}\right) Y$$

The present growth rate is almost 2 percent per year and the present population is about 6 billion people. On the assumption of uniformitarianism, the equation can be solved for Y, the number of years required to generate 6 billion people at 2 percent per year. The equation indicates only 1,100 years or so would be necessary!

---

[24] See *The Biblical Basis for Modern Science* by Henry M. Morris (Grand Rapids, MI: Baker Book House, 1984), 516 p., for a listing of 68 worldwide processes which, even with uniformitarian assumptions, give ages for the earth that are far smaller than a billion years.

It is obvious that 2 percent per year is not the average growth rate for past times. If we assume that past conditions were so rigorous that the population growth was only one-fourth of this rate (i.e., 1/2 percent per year), then the population equation shows that 4,300 years would be required. This number, 4,300 years ago, is the Ussher date for the Flood, when the present population got its start, according to the Bible. All known population data fit these factors very well, indicating the biblical record of population origins is very reasonable and conservative. On the other hand, it is clear that the evolution model is completely unreasonable.

That is, if human populations were to grow at 1/2 percent per year for a million years, the total population would be 10^{2155} people. The impossibility of such a number is pointed up by noting there are only about 10^{80} electrons in the entire universe!

The Bible clearly indicates that both man and his world were created only a few thousand years ago. The best scientific data are completely in harmony with this concept.

Selected books for further study:
Ackerman, Paul D. 1986. *It's a Young World After All*. Grand Rapids, MI: Baker Book House. 131 p.
Austin, Steven A., ed. 1994. *Grand Canyon: Monument to Catastrophe*. San Diego, CA: Institute for Creation Research. 288 p.
Brown, Walter. 1995. *In the Beginning*. Phoenix, AZ: Center for Scientific Creation. 230 p.
Coffin, Harold. 1983. *Origin by Design*. Washington, DC: Review and Herald. 494 p.
Dillow, Joseph. 1982. *The Waters Above*. San Diego, CA: Institute for Creation Research. 479 p.
Howe, George T., ed. 1975. *Speak to the Earth*. Norcross, GA: Creation Research Society. 463 p.
Morris, Henry M. 1993. *Biblical Creationism*. Grand Rapids, MI: Baker Book House. 276 p.
Morris, Henry M. 1993. *History of Modern Creationism*. San Diego, CA: Institute for Creation Research. 444 p.
Morris, Henry M. 1985. *Scientific Creationism*. Green Forest, AR: Master Books. 281 p.
Morris, Henry M., and John C. Whitcomb. 1960. *The Genesis Flood*. Phillipsburg, NJ: Presbyterian and Reformed. 518 p.
Morris, Henry M. and John D. Morris. 1989. *Science, Scripture and the Young Earth*. San Diego, CA: Institute for Creation Research. 95 p.
Morris, John D. 1994. *The Young Earth*. Green Forest, AR: Master Books. 206 p.
Oard, Michael. 1990. *An Ice Age Caused by the Genesis Flood*. San Diego, CA: Institute for Creation Research. 243 p.

Whitcomb, John C. 1986. *The Early Earth*. Grand Rapids, MI: Baker Book House. 174 p.

Whitcomb, John C. 1988. *The World that Perished*. Grand Rapids, MI: Baker Book House. 178 p.

Woodmorappe, John. 1993. *Studies in Flood Geology*. San Diego, CA: Institute for Creation Research. 208 p.

Chapter XX

The Bible and Ancient History

The Unique Nature of the Bible Records

The remarkable antiquity of the Bible records is seldom appreciated as it should be. The Greek writer Herodotus is known as the "father of history," and yet his writings are contemporary with those of Nehemiah and Malachi, the very *last* of the Old Testament writers! The writings of Homer are a mixture of mythology and history, and the line of demarcation between them is quite nebulous, but they date from the same period as the sober histories of Samuel.

The other great historians of antiquity — Manetho, Berosus, Josephus, and others — all date from much more recent periods. More ancient writings are a mixture of philosophy, religion and mythology, interwoven with uncertain amounts of history. In such writings it is essentially impossible to discern where history ends and legend begins.

And yet the Bible records detailed and accurate histories as far back as Abraham and beyond. Abraham's time was at least a thousand years earlier even than Homer!

In all the world, there is no other book like this. The sacred books and the ancient records of other nations fade into dim tradition and sheer mythology only a few hundred years before Christ, but the Hebrew Scriptures incorporate great sections of sober history stretching back to the days before Abraham and, for that matter, back to the very creation itself! No other writing of such antiquity is at all comparable as a book of history, entirely apart from the question of its divine inspiration.

The authenticity of these biblical records, both in the Old

Testament and in the New Testament, has been discussed in earlier chapters. There is good reason to believe, and no reason to doubt (except for evolutionary bias), that the traditional dates and authors were correct and that we have in the Scriptures what amounts to firsthand, eyewitness, accounts of all these great events at the dawn of human history.

Archaeological Confirmations of Biblical Histories

This great antiquity of the Bible histories in comparison with those of other writings, combined with the evolutionary preconceptions of the 19th century, led many scholars to insist that the Bible histories also were in large part merely legendary. As long as nothing was available, except copies of ancient manuscripts, for the evaluation of ancient histories, such teachings may have been persuasive. Now, however, it is no longer possible to reject the substantial historicity of the Bible, at least as far back as the time of Abraham, because of the remarkable discoveries of archaeology.

Archaeology is the science which excavates and analyzes ancient human settlements. Archaeologists unearth portions of structures, pieces of pottery, tools, weapons, and other artifacts, as well as human remains. Often actual inscriptions are found, in one or another ancient form of written language. Through careful study of such data, these scientists attempt to reconstruct the character of ancient civilizations and the events that happened there. It is a remarkable fact that, wherever archaeological studies have touched on biblical places and events, these have been confirmed and illumined, rather than disproved. The historical records of the Bible have been shown to be accurate reports of real happenings, not legends and myths at all.

It is not our purpose here to attempt a detailed listing of archaeological confirmations of Scripture. The discussion would be far too extensive for a single chapter. The interested reader is directed to the books listed at the end of this chapter for this type of study. In general, it can be said that the entire sweep of biblical history, from the time of Abraham onward, has been adequately supported by archaeological study. Although there are a number of unsolved problems remaining as to details of chronology and such like, there is as yet no definite and confirmed archaeological finding which has disproved any single Bible reference. In view of the numerous confirmations of such statements, this is a remarkable phenomenon, and one which gives tremendous support to the doctrine of biblical inspiration.

It cannot be said, of course, that archaeology has confirmed specific events in the lives of individuals; no one would expect that documents or artifacts associated directly with, say, Jacob or Ruth or Elijah would ever be preserved and recovered. There are, however, occasional references to various kings and generals (including King David) that have been found, all of them consistent with biblical mentions. The great value of archaeology has been to show, over and over again, that the geography, technology, political and military movements, cultures, religious practices, social institutions, languages, customs, and other aspects of everyday life of Israel and the other nations of antiquity were exactly as described in the Bible. Correspondence in such details could only have been possible if the writers of the Bible were reliable and knowledgeable observers of real events.

Probably the two greatest 20th century authorities on biblical archaeology have been William Foxwell Albright and Nelson Glueck. Neither of these men was a fundamentalist nor a creationist, but they were universally recognized as of preeminent knowledge in this field. The following excerpts from Albright represent a point of view that was literally forced upon him, contrary to his educational training and early beliefs, by the facts which he discovered:

> When Adam Clarke published his famous 'Commentary on the Holy Scriptures' (1810-26) in which he gathered together all available material for the elucidation of the Bible, nothing whatever was known about the world in which the Bible arose except what could be extracted from extant Greek and Latin authors. . . . Since most of the fragmentary data on the ancient Orient in classical sources was erroneous, the picture then drawn of it was not only very dim and full of great blank spaces, the vague outlines of it were so badly distorted as to be almost unrecognizable to us today. From the chaos of prehistory, the Bible projected as though it were a monstrous fossil, with no contemporary evidence to demonstrate its authenticity

and its origin in a human world like ours.[1]

Then, after thorough discussion of archaeological studies in the lands of the Bible, having shown again and again the substantial accuracy of biblical references to events and situations in those lands, Dr. Albright, even though still maintaining his liberal bias against verbal inspiration of the Bible, does assure us of the following:

> Of first importance is the fact that the history and culture of Israel now form part of the organic continuity of Western civilization, which originated in the ancient Orient, spread westward in the Mediterranean basin, and then flowered in Europe. No philosopher of history can henceforth disassociate the Bible from the historical evolution of our own race and culture. There are innumerable points of contact between the details of Hebrew history, life, and literature, and the world around it. . . . As research and discovery continue (the Bible) will become greater and greater in the widening perspective which they will give to our children.[2]

The above words were written by Dr. Albright in 1936. His revision in 1955 was still more conservative, and he continued to move toward a more completely conservative position on the Scriptures until the time of his death. As far as Dr. Glueck is concerned, we will merely repeat his evaluation of the overall impact of archaeology on the Bible, as follows:

> As a matter of fact, however, it may be stated categorically that no archaeological discovery has ever controverted a biblical reference. Scores of archaeological findings have been made which confirm in clear outline or in exact detail historical statements in the Bible. And, by the same token, proper evaluation of biblical descriptions has often led to amazing discoveries. They form tesserae in the vast mosaic of the Bible's almost incredibly correct historical memory.[3]

---

[1] Wm. F. Albright, *Recent Discoveries in Bible Lands* (appended to Young's *Analytical Concordance to the Bible* (New York, NY: Funk and Wagnalls, 1936), p. 1.

[2] *Ibid.*, p. 43.

[3] Nelson Glueck, *Rivers in the Desert* (New York, NY: Farrar, Strauss & Cudahy, 1959), p. 31.

Before Abraham

For the most part, biblical archaeology has been limited to the study of biblical history during and after the time of Abraham, about 2000 B.C. To some extent, it has been possible to trace still earlier events in Egypt, Babylonia and elsewhere, but these, of course, were prior to the establishment of the Hebrews as God's chosen people, and so do not touch at many points upon the Bible. It is interesting that, while many archaeologists tend nowadays to accept the essentially historical character of the Bible from Genesis 12 onwards, they still tend to regard Genesis 1–11 as largely mythological. This, of course, is primarily due to their fundamental commitment to the dogma of evolution.

A number of biblical archaeologists have attributed the story of the Noahic flood, for example, to a local flood that occurred in the Mesopotamian valley, leaving a deposit of silt in Ur and Kish. There are such frequent references to this so-called "Flood layer" in the literature of biblical archaeology, in fact, that we need to make a special point of emphasizing here that the science of archaeology as such can never expect to find evidence of the Flood or of pre-Flood human settlements. Archaeologists have found, of course, Flood stories in the form of inscriptions made on monuments and tablets *after* the Flood, but the Flood itself was of such worldwide extent and destructiveness as either to obliterate or to bury deep in the geologic column all of the antediluvian habitations and implements. Geology, not archaeology, is the science that must deal with the deposits of the Flood. It is not an eight-foot layer of silt interposed between two cultural zones in Babylonia that identifies the Deluge, but rather the thousands of feet of sedimentary rock that underlie the very first of all such cultural sites. Even the physical anthropologists, with their excavations of supposed primitive men and tools in caves and river banks, are really dealing for the most part only with post-Flood materials. This caution must continually be kept in mind by creationist Christians as they attempt to reinterpret the published data of archaeologists and anthropologists to correlate with the biblical record of pre-history.

Assuming, therefore, that all archaeological sites really relate to post-diluvian cultures, there are essentially only two chapters of the Bible (Gen. 10 and 11) that contain information related to the so-called Paleolithic, Mesolithic, and Neolithic Ages of archaeology. The world was already well into the so-called Bronze Age by the time of Abraham.

Actually, the older "Ages" are largely hypothetical, based on evolutionary assumptions. It is obvious that a given tribe may have a Paleolithic (i.e., "Old Stone Age") culture, using only crude stone implements and tools, at the very same time that nations in other parts of the world enjoy an advanced civilization. The obvious proof of this statement is that such tribes have existed into the 20th century.

The Bible, of course, indicates that before the Flood man did have a high degree of culture and technology. He was able to build cities (Gen. 4:17), practice agriculture (Gen. 4:2) and animal husbandry (Gen. 4:20), fabricate and play musical instruments (Gen. 4:21), and work in brass and iron (Gen. 4:22). These few references would certainly imply that he also could read and write and had a system of weights and measures, as well as accomplish many other things (e.g., build a gigantic vessel capable of withstanding the violence of a world-wide flood for a whole year).

However, all these things perished (2 Pet. 3:6) in the Deluge. When the eight ancestors of all post-Flood men emerged from the ark, they, of course, had to face a drastically changed environment with only the knowledge they had learned and retained in their own minds, along with whatever records and equipment they may have been able to store on the ark. It is no wonder that they were forced for some little time to make use of stone and wooden implements, at least until they could discover veins of metallic ores in the rocks of newly formed lands of the world. Many naturally made use of caves for shelter, until they could find time and materials with which to build more suitable dwellings. No doubt a considerable part of their time had to be devoted to the essential task of providing food for their sustenance. It is remarkable that they could survive at all, let alone set about to develop great civilizations once again. No doubt a great many of the evidences of the so-called Paleolithic and Neolithic cultures of early man, when rightly interpreted, are merely commentaries on the difficult struggle to survive by small tribes in the early centuries following the great Flood and their separation at Babel.

Early Man

The subject of human origins has been severely distorted for over a hundred years by the theory of evolution. Popular displays in museums and magazines, and, unfortunately, even in school textbooks, have persuaded most people that man has an animal ancestry, leading back through a long line of intermediate stages to some form of ape-like creature which was also the ancestor of the modern apes.

But all of this is mere propaganda, endlessly repeated, without a shred of objective evidence in support of it. Great numbers of evolutionists, both professional and amateur, have been searching for "missing links" between man and the apes for over a hundred years, but the links are still completely missing. In the last few years, the most promising candidates have been *Ramapithecus, Australopithecus, Homo erectus,* and *Neanderthalensis*, in ascending order.

However, *Ramapithecus* has now been relegated to the role of nothing but an extinct ape, and so has his somewhat more manlike cousin *Australopithecus*.

> Fossil hominoids such as *Ramapithecus* may well be ancestral to the hominid line in the sense that they were individual members of an evolving phyletic line from which the hominids later diverged. They themselves nevertheless seem to have been apes — morphologically, ecologically, and behaviorally.[4]

Similarly, with respect to the widely publicized Australopithecines:

> It is now somewhat unlikely that australopithecines . . . hailed as human ancestors can actually have had very much to do with the direct human pathway.[5]

It was already known that these animals had ape-sized brains, so there is no reason at all to believe they were anything but extinct apes.

---

[4] Robert B. Eckhardt, "Population Genetics and Human Origins," *Scientific American*, vol. 226 (January, 1972), p. 101.

[5] Charles Oxnard, "Human Fossils: New Views of Old Bones," *American Biology Teacher*, vol. 41 (May 5, 1979), p. 274. Professor Oxnard has long been one of the world's most recognized authorities on the australopithecines.

Homo erectus is usually supposed to be a primitive form of man, but more man than ape at least. These fossils have long been controversial and highly questionable, but, in any case, it now seems probable that these were true human beings.

The most famous of all the supposed ape-men was Neanderthal Man, who was believed by the contemporaries of Charles Darwin to be a brutish, half-stooped apelike evolutionary ancestor of *Homo sapiens*. It is now quite evident, however, even to the evolutionists, that *Neanderthal* (as well as the still more advanced Cro-Magnon Man) was human in every sense of the word, completely *Homo sapiens*. Even such a thoroughgoing evolutionist as Dobzhansky has commented on this.

> The cranial capacity of the Neanderthal race of *Homo sapiens* was, on the average, equal to or even greater than that in modern man.[6]

The reason why Neanderthal Man was somewhat stooped and brutish in structure was not because he was newly evolved from the ape, but because he had health problems.

> Now, at long last, thanks to the investigations of Dr. Francis Ivanhoe of London, who published his findings in the August 8, 1970, issue of *Nature*, the Neanderthal puzzle may have been solved. His review of the currently available anthropological and medical evidence shows that Neanderthal Man was evidently the victim of his decision to move too far north at the wrong time, the onset of a glacial age. In doing so, contends Dr. Ivanhoe, he lost sufficient contact with the ultra-violet rays of the sun and because his diet did not provide the missing nutrient, he contracted rickets, the Vitamin D deficiency disease, which was to deform him for thousands of years to follow.[7]

This picture of Neanderthal Man fits well with the concept of early post-diluvian man struggling to cope with a difficult environment. The glacial period followed soon after the Flood, and was brought on by the changed climatic conditions occasioned by the Flood, prior to which there had probably been a

---

[6] Theodosius Dobzhansky, "Changing Man," *Science*, vol. 155 (January 27, 1967), p. 410.

[7] "Neanderthal Man, Victim of Malnutrition," *Prevention* (October, 1971), p. 116.

global mild, sub-tropical climate everywhere. The most probable explanation for such a universal mild climate, which is suggested by the characteristics of the sedimentary rocks and their contained fossils in all the so-called geologic "ages" prior to the late Tertiary, is a worldwide "greenhouse effect." Such an effect could be produced only by a worldwide canopy of some sort, the most likely nature of which would be a vast thermal blanket of invisible water vapor above the troposphere. Such a canopy is suggested by the "waters above the firmament" of Genesis 1:7, the complete absence of rain suggested in Genesis 2:5, and the establishment of the rainbow only following its dissipation as one cause of the Flood (Gen. 7:11; 9:13).

When the canopy was precipitated at the Flood, the present latitudinal and continental extremes of temperature became established, snow began to fall and the great continental ice caps gradually developed. The resulting glacial epoch probably persisted for many centuries in the northern latitudes, at the same time there were pluvial climates and great civilizations developing in the lower latitudes.

Thus, Neanderthal Man may not have been quite the equal in ability or intelligence of those tribes who were living farther south, but he was certainly a true man, no more different from other groups of modern men than various tribes of modern men today are from each other.

> He had a brain with a capacity sometimes larger than that of modern man. He was a talented toolmaker and successful hunter, even dabbled in art and, most importantly from a cultural standpoint, developed a rudimentary social and religious consciousness.[8]

It is also known that Neanderthal Man raised flowers and buried his dead. Now evidence is beginning to appear that he could even communicate with symbols, and thus was able to write and calculate with numbers in various ways.

> Communication with inscribed symbols may go back as far as 135,000 years in man's history, antedating the 50,000-year-old Neanderthal Man. Alexander Marshack of Harvard's Peabody Museum, made this pronouncement recently after extensive

---

[8] "Neanderthal Man, Victim of Malnutrition," *Prevention* (October, 1971), p. 117.

microscopic analysis of a 135,000-year-old ox rib covered with symbolic engravings.[9]

There seems little of substance remaining in the old evolutionary ideas that man is merely an evolved animal. Both physiologically and behaviorally, man has always been man and the ape has always been an ape. Except for the exaggerated chronologies still employed by the evolutionists, all that we really know of man's early history fits in perfectly well with the biblical implications of the nature and migrations of men after the Flood. There are some extinct apes (e.g., the australopithecines) and some extinct tribes of men (e.g., *Homo erectus*), but there have never been any real ape-men.

Origin of Races and Nations

The Bible is clear in teaching that all present nations, tribes and languages have been derived from Noah's three sons and three daughters-in-law in the few thousand years since the great Flood. It was shown in the previous chapter that the development of the present world population from this beginning is quite reasonable and conservative. However, it might be questioned whether such extreme variations in physical and linguistic characteristics among different groups of men could develop so rapidly. Presumably before the Flood, all men spoke the same language and were of the same race. At any rate, this was certainly true of Noah's family.

There could, of course, have been no development of distinctive tribal or racial characteristics as long as all men lived together and inter-married, with a free "flow" of genetic factors. God had told men to multiply and fill the earth, but for a considerable length of time, they insisted on remaining together in one location. Finally, they united in rebellion against God's commandments, building the great city and Tower of Babel. "Therefore is the name of it called Babel, because the Lord did there confound the language of all the earth; and from thence did the Lord scatter them abroad upon the face of all the earth" (Gen. 11:9).

The accomplishment of this confusion of tongues was undoubtedly a divine miracle. Whatever it may have involved in terms of physiologic changes in man's brain and nervous

---

[9] "Use of Symbols Antedates Neanderthal Man," *Science Digest*, vol. 73 (March, 1973), p. 22.

system, however, it obviously was the most effective possible means of forcing men to scatter around the world as God had commanded. Evidently each little family group at Babel suddenly had its own unique language and was unable to communicate with any other group. No longer, therefore, was intermarriage, or even political union, possible. Each group, therefore, migrated elsewhere, the strongest and most able and industrious families settling in the most desirable locations, the others moving on wherever they could.

It is significant, and completely in line with this inference, that the great early civilizations tended to cluster around the Near East, whereas the so-called "primitive" groups all seem to have located near the edges of civilization, far to the south or north, east or west (e.g., Rhodesia Man, Neanderthal Man, Peking Man, etc.), as well as the African tribes, the American Indians, the Polynesians, and others who first reached the uttermost parts of the earth.

It is known genetically that it is just such isolation and inbreeding that are required for rapid production of individual varieties from a given species. Assuming that all the many genetic factors for all aspects of man's physical structure were present in Adam at creation — and many of them, at least, in the six people from whom the world was to be repopulated after the Flood — then different groups of such characters would soon become more or less permanently established in the individual inbreeding family groups, and soon each would become a distinctive tribe or nation.

Geneticists call this the "founder principle." Dobzhansky discusses it as follows, based on his studies on the fruit fly.

> The founder principle is "establishment of a new population by a few original founders . . . that carry only a small fraction of the total genetic variation of the parental population." Founder events are inevitably followed by inbreeding for one or several generations. . . . Natural selection in experimental populations derived from small numbers of founders resulted in a greater variety of outcomes than in comparable populations descended from numerous founders.[10]

---

[10] Theodosius Dobzhansky, "Species of Drosophila," *Science*, vol. 177 (August 25, 1972), p. 667.

Thus, enforced segregation of mankind into small in-breeding tribal units would generate a rapid development of the distinctive physical characteristics associated with each tribe, and it is very doubtful that any other explanation is feasible at all. The evolutionist may prefer to think in terms of long, slow development of each race by mutation and natural selection, but we have already seen, in chapter 18, that this mechanism is unproductive. Furthermore, this concept of long, slow development of separate races naturally leads to the idea that there are significant evolutionary differences between races, an idea that was widely held by the 19th century evolutionists. In evolutionary biology, a race is an incipient species in the process of evolving into a new species. If this is so, it is obvious that some races are more advanced than others, a thought which has always been at the roots of racism.

Thomas Huxley held this view, in common with Charles Darwin and other leading evolutionists in the days when evolution was being sold to the public, immediately after the American Civil War. As its leading spokesman, Huxley was profoundly influential. On this race question, he had said:

> No rational man, cognizant of the facts, believes that the average Negro is the equal, still less the superior, of the white man. And if this be true, it is simply incredible that, when all his disabilities are removed, and our prognathous relative has a fair field and no favour, as well as no oppressor, he will be able to compete successfully with his bigger-brained and smaller-jawed rival, in a contest which is to be carried on by thoughts and not by bites. The highest places in the hierarchy of civilization will assuredly not be within the reach of our dusky cousins, though it is by no means necessary that they should be restricted to the lowest. But whatever the position of stable equilibrium into which the laws of social gravitation may bring the Negro, all responsibility for the result will henceforward lie between Nature and him. The white man may wash his hands of it, and the Caucasian conscience be void of reproach for ever-more. And this, if we look to the bottom of the matter,

is the real justification for the abolition policy.[11]

Such bold racism is the natural extension of evolutionist thinking concerning the origin of races. It later led, in Germany, to the doctrine of the master race and, ultimately, to Hitlerism. Charles Darwin himself believed that certain human races would eventually eliminate other less advanced races in the struggle for existence.

> I could show fight on natural selection having done and doing more for the progress of civilization than you seem inclined to admit. . . . the more civilized so-called Caucasian races have beaten the Turkish hollow in the struggle for existence. Looking to the world at no very distant date, what an endless number of the lower races will have been eliminated by the higher civilized races throughout the world.[12]

The biblical explanation of national and tribal origins is far superior to such ideas, both morally and genetically. Note that the Bible does not mention the concept of "race" at all, only languages, peoples, tribes and nations.

The most important difference between groups of men, of course, is not skin color, but language. It is only the language barrier that could enforce isolation and inbreeding among men, and it is only such inbreeding that could have produced the many distinctive physical characteristics of the different groups.

As far as the early nations are concerned, the three major groups of nations naturally stemmed from the three sons of Noah. Seventy original nations are listed in Genesis 10, extending evidently to sometime soon after the scattering of the people from Babel. The general accuracy of this ancient document has been attested by none other than Albright.

> It stands absolutely alone in ancient literature, without a remote parallel, even among the Greeks, where we find the closest approach to a distribution of

---

[11] Thomas Huxley, *Lay Sermons, Addresses and Reviews* (New York, NY: Appleton, 1871), p. 20.

[12] Charles Darwin, *Life and Letters, I*, letter to W. Graham (July 3, 1881), p. 316, cited in *Darwin and the Darwinian Revolution*, by Gertrude Himmelfarb (London: Chatto & Windus, 1959), p. 343.

peoples in genealogical framework. . . . The Table of
Nations remains an astonishingly accurate document.[13]

In general, the Table shows the descendants of Japheth
migrating into Europe, those of Ham southward into Africa,
and those of Shem remaining in western Asia. Although not
certain, it seems probable that the Far East was later settled
by certain groups from the Hamitic and Japhetic nations. In
any event, there is certainly nothing in either Genesis 10 or
Genesis 11 that has been disproved by archaeology.

The Antediluvian World

The period from Adam to the Deluge lasted 1656 years,
according to Ussher's chronology, which is based strictly on the
figures given in Genesis 5. It is possible, though unlikely, that
there are gaps in these genealogies (as in the style of the
genealogies recorded much later in Matt. 1). The Ussher date
for the Flood, however (approximately 2350 B.C.), is much
more recent than even most conservative Bible archaeologists
believe is possible, and this suggests that quite possibly there
are gaps in the genealogies of Genesis 11.

The question of an absolute chronology for these periods
is thus unsettled. It is possible that some of the "begats" of
Genesis 11 may refer in some cases to distant descendants
rather than immediate sons. On the other hand, one need not
be overmuch intimidated by the speculations of archaeologists
regarding dates of various sites and events extending far
beyond 2350 B.C. Much of this chronology is based on radiocarbon dating, which, as discussed in the preceding chapter, can
properly be drastically compressed to bring it into line with the
true measured radiocarbon in the environment. Other factors,
such as overlapping dynasties in Egypt, exaggerated claims of
kings on their monuments, and many other uncertainties
render the establishment of firm dates in antiquity a highly
speculative art. Accordingly, this can be left an open question
at this time.

It should be emphasized again, however, that archaeology
can really say little about the antediluvian period in particular. Any human artifacts from the world before the Flood will,

---

[13] Wm. F. Albright, *Recent Discoveries in Bible Lands* (appended to Young's
Analytical Concordance to the Bible (New York, NY: Funk and Wagnalls,
1936), p. 25.

if ever found at all, be found deep in the sedimentary rocks, since these are the actual deposits of the Flood. Almost all the information we can learn about this period must, therefore, be found in the Bible in the early chapters of Genesis.

We have already noted the probable existence of a vast canopy of invisible water vapor above the troposphere during this period. In addition to the greenhouse effect such a canopy would produce, it would also (together with the earth's magnetic field, which was far stronger in the past) provide a highly efficient shield against the deadly radiations perpetually bombarding the earth from outer space. In turn, this effect would contribute markedly to human longevity before the Flood, since it is known that such radiations increase the frequency of both somatic and genetic mutations and, therefore, decrease the life-span.

The greenhouse effect, likewise, would have contributed to a more congenial environment in other ways. Uniform temperatures precluded air mass movements, and thus there were no storms and no rains except a diurnal mist which maintained an equable humidity everywhere. The land surfaces were much more extensive than in the present world, since the oceans now contain the waters drained from the Flood. There were no deserts or ice caps or rugged mountains. With a warm, pleasantly humid climate, all the world was habitable, with abundant plant and animal life everywhere.

There were no earthquakes or volcanoes. With no rain, there was no erosion and therefore no sediments. The earth's covering of rich soil, specially created in the beginning, rested directly on the crystalline crust. Locked within the crust were vast reservoirs of pressurized waters, heated by the earth's internal heat, and emerging to the surface here and there through controlled vents to great artesian springs, which in turn became the sources for the river systems of the antediluvian world.

While none of the above is explicitly taught in Genesis, it is reasonably inferred from what *is* taught there. God had created a world for man's dominion that was "very good" (Gen. 1:31), a beautiful and fruitful world in every way.

The curse of Genesis 3:17 had introduced the bondage of decay and death into the world. Many plants underwent mutations to bear thorns and thistles. Possibly changes also took place in certain bacteria and other micro-organisms, and disease entered the world. Changes in animal structures equipped some to become carnivores. In all creatures, man included, physiological structures became pathological, and they all began slowly to die.

However, the basic structure of the earth and its environment remained unchanged until the time of the Flood. At that time, however, the vapors condensed and fell as great rains from heaven, and the subterranean waters burst their bounds. The tremendous cataclysm that resulted finally, as Peter says, so transformed the earth and its atmosphere that "the world that then was, being overflowed with water, perished" (2 Pet. 3:6).

Although archaeology cannot of itself confirm these biblical inferences, there is nothing in geology or the other sciences that refutes them. This picture constitutes an effective "model" which seems to fit many inferences from both Genesis and geology.

Selected books for further study:

Adam, Ben. 1963. *The Origin of Heathendom.* Minneapolis, MN: Bethany Fellowship. 128 p.

Blaiklock, E.M., and R.K. Harrison, eds. 1983. *Dictionary of Biblical Archaeology.* Grand Rapids, MI: Zondervan. 485 p.

Cooper, Bill. 1995. *After the Flood.* Portsmouth, England: Creation Science Movement. 250 p.

Courville, Donovan A. 1971. *The Exodus Problem and Its Ramifications,* 2 vols. Loma Linda, CA: Challenge Books. 687 p.

Custance, Arthur C. 1975. *Noah's Three Sons.* Grand Rapids, MI: Zondervan Publ. House. 368 p.

Fange, Erich A. von. 1984. *Spading Up Ancient Words.* Syracuse, IN: Living Word Services. 133 p.

Fange, Erich A. von. 1994. *Noah to Abraham.* Syracuse, IN: Living Word Services. 371 p.

Hyma, Albert, and Mary Stanton. 1976. *Streams of Civilization.* Milford, MI: Mott Media. 411 p.

Morris, Henry M. 1989. *The Long War Against God.* Grand Rapids, MI: Baker Book House. 344 p.

Richardson, Don. 1981. *Eternity in Their Hearts.* Ventura, CA: Regal Publ. 176 p.

Taylor, Ian. 1984. *In the Minds of Men.* TFE Publishing. 498 p.

Thompson, J.A. 1980. *The Bible and Archaeology.* Grand Rapids, MI: Wm. B. Eerdmans Publishing Co.

Wilson, Clifford. 1993. *Visual Highlights of the Bible.* Victoria, Australia: Pacific Christian Ministries. 147 p.

Zwemer, Samuel M. 1945. *The Origin of Religion.* New York, NY: Loiseaux Brothers. 256 p.

Chapter XXI

Pseudo-Christian Cults

Introduction

Thus far in this book we have been discussing the many evidences that the Bible is the inspired, infallible, inerrant, authoritative, written Word of God, and that biblical Christianity is the only true way to God and everlasting salvation, through the Lord Jesus Christ — our Creator, Redeemer and coming King. We have tried also to answer the major objections and difficulties that skeptics have brought against these truths.

Now, however, we also need to consider the problem of the pseudo-Christian cults — those groups that profess to believe in the authority of the Bible and in Jesus Christ, but that propose peculiar additions of their own which take them outside the framework of true biblical Christianity.

It is significant that the closing verses of the Bible provide solemn admonitions against such tampering with God's Word — either by taking away from it (as liberals and skeptics do) or by adding to it (as the cults do). Note these fearful warnings: "For I testify unto every man that heareth the words of the prophecy of this book, If any man shall add unto these things, God shall add unto him the plagues that are written in this book: And if any man shall take away from the words of the book of this prophecy, God shall take away his part out of the book of life, and out of the holy city, and from the things which are written in this book" (Rev. 22:18-19).

The Holy Scriptures were brought to completion with these words by the last surviving Apostle, the beloved John, and nothing more is needed until the Lord returns. It is arrogant and presumptuous for later "Christians" to "add unto these things" by writings of their own and then to claim either divine inspiration or divine authority for their new "revelations" or interpretations. Yet that is exactly what the founders and leaders of the many pseudo-Christian cults have done, and they have led multitudes of followers into grievous and dangerous error.

We need to be able to recognize and refute these false teachings, not only to keep other immature believers from being ensnared by them, but also, if possible, to reclaim some of their adherents for true Christianity.

Many followers of the cults are both sincere and zealous in their faith, as well as clean and wholesome in lifestyle, and these facts may mislead themselves and others into believing they are right in their beliefs. The truth is, however, that one may even be a sincere and clean-living atheist or communist, but he is wrong nevertheless. The criterion is not sincerity, but truth, and "if they speak not according to this word, it is because there is no light in them" (Isa. 8:20).

The purpose of this chapter, therefore, is to help identify such cultic groups — not necessarily by name (for they are so many) but rather by use of key guidelines given in the Bible for recognizing truth and error.

Basic Biblical Guidelines

This chapter is intended to identify the main factors by which we may "try the spirits whether they are of God: because many false prophets have gone out into the world" (1 John 4:1). Of the many passages in the Bible that contain information or warnings about false teaching, there are four key New Testament passages that will sufficiently focus our evaluation.

(1)   *2 Peter 2:1-3* lists five characteristics of the leaders of false cults:

They come from "Christian" churches or backgrounds.

They deny the biblical Lord Jesus in some way.

They may become very popular, especially with emotional people.

They will cause important teachings of Scripture to be degraded.

They often use human greed and hidden meanings to attract followers.

These character checks might have been used to quickly identify some of the more notorious "cult" leaders of the 19th and 20th centuries.

Jim Jones of the Guyana mass suicide infamy was an apparently fundamental preacher in California for many years. Joseph Smith, with an emotional religious background, founded what has become the largest "Christian" cult movement in the world, the Mormons. Charles T. Russell, founder of the Jehovah's Witnesses, became disenchanted with orthodox Christianity and began issuing prophetic predictions in light of special signs and mysteries he found in the Great Pyramid of Egypt, and elsewhere. Not only did he make highly publicized, false predictions of the second coming of Christ and the end of the age, but his successors continued to do so for several decades.

The so-called "Health, Wealth, and Prosperity" gospel that attracted so many in the Pentecostal and charismatic movements during the 1970s and 1980s appealed to human greed, and was led by such false teachers and evangelists as Reverend Ike, Benny Hinn, Terry Cole Whittaker, Jim and Tammy Bakker, Robert Tilton, Oral Roberts, and others, whose outlandish dress and behavior were so ostentatious and unethical that the major media networks aired specials exposing their hypocrisy.

Yet these and others like them continue to garner followers and the movements continue unabated. Evidently more serious departure from the biblical ideal is necessary for some to take notice.

(2) *1 John 4:1-3* identifies one major, all-encompassing doctrinal error. "Every spirit that confesseth that Jesus Christ is come in the flesh is of God. And every spirit that confesseth not that Jesus Christ is come in the flesh is not of God; and this is that spirit of antichrist, whereof ye have heard that it should come, and even now already is it in the world." Many of the cults deny either the unique deity of the Lord Jesus Christ or else His true and perfect humanity.

(3) *2 John 7-9* further amplifies this error to include anyone who undermines His teachings, warning that any teacher who "transgresseth, and abideth not in the doctrine of

Christ, hath not God. . . . If there come any unto you, and bring not this doctrine, receive him not into your house, neither bid him God speed." Not only is it blasphemous to deny the deity of Jesus Christ, but it is also blasphemous to deny that which He has taught.

Probably the reader is aware of the anti-Trinitarian teachings of the Jehovah's Witnesses, who view Jesus as a created individual, second in power, but never equal to Jehovah. The public position of the Mormons is more subtle. Mormons pray in Jesus' Name, call Him the Son of God, talk about His death on the cross, His resurrection, and His second coming. What they do not mention openly is the church doctrine that Jesus is the son of Elohim and Mary, brother to Satan, and approved as Savior only after a vote of the Council of gods. The so-called Christian Scientists were a major force of division and schism in the early part of this century, denying the reality of sin and death, and distorting the truth of Christ's deity.

Sadly, many well meaning people are attracted to these and other such movements without ever considering the issue of truth or error. The battle is fought and either won or lost in our minds. Circumstances, feelings, popular acceptance, even miraculous signs are all subject to deceptive manipulation and distortion. Our minds can be deceived.

(4)   *2 Corinthians 11:3* identifies the strategy by which the mind can be deceived. "But I fear, lest by any means, as the serpent beguiled Eve through his subtilty, so your minds should be corrupted from the simplicity that is in Christ." The passage that outlines the "subtilty" of the enemy is Genesis 3:1-7. It specifies a three stage process.

Dispute the *Accuracy* of God's Word. "Yea, hath God said. . . ."

Deny the *Ability* of God to do what He said. "Ye shall not surely die. . . ."

Denigrate the *Actions* of God toward man. "For God doth know that in the day ye eat thereof, then your eyes shall be opened, and ye shall be as gods, knowing good and evil."

All of these elements, the characteristics of false teachers, the position on the deity of Christ and His teaching, and the mental strategy to undermine the accuracy, abilities, and actions of God, can be grouped into three major tests that one should apply to any church, sectarian movement, religious leader, or spiritual phenomena encountered. If we do not "try the spirits," then it is likely that we will be "led away with the error of the wicked, and fall from [our] own steadfastness" (2 Pet. 3:17).

How is the Word of God treated?

How is the person of Jesus Christ treated?

How are the teachings of Jesus Christ treated?

Treatment of Scripture

Earlier chapters have provided evidence of the authenticity, accuracy, and inspiration of the Bible. All of this is powerful foundational information on which to build test criteria. Even more basic is the need to identify departures from the clear teachings of the Bible about itself.

1. Adding to or taking away from God's Word is wrong.

> Every word of God is pure. . . . Add thou not unto his words, lest He reprove thee, and thou be found a liar (Prov. 30:5-6).

> Ye shall not add unto the word which I command you, neither shall ye diminish ought from it (Deut. 4:2; see also Rev. 22:18-19).

2. No other writings are necessary for godliness.

> His divine power hath given unto us all things that pertain unto life and godliness, through the knowledge of him (2 Pet. 1:3).

> All Scripture is given by inspiration of God, and is profitable for doctrine, for reproof, for correction, for instruction in righteousness: that the man of God may be perfect, throughly furnished unto all good works (2 Tim. 3:16-17).

3. The Word of God does not need "secret" or "private" interpretations.

> The secret things belong unto the Lord our God:

but those things which are revealed belong unto us and to our children (Deut. 29:29).

Violations of these principles are easily seen in the major pseudo-Christian cults. The Mormons demand equal authority with the Bible for the *The Book of Mormon*. Jehovah's Witnesses have their own special translation of the Bible, *The New World Translation*. Furthermore, the cults invariably have other writings that "explain" what is "really" meant by God. Mary Baker Eddy authored *Science and Health with Key to the Scriptures* in 1875, and it is still used by Christian Scientists today. The Mormons study *The Pearl of Great Price* and *Doctrine and Covenants*. Jehovah's Witnesses faithfully read *Let God be True, Make Sure of All Things*, and *The Watchtower* to maintain their understanding of "truth."

Even some of the "mainline denominations" and their spokesmen may become guilty of this error. Roman Catholicism insists that the writings of the church fathers, the various encyclicals, creeds, papal bulls, etc., are to be used to properly understand the truth "contained" in the Scriptures. Some Protestant denominations in recent years have been voting approval to statements and creeds that openly defy clear teachings of the Bible, all in the name of "tolerance" and "love." Fringe movements are propagating errors through "letters" to their followers, such as Moses David Berg (founder of "The Children of God" movement) did, or specialized Bible studies like *Power for Abundant Living* used by Victor Paul Wierville to delude followers of The Way, International.

Perhaps the most powerful and far-reaching impact of this sort in the last half of this century has been the result of the explosion and penetration of "Christian" TV. "Revelations" and "visions" and "experiences" have been aired that have nothing in common with Bible truth (the widely promoted 800-foot Jesus of Oral Roberts is an example). TV evangelists have built huge empires preaching "damnable heresies" (2 Pet. 2:1) and leading "captive silly women laden with sins" (2 Tim. 3:6).

Attention to and obedience of the Word of God is the only sure protection against error.

There are certain absolutely clear and basic teachings in the Scriptures that impact the way the entire message is understood. Departure from these clear, broadly taught biblical basics are sure signs of cultic activity.

The creation of all things, from nothing, by the direct fiat of God. With purpose, design, foreknowledge, and divine sovereignty, the creation was accomplished in six solar days (Exod. 20:11), not through some mechanistic and random interplay of cosmic forces. "The things which are seen were not made of things which do appear" (Heb. 11:3). This creation was further planned in the eternal councils of the Triune God, spoken into existence by the omnipotent, omniscient Word of God, and energized by the omnipresent Holy Spirit of God (Gen. 1:1-2; John 1:1-3; Col. 1:16-17). The resultant universe was "very good," all things and every creature perfect in their design and in their nature (Gen. 1:10, 12, 18, 21, 25, 31). Man, both male and female, was created "in the image of God," set in the garden of God to rule the earth and to fill it with other men and women living and ruling under the delegated authority of the Creator (Gen. 1:27-28). All was originally in perfect harmony with and in submission to the Godhead.

Sin and Death constituting an intrusion into the creation. Sometime subsequent to the completion of the creation work of God, Lucifer, "the anointed cherub that covereth" (Ezek. 28:14), rebelled in heaven against God, was cast down to the earth (Ezek. 28:15-17; Isa. 14:12-15), entered the body of "the serpent" (Gen. 3:1-6; Rev. 12:9), and deceived Eve into disobeying God's prohibition against eating of the "tree of knowledge." Adam then also disobeyed God's Word, bringing sin and death into and upon all the world (Rom. 5:12). All the universe, every being and every particle, "groaneth and travaileth in pain together until now" (Rom. 8:22).

The worldwide flood during the days of Noah. This global cataclysm was designed by God to destroy all air-breathing life on the face of the earth (Gen. 6:17; 7:22). Excepted were the "eight souls" of the family of Noah and the graciously preserved seed of the animal kinds kept by God in the Ark (Gen. 7:2;

1 Pet. 3:20). All present life now living on the land has descended from those so preserved in the Ark (Gen. 9:19).

The substitutionary death of Christ on the cross. Jesus Christ died for the sin of the world, and this was followed by His victory over death and bodily resurrection from the grave (1 Pet. 3:18; 2 Cor. 5:21; 1 Cor. 15:1-4; etc.), providing the means whereby God in justice can forgive sin and provide salvation to all who believe (John 1:12; 3:16).

The repentance and salvation of all men as the main objective of God (2 Pet. 3:9). The world is now under the patient maintenance and preservation of the Creator (Col. 1:16-17; 2 Pet. 3:7). God has focused His heart, sovereign will, and active word during this age (1 Pet. 1:18-25), first through the Law as schoolmaster to bring us to Christ (Gal. 3:24-25), then through personal repentance and faith in the work of Jesus Christ on Calvary (Rom. 10:6-17).

The bodily return of this same Jesus to earth. The Creator of the universe, Head of the church, and King of kings is now ruling from His throne in heaven, awaiting the time known only to God (Matt. 24:36) when He will establish His kingdom in righteousness and holiness (Matt. 24:29-31; 25:31-46; John 5:28-29; 1 Cor. 15:50-54; 1 Thess. 4:13-18; 2 Thess. 1:7-10; Heb. 12:25-27; 2 Pet. 3:9-13). We who are now alive and remain, are to "occupy" until He comes (Luke 19:13), working as "stewards" (1 Cor. 4:1-2; 1 Pet. 4:10), "soldiers" (2 Tim. 2:2-3), and as those running a race (1 Cor. 9:24; Heb. 12:1), expecting any moment to be called to account before the judgment seat of Christ (2 Cor. 5:6-11), to be forever thereafter with the Lord (1 Thess. 4:17).

The future great destruction and renovation of the universe. God has promised that He will complete His work in this age (2 Pet. 3:10-12) and then will usher in the eternal "new heavens and a new earth, wherein dwelleth righteousness" (2 Pet. 3:13) under the reign of God's Son, the Savior, Jesus Christ, as the King of kings and Lord of lords (Rev. 19:11-16).

Violation of these key doctrines of the Bible, contained throughout and within nearly every book of the Scriptures, can only result in "certain men [creeping] in unawares, who were before of old ordained to this condemnation, ungodly men, turning the grace of our God into lasciviousness, and denying the only Lord God, and our Lord Jesus Christ" (Jude 4).

Treatment of the Person of Jesus Christ

The Salvation of God, granted through His grace alone, can only be obtained by faith in Jesus Christ of Nazareth, the only begotten Son of God (Acts 4:10-12; Eph. 2:4-10).

Jesus of Nazareth is God in flesh, fully human, fully God, conceived by the Holy Spirit, born of the virgin Mary (Matt. 1:20-23; John 1:1-4, 14; Col. 1:13-17).

Jesus is sinless in nature and in deed (Hebrews 4:15); the willing, innocent, and sufficient sacrifice for the sins of the whole world (Isa. 53:4-6; John 10:17-18; 1 John 2:2; Heb. 10:10-14).

Jesus was resurrected bodily from the grave on the third day as predicted by the prophets of the Old Testament (1 Cor. 15:1-4).

Jesus Christ returned bodily to His Father in heaven (Acts 1:9-11) after completing His early ministry of declaration (John 12:46-50; 17:4-8) and reconciliation (John 3:17; Mark 8:31; 2 Cor. 5:19).

The deity of Jesus Christ is antithetical to cultic teaching. If Jesus really is God, if He is equal in all things to the omniscient, omnipotent, omnipresent God of the Bible, if He is indeed the Creator and King and Lord of all, then what He says cannot be debated. What He demands must be obeyed. What He does will stand forever. False teaching cannot operate under such restrictions. False teachers must deny, distort, or denigrate the person of Jesus Christ if they are to be free to propagate their error. Note the following flagrant examples of cultic error in regard to the Lord Jesus:

When the Virgin Mary conceived the child Jesus, the Father had begotten him in his own likeness. He was not begotten of the Holy Ghost. And who is the Father? He is the first of the human family . . . the same character that was in the garden of Eden, and who is our Father in Heaven.[1]

In *Science and Health with Key to the Scriptures,* Jesus is "the human man," the "divine idea," and was "the offspring of Mary's self-conscious communion with God."[2]

It is beyond the scope of this chapter to include more such quotations from different cults or movements illustrating these various points (but note the supplemental references at the end of this chapter). What is vital to note, however, is that any deviation from full worship of Jesus Christ as the unique God-Man, fully God and fully Man as the Scriptures and the Lord himself teach, is grievous error that can only lead into apostasy.

Treatment of the Teachings of Jesus Christ

The last series of commands from Jesus prior to returning to the Heavenly Father centered around instructions to teach and preach and witness, in every inhabited part of the earth, "all things whatsoever I have commanded you" (Matt. 28:18-20; Mark 16:15; Luke 24:44-48; John 21:15-17; Acts 1:3-8). It is not possible, of course, to include here an exhaustive list of those teachings, nor is it advisable here to presume to codify a doctrinal abstract. There are, however, several unequivocal statements from Jesus about himself and concerning His ministry that are valid checks against false teaching.

> *Belief in the completed work of Jesus Christ secures salvation* for all those who repent of their sins and trust in His substitutionary death and bodily resurrection (John 3:16; 5:24; 6:51; 10:28-30; 11:25-26).
>
> *Repudiation of Jesus' words ensures eternal damnation* (John 3:36; 5:24-29; 12:46-50) to all those who dare to reject the work of God through Christ and deny their desperate need to be "born again" (John 3:3, 18-19).
>
> *Jesus is the only way to the Father in heaven* (John 14:6). All attempts to teach otherwise label such a person as a "thief and a robber" (John 10:1-11).

---

[1] Brigham Young, *Journal of Discourses, I* (April 9, 1852), p. 50-51.
[2] *Science and Health with Key to the Scriptures,* 473:15; 473:16; 29:32-30:1.

The Holy Spirit would bring conviction of sin, righteousness, and judgment (John 16:8-11), glorifying Jesus, not some human agent (John 16:14), who would presume to bring new revelations of divine truth other than the canonical Scriptures.

Christ's human leaders will be distinguished by a servant's heart, not by their demands for power (Matt. 20:25-28; John 13:4-16).

Whenever the doctrine of salvation by grace through faith in the substitutionary death and bodily resurrection of Jesus Christ is diluted, distorted, or disdained, the wrath of God is forthcoming (John 3:36).

Whenever new revelations, visions, prophecies, words from God . . . "or an angel from heaven" teach any other gospel than that clearly revealed in the Word of God, the teacher is to "be accursed" (Gal. 1:8).

Whenever religious leaders attempt to be "lords over God's heritage" (1 Pet. 5:3) or love "to have the preeminence" (3 John 9), they have disobeyed the clear teaching of the Lord Jesus.

The apostle Jude says of this kind of leader, "These are spots in your feasts of charity, when they feast with you, feeding themselves without fear: clouds they are without water, carried about of winds; trees whose fruit withereth, without fruit, twice dead, plucked up by the roots; Raging waves of the sea, foaming out their own shame; wandering stars, to whom is reserved the blackness of darkness forever" (Jude 12-13).

Summary

Each of the criteria discussed in this chapter could be augmented by other applications and examples. The faces of error are many and subtle. The Enemy has his power in lie and doubt. God gives us His power in truth and faith. Although the extrapolations and facets of cultic doctrine and behavior are as varied as the human heart is deceitful and unknowable, all can be discerned by simple application of the following three "tests."

Is the Word of God revered and magnified as the sole source of truth? Is the person of Jesus Christ lifted up as God come in the flesh, the only, unique God-Man? Are the cardinal teachings of Jesus believed explicitly and held unwaveringly?

If the answer to any part of those questions is "no," the person, book, church, movement, organization, or phenomenon, is "not of the Father, but is of the world" (1 John 2:16).

Selected books for further study:

Games, Alan W. 1995. *Unmasking the Cults*. Grand Rapids, MI: Zondervan Publishing House. 96 p.

Horton, Michael, ed. 1992. *The Agony of Deceit*. Chicago, IL: Moody Press. 284 p.

Larson, Bob. 1989. *Larson's New Book of Cults*. Wheaton, IL: Tyndale House Publishers. 499 p.

Lewis, Gordon. 1979. *Confronting the Cults*. Phillipsburg, NJ: Presbyterian and Reformed Publishing Co. 198 p.

Martin, Walter. 1990. *Kingdom of the Cults*. Minneapolis, MN: Bethany Publishing House. 544 p.

Robertson, Irvine. 1991 *What the Cult Believes*. Chicago, IL: Moody Press. 174 p.

Rogers, John Thomas. 1983. *Communicating Christ to the Cults*. Robbinsdale, MN: Religion Analysis Service. 126 p.

Watson, William. 1991. *A Concise Dictionary of Cults and Religions*. Chicago, IL: Moody Press. 300 p.

Chapter XXII

The Old "New Age" Movement

Introduction

All of the warnings and guidelines contained in the previous chapter can also be used to evaluate the so-called "New Age movement." This movement is, of course, anything but "new," containing the essence of the lie first perpetrated on Eve by the serpent in the Garden of Eden; "Your eyes shall be opened, and ye shall be as gods, knowing good and evil" (Gen. 3:5). One of the more obvious common denominators within the myriad facets of New Age teachings is that every individual has the power to reach a state of "altered consciousness" wherein the individual is able to understand the "true" nature of the divine and realize his or her own "potential" within the cosmos.

In all the millennia since the events in Eden, Satan's strategy and lie have not changed. We are encouraged to doubt the possibility of a precise, revealed Word from God. We are then told directly that the information supposedly from God is not all true, and in fact, is a deliberate withholding of information which, when understood and appropriated, will help us to become "as gods" empowering us to become "wise."

The religions of the world all have their roots in the early Babylonian teachings begun under Nimrod (Gen. 10 and 11), and can be traced through Persia, Greece, Rome, Europe, and the West. Central to the modern revival of new age tenets are the belief systems of India and Asia, connected most clearly to Buddhism and Hinduism. For a concise history of the world's religious movements, the reader may wish to study the book

The Long War Against God. That work contains a well-documented analysis of the age-long rebellion against the revealed Word of God, and provides, perhaps, the single most complete tracing of that "war" from the Garden of Eden through the present day.

Exposure of the false message of the New Age is the intent of this chapter.

Scope and Influence

There are no readily available membership lists, no philosophical statements, dogma, or creeds accepted by a majority of identifiable sects, not even a recognizable "denomination" or umbrella group to which one could go for coherent information. Yet as far back as the late 1980s, a significant minority of the population identified themselves as active participants in a group espousing new age teachings. *US News & World Report*[1] estimated that the New Age followers represented five to ten percent of the population, and the *Washington Post*[2] cited a University of Maryland poll concluding that six percent of Maryland's residents identify with the movement.

The numbers have continued to grow steadily since then, and the influence is more widely felt than at any time since the middle ages. Rebecca Nolan, who writes an influential newsletter entitled *Financial Astrology*, brags in a 1996 promotional mailing, "Today, instead of being paid a small salary to lecture students who'd rather be surfing, I'm consulted by heads of state, central bankers, royalty, fund managers, and billionaire owners of major corporations on three continents." John Naisbitt and Patricia Aburdene, authors of the 1990 #1 bestseller, *Megatrends 2000*,[3] say that "New Age followers represent the most affluent, well-educated, successful segment of the baby boom." Naisbitt and Aburdene also estimated that corporations spend some 4 billion dollars on New Age training each year and reference the syllabus of Stanford University Graduate School of Business's "Creativity in Business" course to include "meditation, chanting, and dream work. Yoga, Zen, and tarot cards are also a part of the class."[4]

---

[1] *US News & World Report* (February 9, 1987), p. 69.

[2] *Washington Post* (January 3, 1988).

[3] John Naisbitt and Patricia Aburdene, *Megatrends 2000* (New York, NY, Warner Publ., 1990), p. 317.

[4] *Ibid.*, p. 319.

Although the modern movement has its origins in Eastern mysticism and much of the foundational literature comes from an occult background, the subtle use of Christian terminology has caused an alarming inroad into the professing Church. A popular new age bible, *A Course in Miracles*, has sold well over 500,000 copies since its initial publication in 1975, and several million more people have taken formal instruction from those who teach the *Course*. It openly presents the notes of Helen Schucman, a former Jewish atheist and psychologist who recorded the visions and messages heard from a "voice" who, she remarked, ". . . said it was Jesus."

The book teaches that "reality" as we know it does not exist, that Jesus Christ is not the only Christ, that He was not God incarnate, and that He was not punished on the cross for our sins. We are not "saved" by anything more than our own work and personal holiness, and we are all a part of God "who is all power and glory, and we are therefore as unlimited as He is." Sins are dreams, death is an illusion, and the only way to discover "truth" is to forget all that we have ever learned, put aside all thoughts we have and every preconception we hold, and question our understanding of what things mean and what their purpose is.

In spite of the suspicious origin, the clear contradiction with biblical teachings, the demand to ignore all previous knowledge, and the promotion by openly New Age groups, many churches within the mainline Christian denominations are embracing and teaching *A Course in Miracles* as part of their normally sanctioned information.

The serpent's lie has grown large, and many follow his false promises.

Key Terms and Definitions

Some foundational exposure to the key terms and definitions used within the New Age philosophies will be helpful in understanding the subtle coherence of the divergent manifestations of this movement.

The New Age refers, in today's context, to the *Age of Aquarius*. This new age is said to be the dawning of a new spiritual awareness, a globalization of the utopian dream. Explanations for these "age" changes have roots deep in occult astrology. They are prophesied to occur as certain events are foretold by movements in the heavens, bringing millennial-long shifts in every human endeavor. *The New Age movement* is an informal network of organizations and individuals with common bonds founded in a vision of universal peace and enlightenment brought about in harmony with the Age of Aquarius.

"*God*," when the term is used by New Age adherents, refers to a "higher power" that has "many faces." Depending on the context of the conversation or writing, "God" can mean an immanent being residing in the essence of the whole of reality, or an impersonal force that pervades the whole of the universe. In most instances, "God" is equal to "all-that-is."

"*Spirit guide*," sometimes referred to as a "*Holy Spirit*," is used of an entity who provides guidance through a medium — someone who is capable of "*channeling*" with the spirit guide. These guides present themselves as angelic beings or as "*ascended masters*," human beings who have achieved a state of "oneness" with the universe.

"*Channeling*" is the ability and the process of submitting one's body and mind to be used as a vehicle through which a spirit guide can speak, usually for the purpose of revealing some special or secret knowledge. Those who channel are sought as valuable resources and as means to be introduced to a personal spirit guide. Some famous mediums channel for several different spirit guides. It is the goal of most New Age disciples to make contact with their own spirit guide so that they may "channel" frequently and personally.

"*Cosmic consciousness*" is the point where a person's awareness of reality is said to become linked with the greater reality of the universe. Such an event often produces a profound sense of identity with all things, a transcendence of individuality blending with what is presented as "*ultimate reality*." This reality is said to be the immaterial, spiritual, and eternally living consciousness of "all-that-is." Cosmic consciousness can only be reached through a disciplined process, often assisted by a spirit guide, wherein a person "empties" his or her mind, becomes willing to "let go" of preconceived ideas of reality, and "allow" the new reality to take over.

"Altered state of consciousness" is a new *"level of awareness"* brought about through mental and emotional exercises designed to prepare the practitioner to receive the new awareness. Usually the techniques are related to meditation rituals, and often include such practices as chanting, visualization, and body positioning. The initial experience is normally manifested by a sense of calm, accompanied by a growing feeling of inner peace. Successive sessions bring more rapid results and different information providing "new" insight. Continued efforts to alter the conscious state will bring "mystical" experiences, often accompanied by voices explaining these new wonders, and eventually, introduction to a spirit guide.

"Personal transformation" is the New Age equivalent to Christian conversion. It is a "born again" experience resulting from a psychic shift in perspective, sometimes referred to as a "paradigm shift." Unlike the demands of the Christian gospel which requires belief at the start, conversion to a New Age world view can be engineered through subtle and seemingly innocuous techniques for relaxation, visualization, enhancing creativity, etc. Altered states of consciousness are induced in the hope that a psychic or mystical experience will occur, causing doubt in previously held reality. New Age explanations are then taught to give profound answers for the experience. Personal transformation is usually viewed as a life-long process bringing a growing assurance in personal wholeness and power.

"Visualization" is a popularized psychological technique used for centuries in occult and mystic religions to bring about change in the material realm by the power of the mind. Its widespread use is taught in many public school curricula, promoted throughout the business world in seminars and management training, and is often foisted on the Christian church as a technique to build up "faith." Essentially, the

process is a conscious manipulation of the "self-fulfilling prophecy" cliché: think about something hard enough, clearly enough, and long enough, and it will come to pass.

"Self-realization" is a condition of confident awareness that the individual is autonomous and is able to exercise personal choice with the same power and impunity as a god. Sometimes referred to as *"self-actualization,"* it is achieved when one "knows" that his or her "self" is essentially indistinguishable from "God." The practical outgrowth of this teaching is that every human being has the "right" to do whatever he or she wishes, as long as it does not interfere with another's pursuit of this realization.

The preceding terms do not adequately cover all the beliefs of the new age, but they are the more commonly used ideas and practices of New Age proponents. Use of these key terms during conversations or in writings about psychological, spiritual, religious, or even political matters may be an indication that the proponent espouses some aspect of New Age doctrine.

Basic Beliefs of The Age of Aquarius

Although the New Age movement is an informal mega-network of organizations, philosophies, and individuals that is very difficult to define, there are several common beliefs that can be identified. Each group or individual may stress certain aspects of these basic doctrines, but all share a commitment to these ideals.

"Oneness" is the term most often used to describe the theological doctrine more commonly recognized as *"pantheism."* Essentially, the teaching is that all that exists is God. All of nature, all of reality, all of the universe is "God." The specific application of this "oneness" may range from a mystical "force" that can be tapped by the individual, to an intellectual discussion about evolution coming to "consciousness" in the universe. Western civilization tends to intellectualize and depersonalize this discussion while the Eastern influence tends to mystify and spiritualize it. However the deliberations may vary,

all agree that "all-that-is" is all that is, and that "all-that-is" has always existed, and always will be "all-that-is." That would sound ridiculous except that it mirrors the biblical statement by Jesus Christ that He is the "Alpha and Omega, the beginning and the ending . . . which is, and which was, and which is to come, the Almighty" (Revelation 1:8).

"Unity and Interdependence" extends and differs somewhat from the Eastern emphasis on "oneness" to suggest that while "all-that-is" is unified and coherent, the "whole" is enriched by the diversity of its "parts." Diversity is celebrated as a manifestation of the universe, but "wholeness" comes as each diverse manifestation functions as an interdependent piece of the greater reality. That which promotes unity and interdependence is good, that which does not must be avoided. "Holistic" approaches to ecology and medicine are promoted, and world orders that promise the "common good" are embraced. Businesses that spread the processes of commerce and manufacturing across socio-economic zones or different geological areas are taught as the ideal concept.

"Globalism" or **"globalization"** is the belief in a one-world community, a transformation of human society into a "global village," a single civilization which will ultimately come to a greater state of oneness with all life through an evolutionary ascent towards consciousness. This belief application can be most easily seen in the political realm and the effort behind such institutions as the United Nations. A more esoteric application of this concept can be observed behind various "save-the-planet" movements.

"Evolution" is the order of all things. Whether the evolutionary processes are seen as "directed" by the "consciousness" of the universe, or the random interplay of blind forces, all things have evolved out of a primeval chaos of the eternal essence of whatever makes up the universe. The concept may be popularized and allegorized by making the forces of nature into "gods and goddesses" or given sophistication by attempts to rationalize and intellectualize the mechanical processes by which evolution has occurred, but all levels of the New Age movement hold to evolutionary beliefs. An Omniscient, Omnipotent Creator God who spoke the universe into being is unthinkable and staunchly opposed.

"Survival" is the important foundational belief platform coming out of the adherence to evolution. The applications can be as widely varied as "master race" cults like the Aryan Nation and Neo-Nazis, or vegetarian zealots who refuse to eat a "brother or sister" animal, or democratic political proponents who fight the idea of a one world government out of fear that a horrible dictator would rule humanity. The focal point, the underlying value, is the need for survival; survival of the individual, survival of the race, survival of the planet, survival of the universe. The difficulty of this value system is that it is both nebulous and self-serving. New Age groups are often in conflict with one another as to what best insures "survival," but they will all agree that one must do what one can to obtain it.

"Autonomy," ultimately a logical extension of the "Oneness" belief, has its most obvious expression in the various "individual rights" so popular in democratic societies. This is a very subtle concept, since the Bible certainly teaches *responsibility* and *accountability* for each individual's choices. But the real difference is vast. New Age autonomy would readily sanction abortion, homosexuality, promiscuity, divorce, deception, etc., all within the limitations of "unity and interdependence." That is, each individual has the right to do whatever he or she might wish to do unless and until it interferes with that same "right" on the part of another — or detracts from the common good. There are no absolutes in the New Age thinking, however, so application of this principle is often relegated to a synthesis of the current majority thinking.

"No absolutes" is treated like a *prima facie* statement that justifies all things. Since the universe

is constantly evolving to higher and higher orders of reality, knowledge is both temporal and temporary. Nothing can be known for sure. It is possible to experience certain levels of awareness and to function pragmatically in the environment that we now experience, but it is impossible to find "ultimate truth." Man is always searching, always learning, never able to know. This dogma, of course, is the very antithesis of biblical Christianity. The God of the Bible reveals His absolutes, and we, His creatures, are obligated to obey them or suffer the consequences. New Age believers cannot exist in the same relationship with biblical Christianity. It is worth noting that the Scripture speaks of this in 2 Timothy 3:1-9, noting that those who hold to such "New Age" teachings are "ever learning, and never able to come to the knowledge of the truth. . . . these also resist the truth: men of corrupt minds, reprobate concerning the faith. But they shall proceed no further: for their folly shall be manifest unto all men. . . ."

General Categories of New Age Groups

Eastern mysticism is the category most often thought of as "New Age." These would include the more formal Buddhist, Hindu, and Confucian religions as well as their kindred, the Baha'i and the Hare Krishna. Each of the groups have a more formal worship hierarchy, and tend to practice the mystical methods of meditation and follow established rituals. Although these movements have had an impact in the Western world, it has been more of an indirect influence, than a growth in open followers.

Occult and mystery teachings form a common character for widely divergent groups, ranging from the Church of Satan to the Foundation for Shaminic Studies. Some are focused around specific ancient religions like the Temple of Set (Egyptian), and others are just weird and bizarre like Eckankar, founded by Paul Twitchell and claimed to be the highest pinnacle of wisdom and truth obtainable. In these groups are the magic practitioners (both "white" and "black" magic) and the ancient cults like the Druids. Attention is given to gods and goddesses, stories of "lost" civilizations that held the secrets of the gods, and to astrological signs of the zodiac, all of which provide the promise of learning the deeper mysteries of the universe.

Earth and nature groups worship "Mother Earth" and all forms of nature. Formal groups like witch covens, goddess devotees, and pagan temples are the more easily recognized of this type. The religious worship of the earth goes back to Babylon and Egypt, and has had its followers all down the centuries. Many American Indian religions fall in this category, and the modern revival of these worshipers continues. Much of the passion of the various ecology and "green" movements is founded in the basic tenets of a "worship" of the earth, and is often disguised as a political agenda rather than a spiritual one.

Health and prosperity teachings are very popular among the non-mystic segment of the New Age followers. Indeed, many Christian ministers are known for preaching a "health, wealth, and prosperity" gospel under such pseudonyms as "positive thinking," or "possibility thinking," or "name-it-and-claim-it" faith. But the more readily identifiable cults are the Church of Religious Science (Science of Mind), Christian Science, Scientology (Dianetics), Unity Church, and Unitarianism. The underlying doctrine among all these divergent groups is that each of us has the human potential to "realize" the ideas of our minds. This is the concept that is sweeping the business world through seminars and work-shops on "empowerment" of one sort or another.

Astral and galactic groups would include those who are heavily focused on UFOs, other dimensions, other worlds, and other teachings such as astral travel and out of body experiences (OBEs). Most of the publicity is given to the fringe adherents who talk of being picked up by an alien from a spaceship, but there are many intellectual and professional devotees who seek confirmation of the paranormal or "believe" that mankind is "not alone" in the universe. Millions of dollars are spent in lavish scientific experiments to "search" for communication from outside our solar system. NASA has long had as one of its published agendas the search for life on other planets.

Deceptive Christian groups vary widely from "strange" cults such as the Church Universal and Triumphant (Elizabeth Claire, prophet) and the Unification Church (Sun Myung Moon) to the more well known Mormons and Jehovah's Witnesses. In each case, Christian terminology is woven into the teaching of the "oneness" and "personal transformation" ideas of the New Age. Two world renowned churches, St. James Cathedral in London and St. John the Divine in New York, have become centers for New Age teaching, openly endorsing the bizarre and cultic in the name of "harmony."

The most widely accepted inroad into the liberal churches of the West has been the encouragement of seminars and structured lectures on *A Course in Miracles*, published by The Foundation for Inner Peace. This book, alluded to earlier in this chapter, openly states that the world is an illusion not created by God, denying the deity of Christ and the necessity of Jesus' death on the cross for salvation. It also teaches that forgiveness is nothing but an illusion, merely a kind of "happy fiction" necessary for those who do not know any better. This is true, according to the *Course*, because sins are but dreams bearing no effects at all. One wonders why those who call themselves *Christian* would have anything to do with that blasphemy.

Foundations and Centers for Human Potential are gaining status and impact in the Western world. Often these groups disguise their seminars with such names as "Creative Thinking," "Stress Management," "Success Techniques for Successful People," and "Organizational Development." Other groups take more sinister names like The Omega Group, The Forum (Erhard Seminars Training, now promoted through Transformational Technologies), and "The Association for Research and Enlightenment." All of these groups, in one form or another, chant the mantra, "Be all you can be!" Whether they are esoteric and spiritual like The Theosophical Society of America or ecological and political like John Denver's Windstar Foundation, they all have as the foundational matrix of philosophy the "oneness" of all things and evolutionary progression of all events through "personal transformation" processes bringing about a "greater reality." The emphasis may be pragmatic as in the business seminar or religious as in the earth worship cults, but it is the same doctrine that pervades all.

The Biblical Pattern for Victory

Although Satan is called "the god of this world" and has great liberty and power to blind "the minds of them which believe not," (2 Cor. 4:4), he is not able to act unilaterally. "Greater is he that is in you, than he that is in the world" (1 John 4:4). We are given many promises of our ultimate victory over the lie of the enemy, not the least of which is the great cry of victory from the lips of our Lord Jesus on the cross of Calvary, "It is finished!" (John 19:30). But those promises of our victory, assurances that if we "resist the devil and he will flee from you" (James 4:7), would seem vague and more difficult if it were not for the specific instructions to gain that victory.

Remember the Rules of the Conflict

The battle is for your mind (2 Cor. 11:3; Col. 2:8). The battleground of all spiritual warfare is fought in the mind, not the feelings or the intuition. "Transformation" of the Christian is to take place "by the renewing of your mind" (Rom. 12:2).

The enemy is Satan (1 Pet. 5:8). We are not fighting the *results* of error, we are fighting "against principalities, against powers, against the rulers of the darkness of this world, against spiritual wickedness in high places" (Eph. 6:12).

The strategy of the enemy has not changed (Gen. 3:1-6). The same effort is made to generate doubt of the accuracy of God's Word, embrace the possibility that God is unable or unwilling to do as He said He would in His Word, and to question the character of instructions that would withhold from us knowledge that would make us powerful — as powerful as God.

The weakness of our nature has not changed (1 John 2:16). "For all that is in the world, the lust of the flesh, and the lust of the eyes, and the pride of life, is not of the Father, but is of the world." Eve's fall into deception set the pattern for all subsequent disobedience. "And when the woman saw that the tree was good for food, and that it was pleasant to the eyes, and a tree to be desired to make one wise, she took of the fruit thereof, and did eat, and gave also unto her husband with her, and he did eat" (Gen. 3:6).

Summary

It would be well to remind ourselves that all the power of the enemy is concentrated in lie and doubt (John 8:44). Our power to resist that deception is available only through a confident knowledge of "the truth" as given and granted by "the Word," the Lord Jesus Christ (John 14:6; 12:46-50). The three "tests" detailed in the preceding chapter are applicable to the New Age as well as to the cults. How accurately is the Word of God treated? If it is not revered and magnified as the inspired and authoritative absolute revelation of an Omnipotent God, those who would so disdain it should be avoided with vehemence (Gal. 1:6-9). Is Jesus Christ lifted up and worshipped as God in the flesh? If not, those who would dare to demean Him are to be held as "anti-Christ" and are not to be granted the blessing of "God speed" (2 John 7-10). Are the teachings of Jesus held to be the eternal words of God? If the answer is no, those who reject His "light" are those who love "darkness rather than light, because their deeds were evil" (John 3:19).

Selected books for further study:
Bubeck, Mark I. 1991. *The Satanic Revival*. San Bernardino, CA: Here's Life Publishers. 263 p.
Hanegraaff, Hank. 1993. *Christianity in Crisis*. Eugene, OR: Harvest House. 447 p.
Hunt, David, and T.A. McMahon. 1985. *The Seduction of Christianity*, Eugene, OR: Harvest House. 239 p.
Jones, Peter. 1982. *The Gnostic Empire Strikes Back*. Phillipsburg, NJ: Presbyterian and Reformed. 112 p.
Kjos, Berit. 1990. *Your Child and the New Age*. Wheaton, IL: Victor Books. 180 p.
Kjos, Berit. 1992. *Under the Spell of Mother Earth*. Wheaton, IL: Victor Books. 204 p.

MacArthur, John E. 1992. *Charismatic Chaos*. Grand Rapids, MI: Zondervan Publishing House.

Marrs, Texe. 1990. *Texe Marrs Book of New Age Cults and Religions*. Austin, TX: Living Truth Publishers. 351 p.

Martin, Walter. 1989. *The New Age Cult*. Minneapolis, MN: Bethany House Publishers. 140 p.

Miller, Elliot. 1989. *A Crash Course on The New Age Movement*. Grand Rapids, MI: Baker Book House. 260 p.

Morris, Henry M. 1989. *The Long War Against God*. Grand Rapids, MI: Baker Book House. 344 p.

Morrison, Alan. 1994. *The Serpent and the Cross*. Birmingham, England: K & M Books. 688 p.

Appendix A

Numerical Designs in the Bible

Introduction

A rather intriguing type of evidence for divine inspiration of the Bible is that contained in certain remarkable arithmetical and geometrical phenomena found scattered here and there in its pages. This type of evidence is controversial, and so is included here as an appendix rather than as an integral component of the manifold body of Christian evidences discussed in the main text of the book.

Cautions to Observe

One question is whether or not such phenomena are unique to the Bible or can also be discovered in other books which are not divinely inspired. One cannot prove a universal negative, but the writer has not yet been able to discover such phenomena in other books, nor have others been able to do so, so far as known.

A related question is whether, since there are so many different numbers and other mathematical concepts which exist, and so many different ways in which mathematical patterns might be formed, is it not only to be expected that *some* mathematical patterns would be found in the Bible?

The answer to this question could only be obtained by a sophisticated statistical analysis of the possible number of meaningful, orderly mathematical patterns in, say, the words of a given chapter, in contrast to the possible number of meaningless, random patterns that could occur with the same words in the same chapter. So far as known, no one has yet undertaken such an analysis. Until this is done, one must more or less rely on his own judgment as to whether or not the evidence is meaningful. In any case, there are infinitely more *random*, disorderly patterns possible with a given number of components than there are *orderly* patterns. Randomness is statistically probable; order is statistically improbable. When one deals often with data of any kind on a statistical basis, he tends to develop a sort of instinctive feeling for what is and what is not strictly accidental in the arrangement of those data, even in the absence of a formal statistical analysis.

For whatever it is worth, the writer believes that the many remarkable mathematical patterns in Scripture are too improbable to be explained on a naturalistic basis. If so, this evidence becomes one more striking indication of the verbal inspiration of the Bible.

Another question is whether this type of study might be used to support certain mystical interpretations of Scripture and even to justify strange and dubious doctrines. Unfortunately, among both Christians and pre-Christian Jews, some Bible teachers have done exactly that, imparting unnatural interpretations to certain passages of Scriptures on the basis of the supposed spiritual meanings of the numbers connected with those passages.

But numbers in the Bible should never be used to prove or even to intimate any point of doctrine. The same caution should be observed in connection with any other structural phenomena in the Bible (e.g., types, first mentions, etc.).

One cannot overlook the fact, however, that *some* numbers in the Bible are used in such a way as to indicate that the writer did regard these numbers themselves as being of special significance. The most obvious example is the number "seven," which *all* expositors recognize to be symbolic of completeness; but there are many others (e.g., 10, 12, 40, 70, 666, etc.) which clearly are regarded as significant in various ways.

We must not make too much of the spiritual meanings of numbers — most of them seem to have no such meanings — but neither should we ignore the fact that the Bible writers (and, therefore, the Holy Spirit) did intend such meanings in many cases. The true "literal" interpretation is that which seeks to reproduce what the writer himself (and the divine Author who directed his pen) *intended* to mean.

The following rules seem appropriate to follow in this regard: (1) never use biblical numbers to *teach* doctrine; they should only be used to *illustrate* doctrine, and then only when there is clear and unequivocal teaching related to that doctrine elsewhere in Scripture, and also only when there is clear contextual justification for that use; (2) the primary use of such numbers and mathematical patterns is not doctrinal, but apologetic, providing a distinctive evidence that the Bible writings are uniquely and supernaturally inspired.

With these cautions and rules in mind, we are in position to look at a few of the innumerable mathematical patterns that can be found in the Holy Scriptures.

The Occurrence of Mathematical Phenomena in Scripture

To find mathematical phenomena in Scripture is not as surprising as it may seem at first. The Author of Scripture is also the Designer of the universe. Of the latter, the Scripture says: "Lift up your eyes on high, and behold who hath created these things, that bringeth out their host by number" (Isa. 40:26). "Who hath measured the waters in the hollow of His hand, and meted out heaven with the span, and comprehended the dust of the earth in a measure, and weighed the mountains in scales, and the hills in a balance?" (Isa. 40:12).

The natural world has been very carefully and meticulously planned by God; its structures are highly ordered and its processes precisely controlled. It is significant that man has found it appropriate to develop the science of mathematics to describe these structures and processes. In fact, most scientists would agree that a phenomenon is not really understood until it can be formulated in mathematical terms. Mathematics indeed is the very *language* of science and engineering.

That being so, it is not unreasonable to anticipate mathematical phenomena in God's written revelation, as well as in His natural creation. The full nature of any possible mathematical description of the Word, however, is yet undiscovered. All we can do at present is to note occasional instances where particular numerical relationships emerge to the surface, as it were, from some underlying substratum of mathematical structure which has not yet been identified and explored.

On the other hand, the phenomenon of "Bible numerics," so-called, which has been studied at great length by Dr. Ivan Panin and his followers, is questionable. These writers believe the original Hebrew and Greek texts are filled with numerical patterns in the arrangement of the very words and letters. Panin even developed his own Greek New Testament by applying the criterion of the presence of numeric patterns as the test of authenticity of any particular passage. This evidence has very doubtful statistical significance, however, and some writers have claimed to be able to find similar numeric patterns in other books and documents. In some cases, Panin's approach seems persuasive, but in others it seems artificial. At best, this particular type of numerical study is still quite uncertain and so cannot be cited as a Christian evidence.

The Numbers "Seven" and "Ten"

The most obvious examples of numeric significance in the Bible are associated with the number "seven." This is the most frequently occurring number in Scripture and is very commonly invested with the symbolic meaning of "fullness" or "completion." God created all things in six days, and then marked the seventh day as a day of rest and contemplation of all His glorious work of creation (Gen. 2:1-3). In like manner, man is to do his own work for six days and then rest and honor the Lord and His completed work every seventh day (Exod. 20:8-11).

This primeval emphasis on the number "seven" has been carried over into numerous other applications in Scripture, normally conveying the same basic thought of "fullness." The climax of this "seven-ness" of Scripture is found in the final book of the Bible, in which all the developments of the book are clustered around groups of seven — seven churches, seven seals, seven trumpets, seven vials, seven thunders, seven years, etc.

A number which also is used in a similar sense is the number "ten." In a way, this number is more naturally associated with completeness even than the number "seven." The quickest and most natural way for man to count numbers is by means of his fingers, of which there are ten. Thus, man's number systems have most commonly been structured around the number "ten." The decimal system, the metric system of units, etc., all recognize the naturalness of the number.

The most obvious example in the Bible is the Ten Commandments. Other examples are the ten plagues of Egypt, the ten kings of the prophecies of Daniel and the Revelation, the ten visions of Zechariah, and others. It will be noted that this number seems to be used when the concept is one of "judgment" as well as "fullness." However, the same is also often true of the number "seven."

Combinations of "Seven" and "Ten"

When the numbers "7" and "10" are combined, either by multiplying them to get "70" or by adding them to get "17," two other very interesting Bible numbers appear. The one seems to be used in relation to "judgment" in a special sense as it affects Israel among all the nations of the world, the other in reference to "fullness" in a special sense as it relates to the fullness of eternal life received by those who are redeemed from all the nations of the world.

The original number of the children of Israel as they left Canaan to go into Egypt was 70 souls (Gen. 46:27; Exod. 1:5; Deut. 10:22). Also, there were 70 original nations established by God, as indicated by adding up the names in Genesis 10, the "Table of Nations." That this correspondence of numbers had significance was indicated by Moses in Deuteronomy 32:8, when he said: "When the Most High divided to the nations their inheritance, when he separated the sons of Adam, he set the bounds of the people according to the number of the children of Israel."

Evidently, the Israelites took this statement very seriously, as the number "70" was thenceforth predominant in their judgmental councils. They ordained 70 original elders to judge the people (Num. 11:16, 25); there were 70 scholars designated to translate the Scriptures into the Greek language (the Septuagint Version); there were 70 men on the Council of the Sanhedrin, and Christ sent 70 disciples to the "lost sheep of the house of Israel" (Luke 10:1; Matt. 10:6).

The number "70" was also important in another way in Israel's history. Because of their failure to keep the seventh-year sabbath for the land, for 70 of those sabbatical years, they were sent into captivity in Babylon for 70 years (note Lev. 25:1-4, 26:14, 32-35; Jer. 25:8-11; 2 Chron. 36:15-21). Thus, the people of Israel had despised the Sabbatical Law for 70 x 7, or 490 years, and were thus cast out of their land for 70 years.

This brings before us a remarkable set of 490-year periods in Israel's history. From the time of God's first dealings with Abraham until the final establishment of the children of Israel in the millennial kingdom, there appear to be four 490-year cycles, totaling 1,960 years, when God is dealing with Israel in full covenantal relationship. These years, however, do not include those years when the relationship was suspended, as it were, by Israel's disobedience. Such years were simply lost, as far as Israel is concerned, and are not counted in the covenant years.

The first cycle began with the birth of Abraham. From then until God called him out of Ur was 75 years (Gen. 12:4). There were 430 more years until the giving of the Law on Mount Sinai and the beginning of a new era (Gal. 3:17). However, from this total of 505 years can be deducted the 15 years when Abraham had lapsed from faith in God's promise and went in to Hagar (Gen. 16:3) until the promised seed was finally born (Gen. 21:5). This leaves 490 years during which Abraham and his descendants were abiding under the covenant promise.

With the giving of the Law began a new cycle, which was acknowledged by God through His presence at the ark of the covenant in the tabernacle. This continued until the dedication of Solomon's temple and the incoming presence of God in that new Holy Place.

The years from the Law to the temple seem to total 601. These include 40 years in the wilderness (Acts 13:18), plus approximately 20 years under Joshua, plus 450 years under the Judges, including Samuel (Acts 13:20), plus 40 years under Saul (Acts 13:21), plus 40 years under David (1 Kings 2:11), plus 11 years under Solomon until the dedication of the temple (1 Kings 6:1, 38; 8:1-11).

From this 601-year total should be subtracted these years under the Judges, during which God withdrew His protection and allowed the Israelites to be subjugated by the peoples whom they had, contrary to God's command, allowed to remain in the land. Thus, they were in captivity to Mesopotamia 8 years (Judg. 3:8), Moab 18 years (3:14), the Canaanites 20 years (4:3), Midian 7 years (6:1), the Philistines and Ammonites 18 years (10:8), and the Philistines again 40 years (13:1). These captivities total 111 years, which, subtracted from the 60 years above, leave 490 years.

It is interesting also that this particular cycle of 490 years can be calculated in still a different way. From the total of 601 years may be subtracted the 111 years from the time the ark of the covenant was taken out of the tabernacle until it was set up in Solomon's temple. This includes 20 years under Samuel (1 Sam. 4:22; 7:2), 80 years under Saul and David, and 11 years under Solomon.

From the dedication of the temple in 1005 B.C. to Artaxerxes' commandment to build Jerusalem in 445 B.C. (see Neh. 2:18) are 560 years. Both these dates are accepted in secular history and agree with standard biblical chronologies such as that of Ussher. However, the 70-year captivity in Babylon must, of course, be deducted from this, once again leaving 490 years.

It should be recognized, of course, that chronological data for the above three cycles of Israel's history are somewhat unsettled, especially for the period in Egypt and the period under the Judges. There are several competing schools of thought and the whole subject is technical and complicated. For our purposes here, however, it does seem remarkable that these various numbers, taken primarily from the Bible, yield three such cycles of 490 years each.

The fourth cycle, of course, is the great "70 week" prophecy of Daniel 9:24-27. This prophecy defines a 490-year period to begin with the decree of Artaxerxes and to end with the "consummation" (v. 27), evidently the destruction of the "abomination of desolation" and the fulfillment of God's original promise to Abraham in the millennial kingdom.

The first 69 weeks (483 years) of this cycle terminated in the crucifixion of the Messiah, as we have seen in chapter 14. As a result, God broke off His covenant relation with His people, and there has since been a long period during which, as it were, time is standing still for Israel. The clock will start again when the last 7-year period begins, quite likely immediately following the translation of the Church after the "fulness of the Gentiles has come in" (Rom. 11:25) and, therefore, when "the times of the Gentiles are fulfilled" (Luke 21:24). This will be the so-called "70th week of Daniel," as summarized in

Daniel 9:27, and as expounded fully in Revelation 6–19.

The number 70, therefore, 7 x 10, is a most remarkable and fascinating number in its identification throughout the Bible with Israel, especially with Israel in relation to the other nations of the world. When combined again with the number 7, to make the 490-year cycle, it reminds us again and again both of God's judgment and also of His repeated forgiveness. It seems singularly appropriate, therefore, when we hear Christ telling Peter to forgive his brother, not 7 times, but 70 times 7 (Matt. 18:21-22).

When the two numbers, 7 and 10, are added instead of multiplied together, the intriguing number "17" is obtained. The concept of fullness is now doubly in view, with the idea of full judgment superseded by full blessing. Thus, it seems to be connected with fullness of grace, eternal life, eternal security.

The word occurs first in Genesis 7:11 in connection with the coming of the great judgment of the Flood on the 17th day of the second month. The Flood, of course, while it brought judgment to the world, also brought deliverance and a new beginning to those on the ark, who would otherwise have been inundated in the universal corruption of the antediluvians. It is significant, therefore, that the ark landed exactly five months later, again on the 17th day of the month. The seventh month of the Jewish civil year later became the first month of the religious year (Exod. 12:2). The Passover lamb was always slain on the 14th day of this month (Exod. 12:6). Christ ate the Passover with His disciples on this day, was crucified the next day, and thus rose from the dead on the 17th day of the month, the exact anniversary of the landing of the ark! Both events speak of deliverance and new life, and their occurrence on the same date can hardly be coincidental.

The theme of security and eternal life is stressed in Romans 8:35-39, where there are 17 entities: "tribulation, distress . . . height, nor depth, nor any other creature" listed — all of which are "unable to separate us from the love of God which is in Christ Jesus our Lord." Psalm 23, perhaps the greatest chapter on the believer's security in the Old Testament, contains 17 personal references to the believer (i.e., "*my* shepherd," "all the days of *my* life," etc.).

An interesting number is derived from the number 17

when one adds up all the numbers from 1 to 17. This gives 153, which is also equal to 9 x 17. The digits in the number 153 add up to 9 and the cubes of the digits add up to 153 again. The miracle of the 153 fishes (John 21:11) is the ninth great sign in the Gospel of John, all of which testify that "Jesus is the Christ, the Son of God, and that believing ye might have life through His name" (John 20:31).

The 153 fish seem to have been mentioned by their number in this way because they represent those whom the disciples, as fishers of men, were to go forth into the world to catch with the "net" of the Gospel. "For all there were so many, yet was not the net broken" (John 21:11).

Uses of the Number "Twelve"

The number "12" is also a number which indicates the idea of "completeness," though perhaps the dominant idea is that of "divine government." The natural ordinances for the regulation of the earth are founded upon the sun and moon, which function so as to give the earth a cycle of 12 months per year.

The obvious examples in the Bible, of course, are the 12 tribes of Israel and the 12 apostles of Jesus Christ. This division is to be eternally established as the governmental basis for both the millennial earth (Matt. 19:28) and the eternal earth (Rev. 22:12, 14). Numerous other examples, such as the 144,000 witnesses (Rev. 7:4), could be added.

In the 23rd Psalm, it has already been noted that there are 17 occurrences of the first-person-singular pronoun. Now we may note there are 12 references to the Lord, and that these occur in a rather remarkable geometric pattern. Thus:

"The Lord"	— once in verse 1	
"He"	— twice in verse 2	Testimony
"He"	— thrice in verse 3	
"Thou"	— thrice in verse 4	Prayer
"Thou"	— twice in verse 5	
"The Lord"	— once in verse 6	

The Numbers "Six" and "Eight"

Having already discussed the number "7," we now want to consider the adjacent numbers "6" and "8." The number "6," being as it were short of perfection or completeness, speaks especially of man without God. The number "8," being over and beyond completeness, speaks of a new beginning, of regeneration, resurrection, new life. It is especially identified with Jesus Christ as the One who brings salvation and eternal life.

Man was created on the sixth day, and it was in Noah's six-hundredth year, 1,656 years after the creation that the Flood came to destroy man. There are numerous examples in the Bible of this apparent identification of the number "6" with man, especially as in rebellion against God. The most striking, however, is the establishment of the number 666 as the mark of the Beast (Rev. 13:18) in the coming Tribulation period. The number 666 is a very interesting number. It would be written as chi xi stigma — see the list of the numerical equivalents of Greek letters at the end of the paragraph). In the Greek language (as in Hebrew), each letter was also used as a number. The title "Christ" in Greek is written ("Χηριστοσ"), thus beginning and ending with the letters x and s that appear in the number of the Beast. However, the central part of the name of Christ is forced out, as it were, by the letter, which is in the form of a coiling serpent!

Greek Alphabet — Numerical Equivalents

Greek Letter	Symbol	Number		English Equivalent
Alpha	α	1		a
Beta	β	2		b
Gamma	γ	3		g
Delta	δ	4		d
Epsilon	ε	5		e (short)
Stigma (or vau)	ς	6	(only when used as a number)	s (at end of word)
Zeta	ζ	7		z (or dz)
Eta	η	8		e (long)
Theta	θ	9		th
Iota	ι	10		i, j
Kappa	κ	20		k
Lambda	λ	30		l
Mu	μ	40		m
Nu	ν	50		n
Xi	ξ	60		x
Omicron	o	70		0 (short)

Pi	π	80	p
Koppa	ϙ	90	(not a letter)
Rho	ρ	100	r
Sigma	σ	200	s
Tau	τ	300	t
Upsilon	υ	400	u
Phi	φ	500	ph (f)
Chi	χ	600	ch
Psi	ψ	700	ps
Omega	ω	800	o (long)
Sampsi	9	900	(not a letter)

The Beast, of course, is the Antichrist, the man of sin, who receives his power from the dragon, that old serpent, the devil, and Satan (Rev. 12:9; 13:4). The number 666 is also the sum of the numbers, and 36 is, of course, 6 x 6. The Beast is mentioned by that name exactly 36 times in the Book of Revelation. Actually there are two "beasts" (Rev. 13:11-12) collaborating as one, which perhaps correlates with the repeated appearance of 6 x 6.

The "number of his name" most obviously refers to the numerical value of the name, either the human name or assumed official name, of the man who is to be revealed as this Man of sin. The message of Revelation 13:18 seems to be that one who "hath wisdom" will be able to identify this man before he is openly revealed by "counting the number of his name." Most likely this would involve transliterating his name as pronounced in his native language into the corresponding sounds in the New Testament Greek language, then adding the numbers corresponding to the letters of that name. Probably about one out of every ten thousand names will actually have a value of 666, and one of these will ultimately turn out to be the Beast.[1]

In remarkable contrast to this, the name Jesus (Greek) has the value "888." The name "Christ" has a value of 8 x 185, and the name "Lord" 8 x 100. There are exactly eight combinations of these three names used in the New Testament ("Lord" — "Jesus" — "Christ" — "Lord Jesus" — "Lord Christ" — "Jesus Christ" — "Christ Jesus" — and "Lord Jesus Christ"), and each, of course, has a numerical equivalent which is a multiple of "eight."

---

[1] There have, of course, been many other interpretations of the meaning of 666 in Revelation 13:18. All of them require excessive allegorization or symbolization.

Christ was raised on the "eighth" day, and there are eight resuscitations (i.e., temporary resurrections) from the dead recorded in the Bible (1 Kings 17:22; 2 Kings 4:34-35; 2 Kings 13:21; Matt. 9:24-25; Luke 7:15; John 11:44; Acts 9:40-41; Acts 20:9-12). The resurrection of Christ himself is the eighth of the nine great "signs" around which the Gospel of John is centered.

The Number "22" and the Hebrew Alphabet

Only one other number will be discussed here, although this type of study could be expanded indefinitely. This is the fascinating number "22." There are exactly 22 letters in the Hebrew alphabet, and the Hebrew language is that through which God has chosen to convey His Word to man. The language of the antediluvians was probably the same as spoken in Eden between God and Adam, and was also the language spoken by Shem after the Flood. Since Noah and Shem did not participate in the rebellion of Nimrod at Babel, there is no reason to suppose that their language was among those "confused" by God at that time. This inference is further supported by the fact that the names of the antediluvian patriarchs (Adam, Seth, etc.) all have definite meanings in the Hebrew language, and also by the remarkable revival of the Hebrew language in the present nation of Israel. This is possibly the "pure language" which will be restored to all people in the millennium (Zeph. 3:9).

In any case, the number "22" aptly symbolizes God's revelation to man. The very purpose of language is that God might communicate His Word to man, and that man might respond in praise and thanksgiving to God. The Lord Jesus intimated this when He (who is the Living Word of God) said, "I am Alpha and Omega" (Rev. 22:13). These are the first and last letters of the Greek language, in which, of course, the New Testament was written.

Of direct significance is the interesting appearance of the number "22" in the Book of Psalms. This book is unique in the Bible. Not only is it the longest book, with 150 chapters, located in the middle of the Scriptures, but it is the only book whose chapter and verse divisions are part of the original inspired writing. Each Psalm was separate, with its own specific heading, and its verse divisions were clearly delineated by its poetic structure, right from the beginning.

The Book of Psalms (meaning "hymns of praise") is also known as "the book of the praises of Israel." Thus, it is especially designed to form, as it were, the definitive pattern for man's use of language in the response of praise to God. The theme of *praise* is fundamental in all of man's ability to communicate in meaningful speech, and this is the keynote of the book of Psalms.

Psalms has been divided into five books, the first four ending with Psalm 41, 72, 89, and 106, respectively. Each of these four books ends with the exclamation: "Blessed be the Lord." The fifth book seems to end with a like exhortation, at the end of Psalm 145, instead of 150. Then the last five Psalms form a glorious postscript of praise to all five books. Each of these begins and ends with the exclamatory phrase: "Praise ye the Lord."

This phrase is actually in the Hebrew one word "Hallelujah," which could be considered the key word in the Book of Psalms. It is composed of the verb "hallel" ("to praise") and the name of God ("Jah").

Now it is significant that the word "hallelujah" occurs exactly 22 times in the Book of Psalms, 10 of these occurrences being those in the last five Psalms.

Even more significant is the first time the verb itself ("hallel") occurs in the Book of Psalms. We find it in the midst of the most graphic scene of undeserved suffering and death in the entire Bible, on the lips of the one suffering. Remembering that the chapters and verses in Psalms are themselves part of its Spirit-ordered structure, it is thrilling to note that this first occurrence of the verb "hallel" is in Psalm 22:22! Even more thrilling and praiseworthy does it become when we see that this verse is quoted prophetically by the Lord Jesus himself, right at the very climax of His sufferings on the cross, crying out in victory: "I will declare thy name unto my brethren: in the midst of the congregation will I *praise* thee."

This verse is quoted in Hebrews 2:10-12: "For it became him . . . in bringing many sons unto glory, to make the captain of their salvation perfect through sufferings . . . for which cause he is not ashamed to call them brethren, Saying I will declare thy name unto my brethren, in the midst of the church will I sing praise unto thee."

Therefore, when we assemble together in His name, He is

in our midst (Matt. 18:20), just as He was there with His first congregation, pitiful though it was (John, His mother, the other women, Joseph and Nicodemus) in the darkness surrounding His cross. He is himself the leader of our praises, our invisible song leader as it were, whenever we gather together "by him [to] offer the sacrifice of praise to God continually, that is, the fruit of our lips giving thanks to his name" (Heb. 13:15).

The 119th Psalm

Consider finally what is in many respects the most amazing chapter in the Bible, the 119th Psalm. This is the longest chapter in the Bible (176 verses) in the longest book in the Bible. It is very near the center of the Bible. Psalm 117 (the shortest chapter in the Bible, with only two verses) is the middle chapter, and Psalm 118:8 ("It is better to trust in the Lord than to put confidence in man") is the middle verse of the Bible.

Psalm 119 is a remarkable acrostic Psalm, consisting of 22 stanzas of 8 verses each. Each of the 8 verses of each stanza begins with the same letter of the Hebrew alphabet. That is, each of verses 1–8 begins with the first letter of the alphabet, *aleph*, verses 9–16 each begin with the second letter, *beth*, and so on. Thus, the structure of the Psalm is stamped indelibly with the number 22, representing language, communicating God's Word to man and man's praise to God, and also the number 8, speaking of regeneration and victorious life.

It is by the Word of God, of course, that man is "born again, not of corruptible seed, but of incorruptible" (1 Pet. 1:23). Furthermore, the God-breathed Scriptures alone are profitable to the end that "the man of God may be perfect, throughly furnished unto all good works" (2 Tim. 3:17). The connection of the numbers 8 and 22 in Psalm 119 is thus very appropriate.

Now, the theme of Psalm 119 is simply the praise of the written Word! Almost every verse is an explicit testimony to the Scriptures.

These statements are built around exactly eight different Hebrew names for the Scriptures. Their occurrences follow a most interesting geometric pattern as outlined in the following:

Word (Hebrew)	No. of Occurrences		Word (Hebrew)
Law (Torah)	25	19	Word (Imrah)
Testimonies (Edah)	23	21	Judgments (Mishpat)
Word (Dabor)	23	21	Precepts (Piqqudim)
Statutes (Chuqqah)	22	22	Commandments (Mitsvah)

The word occurring most, plus the word occurring least, add to 44, and so do each of the other rows, as shown, with the total occurrences then being 4 x 44, or 176.

In the first stanza occur the six words — law, testimonies, statutes, judgments, precepts, commandments — all of them speaking to the Psalmist of the demands of God's law which is "holy, and just, and good" and in which he finds "delight in the law of God after the inward man" (Rom. 7:12, 22). However, he also finds he is in "captivity to the law of sin which is in my members," and so has to cry out for mercy and deliverance (Rom. 7:23-24). The first stanza ends with the plea: "O forsake me not utterly" (Ps. 119:8).

In the second stanza, as the Commandments had brought conviction, now the living Word brings cleansing and victory. The remaining two words (both translated "word"!) both occur first in this stanza. "Wherewithal shall a young man cleanse his way? by taking heed thereto according to thy word" (Hebrew dabar), "Thy word (Hebrew imrah) have I hid in mine heart, that I might not sin against thee" (verses 9, 11).

All the remaining stanzas and verses of the Psalm may most effectively be considered as a running testimony of the Psalmist, extending through his whole life, of the continued blessing received from the Word in meeting, experience by experience, every need of his life.

Selected books for further study:
Bullinger, E.W. 1967. Number in Scripture. Grand Rapids, MI: Kregel Publications. 312 p.
Davis, John J. 1968. Biblical Numerology. Grand Rapids, MI: Baker Book House.
Grant, F.W. 1910. The Numerical Structure of Scripture. New York, NY: Loiseaux Brothers Publishers.
Harrison, James. 1994. The Pattern and the Prophecy. Peterborough, Ontario, Canada. 399 p.
Hull, Marion M. 1938. The God-Breathed Book. Findlay, OH: Fundamental Truth Publishers. 48 p.
Johnston, Robert Dougall. 1990. Numbers in the Bible. Grand Rapids, MI: Kregel

Jones, G.E. 1953. *The Significance of Bible Numbers.* Jonesboro, AR: Sammons Publishing Co. 146 p.

Panin, Ivan. 1934. *Bible Numerics.* Ontario, Canada: Bible Numerics. 31 p.

Vallowe, Ed. F. 1977. *Keys to Scripture Numerics.* Forest Park, GA: Vallowe Evangelistic Association.

Woods, T.E.P. 1938. *The Seal of the Seven.* Grand Rapids, MI: Eerdmans Publishing Co.

Appendix B

The Book of God in the Heavens

Introduction

"The heavens declare the glory of God; and the firmament sheweth His handiwork. Day unto day uttereth speech, and night unto night sheweth knowledge" (Ps. 19:1-2).

There is possibly yet another distinctive evidence of God and His truth that deserves to be considered. As in the case of the numerical designs in Scripture noted in Appendix A, this evidence is controversial and should not be considered on a par with the evidences discussed in the main body of the text. Nevertheless, it is most intriguing and does seem to have some support in the written Scriptures, as well as in the nature of the evidence itself. It at least deserves a hearing.

Primeval Revelation

Long before there were any written Scriptures that we know about, men, of course, needed to know about God and their relation to Him, especially His plans for their salvation. There had been prophets of God in the antediluvian world (e.g., Abel, Enoch, Lamech), as well as in the post-diluvian world before Moses (e.g., Melchizedek, Abraham, Joseph). As noted in chapter 4, the various divisions of the book of Genesis give evidence of having been written by the early patriarchs and then edited by Moses later.

Thus, God revealed himself in various ways to early men long before Moses wrote the Pentateuch. These ancient prophecies included the great protevangelic promise of Genesis 3:15, the promise of the coming seed of the woman, who would someday crush the head of the great serpent, though in the process the latter would grievously wound him. There was also the prophecy of Enoch that the Lord would return someday to execute judgment upon all rebellious and ungodly men (Jude 14). Quite possibly there were other revelations and prophecies that have not been preserved for us in written form, but which were important and necessary in ancient times. Both Genesis 26:5 and Job 23:12 seem to refer to divine revelations available well before the times of Abraham and Job.

The prophecies of Genesis 3:15 and Jude 14, as well as other Scriptures, often also seem to be reflected in ancient traditions and mythologies, though, of course, much distorted by later pagan accretions. There must evidently have been a primeval revelation shared in some degree by all ancient peoples, at least up to the time of the dispersion at Babel.

The Witness Recorded in the Stars

The most important of these primordial truths seem actually to have been impressed upon the very stars themselves. It almost seems as though certain antediluvian prophets, in view of the impending destruction of the earth and its civilizations in the coming Flood, desired to preserve these revelations by engraving them upon the only indestructible systems they knew about — namely, the starry heavens.

The heavens were filled with distinctive groupings of stars that had become familiar to all who looked at the night skies. These constellations proceeded month-by-month across the heavens, returning again in the same order the following year. Accordingly, the idea presented itself to someone that these star groups and movements could be utilized to record the great cosmic narrative. Since the stars would be permanent, so would the great saga, and so, hopefully, the primeval revelations and promises would be preserved for all time to come.

The Bible, of course, does not say which of the antediluvian patriarchs may have undertaken the task of inscribing the great prophecies on the heavens, Josephus, the Jewish historian, recorded an ancient tradition that this had been done mainly by Seth and Enoch.

It is even possible that God himself was the Author of this sidereal "Bible." The creation record does state that one of the purposes of the heavenly bodies was to be "for signs, and for seasons" (Gen. 1:14). The Scriptures also indicate that the stars were given names by God (Ps. 147:4; Isa. 40:26).

In fact, the Bible actually refers by name to a number of the stars and their constellations. This is especially true in the book of Job, probably the oldest book in the Bible, if not in the world. Job mentions "Arcturus with his sons" (38:32), the "sweet influences of Pleiades" (38:31), the "bands of Orion" (38:31), the "crooked serpent" (26:13), and the "chambers of the south" (9:9). There are several other references scattered through the Bible.

Perhaps the most important biblical reference to this subject is Job 38:32: "Canst thou bring forth Mazzaroth in his season?" The fact that these words were spoken to Job directly by God, in the context where they are contained, strongly implies that the "bringing forth of Mazzaroth" each season was something that had been designed and established by none other than God himself.

The significant fact is that the word *Mazzaroth* means the twelve signs of the Zodiac and their associated constellations. All scholars and commentators are in agreement on this.

Thus, there is good reason to believe that the various star groupings and their symbolic counterparts were originally used, and perhaps even designed, for the purpose of conveying a continuing message to people of all places and times, that message consisting essentially of God's plans and promises concerning man's redemption.

The Dangers in Astrology

In trying to get at the truth concerning this subject, it is necessary to keep the following facts in mind:

1. The modern system of interpretation of star meanings — that is *astrology* — is unequivocally condemned in the Bible (see Deut. 4:19; Isa. 47:11-14; 2 Kings 23:5; Acts 7:42, 43; etc.), so that we must by all means avoid any association with these particular teachings.

2. Furthermore, astrology is essentially synonymous with ancient polytheistic paganism. The images of "man, and . . . birds and fourfooted beasts, and creeping things" (Rom. 1:23) universally associated with idolatry, have their precise counterparts in the

heavenly pictures associated with the constellations; also the names of many of the figures of pagan mythology are identical with those in the heavens.

3. Still further, this worship of "the host of heaven" is in effect worship of the fallen angels, or demons (Isa. 14:12-15; 2 Kings 21:3-6; Deut. 32:16-17; 1 Cor. 10:19-21; Rev. 9:20; etc.), so that whatever evangelical use may have originally been intended by the "signs" in the stars, they have long since been thoroughly corrupted to the ends of paganism and demonism.

4. Nevertheless, there are still so many points of similarity between the themes of mythology, including astrology, and the prophetic themes of Scripture, that it seems the former must be *corruptions* of the original revelation, rather than raw *inventions* of either men or devils. Thus, to whatever extent we can still recognize the remnants of that primeval revelation, to that extent we have an additional evidence of the truth of the Bible and Christianity.

The Signs of the Zodiac

The most important of the star symbols are, of course, the twelve signs of the zodiac, the *mazzaroth* of Job 38:32. Each sign corresponds to a given month of the year and is referenced to the group of stars which is located on the sun's "ecliptic" (its apparent path through the sky) during that month. These continually change, of course, as the earth makes its annual revolution around the sun.

As a matter of fact, because of the slight "wobble" of the earth's axis, the equinoctial points (the "equinox" is one of the two points during the year when the ecliptic crosses the celestial equator and the days and nights are equal) gradually shift from one year to the next. This "precession of the equinoxes" causes the months corresponding to the respective signs likewise to change very gradually.

If the purpose of the zodiac is to relate a story in the stars, it would, therefore, be important to know the point at which to begin the story. There is no reason to suppose, for example, that the present-day sign corresponding to the month of January would be the starting point.

Furthermore, there are many other constellations that may have been utilized along with the twelve major signs. The zodiacal system has been in use since the dawn of history, and usually the ancient zodiacs (whether in Egypt, India, Greece, Israel, China, or elsewhere) not only exhibit the same twelve major signs, but also 36 additional "decans," or "side-pieces," three secondary constellations accompanying the major constellation for each month.

For reference purposes, these 48 constellations are listed in the table below.

Zodiacal Sign	Decans
Virgo, the Virgin	Coma, the Infant (or Berenice's Hair) Centaurus, the Horse-Man Bootes, the Shepherd
Libra, the Scales	Crux, the Southern Cross Victima, the Slaim Victim Corona, the Northern Crown
Scorpio, the Scorpion	Serpens, the Serpent Ophiuchus, the Serpent-Fighter Hercules, the Serpent-Crusher
Sagittarius the Demi-God Archer	Draco, the Dragon Ara, the Burning Altar Lyra, the Harp Eagle
Capricornus, Half-Goat, Half-Fish	Sagitta, the Arrow Aquila, the Pierced Eagle Delphinus, the Dolphin
Aquarius, the Water-Pourer	Piscis Australis, the Southern Fish Pegasus, the Flying Horse Cygnus, the Swan
Pisces, the Fishes	The Band, or Bridle Cepheus, the King Andromeda, the Chained Queen
Aries, the Ram	Cassiopeia, the Enthroned Queen Cetus, the Sea-Dragon, Leviathan Persus, the Breaker
Taurus, the Bull	Orion, the Huntsman Eridanus, the Fiery Stream Auriga, the Charioteer

	Lepus, the Hare
Gemini, the Twins	Sirius, the Dog, or Prince
	Procyon, the Second Dog, or Redeemer

	Ursa Major, the Great Bear, or Fold
Cancer, the Crab	Ursa Minor, the Lesser Bear, or Fold
	Argo, the Ship

	Hydra, the Fleeing Serpent
Leo, the Lion	Crater, the Bowl of Wrath
	Corvus, the Raven

There are four reasons for suggesting that the narrative in the heavens was intended to begin each year with the sign of the Virgin. These reasons are as follows:

Since the primeval promise of the gospel was contained in Genesis 3:15, it would be appropriate to begin the story with a symbol of the woman whose miraculous seed would someday crush the serpent.

In the key reference to the zodiac in Job 38:32, God had asked the rhetorical question: "Canst thou bring forth Mazzaroth in his season? or canst thou guide Arcturus with his sons?" This seems to be a case of Hebrew parallelism, in which "bringing forth Mazzaroth (the zodiac) in his season" is essentially synonymous with "guiding Arcturus." It is, therefore, significant that the star Arcturus is one of the brightest in the sky and is adjacent to Virgo, in one of her decans.

The symbol of the Sphinx is frequently encountered in ancient cultures, and is found on certain ancient zodiacs. It seems always to be represented as a creature with the body of a lion and the head of a woman. It is shown inside the zodiacal circle, with the woman's head facing toward Virgo and the lion's tail pointing toward Leo.

If the story beings with Virgo, it must end with Leo, the Lion. This also is appropriate; the Lion represents the King (in the Bible, Christ is called the Lion of the tribe of Judah), and the zodiacal figures show Leo as springing on the head of Hydra, the great fleeing serpent, to destroy him.

The Meaning of the Signs

Although we have seen evidence to believe that the star-

signs may originally have been intended as pictorial prophecies of God's future plans for the world and mankind, the story
is very difficult to decipher at this late date. Though some
writers (as listed in the bibliography at the end of this Appendix) have worked out quite detailed correlations between the
"Bible in the Stars" and the written Word, it is obvious that
they have had to indulge in extremes of imaginative symbolization to do so. That this would be necessary is obvious from the
great variety of people, animals, and things listed in the above
table of constellations.

The antediluvian or early post-diluvian peoples for whom
the Star-bible would have been intended would no doubt have
had trouble interpreting its meaning without a set of instructions to guide them. Nevertheless, writing the story pictorially
in the sky surely would make it available to all men, and in a
form conducive to remembering it.

No doubt, one of our major difficulties is that many of the
original symbols have, over the ages, been corrupted in one
way or another, so that modern-day zodiacs may be significantly altered in appearance from the original. They are,
nonetheless, sufficiently similar to the most ancient star-
charts so that there can be no doubt there was only one original,
from which all others have been derived.

The naturalistic explanation of these constellations is
that they developed slowly in the course of cultural evolution,
as records of agricultural cycles of one kind or another. Such
evolutionary explanations are absurd, as is obvious not only
from the imaginative variety of the different signs and the
legendary tales associated with them, but also from the obvious fact that the figures shown on the sky-charts bear no
resemblance whatever to the specific groups of stars identified
with them.

It is rigorously evident that the original symbols were
arbitrarily selected by someone and then arbitrarily identified
with the specific groups of stars that have been associated with
them ever since. This selection could hardly have been capri-
cious; it could only have been because the original author or
authors wanted to tell the story this way.

It is possible that the original author could have been
Satan, or his human followers, the purpose being to establish
an astrological system to encourage men to worship him and

his horde of rebel spirits in the heavenly places. The numerous Babylonian ziggurats, including probably the original Tower of Babel itself, as well as hosts of other pyramids, step-towers, and high places around the world, seem usually to have been designed with shrines at their apexes dedicated to the "host of heaven," represented by zodiacs emblazoned on their walls and ceilings. Its invariable association in later times with paganism, polytheism, and occultism certainly is consistent with the hypothesis of Satanic or demonic origin.

However, on the other hand, Satan has historically always worked as a corrupter of religion, rather than an innovator. The tragic story of man's decline from the true knowledge of God to abominable idolatries is summarized in Romans 1:21-32. It is thus much more probable that astrology is essentially a Satanic corruption of an original representation in the heavens of God's true message to man.

If so, it may still be possible to discern the outlines of that primeval revelation, even after millennia of pagan distortions. It is obvious, for example, merely from a glance at the names of the 48 constellations above, that the story of the cosmic conflict between the Serpent and the Deliverer is the keynote of the entire narrative. It appears again and again in various ways, and this can hardly be a naturalistic accident.

The most ancient zodiacs are probably closest to the original. Certain important differences are noted on some of these. For example, Gemini may originally have been a united man and woman, rather than two male twins. Similarly, Cancer, the Crab, seems originally to have been an enclosure into which people came from all sides. No doubt there have been many such modifications from the original symbols.

To try to recover the original story, we must, of course, adhere firmly to later written revelation, knowing that God would not contradict himself. Also, we should, in so far as possible, try to think in terms of what would be meaningful to the antediluvian patriarchs who presumably first received and transmitted this information.

With appropriate reservations, therefore, a narrative such as the following might be inferred from the 12 main signs and their respective decans.

Virgo. "A Deliverer will come into the human family someday, born as a man, yet supernaturally conceived of a virgin, seed of the woman, yet Son of God."

Libra. "Since man is a sinner and under the curse, an adequate price must be paid to redeem him and balance the scales of divine justice."

Scorpio. "The price of redemption must be the death of the Deliverer, since man is under the condemnation of death, and yet, in dying, He must also destroy the Serpent who led man into sin."

Sagittarius. "To prevent the coming of the Deliverer in the human family, the great dragon will seek to corrupt mankind into a race of demon-possessed monsters and murderers."

Capricornus. "Man will finally become so sinful as to leave no remedy but complete inundation in his entire world."

Aquarius. "The floodgates of heaven will pour forth waters to cleanse an evil world, but representatives of the land animals will survive to fill the earth again."

Pisces. "From the waters will emerge the true people of God, as God retains His kingly throne despite all the attacks of Satan."

Aries. "In the fullness of time, the seed of the woman will come, ready to die as the sacrifice for man's sins, paying the great price to redeem His bride and destroy the works of the dragon."

Taurus. "Having paid the price, the slain Ram will rise as the mighty Bull, to execute judgment on all ungodliness and to rule supreme."

Gemini. "As both Son of God and Son of Man, the second Adam will claim His bride as did the first Adam, taking her to himself forever."

Cancer. "All the redeemed will come to Him from all times and places, secure eternally in His presence, enjoying His love and fellowship."

Leo. "As eternal King and Lord of lords, He will utterly vanquish and destroy the serpent and all his followers, reigning forever and ever."

This suggested original message of Mazzaroth is only a suggestion, of course, but in view of all the unknown factors involved, seems to be a reasonable reconstruction, consistent both with what is known of primeval revelation and with later Scripture. In any case, there seems to be sufficient correlation to indicate the primeval divine origin of this "gospel in the stars," but later corrupted into the pagan tales and symbols of astrology.

Selected books for further study:

Bullinger, E.W. 1979. *The Witness of the Stars*. Grand Rapids, MI: Kregel Publications. 212 p.

Carr-Harris, Bertha. 1933. *The Hieroglyphics of the Heavens*. Toronto: Armac Press, Ltd.

Rolleston, Frances. 1862. *Mazzaroth: or, The Constellations*. London: Rivingtons. 240 p.

Seiss, Joseph A. 1979. *The Gospel in the Stars*. Grand Rapids, MI: Kregel Publications. 188 p.

Spenser, Duane E. 1972. *Mazzaroth*. San Antonio, TX: Word of Grace.

Index of Subjects

Index of Authors

Index of Scripture

- 387 -

The Modern Creation Trilogy

Volume I - Scripture and Creation
Volume II - Science and Creation
Volume III - Society and Creation

Dr. Henry M. Morris and Dr. John D. Morris

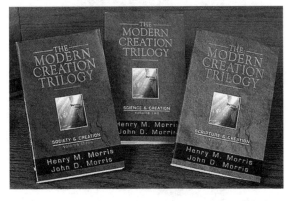

The definitive work on the study of origins, from a creationist perspective, *The Modern Creation Trilogy* examines the evidences for both evolution and special creation. Authored by the prolific father-son research team of Henry and John Morris, this three-volume gift set is a "must-have" for those who believe the Bible is God's plain-spoken Word.

Volume I looks at what the Bible says about origins — man, animal, planet, and universe. Volume II studies the scientific evidences for evolution and creation, contending that the evidence favors creation, since none of us were there in the beginning. Volume III sheds light on the fruits of each worldview — which stance produces better results for all creation? Interest level: Adult.

ISBN: 0-89051-216-7
Gift-boxed set of three • Paperback • 5-1/4 x 8-1/2 • $34.95

Available at Christian bookstores nationwide.

Scientific Creationism

Dr. Henry M. Morris

This book provides an in-depth examination of the research for creation. Covers dating methods, geology, biology, and other areas. Interest level: High school - adult.

ISBN: 0-89051-003-2
Paperback • 5-1/4 x 8-1/4 • $10.95

Available at Christian bookstores nationwide.

Creation and the Second Coming

Dr. Henry M. Morris

Could this be the last generation on planet Earth? Discover the link between creation and the Second Coming, and how political upheaval in the Middle East, the New Age movement, and calls for a one-world government play into the hands of biblical prophecy. Interest level: High school - adult.

ISBN: 0-89051-163-2
Paperback • 6 x 9 • $10.95

Available at Christian bookstores nationwide.